Tea and Grit

A Bicycle Journey along the Silk Road

HELEN WATSON

First published in the UK in January 2026 by
Journey Books, an imprint of Bradt Travel Guides Ltd
31a High Street, Chesham, Buckinghamshire, HP5 1BW, England
www.bradtguides.com

Text copyright © 2026 Helen Watson
Edited by Lucy Ridout and Ross Dickinson
Cover illustration/cover design by Ollie Davis Illustration
Layout and typesetting by Ian Spick
Maps by Lovell Johns
Production managed by Sue Cooper, Bradt & Page Bros

The right of Helen Watson to be identified as the author of this work has been asserted by her in accordance with the Copyright, Designs & Patents Act 1988.

All rights reserved. All views expressed in this book are the views of the author and not those of the publisher. No part of this book may be reproduced, scanned or distributed by any means without the written permission of Bradt Travel Guides, nor used or reproduced in any way to train artificial intelligence technologies/models. Bradt Travel Guides and the author unequivocally reserve this work from the text and data mining exception, as per Article 4(3) of the Digital Single Market Directive 2019/790.

ISBN: 9781804693544

British Library Cataloguing in Publication Data
A catalogue record for this book is available from the British Library
Importer to the EU: Freytag-Berndt u. Artaria KG, Ölzeltgasse 3/10, 1030 Wien, Österreich
Digital conversion by www.dataworks.co.in
Printed in the UK by Page Bros

To find out more about our Journey Books imprint,
visit www.bradtguides.com/journeybooks

Praise for this Book

"A phenomenal journey across an astonishing region, *Tea and Grit* quietly reveals the power of human endurance and connection over thousands of miles. I loved it!" **Anna Fleming**

"Asks powerful questions about why we travel and what we bring home afterwards." **Jonathan Lorie**

"Pure delight. There's something utterly charming and absorbing about this honest account of a precarious adventure along the fabled Silk Road. Grit and tea indeed! Just like the great Freya Stark before her, Helen Watson sets out with an open mind and open heart – and brings news of places that even today are unfamiliar. This is a good old-fashioned journey of wonder through dusty lands, packed with mishaps and telling encounters." **Benedict Allen**

"*Tea and Grit* embodies the essence and value of slow travel. Helen Watson notices and savours the details of ordinary people, ordinary places, from the embroidered dresses and jewel-coloured headscarves of Turkmen ladies and the golf ball-sized yoghurt snacks called *kurut*, to the armies of cleaning ladies scrubbing the streets of Tashkent and the open-top lorries overloaded with sheep on the Pamir Highway. Even on the hardest of travel days, she remains curious and determined, writing engagingly and with humour about the remotest parts of already little-visited destinations. *Tea and Grit* is a valuable addition to contemporary travel writing, especially for Central Asia." **Sophie Ibbotson**

"A cycling odyssey packed with adventure, challenges, and at times, danger and uncertainty. It's also a story that celebrates the power of human connection and the extraordinary kindness of strangers. This beautifully written book – colourful, vivid and poetic – pays homage to the people of the Middle East and Central Asia, their multifaceted cultures and complex histories. A powerful, luminous and deeply personal tale." **Helen Moat**

For my parents, with love

Author

Born in Scotland and raised in Switzerland, Helen Watson is addicted to travel that is both physically and culturally challenging. In 2009–2010, she cycled fifteen thousand kilometres from Scotland to China, inspired by the hospitality of people along the Silk Road – and later dismayed by the subsequent refugee crisis following the Arab Spring. Watson has captured the experiences in her first book, *Tea and Grit: A Bicycle Journey along the Silk Road*. She has previously won travel-writing competitions in *The Telegraph*, twice been shortlisted for the Bradt Guides / Independent on Sunday New Travel Writer of the Year Award and contributed to Bradt's Tajikistan guidebook. Living in the Scottish Highlands with her travel companion and husband, Ed, she works in wildlife conservation.

Author's Note

Names of individuals have been changed throughout this book to protect identities.

Note on the Transliteration of Place Names

There are many ways to transliterate the place names of the Middle East and Central Asia into English. In general, I have opted to use the forms most commonly used in guidebooks at the time of travel and to maintain consistency in transliteration from the same language. Transliterations found in online sources are ever-changing and not necessarily consistent; however, those wishing to find out more about the places en route will find that searching the transliteration of the name provided here will, more often than not, direct them to the right content. It should be noted that Turkey officially changed its name to The Republic of Türkiye in 2022.

Contents

Prologue	VIII
1. Honoured Guests	xii
Syria, February – March 2010	1
2. Your Crazy Choice	3
3. Three Men of Aleppo	11
4. Off the Map	26
5. Yelen, Daoud, Fantastico	41
6. Waterwheels and a Crusader Castle	46
7. The Desert, the Sown and the High Retreat	58
8. Blown Loose	70
9. Earthly and Heavenly Pleasures in Damascus	76
10. The Value of Water	81
11. The Children of Palmyra	91
12. To Raqqa	96
Eastern Turkey, March 2010	107
13. Eastwards	109
14. Bandit Country	117
15. Prepare to Fight	129
Iran, April 2010	139
16. All that Downhill Wasted	141
17. Freedom to Ride	155
18. Tell Them About the Real Iran	168
19. Meetings in Leopard Country	177
20. Money Laundering	182
21. Woman, Life, Freedom	189
Turkmenistan, April 2010	193
22. Turkmenitransit: Across the Karakum Desert	195

Uzbekistan, May 2010 — 203

23. Under the Shade of a Mulberry Tree — 205
24. The Road to Samarkand — 213
25. Stalin's Map — 222
26. Once Bitten … — 230

Tajikistan: The Pamirs, May – July 2010 — 241

27. Pamir Preamble — 243
28. Goodnight from Afghanistan — 251
29. No Room at the Inn — 258
30. Minefields in the Garden of Paradise — 263
31. Praise Be for a Comfortable Bed — 277
32. A Maze of Dashed Lines — 282
33. Just Keep Pedalling — 289

The Long Return — 293

34. Adrift West of East — 294
35. The Moving Ground — 307
36. Homecoming — 311

Notes and resources — 317

Notes on the Chapter Epigraphs and Their Authors — 318
Selected Bibliography — 323
Permissions — 325
Glossary — 327
Kit List — 331
Thanks — 333

Prologue

Tajikistan, June 2010

'There is a light on the Afghan side.' My husband Ed points across the brown torrent. I put my camping bowl of mashed potatoes down and stare hard through the evening gloom at the broken cliffs on the opposite bank. To where I thought there had been no one.

I stand up from the rock I was sitting on and reach into the open tent porch for the binoculars. A man in a pale salwar kameez comes into focus, bending down at the edge of the rushing water. Panning upwards, I can see

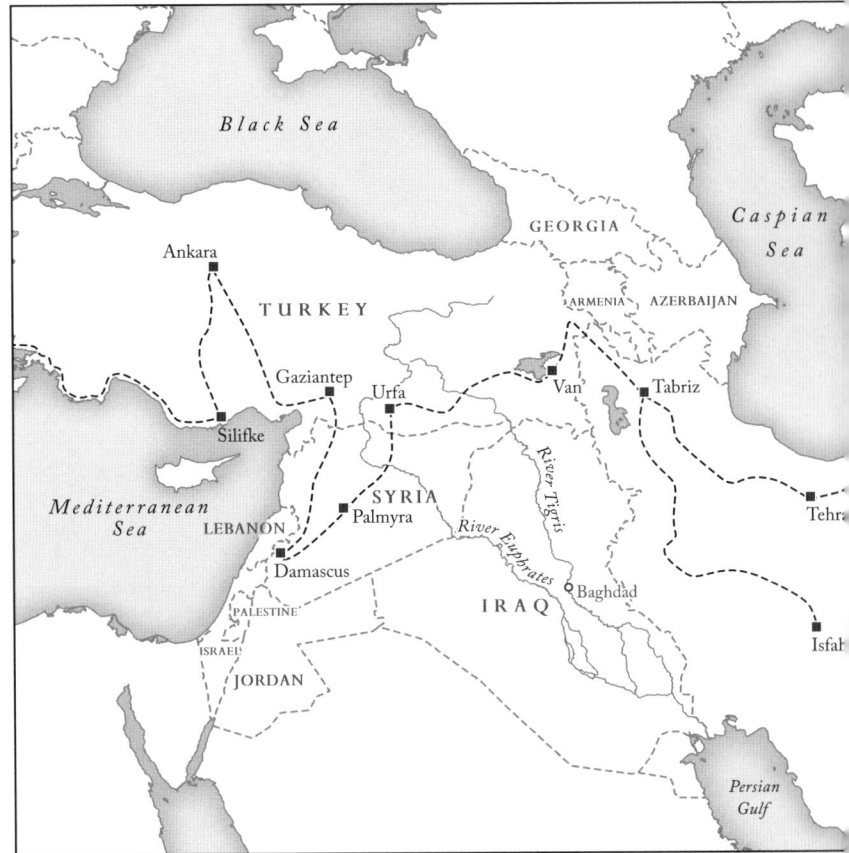

Prologue

two other men sitting on their haunches, the orange glow of a fire between them. They are camped right on the tiny path which clings above the river. There is not a scrap of flat ground. As the crow flies, they are close to us, less than two hundred metres away. Afghanistan is separated from the former Soviet republic of Tajikistan by a narrow void of air churned into icy gusts by the river beneath.

The men have surely seen us, but even if they wanted to call out, the wall of sound between us is as impenetrable as thick glass.

'What are they doing there?' I speak the words out against the cold air and the roar of water, as I pass Ed the binoculars. I shiver, now feeling exposed in our campsite. Earlier, as the shadows were lengthening, we had

congratulated ourselves on spotting a path heading up from the road to a low wall – an old sniper's nest – well hidden from beneath. Together we'd pushed each of our heavily laden bikes up the lumpy incline and swiftly set up camp. We were not expecting anyone on the opposite path.

We have been watching the path since this morning's first glimpse of the sinews of the river Panj from the Shuroabad pass, with the jagged peaks of Afghanistan beyond. Sometimes, the path zigzags up cliffs, and sometimes, it squeezes right along the edge of the river. Mid-afternoon, we saw a cluster of low mud houses with flat roofs – but no people. Even on our side, it is deserted. We have not seen a truck driver in hours, only the rusting carcass of a tank.

'Do you think they could be smuggling drugs?' I say.

The road we are cycling is a major route for trafficking heroin westwards. Surely our bright jackets branded us as one of the foreigners they must have seen occasionally? Surely they could not think we are a handover party? They would not have stopped because of us. Would they?

I ease back onto the sharp rock, agreeing with Ed that crossing would be impossible here, and swill down cold mashed potato with lukewarm tea as we speculate further. The light is fading fast.

'No, it would not be possible to swim, would it?'

'You'd have to fire a rope across or something. It's far too fast for a boat.'

We try to conjure up a plausible solution from a list of James Bond options. I push aside images of the rocket-propelled grenade launchers slung over the shoulders of the Tajik guards we had met at a checkpoint earlier.

'What are they doing there anyway? It's just so weird that they happened to stop right here.'

'Perhaps they are looking for rubies?'

'Or just walking to another village?'

'Or trying to leave Afghanistan?' There are many possible reasons, not least war.

'Or collecting plants?

'It could take days to walk between villages.'

We might as well be watching from a sofa ten thousand miles away; the barriers of tumbling water and rushing sound feel as vast. Eventually, a curtain of darkness falls. It is very cold now, and I imagine the men must be huddled close in blankets. Only a pinprick of light can be seen from the fire.

1
Honoured Guests

All their doors remained simple doors, on/off switches in the flow between two adjacent places, binarily either open or closed, but each of their doors, regarded thus with a twinge of irrational possibility, became partially animate as well, an object with a subtle power to mock, to mock the desires of those who desired to go far away, whispering silently from its door frame that such dreams were the dreams of fools.

Mohsin Hamid, *Exit West*

GLASGOW, SCOTLAND, OCTOBER 2015

I stood at the door waiting to be let into the night shelter. It was dark and the wind was blowing icy drops of rain against my face. Men waited in the shadows around me. One in a tracksuit, a full plastic carrier bag in each hand. Another in a jeans jacket, with a half-empty sports bag. A third carried nothing; his stained T-shirt was too small, exposing belly, but he was seemingly unaware of the cold. He was mumbling to himself. I thought I caught a word in Arabic. I was not sure I was at the right church hall and stood looking at my feet, feeling uncertain. The men did not speak to each other. I checked my phone again, pretending I was waiting on a message. There was none. It was 7.50pm.

'They will come at eight.' The man with the sports bag spoke up in English.

I smiled at him, but his face was tired and expressionless and he did not smile back. More men arrived and waited patiently.

A rusty VW Polo pulled up and a man in low-cut skinny jeans and Converse got out, bunch of keys in hand, to unlock the door. I hovered at the threshold as a wave of men hurried past and into the building's gloomy interior. Many of them were making a beeline for where a male toilet sign hung over a doorway at the end of the corridor.

'I am here to help,' I said to skinny-jeans man, far from sure if I really could. 'I was told to come to the induction today.'

'Ah, okay. I'm James. It's actually pretty full-on at the moment. There's food in the kitchen. Would you be okay just to dive in, sort it out and get dinner on?'

I followed him into a stainless-steel catering kitchen. One of the benches was piled high with donated sacks of rice, lentils and onions, boxes of tomatoes that were going mouldy, a mound of assorted vegetables, and crates of sandwiches and sushi in boxes from Marks and Spencer. In the sink was a plastic basin with bloody chunks of frozen meat sitting in water and on the hob stood a vat of meat that had been boiled grey, congealed fat floating on the water.

'We've been donated all this lamb,' James said, 'but it's very tough. If you can put tomorrow's on now and then make something with the cooked lot, that would be ideal. I've got case paperwork that I need to get to urgently with one of the guys.'

Before he hurried off, I established that there would be twenty people eating and that he'd not had a chance to consult the rota and so wasn't sure if there'd be anyone else helping. He left the kitchen, and I began hunting through drawers. A knife. Chopping board. Onion. Garlic. Two big aluminium pans. Briefly an image of using similar pans in the kitchen of the Glen Brittle War Memorial Hut on the Isle of Skye flashed into my head. Aged nineteen, I'd had my first experience of mass catering there, cooking haggis, neeps and tatties for thirty hungry members of my university mountaineering club after we'd been snowed off the Cuillin ridge on 25 January – Burns Night. If I could do it then, I could certainly do it now. Food, I knew, always made things better.

I set to work with a sense of urgency. The meat seemed like it still needed more cooking and I imagined the men would be hungry. The shelter was only open from 8pm to 8am, meaning that the men were out on the street or possibly in a public building like a library during the day. Glasgow at this time of year was cold, wet and dark. I chopped a heap of onions and garlic, struggled to lift a huge plastic bottle of oil and pour great glugs into the pan, then sweated it all together over a low gas, with a generous helping of curry spice from an industrial-sized packet. I prodded the cooked meat – it looked terrible – and tipped it in.

I stood undecided. Pre-boiling meat for tomorrow in water, as the previous person had done, did not seem a great idea. But was there something I hadn't understood about tomorrow? I tiptoed down the corridor to the common room, but James was on a phone call with one of the men sitting next to him. Sod it. I chopped more onions and garlic, added a different curry mix to the meat with some water. I'd be saving tomorrow's volunteers some time.

The tomatoes all needed to be eaten. I cut away the mouldy bits, chopped them roughly and divided them between the two pans. Then I processed a mound of vegetables: cauliflower into one pan, courgettes into the other.

The fridge was a mess, crammed with leftover bowls of food that looked suspect. I ditched the contents into the bin to make space and sorted through the donations, placing pots of yogurt and cartons of milk into the fridge with a big box of fresh spinach, mopping up an ooze of curry sauce that had leaked across a shelf and throwing out three pints of milk that had curdled.

By now the meat pans were bubbling and I was feeling more at ease. Another volunteer arrived – a politics student. She didn't know how to cook, she said, but offered to wash the pile of dishes in the sink. I wiped down the sticky surfaces while she began to rinse a stack of empty bowls.

A man appeared at the kitchen counter, his hair wet and combed back as if he'd just had a wash. He introduced himself as Mohamed and asked if it was okay to cook the rice themselves. They had a man downstairs who'd been a chef in Aleppo and they liked him to take charge of that. I smiled, relieved not to have the burden of getting the rice right for a group of Middle Eastern diners. Mohamed vanished, then reappeared with Hassan. Together, they chopped more onions and fried the rice grains in oil.

I headed down to the common room, leaving Mohamed and Hassan to take charge of the kitchen. The room was now stuffy and crowded with men sitting on plastic chairs. James was in deep conversation with one of the men.

The men were from many places beyond the outer margins of Europe: Syria, Iraq, Afghanistan, Pakistan and Eritrea. Most had arrived recently, but a few had been using the shelter for two years. Because of civil wars in Syria and Libya and the ongoing wars in Afghanistan and Iraq, the numbers on the move were growing. The Glasgow service had been overwhelmed by the recent influx, but this was just the tip of the iceberg. The refugee crisis of 2015 to 2017 would eventually see Germany process 1.4 million asylum claims and the UK less than a tenth of that.

The stewed meat was still very chewy when we finally dished up, but the rice and sauce were good and for a while there was just the sound of eating. Hassan fetched a pot of tea and poured it into short water tumblers that he handed round. Recalling the smaller tea glasses I'd drunk from in Syria, I smiled. No one was in the mood for talking though; all the men were in a hurry to clear the dishes and get to bed.

We all slept in the sports hall: volunteers on the elevated stage and the men on the floor below. We began taking mattresses from the stack and spacing them out.

'That one is reserved for Daoud. He has some medical problems – you know, his bladder ...' one man said gently, stopping me from handling a mattress with a plastic cover.

I lay in my sleeping bag listening to the snoring for what seemed like hours. Right across Europe, people were sleeping in makeshift shelters similar to this one. Berlin's disused Tempelhof Airport had become an enormous refugee camp. My mother was helping to redecorate an old school in Luxembourg ready to receive people. Refugees were risking their lives to cross borders that my husband Ed and I had pedalled through a few years earlier on our bicycle trip across Western Europe and the Balkans to Turkey, Syria, Iran, Central Asia and ultimately China. In January 2010 I had slept fitfully in the same sleeping bag I was now in on the ferry from Athens to Rhodes, five months into our trip. It was a forty-eight-hour ferry and our budget wouldn't stretch to cabin tickets, so we slept on the floor of the public lounge, which had seemed like a hardship at the time. The lounge was hot, packed with a boisterous group of Roma travellers, and it smelt, as many ferries do, faintly of sick. A smaller boat then took us on to Bodrum in Turkey.

I thought about the sea, grey and rough, and about little dinghies full of people in orange life jackets being tossed and tumbled. Earlier in the evening, Mohamed had told me that he had come by boat. He had not offered further details. I thought about two-year-old Alan Kurdi, found wearing a sodden red T-shirt and navy-blue shorts, lying face down in the sand on a beach near Bodrum, like a discarded doll, just over a month ago, on 2 September 2015. A Kurdish refugee fleeing the Syrian civil war with his family. Drowned.

I had been following the news closely since we'd returned from cycling at the end of 2010. In Syria, peaceful protests during the Arab Spring in 2011 had been crushed by President Bashar al-Assad. Civil war followed in 2012, a conflict that was so complex and involved the meddling of so many foreign factions that the West appeared unable to take any stance. People were being tortured and bombed and began to flood out of the country. We did not have contact details for anyone we had met in Syria – where we had travelled, no one seemed able to give us an email or a postal address and though we'd had a few people's mobile numbers, we'd lost those when our own phones had been stolen (Ed's in Uzbekistan, mine in China). I was sure everyone we'd met would have had their lives shattered by the war. I repeatedly scanned the internet, desperate for news. I once thought I recognised one woman, her head swathed in a familiar headscarf. Her lower torso had been blown off. I stumbled across the image at work and sat in the open-plan office, staring at the computer screen, tears running down my face. Was it her? Could it be? I did not have her photograph.

I wanted to do something, anything. I followed multiple forums, donated money and contributed to the phenomenal local effort in Edinburgh, where we lived, to gather clothes and supplies to send to the camps that were springing up everywhere. There were news reels of refugees fighting over clothing donations, impractical high heels and sequinned tops lying in the dirt, men all dressed in standard-issue grey jogging bottoms. I felt drawn to go and help in Germany or Greece, but I was struggling to get established in my job at an environmental charity, working on the conservation of rare species, and knew I might never get another break if I gave it up. Ed, a geography teacher, had also only just settled in after having worked in three different schools.

It had been tough coming back and I had struggled to cope with the pressures of work and the mundanity of a daily routine. With what little spare energy I had I'd become involved in a group co-ordinated via Citizens UK that campaigned to allow refugees into Britain. The aim was to establish a community sponsorship scheme like that of the Canadian government, which had resettled more than 300,000 refugees since 1979.

Now, as the photograph of tiny Alan Kurdi was being circulated around the globe, the electorate was more forcefully expressing its concern and politicians were at last taking notice. Prime Minister David Cameron had announced that the UK would take 20,000 refugees through the Syrian Vulnerable Persons Relocation Scheme, and Home Secretary Theresa May declared that a community sponsorship scheme would be launched. It was a tiny first victory – the numbers were pitifully low and it was unclear how the community sponsorship scheme would pan out – but that was how I had come to hear about the night shelter.

Somebody shouted out. I started, wide awake, heart racing in the darkness. Someone having a bad dream? Minutes later there was a stifled scream. I lifted my head out of my sleeping bag and peered over the sea of dark shapes lying in the sports hall. There was the pad of footsteps, a groan and then an urgent hushed exchange of words. I lay back down, heart thumping. My bladder was pressing, but I did not make the trip through the long corridors to the loo.

As I lay there in the dark, I knew there were currently thousands of people camped in woodland at border crossings in Serbia. I thought about the night we'd camped in a forest in Hungary, close to the Serbian border, and how we'd been frightened by a stray dog, its fur as black as the darkness, white teeth gleaming. Crossing out of the European Union the next day had felt like a major milestone, striking out into the unknown. Not washing for days, being hungry, always unsure where we'd bed down next – we'd chosen to impose these strictures on ourselves, but they were temporary and, just like Orwell in *Down and Out in Paris and London*, we knew there'd be an escape. There was surely no comparison with the grinding emotional reality of not having a choice, not having an ending in sight. A journey like ours now seemed almost grotesque. I had started writing up the account of our trip but had ground to a halt. I could not get the images of war out of my head. It seemed the world we had visited was lost. Was there anything useful that could be said?

What ate away at me was concern that many people were not receiving the kind of welcome we had received as travellers. People were waiting for help just outside the door into Europe and yet, despite the heroic efforts of many, not enough help was forthcoming. What was the human impact of that?

In the months we'd spent cycling through Europe *en route* to Greece and then Turkey, we'd received help from many people. In France a couple offered us shelter in a rain shower, inviting us on to their barge for ginger biscuits and tea. Our moods were buoyant for hours afterwards. A campsite owner in Austria rented us a holiday chalet for the price of a camping pitch because the nights were getting cold. Fishermen beside the Danube in Serbia poured us shots of rakia, their local brandy, and stoked up their fire for us before they left for home. Families in Bosnia allowed us to camp in their gardens so we would avoid landmines. A priest in a remote part of Greece bought us coffee, gritty with grounds and thick with sugar, as we sat sodden and frozen in a café. These gestures moved us and boosted our morale. The hospitality intensified the further east we got. During our eight months in the saddle between Turkey and China we were invited in for endless cups of tea and plates of food. Beds were rolled out for us to sleep in and we were often treated as honoured guests. We were trusted by people even when some of them clearly distrusted or disapproved of our culture, and we were looked after by people who could easily have attempted to profit from our relative wealth but did not. The people that we met were not saints, and some were scoundrels. They were just people like us. But the culture of hospitality given so unquestioningly was overwhelming and touching and allowed us a privileged glimpse into their lives.

I felt terrible. What would those arriving in the UK be thinking of us? What was I doing to help?

It was raining heavily as I drove home from the night shelter at dawn. The radio was turned up loud to keep me awake. A reporter was talking about the construction of a vast refugee camp built from shipping containers. He was broadcasting from the Turkish town of Kilis, at the border with Syria.

SYRIA

 FEBRUARY – MARCH 2010

Tea and Grit

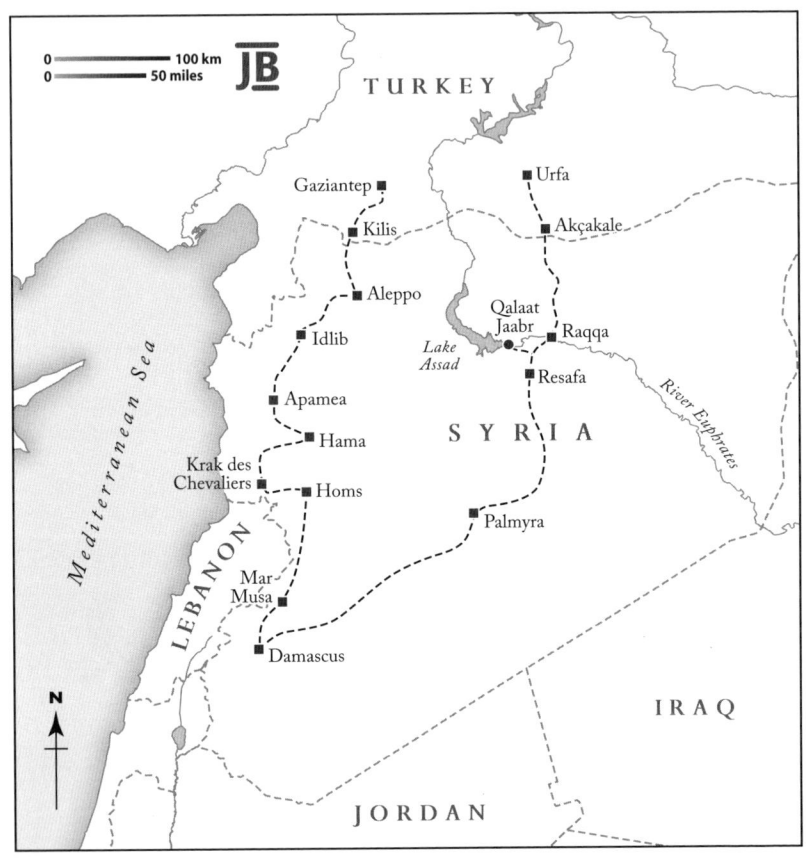

2

Your Crazy Choice

People are going back and forth across the doorsill where the two worlds touch.
Rumi, trans. Coleman Barks, from 'The breeze at dawn', in *Selected Poems*

7 February 2010

The road descended steadily from the Turkish town of Kilis towards the Syrian border. I turned the pedals of my bicycle slowly in high gear, enjoying the feeling of rolling swiftly without having to put in much effort.

Two women in dark dresses, their headscarves standing out white against the terracotta soil, were bent down in a field, at work. A man was pivoting a donkey and a wooden plough beyond the fence of thorns which lined the road. A car overtook us, rushing along the ribbon of asphalt ahead. Then the landscape was empty. Even the rows of olive trees and seedling crops had given way to the shrubs of no man's land stretching to the horizon. There was a big blue sky above us. The gentle downward gradient and the weight of my laden bike was doing most of the work.

Despite the spring rays of sunshine that radiated warmth through my black fleece gilet, a chill breeze stung my face. The last few weeks had been bitterly cold, and even though we'd tried to avoid the worst of the Turkish winter by cycling east from Bodrum via the 'warmer' route, which took us along the Mediterranean coast as opposed to through Turkey's freezing interior, we'd still spent several nights at minus 15°C. It was warmer now, above zero, but the threat of winter was not gone. I reached down to take a swig of icy water from the bottle on my bike's frame. My stomach was churning with anxiety. The border to Syria was close and I was afraid. Syria offered the promise of respite from the Turkish winter, but among the images of desert oases and camels, there were other visions.

Syria (along with Iran, one of our next stops) was routinely referred to in the UK as being part of the 'axis of evil', and the sort of phrases that popped into my head were 'state sponsors of terrorism' and 'next flashpoint in the Middle East'. The West's so-called war on terror had dominated my adult life. The 9/11 attacks on the World Trade Center and other US sites in 2001 had happened the week before I left home to become a student in Scotland, followed soon after by the invasions of Afghanistan and Iraq. When I arrived at the University of St Andrews, the skies screamed with the sound of the jets at nearby RAF Leuchars preparing for war. I had entered adulthood and, in an instant, the world had changed. Could something so awful unite rather than divide, I wondered? Then came the war on terror and the answer seemed to be a resolute no.

I did not like the black-and-white rhetoric of good versus evil, and the media's portrayal of people from some of the places we were at war with was at odds with my experience. Having moved to Switzerland from Scotland as the five-year-old daughter of a British mother and an Anglo-Swiss father, I grew up as an outsider; an outsider who played with Afghan, Turkish, Kurdish, Ukrainian and Russian children and was interested by what she saw inside their houses. In planning our trip, I knew I wanted to cycle east, a transect across Europe and into Asia, to understand more about how, on our joint land mass of Eurasia, 'us' became 'them'. 'Eurasia' – a logical geographic grouping but a rarely used term. No other continents are as hard to delineate as Europe and Asia. The Urals, for example, a line of mountains which runs north–south through Russia, from the coast of the Arctic Ocean to northwestern Kazakhstan, is the divide between European and Asian Russia. Extend that line south and most of Iran and all of Saudi Arabia, which few recognise as Europe, would fall on the European side.

In the five months of our trip thus far we'd already had some watershed cultural moments, not least riding into Sarajevo at dusk on a wet October evening as the call to prayer echoed through the valley from a hundred needlepoint minarets piercing the low cloud. But crossing from Greece to the Turkish town of Bodrum had actually revealed much similarity. What was 'west' and what was 'east' anyway? What was 'us' and what was 'them?' Where did it begin or end either notionally or geographically?

Whichever way it was turned, there was no doubt that Syria was the start of a 'them' on Europe's doorstep. I had barely met anyone from Syria or anyone who had been there. That we'd decided to go there ourselves, to avoid the worst of the Turkish winter, was almost entirely thanks to a Syrian pizza-kebab shop owner we'd met in Austria who had assured us it was safe. 'If you are going to Turkey,' he'd said as he sprinkled on our pizza toppings, 'you must go to Syria. It's not like Turkey or Iraq and there are lots of policemen everywhere. Sometimes they give problems for local people, but the Syrian people love tourists. You have my word, you will be 100 per cent safe.'

We'd laughed at his insistence on the touristic benefits of a police state. Though there might have been some truth in that, it wouldn't mitigate my father's concerns about suicide bombers and kidnappers, concerns that were fast becoming mine too. When I'd finally broken the news to my parents that we were cycling to China, the only thing my father had said was, 'Oh no,' in a tone which conveyed both resignation and disappointment. He had not spoken to me about it since. My mother was (somewhat covertly) slightly more encouraging. She had a keen sense of romanticism, honed by a year in Venice in the seventies spent working as an au pair, and she liked to recount tales of the crumbling palazzo, once visited by the poet Byron, which was owned by her host family. She understood 'the allure of the East'. However, I was starting to wonder if it was my father who was right.

The acid was still swirling in my stomach, which had started cramping too. I stopped my bike and Ed drew up beside me.

'Border crossings are always the worst,' my cycle-touring friend Jarrod had advised us in Edinburgh before we left. 'No matter how hard I try or how many times I've done them before, I'm always convinced that the next country is going to be completely different. Full of murderers and bandits. And then it's always fine.'

'That's great.'

'Well, I mean, it's normally fine. There was that one time I was nearly stoned to death ...'

A border meant nothing but it also meant everything.

Ed was looking at the map and munching dried fruit. Feeling suddenly hungry, I reached into my bar bag, pulled out a handful of the walnuts and dried apricots we'd stocked up on in the bazaar at Gaziantep and rested my head on his shoulder to check the map too. Just five kilometres to the border.

Within minutes we were there. A battered orange BMW coach had pulled up onto the dusty verge opposite the border post. Its doors were open and a group of women stood next to it in the sunshine, clasping their chadors. The black cloth flapped and tugged around them in the persistent breeze. The flags of Turkey and Syria whipped the air on high poles above. A sign on the bus said 'Tehran–Halep (Aleppo)'. I felt the women's eyes on me as I rolled to a stop, swung my leg over the crossbar and unclipped my helmet.

Feeling underdressed, I smoothed down the sleeves of my shirt and wrapped a scarf around my neck. We'd chosen trousers and long-sleeved shirts rather than Lycra shorts and tops as our cycling clothes for just this sort of situation, so that we might blend in more easily when off the bikes, and to prevent sunburn. We left our bikes in the sunshine and entered the darkened building. Marble floors and rows of plastic seats gave it the feeling of an airport lounge. Two queues of men, almost all dressed in dark trousers and jackets, snaked up to the glass-fronted tills. We hung back momentarily, unsure which queue to join. Many of the men were clasping piles of passports. More women swathed in black, and children, spilt out across the seating area.

'Come! Come!'

A man grabbed Ed by the arm and pulled him towards the front of the queue, exchanging a few words with the people who were waiting. From the large bundle of papers he was carrying, I assumed he was the tour guide from the bus and that the others in the queue were his group, presumably Iranians on a pilgrimage to Damascus, to the Shia shrine of Hussein, grandson of the Prophet Muhammad and founder of Shiism. Shia and Sunni had fallen out over lines of succession following the death of the Prophet in 632. Iran was a Shiite state, while Syria, like most of the Muslim world, was predominantly Sunni. Confusingly, Syria had an Alawite president, Alawites having fallen out with the Shiites over lines of succession.

The portrait of the current president looked down on our throng. Bashar al-Assad, a London-trained eye doctor, had been in power since 2000, taking over from his father, Hafez, who'd ruled Syria with an iron grip since 1971. Bashar's wife Asma, born of Sunni Syrian parents and raised in London, was a financial analyst and beautiful. She went about unveiled and seemed to model herself on Princess Diana. Clearly serious about her role as first lady, after her honeymoon she took a road trip around Syria to learn where she should direct future policies. Bashar had actually been his father's third choice of successor, after his uncle Rifaat, who'd been banished for trying to seize power when Hafez was ill, and his brother Bassel, who'd been killed in a car crash. With his soft jawline and brush moustache, serious eyes below a furrowed brow, and dark suit and tie, President Bashar looked more geek than general.

The tour guide pushed across the man at the front of the queue and tapped on the glass to alert the uniformed guard, who was writing something down on the other side. The guard handed two forms out and gestured that we should wait for him to finish.

'As-salam ... alaykum,' Ed stumbled when it was our turn.

'Wa-alaykum salam. Hello. Passport,' came the reply from the official with a smoothly shaven jaw. 'You tourist?'

Ed nodded.

The man looked up at us and then scrutinised the entry forms. 'Hotel?'

Ed nodded again.

'Okay. Hotel where? Hotel Damascus?'

'I think he wants to know where we're staying,' I whispered to Ed.

'Ah, okay. Aleppo ... Hama ... er ...' Ed turned to me. 'What's the other one with an H?'

'Homs.'

'Homs, Damascus, Palmyra. All hotel.'

Ed gave the reply that we thought the man wanted to hear. It was perhaps not obvious to the official that our bikes were waiting outside or that the route we had given him was rather ambitious. We were planning on cycling a big V-shape across Syria. First heading south to the cities of Homs, Hama and the capital Damascus and then turning northeast through the desert to the Unesco World Heritage Site of Palmyra before returning to eastern Turkey at the border near Urfa. It was to be a loop of at least a thousand kilometres that would take the month of our visa and would hopefully mean that Turkey had defrosted by the time we returned. But we were not going to overcomplicate matters with details.

Five minutes later, we swung our legs back over the crossbars of our bicycles and set off into Syria, blinking in the sunshine. The road looked little different from before, a dusty ribbon fringed with scrub. Above, the same chocolate-box blue sky. The orange bus overtook us after a while. It was driving slowly with its doors open and we waved as it drew even with us. The driver leant across his steering wheel and shouted for us to jump in with them.

We waved and shook our heads.

He lifted both hands off the steering wheel, causing the bus to swerve towards us, and raised them up to heaven as if to say, 'Your crazy choice.'

The faces of the women pressed against the windows, watching as we shrank away behind them, pedalling hard.

There were around sixty kilometres between us and Aleppo, the second biggest city after Damascus, and we planned to reach it by nightfall. For the first time in a long time I began to feel sweat building on my back and I savoured it. The day was moving on, but we had also lost quite a bit of altitude as we descended towards the Fertile Crescent – the great plains that stretch between the Tigris and Euphrates rivers, which rise in eastern Turkey, drop through valleys and gorges to the uplands of Syria and northern Iraq, stream out onto the alluvial plains of central Iraq and then discharge into the Persian Gulf. We were crossing an ancient borderland to the cradle of civilisation, birthplace of the wheel, the alphabet and domestication, a land coveted and contested for most known generations of modern human history. There are sites here that date back nine thousand years. Here too is the world's oldest known border post, incised with cuneiform instructions and erected by the warring Sumerian city states of Umma and Lagash in 2400 BC to mark a boundary between the Tigris and the Euphrates.

Syria was at the crossroads of several ancient civilisations. In addition to the Euphrates–Tigris system in the northeast, there was the Nile in Egypt to the south, to the far east the Amu Darya and Syr Darya rivers of Central Asia, and to the west the Mediterranean civilisations of Greece and Rome. It was hard to believe, looking around us, for the land was barren and dry.

The sun had a stronger warmth in it now and over the next hour my pleasure at it began to unravel. Perspiration rose on my face and, mixed with suncream, started to irritate my eyes. I took another swig of water and resisted the temptation to rub my eyes with a dusty hand. My shirt was getting damp. The road was still empty and there were no farms, just dirt and thorns and the odd discarded plastic bottle.

An hour later, the township of Azaz emerged on the road as a scattered collection of low, flat-roofed concrete buildings. A group of men was lounging by a wall. I glanced over my shoulder; Ed was close behind me. Just as we drew level with them, I heard a shout and a man rushed out towards us.

I waved cheerily but pedalled a little harder, not sure at all.

I looked over my shoulder again. Ed was now standing astride his bike, surrounded by a gang of men in leather jackets and paint-stained jeans, with crew cuts and dark stubble beards. I took stock at a distance, my heart racing.

Had they made him stop? Was he in trouble? I slowed down and did a U-turn beside a tumbledown house in the empty road, careful not to jerk the bike round too fast and have the panniers trip me over. I could see now that Ed was shaking hands with everyone. I stepped off my bike and walked towards the group, placing my hand on my heart in a greeting that was returned.

There was a babble of voices and questions
'Where from?'
'Where to?'

A stool was brought from beside the wall and placed on the pavement for Ed to sit on while the men crouched on their haunches, asking him things and peering at the map of Turkey and northwest Syria that was on his handlebar bag.

One of the men fetched a teapot and tiny glasses from a neighbouring house. Feeling ignored as I sipped the hot and intensely sweet tea, I asked a thin teenage boy with a moustache next to me if he was from Azaz. He coloured and gave Ed a sideways glance, as if to gauge his reaction, as if he was asking permission from my husband to speak to me, then nodded.

'I wasn't sure which way that was going to go just then,' Ed said half an hour later when we had got back on our bikes amid a lot of well wishes and (in Ed's case) hugs.

The turning on to the two-lane highway to Aleppo and Damascus was announced by a crumbling concrete archway, the only monument in the dusty landscape. We pulled on to the side of the road and ate lunch, resting our backs against a concrete barrier, legs stretched out in front of us. The sun was now hot and drinking the sweet, tannin-rich tea on an empty stomach had left us feeling shaky and thirsty. Trucks rumbled past us, kicking up dust as we munched on dried bread and white Turkish feta.

Ed was passing me our pocketknife when I looked up to see a large truck reversing backwards up the highway.

I prodded Ed to alert him.

The truck stopped in front of us and a man got out. We watched without trying to stare as he opened the cargo door. Then he walked towards us and my concern started to mount.

'What's he coming for?' I whispered.

Before we had a chance to remember a greeting, the man set down two cans of orange juice in front of us.

'Welcome to Syria!' he said as he hurried away.

3
THREE MEN OF ALEPPO

Is it an aberration, sister, for an apple to kiss an apple?
Nizar Qabbani, trans. Nayef al-Kalali, from 'The Evil Poem: 1956', in Lisa Kavchak (ed.), *Republic of Love*

The heat of the previous afternoon had turned to cold, heavy rain, dissolving the dust on the streets of Aleppo to mud so that the inhabitants had to lift the hems of their long clothing and skip across pools in their slip-on sandals. We had entered a new world. Men walked the streets wearing coffee-coloured dishdashas (long-sleeved shirts which reached down to the ankles) and on their heads red-and-white-checked shemaghs wrapped in a number of ways. Folded to a triangle, the square cloth could be kept in place with a coil of black rope – this seemed to be the most formal style. Men on motorbikes, with the hems of their dishdashas hitched over the crossbar so that their jeans showed underneath, rode with their faces swathed completely in red-and-white check, only their eyes showing. Many rolled the ends of the scarf back round their head like a turban and a few old men tied them under the chin, which made them look grandmotherly.

We browsed the stalls selling huge selections of shemaghs, differing in pattern and quality. 'This Palestine, this Bedouin, this tourist,' a stallholder told us, laughing, pointing in turn at a black-and-white, red-and-white and then multi-coloured 'Palestinian scarf' of the kind you would find in an H&M fashion store back home. A woman browsing rolls of pink sequined fabric wore the same Bedouin scarf bound tightly around her head and below the chin. Her leathery face was tattooed with indigo X marks and her blue eyes were smudged with kohl. I felt sure she had come from deep in the desert. Many women, however, wore headscarves in lively colours to match embroidered floor-length dresses; the rest were enveloped in more subdued blacks or greys and wore the niqab, the full-face veil, so that only dark eyes showed through the slits. No one that I could see was wearing trousers like me.

Mahmoud wore the uniform of young men: jeans, a pink T-shirt tight against his skinny torso, a leather jacket, gelled hair and slip-on leather shoes. He told us, in perfect English, that he wanted to be a translator in Saudi Arabia. He'd waylaid us in Aleppo's vaulted souk and led us to a friend's fabric shop to sit and drink tea tucked in among the bales of material. 'It is very good to find people to practise my English with. I have met some Dutch and just yesterday some Germans, but you are the first native speakers.' He had just finished telling us how he'd been awarded the highest grade in his English class when he announced, 'You must come to my house and visit my family.'

'Really? Thank you,' Ed responded, caught off guard by the offer.

'Are you sure?'

'That's very kind.'

We stumbled over each other, unsure whether this was a genuine invitation and whether we should accept.

'Good!' He beamed. 'My uncle likes meeting foreigners. I will just let them know.' He lifted his mobile phone to his ear.

We sat in polite silence and I ran my eyes across all the fabric patterns surrounding us as we listened to a stream of Arabic on three separate phone calls.

I shifted in my seat and shot a sideways glance at Ed. Were we being naive? Was this some sort of scam?

'Is it far to your house?' Ed asked casually.

'Not far at all. Maybe twenty minutes by bus. Shall we go?'

'Bus?' I echoed.

Ed and I looked at each other. I did not like the idea of going somewhere we could not easily find our way back from. I'd had my fair share of uncomfortable experiences, not least while travelling solo at nineteen in Fiji and having to ward off scary, unwelcome attention.

I sized up Mahmoud – slight, boy-band-ish and probably harmless, if rather persuasive – and then looked at Ed, who was taller, with the wiry build of a climber. I was fairly sure he was stronger. Plus it would be two against one – for now at least. Anyway, it would seem rude to back out now.

Half an hour later, we were bouncing along at high speed, crammed into the back of a minibus alongside two schoolgirls in matching white headscarves and long tunics and some old men wrapped in their shemaghs. The densely packed concrete tower blocks of the city, with their shopfronts at street level selling bottled water, motorbike spare parts, plastic shoes, piles of oranges and falafel, began to thin out, as did the flow of yellow taxis, cars and motorbikes, and soon the city was vanishing behind us as we sped along a highway flanked by fields and muddy tracks that ran off at right angles to small villages. As we pulled to a stop to let the girls off, a man in jeans and a shirt, who'd presumably just come down a track to hail a bus into town, bent down to polish the mud from his office shoes.

Mahmoud's teenage sister Miriam and aunt were waiting for us at the entrance to a single-storey brick house. They rushed over and embraced me so tightly that I immediately felt ashamed for having been suspicious. We left our mud-coated shoes in the courtyard and were led straight into a long, carpeted room.

'This is my father.' We were directed to sit on the floor next to a small man in his forties. The aunt and a sister sat at a distance, and an older sister brought us tea. 'My aunt is my father's wife,' Mahmoud said simply. 'My mother died and my father married my mother's sister.'

'I am sorry to hear that,' Ed started.

'It was a long time ago.'

'Please thank your family for inviting us to visit. It is very kind.' I shifted awkwardly on the floor, causing Miriam to jump up in a fluster and offer me another pillow.

'My father says you are very welcome.'

Everyone beamed, unsure what to say.

I tried to still my anxiety at the silence. We'd been invited into local homes a few times on the trip so far and were becoming used to searching for mutual topics of conversation in fragments of common language. I glanced around the room. There was no furniture apart from the cushions on the floor and a dresser with a TV. The father turned it back up a notch once we had exhausted an exchange of questions mediated by our translator.

Mahmoud went to a sink in the corner of the room, washed his face, then selected a couple of starched dishdashas from a hook, one in brown and the other in grey.

'Which one do you think I will look more beautiful in?' he asked, brandishing the two outfits at Ed. Ed having diplomatically expressed no firm preference, Mahmoud disappeared for a while before returning in the brown one, now looking quite different from the young man who earlier would not have seemed out of place on the streets of Edinburgh. 'Later we will go and visit my uncle. The whole village gathers at his meeting room, but first we must eat.'

A big circular dish of carrot and potato bake was brought in by the women. Mahmoud tore up the flatbread and handed pieces to us and his father.

'We eat with our right hand, but there are spoons if you would prefer.' He seemed to understand that Europeans might struggle with certain aspects of etiquette.

I was glad that I knew this and other basic rules for travel in Muslim countries: never accept anything with the left hand or use it to eat; never walk into someone's house with your shoes on (incidentally, a cardinal sin in Switzerland too); and don't make physical contact with anyone of the opposite sex.

The aunt sat watching at a distance with her legs tucked under her. Miriam had obviously been sent away, perhaps because it was improper for them to even observe us eating.

After the meal, Miriam, who had a pale oval face and wore an orange sequined dress, giggled enthusiastically as she directed me to put on a pair of plastic sandals to walk to the outdoor squat toilet. She was waiting for me when I emerged and hugged me and shook her head when I tried to ask her some questions.

Later, as we were leaving, she presented me with a child's necklace with an initial M for her name, pressing it into my hand and whispering something. Mahmoud rolled his eyes, embarrassed. 'She wants you to have this to remember her by. It is just a silly thing, though.'

'Please tell her that it means a lot to me.' I gave her a hug and apologised that I had nothing to give her in return.

Mahmoud's father drove us across the rutted, mud-swamped paths of the village in his flatbed pick-up. We were crammed four abreast into the front of the two-person cab. I was between Ed and the door, a point which required some discussion to ensure I was not sitting next to one of the men. 'Women normally travel in the back,' Mahmoud said once we were all seated.

We picked our way across the muddy path and entered another low building, walking directly into a room full of men. It was bare save for a carpet, cushions, a couple of low wooden rests designed for leaning against, a coffee unit and a vast flat-screen TV. An embossed metal plaque of the ninety-nine names of Allah hung on a wall.

Mahmoud ushered Ed round the introductions to three men, all in dishdashas, and his uncle, a portly man with a greying moustache, who was seated in the centre of the room. My trekking trousers and thigh-length tunic, which I had bought in Turkey and which seemed conservative enough for walking the streets of Aleppo, now seemed both scruffy and skimpy in this setting where all the men appeared to be dressed up and from which women were entirely absent. Perhaps thinking the same thing, the uncle commanded Mahmoud to fetch his heavy black cloak, which was lent to me. Had he sensed my discomfort, even though no one had stared at me? Did my state of dress offend his propriety? Or was he worried I was cold? I was asked more than once if I was. Whatever the reason, I felt considerably more at ease once I disappeared into its folds.

I had thought carefully about what to wear on this trip. Clothing is perhaps three things: a tool of practicality, a symbol of wealth and a symbol of culture. Clearly, functionality when cycling was key, but for me so was blending in. I felt torn about doing this in places where certain types of dress were effectively compulsory for women. We had stayed with a Muslim family in a homestay in Albania's capital, Tirana. Upon seeing me in my baggy trousers and long-sleeved shirt cycling get-up, the father of the house had turned to his eldest daughter and, waving his hand at her vest and shorts, said, 'Why can't you dress more like her?' I felt an instant traitor.

Once we were seated on a pile of cushions offered from all quarters, a boy of six or so carefully carried over sweet tea in tulip-shaped glasses. A two-year-old boy, Mahmoud's youngest cousin, crawled around in the corner, alternately entertained and ignored by his father. Mahmoud's uncle had turned to speak to two darker-skinned men, both in red-and-white shemaghs. The uncle himself wore one of pure white held on by a coil of black rope. Mahmoud explained in a whisper that the men were also visitors 'from a long way, another tribe'. Another group of men were listening from the corner – an assortment of uncles and cousins. We relaxed into a stream of tea, saying little, with Mahmoud occasionally whispering to us that the men were talking about livestock, or politics. He was obviously concerned that we might become impatient or offended at being ignored.

There appeared to be a strict sense of hierarchy here. How close you sat to the uncle, who offered you their place, and who offered you coffee or tea seemed to be carefully choreographed. Mahmoud, who had before been self-confident and buoyant, was now nervous and deferential. This made it even worse when the rounds of coffee started and Ed accidentally spilt the tiny cup that the uncle himself had risen to serve. There was an embarrassed silence in the room and Mahmoud's cheeks flushed red, but the horror on our faces and our profuse apologies seemed to make it evident that this was not a deliberate slight. After a brief pause the uncle laughed and told us to stop mopping the carpet. The oldest boy went back to the coffee unit to pour some more.

The unit was an embossed brass box containing burning coal and with a series of curve-spouted Arabic coffee pots, or dallah, of different sizes heating on top. Coffee drinking in Syria seemed to have more of a ceremonial quality than tea, which was offered everywhere, and the ritual of preparing, serving and drinking it was a sign of hospitality, generosity and wealth. The hot, dark, bitter, cardamom-scented coffee was decanted from one brass pot to the next in an aromatic stream, to concentrate it, and when eventually served was just enough for a tiny sip, covering the bottom of a small bowl.

Some of the men went into a corner of the room to pray and we sat in silence, listening to the chanting as they prostrated. After that a nargileh was lit with an ember from the coffee fire and Mahmoud started the water pipe, ensuring that it was drawing well before offering it to Ed. In Syria, he explained, everyone smoked their own pipe; it was not customary to pass it round as tourists did. In fact, since no one else smoked, it seemed that Ed was offered the pipe to satisfy our touristic expectation.

The uncle appeared to have finished the business with the strangers and now began to speak to us with the aid of his nephew's translation.

'My uncle asks what do you think of George W. Bush?'

We expressed the hope that Barack Obama, by now one year into his tenure as US president, would make a better leader than his predecessor, whose response to the 9/11 attacks had been the war on terror and the invasions of Afghanistan and Iraq. In the UK, Gordon Brown had taken over from Tony Blair, Bush's key ally.

'My uncle says we don't mind America, but we are afraid of Israel because they have nuclear weapons and they always have America on their side.'

And then:

'He asks what religion are you?' Mahmoud saw us hesitate and prompted, 'You are Christian?'

'Yes,' we said, genuine in the cultural sense. 'Is it a very bad thing in this country if you say you have no religion?' I asked Mahmoud quietly, the uncle having momentarily turned to talk to someone else.

'Yes.' He stared hard at me. 'This is a very bad thing and it is better never to say this.'

'My uncle would like to know are there Muslims in your country?' Followed by: 'Is it true that some people in your country eat the meat of the pig?'

Mahmoud was genuinely shocked when we replied in the affirmative.

'But it is dangerous!' he squeaked. 'It is full of disease.' And now he coloured a little pink. 'We hear,' he said bashfully, 'that sometimes in Europe men and women … they … have children together, but they do not get married.'

'Yes,' I said, 'it is true. Many people my grandparents' age think this is bad, but now many younger people do not think marriage is so important. A lot of people are also married, though.'

The uncle nodded.

'Can I ask your uncle, is it possible for a man to marry more than one woman here?'

'Of course. My uncle has four wives.'

It turned out that most of the men in the room were married to multiple women.

'So are you married too?' I asked Mahmoud.

The reply I received from our twenty-one-year-old translator was unexpected. 'No, I am divorced. My wife, she was, you know, a village girl. Not so intelligent. It was not a good match.'

'And will you get married again?'

'Oh, yes. I am planning to marry a teacher from Aleppo. Maybe in a few months' time. I am in love.'

'When did you meet her?'

'I have not met her yet. A friend has sent me a picture.'

There was a murmur of conversation among the men.

'My uncle asks how much do wives cost in your country?' Mahmoud said to Ed.

'They cost nothing. They are free.'

'So you paid nothing to marry Helen?'

'No.'

A roar of laughter went round the room once Mahmoud had translated.

'This is very strange to us.' Mahmoud laughed.

I looked around the room of men in dishdashas and shemaghs lounging on cushions as clouds of steam hissed from the dallah and wondered what their multiple wives and daughters were doing just then. What of Mahmoud's ex-wife – was she free to remarry? Would she be considered only co-wife material from now on? What lay ahead for his sister Miriam? Did the teacher in Aleppo know that a marriage proposal was coming? These things were strange to me.

The alleys of the al-Madina Souk, the largest covered market in the world, drew us back again the following day, into its thirteen-kilometre-long maze.

At the entrance stood a small cart with mouth-watering falafel, freshly fried and wrapped in flatbread with coriander and mint. Nearby, another seller was serving small metal cups of hot salep, sweet milk thickened with orchid root and flavoured with cinnamon. The cups were given a cursory rinse in a bucket of water and then passed on to the next customer. Fresh food stalls displayed piles of black olives, white cheese, pomegranates, apples, lemons, oranges, dried apricots, cherries, sunflower seeds, almonds, dates, fresh herbs, bloody meat and tinned produce.

Everywhere, I could smell the scent of olive-and-laurel-oil soap, which had been traded out of the souk for centuries, since well before the Crusades. Blocks of it were piled up in pyramids, some of them cut open to show the change in colour affected by at least six months of ageing – brown-gold on the outside to green in the centre. The highest-quality soap, reserved for the face and hair, was the darkest.

Next to the soap stalls were others selling angular chunks of rock salt and spices, everything from fine yellow turmeric powder to green za'atar, a mixture of thyme, sesame, sumac and salt, commonly eaten for breakfast with hot flatbread (khobez) dipped in olive oil.

We wandered the cobbled alleys, past stalls selling underwear, nightdresses hung up high. A shopkeeper was lifting one down with the help of a pole for a group of women. There were heaps of headscarves, plastic sandals, children's T-shirts, prayer mats, alarm clocks, framed inscriptions of the ninety-nine names of Allah, mobile phones. There were stalls that sold rolls of fabric for women's long dresses and a whole section of shops staffed by young men with gelled hair that specialised in jeans, leather jackets and shirts. To find more traditional attire you had to venture into the traffic of the vaulted central walkway, where shopkeepers would measure a man for a dishdasha of coffee-coloured cotton, while other stalls sold heavy black cloaks and shemaghs of various patterns and quality.

There were tourist trinkets – silver earrings, postcards, and silk scarves too bright and small to be of use to local women – but the souk was no slave to tourism. After all, silk had been bought and sold there for centuries, along the huge network of land and maritime trade routes that stretched from eastern China to the Mediterranean – the Silk Road.

The multitudes of pilgrims that visited the mirrored white marble courtyard of the nearby Great Mosque and cried at the shrine containing the remains of Zechariah, the father of John the Baptist, constituted only a fraction of the souk's customers. We too had been to see Zechariah's coffin, which was bedecked in gold damask, illuminated by filigree lanterns hung from a gilded beam and protected behind a copper grille. According to the Qur'an, and to Luke of the New Testament, Zechariah was struck dumb by the Angel Gabriel for doubting that he and his wife, who were childless and of advanced years, were to have a son who was to be the forerunner of Jesus. Pilgrims pressed themselves against the grille, but we as non-believers could only glimpse the coffin from the doorway.

The souk was where locals came for wedding gold, baby clothes, televisions, toothpaste, the day's ingredients and gossip. In the blacksmith's alley, young boys worked at an art untouched by time, beating sparks from white-hot metal. I came to a halt, trying not to stare. One of the young blacksmiths had a shock of ginger hair just like mine, and pale skin burnt savagely by the sun. As the only redhead in my family, I knew that the redhead's recessive gene could skip generations and wondered if his ancestors could be traced back to the Caucasus, had Jewish roots or had connections with the Crusaders from northwest Europe. Was his hair colour a source of comment, mockery and scorn here in Syria, as I knew from personal experience it was in the UK?

Although predominantly Sunni Arab, Syria is home to a diversity of other cultures, but as outsiders it was extremely hard for us to discern people's ethnic identities unless they told us directly or there were obvious outward signs, like a woman not wearing a headscarf, which may have indicated that she was Christian. Around 10 per cent of the population is Christian, many of whom live in the western mountains of the Syrian Levant, and a similar percentage are Kurds, with their main centres of population in the north of the country and contiguous with those in southeastern Turkey (northern Kurdistan), northern Iraq (southern Kurdistan), northwestern Iran (eastern Kurdistan), and broadly spanning the Zagros and Taurus massifs. This simple summary hides an array of ethnic and religious groupings – Shiites, Alawites, Circassians, Ismailis, Druze, Yazidis, Turkmen, Maronites, Mandaeans, Melkites, Greek Orthodox, Syriac Orthodox, Armenians, Jews, as well as more recent immigrant communities from Palestine and Iraq – all of whom bring their own faiths. A rich tapestry that was later to be the complex and tragic backdrop for the Syrian civil war.

In March 2011, just over a year after we were in Aleppo, protests were rippling across the Arab world and regimes were toppling. A schoolboy called Mouawiya Syasneh, from Daraa in the south of Syria, spray-painted a wall with 'Your turn is next, Doctor', the doctor in question being President Bashar al-Assad. Mouawiya and other schoolchildren were detained and tortured by security services for forty days, triggering large-scale protests and pro-democracy rallies across Syria. The al-Assad government cracked down lethally on what were initially peaceful protests. What followed was a descent into a multi-sided conflict supported by state-sponsored and non-state actors from outside the region (including Nato, the Cooperation Council for the Arab States of the Gulf, Iran, Russia, Turkey, Hezbollah and al-Qaeda) as well as mercenary fighters. By 2014, the terrorist group Islamic State, which grew out of al-Qaeda and the aftermath of the 2003 invasion of Iraq, had taken advantage of the chaos in Syria and seized control of large areas of western Iraq and eastern Syria (occupying key Kurdish areas). By 2015 it controlled an area of some twelve million people, on whom it enforced its brutal and oppressive interpretation of Islamic law. From 2015 onwards, significant military intervention, including heavy air strikes in support of the al-Assad government, was conducted by Russia. By 2019, after years of intense combat with American, Iraqi and Kurdish forces, Islamic State had lost all its territories and returned to insurgency tactics. By 2024, it was estimated that the war had cost some 500,000 lives and created fourteen million refugees and 7.2 million internally displaced people.

In 2010, during what would become a month in Syria, we discerned almost nothing of the political or religious tensions that would boil over so tragically within just a few years. We were met with hospitable curiosity at every turn, not least in Aleppo. In a different section of Aleppo's great souk, we were called over by another young man who spoke English.

'You must be from the UK – correct?' He leant on one elbow on a brightly coloured bundle of scarves. 'Where are you from?'

'Edinburgh,' I replied, imagining he would never have heard of it.

'Oh, Edinburgh!' the young man squealed. 'My uncle used to live on Broughton Street.'

'In the New Town?' I pictured the steep road lined with austere Georgian townhouses in blond sandstone, trendy bars and organic food shops – a world away from Aleppo. 'What was he doing there?'

'Well, he was living' – the young man gave a sly glance to either side; presumably, I thought, because he was going to confess to the terrible sin of living with a girlfriend – ' with his boyfriend!' He beamed.

'Oh!' I grinned.

'Ha, ha, you know, "We are the only gays in the village!"' he said to my surprise, quoting the sitcom *Little Britain*. He winked. 'This is my uncle.' He gestured behind him. 'He's gay. I am gay, and my cousin, he is bi-gay, not decided yet.'

'Shh,' said a middle-aged man – presumably the uncle – stepping out from the back of the shop, looking bashful. 'Someone might hear.'

Homosexuality is illegal in Syria and, having been warned by our Syrian–Austrian pizza seller, we knew the whole country was kept under close watch by President Bashar al-Assad's security service, an architecture of control inherited from his father, so we did not probe further. The current president and his father were both observing us, since their portraits looked down at us from above the stall of bright silk scarves. Their portraits were side by side in every shop and displayed in the back window of all of the yellow taxis, as if everyone wanted to make sure their fealty went undisputed.

It seemed that everyone in Aleppo wanted to talk to us about sex, rather than politics. Not least the receptionist at our hotel, a man in his thirties called Ali.

'Any friend of yours is a friend of mine,' Ali said when we apologised for having invited in Mahmoud's uncle for a cup of tea the previous night.

'They'd been so welcoming to us. We felt we had to reciprocate.'

'Yes.' Ali gave a small smile and set our room key on the front desk. 'I am glad you found our hospitality, but in truth I am not normally a friend of these men – these men with two wives.'

'Oh, really?' I paused, hoping he might shed light on last night's conversations but not sure whether to push him.

'No.' He shook his head and sighed. 'I also don't like these men that hide their wife in part of the house from me when I come to visit, or make their women wear the veil completely over their face. I am a Kurd. We don't do that.'

Until the 1970s, the face veil or niqab had been largely exclusive to Muslim women in Najd, a region in present-day Saudi Arabia, and in some Arab countries of the Persian Gulf. The wearing of it has grown in popularity among the Sunni Muslim community due to the sponsorship by Saudi Arabia of mosques throughout many Muslim-majority countries, leading to the increased adoption of Wahhabi and Salafist forms of Sunni Islam.

'Have you seen these women eating ice cream?' he asked, smirking as he mimed lifting up the face veil and taking a lick before putting it down again.

I blanched, both shocked and amused at his mimicry, which made him laugh.

'How stupid, making your wife do that,' he said. 'Many of them just never eat in public.'

I recalled how earlier that day I'd seen an elegant woman, exuding affluence, battling with an ice cream from beneath her niqab. She was sitting with her husband in front of Aleppo's great citadel, one of the oldest and largest castles in the world. The sun was glaring off the massive white limestone ramparts as she sat at the foot of the great entrance bridge, stilettos poking out from under layers of diaphanous fabric, and it was melting her vanilla ice cream, which seemed dangerously close to sticking to the black veil as a gust of wind took it.

'These wealthy women are a real problem.' He nodded, warming to his topic. 'One lady asked me to come into her hotel room while her husband was out. "Come quickly and make love to me!" she said. "Don't be stupid, I don't want to die," I told her. These women are so miserable with their horrible husbands. Many of them become lesbians and they get together to watch pornography with their girlfriends.'

I raised my eyebrows questioningly. Having witnessed the reactions in Scotland to a female friend coming out, I was familiar with the narrative, often espoused by heterosexual men, that lesbianism is a natural response to not having met the right man. How would he know such details anyway?

'Yes, yes. All true,' he said, reading my thoughts. 'I was invited once to a party like this – and said no, of course. Yes, there are many lesbians here.'

My brain was whirring. The conservativism of last night now seemed at odds with today's conversations. I glanced over at Ed to try and gauge what he was thinking, but his face wasn't giving anything away.

Ali clearly had more to tell us.

'Women tourists are even worse. I have had two offers of marriage.'
'Really?'
'Yes, yes. One French woman aged sixty said she would marry me to give me a visa and she did not mind if I had girlfriends so long as I looked after her every day ... you know?'

Ed and I both mumbled something non-committal, avoiding eye contact.

'One German woman came up to me in the middle of the night while I was sleeping behind reception and asked me to go to her bed – just like that! Now! She said she was lonely and was very angry when I said no. What do they think we are?'

I shook my head, embarrassed. Then wondered if that was really true, and then felt guilty.

'Some men in the souk, however ... Oh! They love all of this. Mr S., who owns a jewellery company in the souk, he is married, but, oh, he has many girlfriends – and he sells many jewelleries to them!' He laughed. 'He had one Japanese girlfriend he sold so much gold to. Oh yes! He asks her if she want a foot massage in his shop ... Heee heeeeeeeeeee!' He imitated the squeal of a Japanese schoolgirl. 'Eeeughhh, how horrible.' He pulled a face of utter disdain. 'Of course, you know these Japanese women don't ever wash their feet,' he added, as if this was a universally acknowledged fact. 'And they smell.'

He wrinkled his nose. It sounded as if Mr S. had confided quite a bit in Ali.

'She was delighted as he stroked her ... ahhh ... little fingers of the feet! How disgusting. But anyway now he is a very rich man.'

I told him that a seller in the souk had tried to hug me the previous day. We'd just bought some dried apricots and hazelnuts, and then the man, who'd been perfectly affable and polite until then, unexpectedly grabbed me and kissed me hard on both cheeks. This was how Syrian male friends greeted each other, but even after just forty-eight hours in the country I knew that it was absolutely not what was supposed to happen between a man and his female customer. As the shopkeeper had moved towards me, there was a lull in the bustle of the alley and I felt the eyes of disapproving shoppers turn on me. It had happened so fast, and I was too polite, too British and too embarrassed to make a fuss. I just wriggled free and hurried away from his stall, eyes on the ground and cheeks aflame.

'Disgusting!' Ali said. 'Next time, if a man even so much as brushes against you, you say "HALAS!" and spit in their face! That is what all nice girls here do. Otherwise, they may think you are a Russian prostitute, especially on account of your red hair.' He smiled up at us, and said, 'I myself of course am going to wait for a nice girl,' and turned back to his paperwork.

'Nice', that word of barbed meaning, I thought as I climbed the stairs to bed.

4
OFF THE MAP

I found it
after a long wandering
it was a tender evergreen bough
where birds took shelter
a bough bending gently under storms
which later was straight again.

Fadwa Tuqan, trans. Patricia Alanah Byrne, Salma Jayyusi and Naomi Shihab Nye, from 'I Found It', in Marlé Hammond (ed.), *Arabic Poems*

We were beginning to learn that there was no easy way to hurry in Syria. As we headed west from Aleppo the landscape started to rise and we found ourselves on a quiet road atop a gently rolling massif. The soil was orange and arid, but tiny green seedling crops grew in lines across it. Above was a powder-blue sky milky with humidity despite the occasional cool breeze. We stopped and rested on our handlebars, munching biscuits and breathing deeply as we surveyed the scene, glad to be on the move again and free of the mayhem of the city.

We had stayed a day longer than planned in Aleppo to make sure we were properly supplied for the trip ahead. One of the key challenges had been finding a map. It is very easy to take maps for granted. For most of the trip we used German Reise Know-How country maps, which were generally 1:1,000,000 to 1:2,000,000 in scale and which had, in Ed's words, 'excellent cartography' and were printed on light but indestructible waterproof paper. We had Nokia 'brick' phones only – relatively few people had mobile phones at all – and though we'd considered carrying a GPS we'd rejected that as being more of a risk than a benefit, since it could have been taken for the apparatus of a spy. This paranoia would turn out to be not unfounded.

We'd not been able to find a map of Syria in Turkey and since we'd made the decision to come to Syria quite late on, cementing our plans as we faced the Turkish winter, there hadn't been time to get my mother to post us one before we crossed the border. Instead, she had mailed it to post restante in Damascus, so for the time being we had to make do with the only map we'd been able to find in Aleppo – a fold-out leaflet provided for free by the Syrian Arab Ministry of Tourism which fitted the whole country onto one side of A2. It showed the major roads and listed key archaeological sites, of which there were an enormous number, from the Bronze Age cities of Ebla and Mari to the stone remnants left by successive civilisations of Achaemenid Persians, Greeks, Romans, Byzantines, Umayyads, Abbasids, Crusaders, Mamluks and Ottomans. The map also had pictures of a robed Bedouin and camel trotting eastwards across the desert towards Iraq, a windsurfer in board shorts frolicking on the Mediterranean coast and a table laden with hummus and falafel.

We were now cycling in a region called Taftanaz, aiming for the Byzantine ruins of al-Bara and Serjilla, from where we planned to head to the Roman ruins of Apamea. The road marked on the map looked rather approximate, however. Within two hours, we were ambushed by a group of villagers. A man ran out from a group sitting by the road, shouting and beckoning to us. This time, I was much less nervous; accepting Syrian hospitality was beginning to feel like a familiar routine of greetings and hot, sweet tea.

As we introduced ourselves to the leather-jacketed men, a woman in a maroon dress and headscarf yelled from a nearby doorway, rushed towards me, hugged me and dragged me back to her house. I complied with pleasure, glad at the prospect of some female company.

Inquisitive faces peered at me from across the threshold as I fumbled with my shoelaces. My guide, who had introduced herself as Manoor, led me across a sea of pink and purple plastic sandals and along a corridor to an unfurnished room packed with women and children. One of the women was lying on a mattress on the floor in a fleece nightdress, her cheeks flushed very red, as if with fever, as she breastfed a baby. I worried for a moment that I was going to be asked for a diagnosis. When visiting a remote region of Ladakh in India in 2000, I'd had to fend off requests from villagers for antibiotics to treat conditions like colds and sprained wrists. I knew that some travellers unscrupulously handed out vitamin pills or paracetamol to keep persistent locals happy in such circumstances, but to me that simply fuelled the notion that tourists came with medical magic. Famously, the British desert explorer Wilfred Thesiger, who had no formal medical training, set himself up as a medical doctor during the seven years that he spent with the Marsh Arabs of Iraq. His speciality became male circumcision, an obligatory ritual in the religious traditions of Islam. Prior to his arrival, circumcision had been carried out by peripatetic surgeons operating with a rusty razor, a piece of string and no antiseptics. Thesiger, who employed a sterilised scalpel, anaesthetic and penicillin, soon became the favoured operative, even carrying out other procedures like amputations. That was the 1950s, though, and thankfully the lady just smiled weakly.

I was seated on the floor with numerous cushions and surrounded by a crowd of peering girls and boys. A round of introductions began and I stumbled over the unfamiliar names, trying desperately to remember them. Manoor spoke good English, having learnt it at school, and I was soon answering lots of questions about my life with Ed. Manoor, it turned out, was twenty-seven like me, born in the same month, and had four children, the youngest of whom was just a month old. We joked about being twins and how different our lives were. Why, everyone wanted to know, given that Ed and I had been married for two years, did I not have any children?

Ed and I had met as students at St Andrews, while out climbing on the sea stack called the Maiden, and from almost as soon as we'd become a couple we'd been scheming to go away on an adventure. Eight years on, and most of my PhD colleagues were by now busy starting postdoctoral positions, while other friends were having babies. Since our wedding, hints had been dropped about it perhaps being time for Ed and me to settle down, but children had thus far been ruled out by mutual consensus. This was something I ruminated on a lot while I was in the saddle. For now, however, our goal was China, to be reached in a relaxed fashion, without a cast-iron schedule of times or routes. Our goal was China but our purpose was the way there. All of which was quite a lot to explain, both because of the significant language barrier and because I wasn't sure I fully understood it myself. So I settled on summarising this with that ever-useful Arabic expression 'Inshallah' (God willing), smiling with a slightly serious expression, and moving on.

A large lady called Fatima pinched my thigh and told me that I was too thin and then joked that maybe she should take up cycling. She grabbed my wrist and held it up, circling it with her plump fingers, and there was a general murmur of agreement that I was too skinny. My friends in the UK sometimes commented enviously on my ability to snack and not gain weight, but I knew being thin was often taken as a sign of poverty in countries where food was scarce. Fatima tugged at my long shirt and asked me if I liked cycling. I looked around at the women, who were dressed, despite the rural setting, in satins and sequins, material that I associated with formal occasions and parties. Fatima herself was in crushed purple velvet, with a white hijab draped over her expansive bosom. I laughed, realising that she assumed my husband had dragged me along on this trip against my will, a trip that required me to wear unglamorous clothing and that had caused me to lose an unappealing amount of weight!

'Yes, I like!' I protested. 'I like to see the world and your beautiful country and meet you!'

Fatima patted my hand, clearly not convinced.

Tea was brought, together with a big bowl of oranges and yellow apples. Manoor insisted on peeling an apple, removing the bruised bits and slicing it for me. She did the same with an orange, picking the pith off carefully before handing me the first segment and then the rest to the others. A small, solemn-faced boy of perhaps ten came to sit next to me and showed me his English homework. After a few minutes of me listening to him read, he declared that he loved me, much to the mirth of the women.

Eventually Ed and I set off again, having politely refused repeated offers of accommodation for the night. As we were packing up, Manoor forced a package into my hand, making me promise not to open it. I hastily dug the only thing out of my panniers worth giving her: some earrings that Ed had bought me for Christmas on Crete two months ago. Then came the departure photo. Manoor's husband and the three older children sat together on the back of his motorbike; she held the baby, dressed head to toe in pink fleece, and then perched side-saddle on the back. She spent some time arranging her family, telling her son to sit further forward on the bike's steering column, straightening her daughter's jumper and wiping a mark off her younger son's face. At the last moment she moved off to one side, indicating that she did not want be photographed. Taking photographs of women can cause offence in Syria and I did not press her.

That evening I discovered that she had given me a nightdress – long white satin, and with long sleeves and shoulder pads. I smiled. Perhaps she thought that I would need it to keep Ed interested during our biking escapade. In my diary, from which she had seen me take family photographs to show everyone, a poetic message spidered across the page in Arabic.

The flowers exuded freshness and fragrance.
The sun and moon are pure and pure.
I love you so much and hope to see you again.

I don't know if this is a classic Arabic verse or Manoor's own words, or if the translation is faithful or poor. Poetry occupies a central position in Islamic culture, dating back millennia as an oral tradition that came out of desert communities and was used as rallying calls for shared values and war, a practice which underpinned and amplified the spread of the written Qur'an and literacy to the four corners of the vast Abbasid Empire (750–1258). There is, for example, poetry in the adhan, the call to prayer traditionally issued five time a day from a minaret, which includes the repeated, hypnotically alliterative phrase 'La illaha illa 'llah' (There is no god but Allah). Memorisation of the Qur'an is considered to be a religious act and those who achieve this feat – and millions of people do – are bestowed with the title of hafiz (for males) or hafiza (for females). The Qur'an's influence on literature is equivalent to (and indeed exceeds) the influence of the Bible on the English language and its literature.

A Hadith, a reported saying of the Prophet, states that 'underneath the throne of God lie treasures, the keys to which are the tongues of poets'. The early Muslims valued poetry so highly that seven poems – the Mu'allaqat – were written in gold on pieces of linen and hung on the curtains which covered the Kaaba at Mecca. There were even journalists who wrote political articles in rhymed prose into the early twentieth century.

We reached the outskirts of the town of Idlib fifteen kilometres later, as the light was fading from the sky, and began to regret not having accepted Manoor's offer to put us up. It was quite built up here and we did not feel brave enough to camp. The town was an unprepossessing mix of concrete tower blocks and shops with corrugated-metal fronts jumbled together along dusty streets edged with the usual deep drainage channels that seemed designed to be traps for cyclists. A regular town where people lived out their daily lives, a town that did not feature in the guidebooks and that we were therefore in a way privileged to see, as cycle-tourers unable to whizz from tourist hotspot to tourist hotspot. During the civil war, Idlib was to become a significant rebel stronghold, holding out (under changing hands) against being retaken by the government and becoming a proving ground for President Ahmed al-Sharaa, who would finally do in 2024 what most thought was impossible, and overthrow Bashar al-Assad, ending fifty-four years of Assad family rule. Idlib paid heavily for its rebel status. In 2017, the town of Khan Shaykhun in the south of Idlib province suffered the deadliest sarin gas attack of the war, which killed at least eighty-three people, many of them women and children. An attack the UNHCR's (the UN Refugee Agency) independent commission of inquiry concluded had been conducted by the Syrian Air Force.

A white 4x4 slowed next to us. A black window slid down and a man in a suit asked if he could help us.

'Salam,' Ed said. 'Yes, we need to find a hotel. Can you recommend one?'

'The best hotel is on the other side of town. It is expensive, though – one hundred US dollars per night.'

'A hundred dollars? That is very expensive.'

'Yes, it is. It is much.'

'You don't know of anywhere cheaper?'

'Come.' He waved for us to follow.

We pedalled fast behind the car as it sped off, riding deeper into the town, past buildings that looked like military or police barracks. The streets became busy with cars and motorbikes and then the evening call to prayer (the adhan) began to sound out. Long, wobbly shadows were being cast by the golden sunlight and we were swept along with a flock of motorbikers, who waved to us as the muezzin's call bounced from one minaret and the next, proclaiming the greatness of God and hastening the faithful to prayer. We eventually came to a halt at a square that was little more than a roundabout and the 4x4 driver motioned for us to wait while he entered a concrete building with a few cracked plastic chairs on its veranda. We leant on our handlebars, surreptitiously watching from behind our sunglasses the men who'd stopped on the street to watch us. From the stares, I doubted many tourists ever made it further than the luxury hotel out of town.

'You will be okay here,' our man said when he came out again, handing Ed a business card. 'Any problems, you can call.'

A sullen attendant helped carry our bags through the restaurant, where two men were watching TV and smoking. We followed him up a dirty concrete staircase to a room which smelt of cigarettes and whatever was emanating from the en-suite squat toilet and shower combo. I peered at the sheets and wondered if we might have been brought to a brothel. The manager had apparently been loath to take us, but our 4x4 man had insisted and had then negotiated a decent price on our behalf.

We asked about food and were told that there was none, so we set up our stove on the small balcony that overlooked the roundabout and made pasta. We lay in bed watching a Bollywood movie, hearing voices and TVs in other rooms and the scurrying of feet when the call to prayer rang out again at 4am. We checked out soon after.

By 9.30am our stomachs were growling and the road had begun to climb again. We stopped, ten kilometres out of Idlib, at the first open shop we'd seen and I waited with our bikes as Ed went in.

He returned holding a bowl of brown porridge-like substance and a spoon. 'The guy in the shop gave me this,' he said.

It was sweet and good and something like bulgur wheat. We stood in the sunshine, taking turns with the spoon, and I felt my hunger pangs dissolve. When we both went inside to thank the shopkeeper his eyes widened when I greeted him. Immediately he called out to the back of the shop and a woman appeared and gestured for me to follow her. From a distance, he'd thought I was a man. I could understand why. I'd not seen a single woman on a bicycle since Athens, more than two months ago, and no woman wearing trousers since we had crossed the Turkish border. My long shirt covered my bottom and upper thighs and I wore an olive-green headscarf under my helmet to keep the sun and dust off. In a country where both men and women wrapped their heads, I could see why at the first sight of my heavily laden bicycle he'd assumed I was a man. The thought gave me comfort.

As I stepped through the low hatch, a fit of giggles erupted from a teenager holding a baby on the other side.

'Salam.' I beamed brightly.

'Salam.' She composed herself and smiled as I took her hand.

The older woman had come through behind me and was trying to stifle her giggles too.

'Arabi?' the younger girl asked. She was breastfeeding.

I shook my head. 'Inglesi.' Scottish travellers will be familiar with the difficulty of explaining the nuances of the United Kingdom. Since I was frankly in the early stages of understanding the differences between Kurds, Turks and Arabs, it seemed to me that 'England' provided sufficient reciprocal geographical precision.

I opened my bar bag, the bag that clipped on to my handlebars and held my most essential possessions, and pulled out my diary, which had the photos of my family in the back. I flicked to the one of my parents standing on top of a hill and pointed to my mother and then me. 'Amma.' I pointed at the older woman and the younger woman and repeated, 'Amma?'

They shook their heads and laughed. The girl was the daughter-in-law and the baby was her first. She was sixteen. A younger girl appeared with a tray of tea and a bowl of dried fruit. The women crowded close into me and peered at the photographs, which must have seemed strange to them: my parents in hiking trousers and carrying trekking poles; my brother and parents on a mountain in Norway; my family sitting on a sofa; and lastly a photograph of our wedding in Braemar two years previously, me wearing a strapless wedding dress and Ed in a kilt. I looked at it now, thinking we both looked underdressed by local standards, since even men did not show their knees in Syria, but the younger girl took it from my hands, examined it and mimed her request to keep it, to which I agreed, bemused. She pressed it to her heart and then placed it into a pocket under a fold of her abaya. In my family we preferred informal pictures of ourselves on the tops of mountains, but the photos of us in formal dress always seemed to garner more approval, perhaps because they better fitted a stereotype of affluence.

'Helen?' Ed's voice came through the hatch. 'We should probably leave now.'

He was loading the shopping into my front pannier when I came back out.

'We are really going to have to find a way round this,' he said. 'The shopkeeper wouldn't take payment for any of these groceries.'

People just seemed to want to give us things and it felt really wrong. No sooner had I innocuously admired a girl's headscarf at our hosts' house the previous day than she began to take it off to give to me. I had to fight to get her to keep it.

Rising out of the hand-ploughed orange earth and set between drystone walls and the silver foliage of olive trees was a series of square, blocky structures with doorways and tapering pyramidal roofs. This was the settlement of al-Bara, which back in the fourth century had been a centre of wine and olive-oil production on the trade route between Antioch (current-day Antakya in Turkey) and the Roman city of Apamea, some twenty kilometres away. It is the largest of the so-called Dead Cities, seven hundred such settlements dating from the first to the seventh century that are scattered across the limestone massif of northwest Syria and are under Unesco World Heritage Site inscription. The villages were all abandoned between the eighth and tenth centuries for reasons that aren't clear but may have included changes in the price of olive oil, the shifting of trade routes and earthquake damage.

We stopped by a tomb whose pyramidal top was as steep as a witch's hat and sat under the shade of an olive tree for our lunch of flatbread and tinned sardines. The tomb was made of hefty blocks of orange rock crusted with grey lichen, its size presumably testament to the wealth of its owner. I ducked under a low archway, savouring the slightly damp air. Light shone in from four high windows cut into the side. Around the walls lay five sarcophagi hewn from the same rock and topped with heavy lids covered in green moss. Some of these were cracked, possible evidence of tomb-raiding attempts, but otherwise the whole building was remarkably intact. Each sarcophagus was embossed with a central six-spoked wheel wreathed in leaves, flanked to left and right by a smaller wheel. The same design was repeated on the cornices inside and out and was accompanied by scrolling of deeply cut foliage resembling thistles or cardoons.

A man herded a flock of sheep past and later a taxi pulled up, disgorging some local tourists to take pictures. When they moved on, the only sound was the distant call of the shepherd in the still air. I took another bite of flatbread and thought how good it was to be eating just in our own company. The experiences of the last couple of days had been exhilarating but required a constant state of alertness, reading people's intentions and reactions, especially at mealtimes, to ensure we were not committing any faux pas.

The road continued climbing. We were on a vast limestone plateau of rolling, barren hills devoid of most vegetation other than the crops and olive trees planted in sparse rows that struggled out of the rocky orange clay-rich soil. The air was still humid. As we got higher, the scatter of villages disappeared and only an occasional car passed us on the road. As I turned the pedals, sweat rose on my forehead, but I was enjoying cycling away from traffic and people once again. We rode two abreast.

By mid-afternoon we'd reached the Dead City of Serjilla. The ruins here were more substantial, comprising many two-storeyed buildings spread across a hillside of cropped bright green grass dotted with fallen limestone blocks. The most striking building had a three-columned portico on both storeys, one line of columns still balancing improbably on top of the other, even after more than 1500 years. This was the andron, or men's meeting house. As we picked our way towards the ruins of the substantial bathhouse, a large flock of brown and white sheep with dreadlocked coats and big floppy ears poured around us and through the cracks in the building. Behind them wandered a small boy, whistling.

There were perhaps five or six other tourists fanned out across the site, each on an individual mission of discovery with their digital camera in the still afternoon. We drifted close to a group of young Syrian men, perhaps still teenagers, all tight T-shirts, leather jackets and gelled hair. A waft of cologne hit me as we passed. I looked round as I crossed a ruined threshold to see that they were following me, shoving each other and laughing, two holding their mobile phones aloft.

'Why are they filming me?' I muttered, catching up with Ed. In my grubby trekking trousers and baggy shirt, I wasn't exactly model material. We sauntered further into the ruins and I could hear their voices getting closer.

'Just ignore them,' Ed said.

To me, their behaviour seemed harmless but rude. So far in Syria, each of my tentative requests to take photos of the women I'd met had been met with a polite but very firm refusal. The men enjoyed posing for photographs and having their children's photos taken, but, as with Manoor, we got the distinct impression that photographing the women would cause offence.

'Let's take a photo of them, give them a taste of their own medicine,' I said, irritated.

We wheeled round and walked right up to the group. Mobile phones were lowered and they laughed nervously.

'Salam. Photo?' Ed lifted his camera and began directing them to stand together.

Looking uncertain, the boys assembled, arms draped over each other. They spoke to each other in Arabic and one of them was shoved forwards.

'Where you from?' he asked.

'Scotland. And you?'

'Damascus.'

There was more chatter.

'Sister?' He gestured at me with an upward jerk of the chin. They laughed.

This was not to be our last such encounter that day.

We cycled off, along the crest of a wide hill. The roadside was dotted with small bushes and we passed a family picnicking in a lay-by squeezed under their shade. A bird tweeted and the surrounds seemed suddenly lush in comparison to the dust of the last few days.

I heard the splutter of a motorbike engine coming up behind us. Two young men on a Honda drew level.

'Salam,' they called out.

'Salam.' We waved in reply.

'Where are you from?' They addressed Ed.

The man riding pillion uncurled his arm from around his friend, pulled a phone out of his jacket pocket and began filming me.

I fixed my eyes on the road, the colour rising to my cheeks, suddenly nervous and acutely aware of every pedal stroke.

'Hello,' the photographer called out to me.

I stared straight ahead and pretended I couldn't hear, thinking that was what a local woman would do.

Eventually they got bored and roared off.

Later, we pulled up outside a shop in a small village to buy supplies for dinner.

'Perhaps you'd better go in,' Ed said as a group of young men who'd been standing outside a house further down the road hopped on their motorbikes and congregated round us.

I unclipped my helmet, stowed my sunglasses and crossed the road, screwing my eyes up against the low evening sun. Two teenage boys who'd been lounging on the step of the shop followed me inside. The older turned to the younger one and gestured that he should leave, at which point he fled across the road to join the growing crowd that had surrounded Ed.

The older boy took up place behind the counter, watching me closely as I walked around the shop picking up flatbread, tinned fish, eggs and bottled water, then followed me outside again as I negotiated my way back to the bicycles. A group of boys were leaning over the map on Ed's bar bag and others were testing the brakes on my bicycle. They stood away respectfully as I began stowing the shopping in my front panniers and stacking the water bottles under the bungees on the bike racks.

'Apamea, this way?' I could hear Ed saying.

'Yes, yes. Come.' One of the boys patted his motorcycle engine.

'Are we lost?' I called across to Ed.

'I can't seem to make sense of where we are right now. This junction has more roads coming off it than the map suggests. If I've got it right, we're not in the correct town. Basically, this map is crap.'

'Does he know the way?' I nodded at the boy who'd spoken.

Ed shrugged. 'No idea.'

There was clearly going to be little choice about the assistance anyhow and we set off with a convoy of three motorbikes, each loaded with a pair of teenage boys. I cycled close behind Ed as they flanked us. They looked young, friendly and harmless, but I still didn't fancy a party helping us set up camp.

Everyone in Syria seemed to drive the same make of motorbike: Hondas with red or cobalt-blue bodywork, wide-set handlebars, serious front suspension, a long, cushioned seat with a low backrest, and chrome metalwork and foot rails. They were designed to be workhorses and it was not unusual to see three grown men or a family of five bumping along, one child on the handlebars and two sandwiched between the father at the front and the mother riding side-saddle at the back. Despite or perhaps because of their slip-on shoes and headscarves, the drivers (always men) emitted an unaffected machismo that made the leather-protected super bikers who tore up the A82 to Fort William in Scotland seem unmanly in comparison. Some riders adorned their steering columns and handlebars with garlands of plastic flowers, presumably to appeal to the ladies, and many had saddlebags made of patterned kilim rugs.

The swarm of bikes accompanied us through a number of junctions at small villages scattered along the hillside. The boys talked to Ed as I struggled hard to keep up, sweat rising on my forehead, my throat dry. Eventually, just as the sun was setting, we reached the brow of the hill and they pointed downwards and said their goodbyes. Our road descended to a main road along a flat plain.

'Bugger,' Ed muttered. 'I think we've dropped down off the hillside the wrong way and now we're going to have to skirt round it.'

Ed is an exceptional map reader – I know from experience that he can navigate a white-out on the featureless plateau of the Cairngorms in the Scottish Highlands, counting out paces on a bearing to a ring contour or a catching feature – but for that he needs an accurate map. At this point, somewhere in the approximate vicinity of Apamea, we had just the tourist sketch-map.

'How far do you think it is?' I asked, my anxiety building.

'Not sure. Another hour at least.'

Ploughed fields abutted the roads. Heavy clay in furrows. We cycled under an opaque, pinkening sky that intensified the lush green of the seedling crops. The air was still and damp and a coolness was creeping into it. In the distance the call to prayer started.

We pedalled in silence, past isolated mud houses, the colour of the ground. Past groups of women walking in from the fields. I hoped we wouldn't have to ask at a lone house to camp. I always felt more secure if we were either totally on our own or in a village. And anyhow it was difficult to see where in the heavy clay furrows there would be space to camp, so we would be practically inviting ourselves into their house for the night.

I gazed at Ed pedalling in front of me, feeling detached, as if I was watching us on a TV screen, cycling along this rutted road, avoiding pot-holes of mud, swerving as the occasional car or motorbike passed. I could switch this off and be at home, I thought idly.

A young couple on a motorbike overtook us, the woman riding side-saddle on the back, her headscarf and long dress tugged out in the breeze. 'I love you,' she shouted, waving as she passed us, balancing herself against the rack with her other hand. I waved back enthusiastically, snapping myself back into the scene. My wrist crunched towards my handlebars as, momentarily distracted, I jolted over an unnoticed pot-hole.

Half an hour later it was dark.

I came to a stop and Ed pulled up next to me. We peered at the map in the gloom.

'Someone's coming,' I said.

The engine sound grew louder and a pick-up stopped alongside us. A man leant out of the window.

'Salam.'

'Salam.'

He stared at us and I squinted back at him. He seemed to be alone. He twisted his hand, turning it from palm down to palm up, the Syrian gesture for 'What's up? What the hell …?' People often did that as they passed us on the road.

'Apamea?' Ed answered.

The man indicated that it was still a way off. 'Welcome, welcome. Yes.' He waved at the back of his pick-up.

Ed looked at me and I nodded. It seemed like a reasonable option.

'Okay. Taxi,' Ed said, indicating that we wanted to pay him for the detour.

Hurriedly, we unclipped all eight panniers from the bikes as the driver dropped the side of the pick-up. While Ed was checking that everything was loaded, the man waved for me to climb into the cab next to him.

'Hello.' He waved at me again.

I pretended not to notice and slipped into the cab after Ed so that he was the one straddling the gearstick. A warning light switched to amber in my brain.

5
YELEN, DAOUD, FANTASTICO

If you are distressed by anything external, the pain is not due to the thing itself, but to your estimate of it; and this you have the power to revoke at any moment.

Marcus Aurelius, *Meditations*

As the engine started up, I remembered that our bar bags were still attached to the bikes, in the flatbed of the pick-up.

S***, I thought, doing a mental inventory. I was carrying three hundred dollars in my bra, and Ed another two hundred hidden in his belt, but credit cards, mobile phones and passports were in the bar bags in the back. Idiots. Stupid idiots.

The driver, I could now see, was around forty and dressed in a brown dishdasha with a tatty shemagh wrapped around his head. His moustache was greying and dark stubble grazed a flabby chin. He spoke in a rapid volley of words: basic English, Arabic and seemingly Italian.

'Welcome, yes. Yes, welcome to Syria. United Kingdom, very good … very fantastico. You are welcome, my friends. Inshallah, you are welcome here. Ahlan wa sahlan – welcome. Where are you from? Yes, yes. Scotland.'

Was this outpouring a distraction tactic?

'Fantastico. My name is Mustafa. My name is …?' He leant across Ed and tapped me on the knee.

'My name is Helen.'

'My name is Edward.' Ed pointed at himself, sounding strangely like a spare wheel.

'Yelena, Daoud, good. AHLAN WA SAHLAN!' He seemed particularly pleased with the alliteration.

'Zawja? (Wife?)' Ed pointed at the man.

The man waved dismissively and did not return the question.

'Yelen, Daoud, fantastico.' He began to sing in Arabic, punctuated by expressions of 'AHLAN WA SAHLAN!'

I tried to shoot a sideways glace at Ed, but we were both squashed in, facing forwards, and all I could see was the view past his profile of the driver's red-and-white shemagh in a roll around his forehead, and his grizzled chin. I did not dare squeeze Ed's knee.

The vehicle bounced as we took the pot-holes.

'Yallah. Yallah.' The driver laughed. 'Good. Good.' He leant across Ed again, thrusting a tape at me. 'Music. Good.' He waved at the tape deck, giving my knee another pat.

Ed tensed next to me.

'Watch him,' I muttered. 'Can you help me sort this out?'

'I am,' Ed muttered back as he jabbed the play button. 'Good music,' Ed said loudly.

'Good, yes. You like Syrian music.'

As we bumped along, I strained my eyes, trying to make out something, anything, in the darkness. The conversation had died and the driver sang snatches of the song to himself.

'Do you think we're going the right way?' I asked Ed quietly, hoping his innate sense of direction would keep us safe.

'Yes, probably,' came the terse response.

We passed through a village, its roadside lined with a few tatty shops, fronts lit by faint sodium lights, some men standing in an open doorway, their long robes luminous. We slowed and the driver tooted and waved at a group of men in leather jackets, who stared back. At least there would be some witnesses, I thought.

We jolted back into the darkness and the driver lifted his mobile phone to his head.

What he's up to now? I wondered. The driver leant across and tapped me on the knee again, indicating that I should turn the music down. Ed reached for the knob. The driver was laughing into the handset.

'Telefon.' He pushed the handset towards me.

I stared ahead impassively, not wanting to be drawn into whatever he was planning.

'TELEFON.' He tapped me on the shoulder and when I still pretended not to understand he patted my thigh with it.

I took it reluctantly and held it to my ear.

'Talk. Talk,' he urged.

'Salam alaykum.' I recited the formal greeting into the handset.

Male laughter echoed back. The driver had told them that he had a European woman in his car (perhaps even his girlfriend, I thought cynically) and now they wanted him to prove it.

'Talk English.' The driver nudged me as I stared ahead, saying nothing into the handset.

I passed it back towards him.

'Talk English.' He pushed it away.

'Hello. My husband and I are travelling around Syria. We like your country very much,' I said dumbly. There was more laughing as I passed it to Ed, indicating he should take over.

'Okay. Okay.' The driver took the handset from Ed.

We turned off the main road and began to head uphill, the pick-up jolting over deep pot-holes.

'Do you think this is right?' I whispered.

'It makes sense.'

Five or maybe ten minutes passed and then we stopped in the middle of the road. I peered out of the window to see a line of white Roman pillars marching off into the night.

'Apamea,' the driver announced.

'Thank you. Shukran.'

We burst out of the passenger door and hurried to unload everything from the pick-up. I stood close to Ed and helped him lift the first bike over the side of the flatbed and then I wheeled it to the edge of the road as he dealt with the second one. As I turned round, I found the driver beside me. He reached out and pulled me towards him.

I froze in shock for a split second, my face inches from his. Long enough to feel his breath coming fast and to see his moist lips moving mechanically as beard hairs brushed my cheek.

The split second passed.

'HALAS!' I hissed, pushing him with all my force.

To my surprise, he let go. It was as if uttering that phrase had supercharged me with electricity. He stepped backwards, arms raised. I looked round and saw that Ed was leaning into the pick-up, adjusting something. I stood in shock as Ed counted out some notes for him and shook his hand.

The truck started up and with a toot drove off into the darkness.

'Cheeky bastard asked me for my sunglasses as well,' Ed said once the engine sound had died away.

'Did you see what he did?' I said, shaking.

'Yeah, I thought he was overstepping the mark a bit.'

'A BIT?' I choked, suddenly apoplectic with rage, my heart racing. 'He just grabbed me and tried to kiss me.'

'What?'

'Yeah. I just managed to avoid it. I can't believe you paid him.'

'S***. I thought he'd just come too close to you. Are you alright?'

'I'm NOT alright.'

'Bastard. I just wanted to get rid of him quickly.' Ed pulled me towards him and I shook with fear and rage and self-loathing for having somehow invited this behaviour.

Next time, if a man even so much as brushes against you, you say 'HALAS!' and spit in their face! That is what all NICE girls here do. Clearly not NICE enough.

'We better find somewhere to camp.'

'Do you think he's going to come back?'

'That's what I'm worried about. I doubt it, but still …'

A light shone out a short way up the road. There was a house and we could hear women's voices.

'I'm going to ask about camping,' Ed said, heading towards the light. He returned five minutes later. 'It's okay. She says we can camp in the ruins.'

We pitched the tent and cooked a hasty dinner of scrambled eggs. The white pillars of Apamea's main colonnade gleamed in the moonlight and on a distant hill a few lights twinkled. I pulled on Ed's bulky down jacket and a shemagh scarf, feeling safer in the knowledge that from a distance I would be taken for a man.

'Perhaps if you had reacted to him touching me in the cab, he would have backed off,' I said as we lay in our down sleeping bags, listening to the road. I'd been trying to work out the apparent contradictions in behaviour in this country.

'Yes, but we were kind of trapped, Helen. That's why you didn't react either. I mean, maybe we were stupid to get in the pick-up in the first place, but neither of us wanted to piss him off after that.'

'Just think how a man here would react if another man touched his wife. I don't know if you essentially sanctioned his behaviour …'

'I'd find it hard to go ape every time a man brushed against you, but if I'd seen him try to kiss you, that would have been different.' Ed propped himself up on one elbow, emphatic now. 'I have never treated you like my property, Helen, and I don't intend to start doing that now just because we're here.'

The truth was, I wouldn't have been there at all if it hadn't been for Ed. Not because, as Fatima had wrongly surmised, Ed had made me come. Absolutely not. It had always been a joint project. But I wouldn't have come to Syria alone and by bike. I'd done my fair share of solo, independent travel, including tramping New Zealand's trails by myself. My nineteenth birthday was spent alone on Stewart Island's Northwest Circuit, one of NZ's more remote hikes. It was winter and I trekked through a creaking forest, wind howling, pushing past punga ferns with a backpack weighed down with ten days' food and a stick to haul myself out of the frequent pools of mud. The Southern Ocean's white teeth bit at isolated yellow beaches, and bones of pilot whales littered the shore. At the huts on the first night I met nine hunters (all men, of course), who fed me and told me that the huts were haunted. I didn't see another person until day eight. When staying at the huts, I took the axe off the woodblock and stashed it under my bunk, but I found it hard to be afraid. The beauty was too overwhelming and I generally felt at ease on my own.

Ed would often say, though, that there was a big difference between being alone with nature and being alone with other people. 'I can read mountains, but people are so unpredictable.'

The latter were definitely our bigger fear. Not only did us travelling together give me, give us, the courage to visit places we might otherwise have avoided, but also, fairly or not for a feminist, I was relying on him to protect me from the worst sorts of men.

I took Ed's hand in the darkness and drifted into an uneasy sleep.

6

WATERWHEELS AND A CRUSADER CASTLE

Life is a flame that flickers in the wind,
A bird that crouches in the fowler's net -
Nor may between her flutterings forget
That hour the dreams of youth were unconfined.

al-Ma'arri, trans. Henry Baerlein, from 'Diwan', in Suheil Bushrui and James M. Malarkey (eds.), *Desert Songs of the Night*

Birds had chirped in the ruins all night and we woke early, feeling exhausted, to the line of white pillars marching off into mist and the grass glistening with a heavy dew in the pale sunlight. We sat in the porch of the tent drinking tea and eating stale flatbread with jam as we watched the mist dissipate. In the daylight the anxieties of the previous night seemed less pressing and by the time we had packed up the bikes and spent an hour wandering the deserted colonnades of Apamea, I had begun to remember why I was here.

Apamea's Great Colonnade is a vast avenue of almost two kilometres, the longest in the Roman world. It was completed during the reign of Marcus Aurelius (161–80), the Roman emperor who was also a philosopher of the Stoic school and whose inspirational writings, published as *Meditations*, endure to this day. Syria had been annexed to the Roman Republic since 64 BC and Antioch, 150 kilometres to the north of Apamea, was the third most important city of the Roman Empire after Rome and Alexandria.

In its heyday, Apamea and the surrounding villages would have been home to half a million people, with Rome's II Parthica Legion, five thousand men strong, garrisoned there too. Now it was utterly deserted. There was no ticket office in sight and no explanatory signs; the only person who found us among the ruins was a boy on a motorbike with a child's face and the fluff of an incipient moustache. Whether we wanted it or not, he was going to be our guide. Together we trod the great paving stones of the broad cardo maximus, the main street, which ran north–south beneath the high columns that had been restored by a team of

Belgian archaeologists. The grass to either side was thick with silk webs and hundreds of black caterpillars with orange spikes marched across the avenue in a grotesque conglomeration, dwarfed to specks by the towering pillars. Our guide pointed upwards to the twisted fluting adorning a section of columns, a feature unique to Apamea. I squinted up, their spirals making me dizzy, my face in the bright sun. It was going to be a hot day.

We pedalled back down the road that we'd been driven up the night before. The plains stretched out before us into the haze. So far the skies in Syria had seemed permanently milky, as if a veil had been drawn over the far landscape. Now, in the light, we could see muddy fields of seedlings cut up by dirt tracks and low, flat-roofed houses of mud or concrete. The fields were speckled with the dark figures of women at work. We hurried through the town at the junction lest we encounter the pick-up driver from the previous night, but no one stopped us for conversation.

By mid-morning the ground was rising gently. The outline of a small hill appeared and soon we could see the citadel town of Shaizar perched on its crest. A giant wooden waterwheel or noria came into view at the foot of the hill, turning lazily under the power of a narrow, grubby stretch of the Orontes River, plastic bottles strewn across the bank. Aside from the hill and some gangly telegraph pylons, it was the highest object in the landscape. Many of the norias found along the Syrian extent of the Orontes River date from the twelfth or thirteenth centuries, but waterwheels may have been operating around here in some form since as far back as the middle of the fourth century. They were used to lift water into aqueducts and irrigation channels. Norias were depicted in Roman mosaics, including in one that was illegally excavated from Apamea in the first months of Syria's civil war, which might be the oldest known representation of a waterwheel, likely dating from the reign of Emperor Constantine the Great (306–37). The Sufi saint and mystic poet Rumi (1207–73), who spent time in Syria, eventually living in Konya, Turkey, was familiar with them too …

Stay together friends
Don't scatter and sleep
Our friendship is made

Of being awake.
The waterwheel accepts water
and turns and gives it away
weeping.

Rumi, trans. Coleman Barks, 'Waterwheel', in *Selected Poems*

The road beyond Shaizar was lined with tents. Low, long, rectangular and made of discoloured grey cloth, they clustered on the dusty ground to either side. The cry of a child went up and a group of small figures raced towards us. The children, three of them, walked alongside us as we toiled up the slope. They were dirty and barefoot and as we stood on our pedals, the boy, who was no more than five and tiny and thin, with a shorn head, broke into song. His voice was high and eerily strong for such a little body. Seeing us smiling, he began a comical dance and clapped as he sang. His sisters, if that was who they were, smiled but said nothing. We stopped to rest halfway up the hill and clapped with him as he finished the song. Then a woman's voice called from by the tents and the children were gone.

As we reached the brow of the hill, the tents were closer to the road and an old man who was sitting on a plastic chair outside one of them waved us over, shouting, 'Chai! Chai!' We pressed our hands to our hearts and waved back, shouting our thanks before we cycled on. It was too soon for another tea stop and we still had twenty-five kilometres to go before we reached Hama.

It was only a few minutes later, when I had gathered my breath, that I realised that the high barbed wire surrounding the encampment meant these were refugees, not nomads. Syria was home to around half a million Palestinian refugees in 2010 and I later discovered that this camp had been erected in 1950 to house Palestinians made homeless by the first Arab–Israeli war in 1948, the war that followed the adoption of the UN's Partition Plan for Palestine. This plan aimed to divide the territory into an Arab state, a Jewish state, and the Special International Regime encompassing the cities of Jerusalem and Bethlehem. The newly formed State of Israel controlled the area that the UN had proposed for the Jewish state, as well as almost 60 per cent of the area proposed for the Arab state, and West Jerusalem. The original inhabitants of the camp had fled from the villages surrounding Haifa and Acre in northern Palestine and when we passed it was home to thousands of Palestine refugees, many of whom were descendants of the first inhabitants. Refugees in Syria have never been given the status of full citizens and many had lived for generations in camps like the one outside Shaizar.

It was a straightforward ride to Hama along a dusty dual carriageway and that evening we made the most of being in the city again as we sat on a bench in a small park in the centre, devouring roast chicken and potatoes from a shop across the road. The heavenly smell of the chicken infused the balmy evening air. We were not the only people having take-away – most of the benches were occupied by people eating from parcels wrapped in paper. Two large noria waterwheels stood motionless in the static canal water beyond. Hama is famous for its noria, having seventeen in total, including the great Noria al-Muhammadiya, which supplies Hama's Grand Mosque and for nearly five hundred years was, at twenty-one metres in diameter, the tallest waterwheel in the world. (It was surpassed only in 1854 by the slightly higher Laxey Wheel on the Isle of Man, which was used for the mining industry.)

We were in Hama's old town, the tourist centre, which looked like it had been quite recently restored. There was a reason for that, since much of the city had been destroyed in 1982 when Syria's then president, Hafez al-Assad, had bombed it, killing between ten thousand and twenty-five thousand of his own citizens in an attempt to quell an opposition uprising by the Muslim Brotherhood. At that time this was the worst bombing of civilians in history. Many of the city's mosques, churches, archaeological sites and infrastructure were destroyed. A stern lesson had been issued to the Syrian people not to agitate for change.

Today's streets were lively with people, but few seemed to be tourists. I looked up from tackling a chicken wing and noticed we were being watched. A group of youths had sidled up to the bench opposite us and were glancing over to us while they talked. The sound of their laughter carried through the still air and I began to feel self-conscious as I fished around for the last deliciously greasy roast potatoes and licked my fingers. We'd not eaten anything meaty or fatty for a number of days and I was really beginning to crave fat for the first time in my life. The youths were still watching us.

'Why is it that women don't eat in public?' I said to Ed. 'Is it too carnal?'

We answered a wave of questions. Then an elderly man invited himself over and in English began a long monologue about the city. It irritated me that he was impeding our chance to understand more about these young people. They, however, treated him with utter respect. 'He is a very good man,' one of them said when he left and I instantly felt guilty.

We tried and failed to invite the youths to come for tea with us. There were shops selling a local dessert made out of cheese nearby and we wanted to sit and talk further over tea and pudding. They fidgeted and looked awkward at our suggestion and then point-blank refused. When we finally left them, they presented us with sweatbands bearing the Syrian flag. One of them had nipped to a tourist stall to buy them while we were talking.

As we sat eating the sweet and sticky dessert by ourselves, it dawned on me that Syrian hospitality dictated that they could never accept an invitation from a foreigner. They had refused because they didn't have enough money to pay for us – thank goodness for that. It seemed impossible to repay any of the hospitality we received, but we were still desperate to try.

Fuelled only by a stingy hotel breakfast served on a stainless-steel tray with separate compartments for the single triangle of white cheese, the three olives and the lone slice of flatbread, we took many wrong turns as we made our way out of Hama, through farmland to the town of Masyaf and then on to the sizeable town of Bait. As we bumped along a dirt track, we were mobbed by a bunch of primary-school children. I stopped to speak to a little girl with a pink hair bobble and soon children were pressed around me, hands running over the bicycle and fiddling with our bags. The girl peered over my handlebars and another tugged my hand. Most wore a loose uniform of a royal-blue tunic over sportswear or sweatshirts. A few of the boys started to shove our bicycles, excitement tipping over into mob mentality. One boy kicked out Ed's spokes, at which point we extracted ourselves quickly, giving them a cheery wave as we continued down the hill. Ed's back wheel began squeaking ominously, which worried us for the rest of the day until we realised that it was only the edge of the mudguard that had been bent inwards.

We got hopelessly lost, missed a turn-off and stopped often to ask for directions to the Krak des Chevaliers castle, or Qalaat al-Husn, careful to take time with each person, dismounting, shaking hands, doing introductions, attempting to ask after people's health and then getting to the business of calling out 'Qalaat al-Husn?', gesturing with both hands to the sky, then tapping with left palm to the right bicep indicating 'Go right?' or right palm to left bicep indicating 'Go left?' We'd learnt that sign language could be the false friend of the traveller, given the tendency to assume that gestures are universally understandable. We'd managed to stop ourselves from using the thumbs-up sign several weeks ago – it meant 'penis' – but pointing did not seem to be understood either, or was possibly rude.

One man peered at our map, looking confused, as if he did not understand its relevance to our question. Another pointed confidently to Damascus, informing us adamantly that that was where we should go, before blowing his nose loudly on a corner of his shemagh. We asked for directions again, indicating 'Is it left to Qalaat al-Husn?' and receiving 'Yes' in reply, then indicating 'Is it right to Qalaat al-Husn?' and also receiving a 'Yes' in reply.

A group gathered round. Some further questioning established that we were in the wrong valley. We were sent up a steep hill, much of it 20 per cent gradient, requiring us to get off and push. Boys in leather jackets and on Honda motorbikes adorned with plastic flowers cruised by, shouting encouragement. A middle-aged man who had helped us twenty minutes previously returned on his motorbike to check we were still on the right path. Higher up the hill, two boys on a motorbike assigned themselves as our guardians. They spoke no English but drove alongside, so I could see a bunch of plastic roses out of the corner of my eye for half an hour until we reached a junction that they pointed us down.

Finally, the road flattened out and we reached a sign that declared it was twenty-eight kilometres to the castle. Happy to be on the right road at last, we stopped on a flat terrace high on the side of a hill and set up camp, exhausted. I cooked pasta as Ed set up the tent and we sat overlooking groves of olive trees, talking about how far we'd come. It was

Valentine's Day, exactly seven years since we'd got together on a student mountaineering club night out at the dubious St Andrews University Union club, which was known as 'the Bop'. A place best visited after a few drinks had rendered the stickiness of the floor unconcerning.

'What if I'd decided not to go out that night? I almost didn't.'

'I know. I don't like thinking about it.'

'You might be doing this trip with someone else.' I laughed and adopted a mock Sheffield accent in imitation of Jarvis Cocker, the frontman of Pulp, a band we both loved, repeating it to the tune of 'Something Changed'.

'I doubt it, Helen.' Ed laughed too. 'Gi' us a kiss.'

We teased each other, but I doubted it too. Travelling day in and day out with your partner is testing in a way that sharing a house and the working week with them is not. I could not imagine being able to tolerate any other person, apart from perhaps my brother, Mark, for that amount of time.

What had first attracted me to Ed were his blue eyes, mess of blond hair, constant three-day stubble and jokey but caring nature, but our relationship was cemented over a shared love of the outdoors. Our first trip away together was to Culra Bothy when we climbed Ben Alder in the remote, boggy wilderness of the central Scottish Highlands. That summer I took him to the Swiss Alps to visit my grandparents. Ed had already been to Switzerland to climb some of the 4000ers, and my Yorkshire-born grandmother, who had taught me to ski and camp and did not mince her words, approved. Ed was a couple of years ahead of me and by the time I graduated he'd started teaching in Dingwall, north of Inverness, while I went on to do my PhD in Evolutionary Genetics at the University of Edinburgh. For four more years we spent weekends on trains and buses, drawing lines across Scotland to see each other or meet in the hills.

One weekend, we'd hiked into Barrisdale Bothy on Knoydart and were standing on Luinne Bheinn looking out to where sunrays were making mercury pools on the grey sea between the islands – to Rum, which we'd revisited together that summer, and to the strange fin of Eigg. My ear was scratching Ed's waterproof jacket as I hugged his chest, his arm around me against the chill wind, and I noticed that his heart was thumping very loudly, audible over the wind in my other ear and through all those layers of clothing. Perhaps, I thought vaguely, he's actually a bit exhausted – unlikely, though, with all that Wednesday fell running. The mist was wrapping a little thicker over the ridge, and the waters gleamed palely through drifting wisps. A spot of rain hit my cheek and I shivered.

'You know, it's strange, but your heart's beating so loud that I can hear it.'

There was a pause.

'That's because there is a question I've been wanting to ask you.'

And somehow he was on one knee in the wet moss and, in Knoydart, a second heart was now beating strong.

As soon as we were married, we started to bank all of my PhD stipend and lived off Ed's junior teacher's salary, relocating to a small flat near Haymarket in Edinburgh so that Ed could get to his new job in Glasgow. The trip took shape in our flat one evening. I had a succession of long-distance hiking heroes and was initially inspired to try and do something similar. There was Ffyona Campbell, who'd walked across Africa, at times accompanied by boyfriend, bodyguard and all-round outdoors hero Ray Mears. Benedict Allen, all of whose books I'd read, detailing his hazardous journeys to Papua New Guinea, the Amazon, the Skeleton Coast and the Gobi Desert. And Nicholas Crane, who'd set off shortly after his honeymoon to spend two years walking alone across the mountains of Europe to Turkey, carrying an umbrella.

We discussed hiking the Appalachian Trail in the eastern US, but we both agreed that the problem with hiking was that in a year we wouldn't cover that much ground.

'We could cycle South America end to end.'

'Okay,' I said, 'but I'm not sure about South America. What about cycling to China from here? I like the idea of leaving from our own front door.'

Neither of us had cycled much before this point, but we trusted in the fact that our ability to not just survive but thrive in the outdoors was a good start. I bought a cheap mountain bike and began cycling up the steep hill to work, and we both booked ourselves on to cycle maintenance courses.

We packed up our olive-grove camp early the next day and cycled twenty kilometres through terraced mountains until we reached the final approach to Qalaat al-Husn, or Krak des Chevaliers, the Castle of the Knights, built in 1031 and rebuilt in 1142 by the Knights Hospitaller during the Crusades. We stopped at a small bakery for a breakfast of flatbread with thyme and then, to the amusement of local residents, slogged up the final vertical road to the castle. The day was already close and thunder rumbled from heavy clouds to the north. The limestone castle glared down at us from a hot, dull sky.

The castle guards the Homs Gap, a valley which traders and invaders have used for centuries as it is the easiest route from the Mediterranean coast and current-day Lebanon to the Syrian interior. The castle was solid, with towered ramparts in a double ring, its smooth exterior undamaged and seemingly impenetrable. The Crusaders had briefly occupied the site – then a small Kurdish fort – on their first march south down the Orontes from Antioch on their way to Jerusalem, which they proceeded to capture with much brutality in 1099. In 1142 the Krak was given to the Knights Hospitaller, a Christian order whose original remit was to minister to travellers to the Holy Lands by means of a network of hospices that served men and women of all faiths and acted as travellers' rests, hospitals and homeless shelters. The order had been placed under the direct protection of the Pope in 1113 and by 1136 had become militarised, perhaps in response to increasing unrest following the First Crusade and the establishment of the Knights Templar, which had military objectives from the outset. The Knights Hospitaller grouped their properties into 'commanderies', clusters of local farms and other assets like mills, and received donations from the pious, thereby amassing considerable wealth; the Krak was the largest of the 140 properties they acquired.

We left our bicycles in the care of a one-legged warden and spent a few hours exploring the vaulted main hall, peering over the moats and into Crusader latrines. Desert explorer, archaeologist, Arabist, diplomat and spy Gertrude Bell had been put up here in a thunderstorm in 1905, staying in one of the towers, feasting with the governor and smoking nargileh with his wife and her ladies. The castle was no longer lived in and we were once again back in the company of a handful of tourists and sightseers. I gazed out across the ramparts to greened limestone hills and the Homs Gap. What motivated the Crusaders on an individual level, I wondered? Taking part in the Crusades was considered an act of religious piety that would lead to salvation, but among the other reasons to join up, including the promise of earthly wealth and status, surely there was also, as for us modern-day tourists, adventure for adventure's sake?

When Jerusalem was recaptured from the Christian Crusaders in 1187 by Saladin, a Sunni Kurd and founder of the Ayyubid dynasty, the Knights Hospitaller moved their headquarters northwest, to Margat on the Syrian coast, and later to Acre in the north of today's Israel. Rather than make attempts on major strongholds such as the Krak, Saladin focused on poorly defended positions. He fatally weakened his enemies, but the Knights Hospitaller managed to hold on to the Krak into the thirteenth century, its massive ramparts surviving two major challenges in the late twelfth century. The castle eventually succumbed to a siege by the Mamluks (a caste of slave soldiers, many from Central Asia, converted to Sunni Islam, that constituted the military backbone of the Ayyubid dynasty and would later overthrow it), and its defenders were granted safe passage to Tripoli on the Lebanese coast so long as they promised not to return. The Mamluks took over the Krak as a base, but as the Crusader threat dwindled it gradually fell into disuse as a military stronghold, eventually becoming a village. In 1934, under the occupation of the French, the village was relocated. The castle was a centre of fighting between rebels and government forces during the Syrian civil war and was shelled by the Syrian government. As of 2025, it is on the Unesco List of World Heritage in Danger sites.

Just how close Krak des Chevaliers was to the Lebanese border and the strategic ports and shipping routes of the Mediterranean was impressed upon us soon after our leaving the castle. We freewheeled down to a fertile plain and the highway to Homs, which rumbled with lorries and buses, and eventually located a quieter road to the south that was marked on our map. We had cycled no more than three kilometres when some men began waving and shouting to us up ahead. Anxious about the remaining afternoon hours, we pedalled harder, prepared to pretend not to understand this tea invitation and cycle by with a friendly wave. But when one of the men lifted something down from his shoulder, something that looked very much like a machine gun, I drew to an abrupt stop. Ed crunched to a halt next to me.

The men, whom we could now clearly see were in uniform, inspected our passports and with a friendly greeting sent us back the way we'd come. Back to Syria. Unbeknownst to us, we had been in Lebanon since shortly after leaving the highway.

We reached the edge of Homs with the fading light and carried on through traffic fumes and the evening call to prayer, the first call being joined by call upon call from all directions across the city night.

Two young men ran across the road towards us, dodging the flow of traffic and shouting, 'Hello, can we help you?' One of them was weighed down by the grey box of a computer hard drive. They were science students at the university and were excited to meet foreigners.

We walked our laden bicycles and computer parts together along high pavements, paying little attention to the modern tower-block maze of Homs. Once the two students were satisfied that our hotel was 'a good place' (though in reality it was dirty, with doors that didn't shut properly and men smoking in the corridors), we sat and ate kebabs together in a café where young men played pool and puffed at nargileh.

'No, you are guests in our country' was the response when we'd tried to pay for dinner. Back out in the busy night, we all stopped at a fava bean stall to be taught how to shuck tough skins from the giant beans and dip them in salt. A patter of Arabic flowed between our guides and the curious crowd that had gathered. 'The seller asks if you drink ful?' We nodded, unclear what we were agreeing to, and accepted steaming glasses of bean stock ladled from the deep cauldron. Expectant faces beamed as we drank down the sharp, salty liquid. I could feel my weary muscle cells rehydrating.

Then we took a taxi ride across town to their student flat.

'So you walked us all that way to the hotel even though you don't live near there – and with a computer?' we exclaimed.

They laughed, slightly embarrassed.

We sat on cushions on the floor, sharing bowls of maté, the bitter, green-tea-like drink from South America that is brewed in a bowl, passed round communally and drunk through a metal straw. Syria is apparently the biggest importer of maté in the world, a habit picked up from Syrians who moved to South America during the late nineteenth and early twentieth centuries. We discussed the young men's plans to travel to Saudi Arabia to study and find their fortunes, and their hopes to marry their girlfriends, and they asked us about our journey and how we had met. It was late when they finally hailed us a taxi off the street and said goodbye. We drove through the quiet night-time city, all the shops shuttered behind aluminium fronts.

Our student friends' dreams of further studies, marriage and a better life will have been shattered by the war, assuming those two young men have even survived it. Those students of computing were not born fighters but may have been forced into joining up anyway. When the war broke out, there was strong resistance in Homs, which was subjected to a siege by government forces that lasted three years, from May 2011 to May 2014. 'A major assault on Homs took place yesterday,' Ban Ki-moon told the UN General Assembly in New York City on 2 March 2012. 'Civilian losses have clearly been heavy. We continue to receive grisly reports of summary executions, arbitrary detentions and torture. This atrocious assault is all the more appalling for having been waged by the government itself, systematically attacking its own people.'

In February 2012, exactly two years after we had visited, I sat at my computer in Edinburgh watching a news report. The streets still seemed familiar, despite shaky footage of raw gashes in the concrete. It was daytime, but all the shops' aluminium shutters were down. The camera focused on women who were running for cover. Then the footage switched to government tanks rolling through rubble and to plumes of debris rising from shelled buildings. The red-and-white-checked shemaghs normally used to protect faces from the sun and dust were now masking the identities of the Kalashnikov-bearing members of the Free Army. Journalist Paul Wood interviewed people hiding inside their flats for the BBC: men, women, children and … students were under siege. Afraid. Deserted. Men between the ages of fourteen and fifty were being rounded up by the government. There was talk of executions. The camera footage switched back to the bombed-out street. A young man was running down it, calling out. He was calling for God's help. The bundle in his arms was not a computer.

7
THE DESERT, THE SOWN AND THE HIGH RETREAT

Jesus said, 'Be passersby.'
Gospel of St Thomas (42), trans. Stephen Patterson and Marvin Meyer, in Robert J. Miller (ed.), *The Complete Gospels: Annotated Scholars Version*

So far in Syria we had traversed the settled, 'sown', urban and agricultural regions; now we were headed for the desert. The Homs–Damascus highway led us out into a wasteland of dust and broken rock. This was the desert, but not that of dunes and sand seas. Instead, clumps of weeds struggled out of the cracked ground and dry thorns collected scraps of plastic bags, torn to shreds, bleached pale and decayed by the sunlight. Disposable nappies and plastic bottles were a common sight at the edge of the road, as they had been since Serbia. We were becoming immune to the presence of rubbish, but it was more striking and depressing in this empty landscape.

We were cycling along the hard shoulder when two shepherd boys waved us over. They were sitting on a small hillock next to the road and their sheep were grazing on scraggy vegetation growing in the baked ground of a dried riverbed. Syria had just experienced a three-year drought, particularly in the north and east, the worst on record, and it showed. Some of the sheep were congregating in the shade of the underpass designed to carry the floodwater, when it came, under the road. A track led off the road, over the hillock to a building beyond and we turned on to it to go and speak to them. The ground was littered with hypodermic needles. Was the building a hospital, I wondered?

The boys were sitting by a small fire of twigs. A kettle was in the embers. The oldest, who was about fifteen, wore a shemagh loosely wound around his head. He removed his green combat jacket and placed it on the ground, indicating I should sit. Embarrassed, I waved that he should take it back, but it lay there waiting as we four crouched around the fire. The younger boy stared at us uncertainly when I smiled at him. He ran off to call back his donkey but returned to the fire. Every now and again he would stand and throw a rock, with extreme accuracy, at the flank of a wayward sheep to send it back into the herd.

'Chai?' The older boy swilled a small amount of tea around two small glasses and poured for us.

We offered them some dried fruit and biscuits. Ed pointed at the sheep and counted out on his fingers to ask how many they had. The answer, 0•, was scratched into the dirt with a twig, the dirt first patted flat by a deeply tanned hand. The dot represented zero – zero being an invention of the Fertile Crescent from around 2000 BC. Arabic numerals were introduced to Europeans only in the tenth century, Europeans having to this point used Roman numerals, absent a zero. The 0 symbol represented the number 5, making it fifty sheep.

Ed showed them some pictures on the screen of his digital camera to explain where we had been and they posed for some photos, faces serious, scarves arranged. They grinned at the results and ran to fetch the donkey, which had strayed back towards the grubby underpass, for a portrait.

As we made our bicycles ready, a vehicle that was driving away from the building came to a halt. A window slid down.

'Why you stop here?' the man in uniform said. Other uniforms peered at us from the car.

'We took a break for chai and now we're going to Damascus.'

The official jerked his head towards the boys, wrinkled his nose and drove off.

I suddenly remembered the hypodermic needles in the dust, feeling sick. Hospital ... or prison? The police state was notorious for incarcerating, torturing and executing its people.

The highway climbed and passed between two rocky outcrops. We had not seen a house for some time. The road was straight and trucks rattled past us, kicking up dust and sending plastic bags cartwheeling into the desert. We were pleased when a track turned off the main road and ran in parallel to it across the broken red ground and through a village. A man was sitting in the shade outside one of the houses and we stopped to ask if there was a shop. It was hot and we both fancied a drink of ice-cold Coke.

Within a few minutes we were sitting inside his front room. Unusually for the houses we had been in so far, it was furnished with sofas. I shifted uncomfortably on the velour, aware of my dusty clothes, damp shirt and fraying socks. My bar bag sat incongruously on the patterned carpet. There was a large framed picture of the Kaaba in Mecca on the wall. Pilgrims in white surged around the black-clothed cube.

'Is that the haj?' I asked, not sure what to say.

Our host nodded.

'You have been?' Ed took up the conversation.

'Yes, two years past.'

'Congratulations. It is a long way to travel.'

The man responded with a broad smile.

He wife brought in a plate of dried fruit. Tea was poured and our host told us about his son who was studying IT in Damascus. An hour and a half slipped past. Fresh fruit was brought and peeled for us.

'Eat with us. Sleep here,' the man said as we stood up to leave.

We shook our heads. It was time to get going.

We'd been hoping to make it to Mar Musa that night, an eleventh-century monastery high up in the mountains, but by five o'clock we were still at least fifteen kilometres away, and there were likely to be hills ahead. Plus the monastery didn't accept guests who arrived after nightfall. I was regretting our tea stops and began wondering if we'd find any cover for camping.

'Here?' Ed called across to me two hours later.

From where I was standing with the bikes, only his head torch was visible in the darkness. Its light shone out across terrain strewn with stones which cast long shadows. The beam swept around in a circle then dropped downwards. Ed was crouching, examining the ground.

'Fine,' I called back.

I wanted to leave the road before someone drove past me. There were lights on in a small row of houses that stood back from the road. Far enough away that we wouldn't be disturbed, hopefully, but close enough to deter anyone from trying to rob us, I thought. At night the world always seemed more threatening.

We jolted the bikes down the bank and out into the darkness.

Once the shell of the tent was up, I began unloading the panniers inside the porch. Ed went round banging in more pegs and tensioning the guy ropes. I pulled out sleeping bags and Therm-a-Rests and flung them into the inner tent, along with the dry bag Ed stored his pants and

T-shirt in, my mesh bag of pants, socks and thermals, our down jackets (for pillows), diaries, book, map, toothbrushes and toilet paper.

I primed the stove and lit it, sending soot-fringed flames up into the porch. Once they had died down, I set the kettle on the blue flame. Dogs were howling in the distance, but despite our vulnerable position, the tent and the chug of the stove never failed to give a sense of security. I began to relax as I chopped up some carrots to add to the stock, rice, herbs and tin of butter beans in tomato sauce.

By now, six months into our trip, we had a well-established camp routine. Most nights not spent in cities had been spent in the tent. In Scotland we had wild camped, as we always did, due to the rights of (responsible) access enshrined in the Land Reform Act of 2003, but in built-up Western Europe we had spent most nights in campsites, generally only wild camping in higher mountain areas. As we'd moved further east, we stayed in cheap hotels or hostels in urban areas, for security reasons, but in rural areas we wild camped.

It had now become apparent what our respective roles on this expedition were. Back in the early days of the trip, in Luxembourg, I'd noted in my diary that:

Ed does bicycle maintenance while I do the cooking. I am slightly disappointed in this traditional divide but not enough to want to swap roles. Despite my best intentions to learn, Ed has a natural knack for mechanics. His strong fingers are also always needed for levering off tyres. I am reduced to assistant status: holding patches, keeping screws safe, polishing off dirty parts and handing him tools. If I'm totally honest, I'm just not that interested in how the bikes work. On the other hand, I spend a lot of time wondering what to eat for dinner. Food is a big motivator for us both and we are forever hungry.

We are both settling into the rhythm of the journey much more now and adopting our respective roles has helped a lot. We are finding that there is an awful lot to fit into the day: cycling of course, but also route planning, cycle maintenance, cooking, eating, shopping for food, diary writing and maintaining other pieces of kit like the stove. This all takes up a lot of time. Before we set off, I had imagined long afternoons of reading my book and learning Turkish, but right now I have neither the time nor the energy. When my head hits my down-jacket pillow in the evening, I am so exhausted that I fall to sleep instantly.

Nothing had changed.

'Shift over,' Ed said as he ducked into the porch. 'I'll sort out the Therm-a-Rests.'

Ten minutes later, I was still tending the stove, stirring constantly now that the gloop had thickened, to stop it sticking to the bottom of the pan. It was impossible to regulate the flame to any other setting than 'fierce'. I was hoping the carrots would be ready any minute now, when Ed hissed at me.

'Shhhh!' he whispered again urgently.

I immediately reached out into the porch to turn the stove off. We'd avoided using a torch, to minimise the possibility of being spotted. As the great Edinburgh writer and explorer Robert Louis Stevenson remarked, 'If a camp is not secret, it is but a troubled resting place.'

Blackness cloaked us.

Now that the stove was silent, we could hear the sound of men's voices. They were getting louder, and there was the crunch of footsteps too.

We were camping with the porch facing away from the road, again so that there was less chance of the stove being seen. But although it was sheltered by a wind guard, it still glowed through the crack.

Ed stuck his head out of the porch. 'Someone's coming,' he said, dropping back inside and putting on his jacket.

I moved the stove aside, put the lid on our half-cooked dinner and fished my headscarf out of a side pocket. Ed stood up, blocking the porch, as I sat back in the tent. There were two bicycles in front of the tent and we knew that until whoever was visiting saw me, they would assume we were two men. Better to have the edge for as long as possible.

'As-salam alaykum,' I heard Ed say.

Two male voices responded.

'Scotlanda ... Mar Musa ...' Ed was explaining our journey.

And then:

'No problem. We will sleep here. Tomorrow we will go to Mar Musa.'

Moments later, the faces of two young men were peering inside the tent.

'As-salam alaykum.' I placed my hand over my heart.

'Malaykum as-salam,' came the response, and I caught one word in the sentence that one of them exclaimed – 'Zawja', which meant 'wife'.

The discussion was continuing outside.

'You must sleep with us.'
'Thank you, but, please, we are fine here.'
'It is dangerous.'
'We are not afraid. It seems safe here.'
'No, there are dog – wild animal … bad men with gun – boom!'
Ed laughed.
'No, you must come. Please.'

Ten minutes of conversation later and Ed had been forced to relent. 'We'll just be pestered if we don't agree,' he said as he stuffed his sleeping bag away. 'They seem okay. I get the feeling they really just want to talk to us.'

I was exhausted and hungry and the prospect of having to be an entertaining guest was not particularly appealing.

We collapsed the tent, accepting tent pegs and poles out of eager hands, then scanned the ground with a torch, worrying that in the hurry to pack up in the dark we might have missed things. We pushed our bikes back to the road and up towards some houses on the other side. Entering a dark courtyard, we were told to leave our bikes and then mounted some steps to a concrete balcony. The building was a shell. Leading off from the balcony was a bare room lit with a single bulb and ten young men sitting cross-legged on the floor. We left our shoes at the door and I stood, feeling self-conscious, as Ed received a long round of introductions.

The men, some barely teenagers, were a group of friends. They were students or worked – one was a barber, one a mechanic, one a shopkeeper. The house belonged to an uncle of Ahmed's, one of the boys who had come out to our tent, and they came here to hang out together. I was offered a pile of cushions and told to sit down. When I asked for the toilet, Ahmed dispatched his brother Aziz and another boy on a cleaning mission. They were both waiting with a jug to pour water over my hands and pass me soap once I had finished.

A charcoal barbecue was lit on the balcony and pieces of chicken grilled. We gathered round the glowing embers as we looked out over the sea of darkness. No wonder they'd spotted our tent. In the distance the lights of the town of al-Nabek twinkled and stars shone in the moonless black above. I felt the tension of our 'rescue' lift from me a little as I nibbled a scalding piece of chicken wrapped in flatbread.

Soon after, I excused myself to go to bed, leaving Ed to sit up with the young men. Two of the boys hurriedly laid out some mattresses for me in a second room off the balcony, asking repeatedly if I would be comfortable, offering more cushions. Within moments of crawling into my sleeping bag, I sank into a half-sleep visited by the sound of voices and the smell of food cooking.

In the morning, I felt more relaxed and allowed myself to laugh and joke a little with Aziz and some of the other boys. They were young and spoke to me in a deferential way, perhaps because I could almost have been their mother.

Aziz asked Ed if it was okay for him to show me how to wear a scarf the Bedu way. To which he responded, 'Ask Helen.'

'Okay,' I said, not entirely sure.

Aziz took off his red-and-white shemagh and then, carefully, without actually touching me, arranged it on my head, twisting the corners round and round, crossing them behind my head and tucking them one behind the other, creating a cascade of cloth down one shoulder.

I took from this that these boys considered themselves to be Bedouin. Bedouin (in English) or Bedu (in Arabic) are the Sunni Arab populations which dominate the sparsely inhabited Syrian desert that stretches east from Hama, Homs and the mountains northeast of Damascus and beyond the Syrian border into vast areas of Jordan, Iraq and Saudi Arabia. The desert region is called the Badiya or Badawah, hence the name of its people, while the watered and therefore settled and sown areas of the Fertile Crescent are the Hadarah. Today and through the course of history, the people of the Badiya have moved to agricultural or urban Hadarah areas in search of livelihoods and education, but the tie to the desert is strong. Town dwellers may still be involved in camel, sheep or goat herding, outsourcing it to others, even if it is not their main source of income. The traditional Bedouin sports of camel riding, horse riding and falconry are multibillion-dollar industries in the Gulf states. The roots of the desert are strong in the psyche, if not always in everyday lived reality. In his piece 'Arabs and Non-Arabs' (trans. John Dumis in *Desert Songs of the Night*), the Iraqi writer al-Tawhidi (c. 923–1023) is clear that it is the harsh desert origins that forge the virtuous spirit:

They are people from a poor land, deserted from mankind; everyone among them in his loneliness, has need of his thought, his contemplation and his mind. They knew that the livelihood came from the plants of the earth, so they marked them and attributed to each of its type ... They knew that drink was from the heavens, so they invented for them the constellations ... They needed to spread out on earth so they made of the heavenly stars guides for the sections of the earth and its regions ... This is why I said they are the most intelligent nation, because of the soundness of natural endowment, correctness of thought and acuteness of understanding.

Something of the European notion of the 'noble savage' perhaps, simultaneously admired and looked down upon by the settled. The disdainful response of the officials in the car to the shepherd boys we'd had tea with earlier in the day had given us a sense that describing someone as Bedu could be problematic, so this was not a question that we asked.

'Come, I want to take a photograph of you on the roof,' Aziz said.

I shot Ed a look, but his attention was being monopolised by Ahmed. I followed Aziz and another boy up a narrow staircase and onto the roof in the glaring sunlight. The morning already had plenty of heat in it. There was a large cage of rabbits and he opened the lid and fished around for a bunny.

'Look. So soft.' He passed it into my hands.

Ed was called up by the other boy to take the photographs.

'Hold it close.' Aziz gestured that I should cuddle it up to my cheek.

'Okay, that's enough!' I said once a few photos had been snapped. I handed over the rabbit as the others filed back down the stairs.

Aziz shut the hutch and then grabbed my hand.

'La! (No!)' I said, trying to free myself.

'Habibi. (Beloved.)'

'La habibi.' I pulled my hand free.

'Habibi,' he pleaded, reaching for me again.

'Halas!' I deployed Ali's advice again, and he stepped back as if struck by lightning.

I hurried down the stairs to rejoin Ed and the other men, sad that the meeting with Aziz had had to end that way. I felt fond of these boys who had adopted us, keen to learn more about foreigners, and who had, notwithstanding this exchange, treated us so politely. Again, it seemed that 'nice girls' were to be held responsible for keeping boundaries uncrossed.

We were soon tackling a series of steep switchbacks and sweating under the strong sun. The landscape was red and an ocean of broken rock stretched before us. From the cusp of the hill we looked over into a world that seemed stark and empty. The road we were following ran straight out into the desert towards craggy hills, purple in the hazed distance. A few tents were scattered across the void, flocks of sheep in motion near them.

We freewheeled down the other side, enjoying the cooling feeling of the wind, but when we hit the plain below it soon became apparent that this was not flat at all. We began to struggle upwards on seemingly level ground, as if we were on a giant undulating wave, having lost all reference of what was horizontal. We turned off the main road and headed back up the hill we'd just come down off, the road steepening at every pedal turn until it finally terminated at the base of some cliffs. A path snaked up the side, leading to the monastery of Mar Musa on the clifftop.

We planned to spend a couple of nights at Mar Musa, providing the monks were happy with that. Having sorted out what we'd need, we locked our bicycles to a signpost with an explanation about the monastery and started up the steps.

The mountains of Syria have long been a place of refuge, both for religious groups pushed into hiding because of the comings and goings on the plains, and for ascetics and monks deliberately choosing seclusion. The monastery, known in full as Deir Mar Musa al-Habashi or the monastery of St Moses the Abyssinian, is thought to have been present on the site since the sixth century, with the structure of the current church dating back to the eleventh.

Two men in belted charcoal robes greeted us on the terrace with tea and water. One of them was Father Paolo Dall'Oglio, the Italian Jesuit priest who had restored the monastery in the 1980s, after it had been abandoned in the 1830s, and founded the al-Khalil monastic community.

The monastery was made from stones hewn out of the surrounding rock and emerged from the edge of the escarpment as a set of stepped buildings with a panoramic terrace affording a vast vista across the desert. A perfect position for observing one of the main roads between Palmyra and Damascus, a key artery of the Silk Road. The terrace was sheltered by a recently constructed hand-cut wooden awning, decked with rough fabric of charcoal-coloured camel hair of the kind used for Bedouin tents and furnished, incongruously for such an ancient place, with white plastic picnic chairs and tables.

Aside from the welcome and invitation to evening prayer, we were not given any instructions and the monks seemed busy, so for the next two days we settled into the community routine guided by a ragtag bunch of other travellers comprising an American theology student, a small group of Danish circus performers on a break from teaching skills to Palestinian refugee children, and a German backpacker who had come overland from Mongolia. There were only a handful of community members, distinguished by their attire.

We attended evening hour-long silent meditations followed by Mass in the church and during the day helped with kitchen chores or tended the herb garden of thyme, rosemary and oregano at the foot of the cliff. For meditation and Mass we all sat cross-legged on a patchwork of tribal rugs in the cool dark of the chapel, light filtering in through small, high-set windows. In the centre of the nave, in front of a modern wooden screen obscuring the apse, was a hairy black-and-white goatskin of the sort I imagined Jacob might have used to dupe his blind father, Isaac, into thinking he was the hairier favourite son, Esau. On top of it stood two vast Bibles, held open by X-shaped wooden book rests. An oil stove stood, unused, in the middle of the chapel, ready for chillier days, and a filigree oil lamp hung above the Bibles. Every surface of the small chapel, including the insides of the low arches between the aisles, was painted with frescoes that dated from as early as 1058. Nearly all of the paintings were of people, most of them saints robed in maroon or white, carrying yellow halos against an indigo background. In one of the earliest murals, Samson, in a white tunic with long hair tumbling down his back, wrestled an orange lion. A few of the frescoes had been damaged, their faces perhaps deliberately scratched out by iconoclasts.

As I tried to resist the temptation to wriggle so as to alleviate knee and hip pain from sitting cross-legged for so long, my eyes wandered to a large, almost intact fresco depicting the Last Judgement with lines and lines of people – the saved on the left and the damned on the right. To the left, Jacob, Isaac, Abraham and Mary gathered lost souls in their cloaks. The damned were represented by sinners with swords, mirrors and moneybags and a row of naked and chained writhing men, and women with serpents entering their bodies through their eyes and mouths. Those of other religions were also entered on this side, some wearing turbans and scarves (Muslims and Jews) and others, tellingly, with crosses. There were major schisms between the Syrian Church and other Christian sects, not least at the Council of Chalcedon in 451, where the Syrian Church together with the Coptic Church found no agreement with the Churches of Constantinople or Rome. The debate centred on the nature of the Trinity and whether Jesus was simultaneously both fully divine and fully man. Chalcedonian beliefs around these concepts were and are upheld by more than 95 per cent of Christians, including followers of Catholicism, Eastern Orthodoxy and Protestantism, but not by the Syrian Church. The rift was to result in Christians persecuting other Christians for the first time.

The modern-day al-Khalil community at Mar Musa welcomed men and women of all faiths and none. 'Al-Khalil' is a Qur'anic reference to Abraham, Khalil al-Rahman, or 'Friend of the Merciful', the prophet who is the founder of the Abrahamic religions of Judaism, Christianity and Islam. The community was dedicated to prayer, work, hospitality and interfaith dialogue. I was grateful to see the workings of this thoughtful community. To have time to stop and reflect and become, in an infinitesimal way, part of the succession of those coming here to contemplate life over millennia.

I understood something of faith. I had been brought up a Christian and as a teenager had chosen to be baptised, used to read the Bible and was heavily involved in an evangelical church. I always had a lot of questions about the world, which were initially answered by the Bible, but, eventually, looking for answers created more questions than it could answer. The death of a baby cousin unleashed in me a dark anger about suffering, and there were other questions raised when I observed the anguish of a church friend who came out as gay. I also began delving into evolution, an interest that became such an itch that I would eventually go on to major in it at St Andrews and subsequently do a PhD about it. My youth-group leaders told me to pray to make it better, but by the time I was eighteen the darkness had become unbearable and so one day I said into the void, 'I need to go now. If you are really there, then I am sure I will return one day.'

I looked out over the desert to where the sun was setting, folds of escarpment glowing in the soft light of evening, a first star pricking the firmament. For me, meaning was not to be found in city life or in the cocoon of the still chapel but looking outwards as much as possible, to the breathtaking diversities of places and people, for this limited time I would spend on earth. It was the open road and the desert that were calling.

8
BLOWN LOOSE

And it came to pass, that, as I made my journey, and was come nigh unto Damascus about noon, suddenly there shone from heaven a great light round about me.

Acts 22:6, The Bible (King James Version)

The wind was so strong, we were struggling to stay upright. I stood up on my pedals, forcing a downwards stroke with the full weight of my body. The air felt solid as it roared out of the desert, sucking up dust. I gritted my teeth and stared in front of me. Ed was waiting a few metres ahead. I had lost his slipstream by slowing too much. Beyond him the sky was an angry orange – the colour of a desert storm.

That morning the sky had been dull with cloud when I looked out from the balcony of the monastery. A breeze had tugged at the terrace awning and a gust had sent a plastic chair skidding, but to a person accustomed to living in windswept Edinburgh this had not seemed unusual. The wind had gathered strength hour by hour, forcing us to take shelter in the lee of a gravel pit at lunchtime. We ate hurriedly – tinned hummus and stale bread that we'd bought before our arrival at Mar Musa, guarding it from air-blown grit. After that, conditions had worsened.

I caught up with Ed and we set off again, my front wheel only centimetres from his rear wheel, to maximise the benefit of the shelter he was creating. I pressed my weight down hard with every pedal stroke, but lack of momentum was causing my bike to wobble, leaving me at the mercy of the violent gusts. Our faces were wrapped completely in cotton headscarves, a timeless solution to life in the desert environment. My mouth and nose were covered, and the slit for my eyes was shielded by sunglasses so that my field of vision had shrunk to a narrow tunnel: the road ahead.

A plastic bottle skidded down the verge towards me.

It felt like someone had switched on a vast hairdryer and my mouth was sticky and dry. The world had been reduced to the next pedal stroke. I had to keep up with Ed, who was in his own private battle with the elements.

Cars hurtled past. Lorries charged by, creating strong vortexes that kicked up dirt and sucked sideways at our wheels. The wind was so loud that we did not hear them approach until they were next to us. A people carrier zoomed off into the distance, stirring up a shredded carrier bag that whirled like a dust devil on the road until the next car ploughed into it. Its passengers were in a cocoon of calm, no doubt passing each other sweets, listening to music and exclaiming how strong the wind was. I expected someone to stop and ask if we were okay, but no one did. It probably didn't look nearly so bad from inside. Either that or they didn't want to get coated in dust.

I wanted this to end. In Serbia we had sensibly turned back from a snowstorm and taken refuge in a hotel when our hands became so numb we could no longer squeeze our brakes. Here, on the way to Damascus, our options were to give up and camp by the road or to reach the capital. In Mar Musa we'd looked at the map and thought we'd arrive by lunchtime; an easy ride. It was always like that with tough days. I stared up at the dull orange heavens, angry with storm clouds. It seemed unlikely there would be divine intervention today.

Damascus was an unspoken milestone. After months of cycling through Europe it represented a worthy destination. Being able to say that we had cycled to this iconic city of the Middle East from the cold sandstone grandeur of Glasgow would feel like an achievement. A justification for having given up jobs and stuffed up career chances. Perhaps it would be a comfort to my mother, who spoke urgently of the recession, caused by the banking crisis, every time I called her, hinting we should return before things became too tough.

Damascus was not just a goal, it was the turning point. The pivot. From here we would have to turn northeast and commit to the journey back across the desert towards the high peaks of eastern Turkey and then Iran. Beyond lay the deserts and mountains of Central Asia and then China, places that were almost out of grasp in my imagination, behind a veil of sand and snow and yet more sand. The wind howled. The next tiny step was getting to Damascus, and every pedal stroke was a battle.

'Stop!' I shouted forward to Ed, overwhelmed by frustration. But my voice, muffled by the fabric over my mouth, was thrown behind me by the wind. 'Stop!' I cried, but I lost the energy to shout a third time.

I wanted to drink and eat a bit and maybe discuss the options, such that they were, but it actually seemed unthinkable in the wind to do anything other than keep pushing forward. My exposed wrist was plastered in a brown film of dust. Dust sticking to sweat. All the dirt, dried sheep droppings and plastic rubbish that had lain baking for months on the hard earth was now being hurled into the air and deposited somewhere else, until the next storm.

My thighs were burning with the effort. I sucked in the hot air, my throat rasping, and pushed down. Should I try and drink some water? The teats of the bottles on my bicycle frame were also plastered in dirt. Trying to drink on the move would almost certainly throw me off balance, and stopping ... I'd have to try and get Ed to stop as well.

Just keep moving.

My baggy shirt was flapping wildly against my ribcage, chafing with each tug. I felt thin and hungry and at the limits of exhaustion.

I need to stop and eat.

Our meals were erratic and limited to things that could easily be bought, carried in the heat and then cooked – rice, pasta, tinned beans, tinned hummus, olives – or cooked food like falafel or bread that was widely available from roadside stalls. When we were invited into people's houses, I battled the temptation to eat too much, knowing that the more we ate, the more would be set before us. There was little room to store any calories before they were siphoned away into pedal power.

Despite having eaten lunch, my stomach felt empty, hollow, tickling with acid. I began fantasising about the food possibilities in Damascus. Fresh fruit, salad, maybe roasted chicken like in Hama, maybe falafel with coriander like in Aleppo, ful like in Homs, shops laden with baklava ...

But first a shower.

My skin was crawling with sweat and dirt.

A hot shower, food and then sleep.

Another pedal stroke.

If we get there.

Ed was still just ahead of me, my view unchanged: the dirty verge of a dual carriageway, a dark orange sky, vehicles whizzing in and out of my field of vision, the oppressive buffeting of the wind.

The wind was hot. My heart was thumping.

Another pedal stroke.

I wish I could have a drink.

My exhaustion was deeper than a deficiency of food and sleep. I felt guilty admitting it, but I was beginning to find the hospitality we were encountering smothering. For the weeks since we'd been in Syria, I had barely had time to think when off the bike. We only had to stop momentarily to look at the map for people to approach us, wanting to talk, ask questions, offer help. And there was so much to think about. I was fascinated by the Syrian culture and people's reactions to us. We wanted to meet and talk to as many people as we could; after all, what was the point of travel if not that? But late nights and lunchtimes filled with faltering conversation, the need to be constantly on guard for points of etiquette, and the feeling that we needed to be animated in order to be good-value guests were giving me mental burnout. Sometimes it felt like we were trying to pedal against a vast tide of embraces and sickly-sweet tea. The day before we reached Mar Musa we had actually hidden in an underpass to enjoy a bar of melting chocolate in silence. No, it was the most wonderful thing about Syria, a hospitality that was perhaps unrivalled for the rest of our journey, but I also had to admit that I had a need for solitude. Did this really define northern Europeans? If so, why? I cringed at the contrast in experience a Syrian tourist to Scotland would have.

Balls of thorny tumbleweed were blowing around ahead of us, rolling just like footballs along the road. I'd only ever seen that in Westerns.

Abruptly and without thought, I dismounted, balanced my heavy bike by the handlebars and walked. Walking seemed faster. Ahead of me, Ed stopped too and began doing the same. Every muscle was straining against the storm. Ed was metres ahead in the whirling dust. Soon my back and shoulders ached as the bike pulled against them.

A plastic bag carouselled along the road, collided with my spokes and flapped madly as it was chewed into by the chain.

Not this.

I attempted to pick it out with one hand while steadying my bike by the crossbar against the wind with the other. The heavy panniers on the front rack meant the handlebars twisted as soon as I let go of them. Ed shouted something at me through the orange distance. I shouted back, suddenly furious.

'I can't do this!'

Can't do this. The storm roared.

The plastic came free. A lorry raced past, nearly knocking me over with the suck of its vortex. Hot tears wet the scarf around my face.

I needed to pee. I needed to eat. I needed to be somewhere else. 'I can't do this!' I shouted at Ed again when I reached him. I could not see any of his face and his checked shirt was stained brown.

'What do you want me to do about it, Helen?' he shouted back.

We trudged on into the storm. Ed in front. Me behind.

Minutes or perhaps an hour later, a blue road sign materialised out of the orange gloom. A few metres closer, I made out 'Damascus: 15 kilometres'.

My heart sank.

Fifteen kilometres – three or four hours.

'Stop!' I yelled pathetically.

At this pace, it would take far too long, surely. I struggled towards Ed and lifted his arm to peer at his wristwatch. Two o'clock. Not too late. We set off again, plodding into the howling orange dust.

The force of the wind eased once we reached Damascus at dusk, the walls of the buildings giving shelter, and there was less dust in the air. We propped up our bicycles by a roadside stall and ordered two falafel wraps each. They came with American burger-style gherkins and pickles instead of the dreamed-of coriander. We sat on plastic chairs, hearing ourselves chewing as the wind rattled across the roofs above. Despite this, it felt as if we had entered an oasis of calm. Some backpackers were sitting by the window on a cushioned bench in a café opposite, smoking a nargileh pipe. I looked at Ed, whose clothes were brown with dust. He had a brown stripe of warpaint across each cheekbone, in the gap between where his glasses and scarf had been, and his ears were brown. I scratched my head, feeling grit.

'We look a state.' I laughed.

At the second hostel we found a room. The owner let us park our bicycles in the backyard and the showers had hot water. Half an hour later, I lay in bed on my back next to Ed, my ears ringing from the silence as I watched the light from the inner courtyard fall into the room through carved wooden grilles. A heavy ache radiated across my limbs.

The wind was still strong the next morning, but the dust had all but vanished from the air. Our hotel breakfast had been set down on a tin tray in the covered courtyard and, as always, it was meagre, comprising just a small piece of flatbread each, a boiled egg, some white cheese and a few olives. It required some supplementation, so I hurried up the alley to a nearby bakery, paid for two fresh rounds of bread, and raced back towards the hotel, keen to get them back quickly and to get out of the wind.

I felt it hitting me first, and then I heard the smash.

Grit fell out of my hair and down my shirt as, instinctively, I raised my hand to my head, which, for the first time in days, was unprotected by a bicycle helmet. I looked down to see a large mud brick between my feet, then up at a gap in the roof edge whence it had fallen, rubbing my head as an adrenaline surge coursed through me. I'd been hit by the mortar that had come away as the brick was blown loose. I took one more look and ran all the way to the hotel, heart pounding harder than the previous day.

Had I been half an inch closer … The brick had been big enough. Terrorists, lorries, illness – all of these were things I had lain awake at night worrying about. Something falling out of the sky, however, had not been on the list.

9

EARTHLY AND HEAVENLY PLEASURES IN DAMASCUS

Such is the Paradise promised to the righteous; streams run through it; its fruits never fail; it never lacks shade.

Qur'an, Sura 13 'Thunder' 35

In Damascus we ate. We scooped ful from a giant copper cauldron balanced on a bicycle cart at a busy intersection surrounded by concrete tower blocks, tearing off the tough skins with our teeth, squeezing lemon over the beans and dipping them into salt and cumin. The vendor was delighted at our enthusiasm. We slurped the savoury water they'd been cooked in. I still felt desiccated from the desert and the salty liquid tasted good.

I was sore from pedalling and also glad to be wearing my city clothes – a long fleece top that I had haggled for in a stall in Gaziantep, and jeans – and playing at being a more usual sort of tourist. It was a relief to be walking unencumbered by bicycles and kit in warm spring sunshine.

We went to the souk to find ice cream. It was stiffened with mastic gum to stop it melting and scented with rose water. We drank dark red pomegranate juice freshly squeezed into metal goblets which were washed out in a bucket of water. Then at a café with plastic chairs and fruit lined up in a glass display counter we stopped by for smoothies of yogurt, avocado, nuts and honey.

In the souk's main thoroughfare the light shone through old bullet holes put there during the 1925 revolt against French occupation. Syria had many regime changes in the early part of the twentieth century. Five hundred years of Ottoman (Turkish) rule came to an end after the Turks sided with the Germans during the First World War. The British, then based at Suez, in a campaign spearheaded by Col. T.E. Lawrence (of *Lawrence of Arabia*), encouraged Arab forces under the Saudi-born Emir Faisal to seize Damascus from the Turks. The French did not like this one bit and forced the emir into exile. Although France and Britain were allies, fighting Germany in the trenches together, there was deep paranoia on both sides about how the spoils would be divided up after the war. Later, the French were formally awarded the mandate to rule Syria by the League of Nations. This was the Sykes–Picot Agreement, drawn up in 1916, which divided the Ottomans' Middle Eastern empire along a diagonal on the map that ran northeast from the Mediterranean coast to the Persian frontier, 'from the "e" in Acre to the last "k" in Kirkuk'. Territory north of this line, including Syria and Lebanon, would go to France, territory to the south to Britain. Neither party could agree on the control of Palestine, so this was put into international administration. Syria had continued to be controlled by the French since the 1925 revolt that put the bullet holes in the roof of the souk, but when France fell to the Germans in 1940, British and Free French forces took over and Syria was promised independence. This was delivered five years later, but only after violent clashes and bombing by the French in 1945 had led to further British intervention. Syria's first democratically elected president, Shukri al-Quwatli, oversaw the transition; a few years later, in 1949, he was ousted in a military coup that was backed by and allegedly co-planned with the CIA. Quwatli had blocked the building of the Tapline, the 1648-kilometre-long Trans-Arabian Pipeline; this was duly completed in 1950, connecting the oilfields of Saudi Arabia to the Lebanese coast, and would remain operational until 1976. In the two decades following Quwatli's removal, Syria endured at least another nine coups, ending in 1971 with the arrival of Hafez al-Assad, head of the Ba'ath Party.

In the souk we stocked up on food for the next leg of the journey: bags of dried apricots and almonds, fresh tomatoes and cucumbers, rounds of flatbread, tins of tomato puree and stuffed vine leaves, packets of macaroni, cheap, overly sweet biscuits, bad chocolate and plastic cheese triangles. We could not find rice or flour in small quantities.

It was also hard to source suncream. Not finding any in the soap stall in the souk, we went into some smarter-looking pharmacies, only to be pointed towards skin-whitening creams. Many adverts for products seemed to feature very pale-skinned people, a trend that is endemic across all of Asia. I became careful about applying suncream, only doing it in private in case onlookers thought it was an attempt to remain pale.

We went to the central post office to collect our poste restante. My mother had sent us a parcel more than two weeks earlier, containing, among other things, a proper map. We queued in the echoing hall of the large concrete tower block adorned with Syrian flags and pictures of the president. The package was not there. The A2 fold-out tourist leaflet that we'd picked up in Aleppo was now dog-eared and coming apart at the seams. The lack of a map was worrying. We had learnt from our close call with Lebanese guards that the border demarcations could be vague. The roads around the Dead Cities and Krak des Chevaliers had been drawn on approximately, missing out minor side roads, but at least there had been people to ask. Where we were heading now, east, the map showed many roads that started off as solid lines only to dissolve into dashed lines crossing a vast expanse of desert.

We scoured bookshops and the souk, but maps were not on offer. Police states favoured keeping their populace in the dark about cartography, it seemed. In the end we had to settle for repairing our leaflet map with sticky tape supplied by the owner of our hostel. We would cross out of Syria without a proper map. Meanwhile, the Syria map would be diligently sent back by the post office in Damascus, to sit waiting for us when we returned to Scotland some nine months later.

We packaged up some parcels for the UK, including a damask silk scarf for my mother. This characteristic woven brocade, a reversible fabric patterned with floral motifs, was named for Damascus, its city of origin, and was a major trading commodity of the Silk Road. I had bought mine at a stall in an area where there were stands of fine Armenian silver jewellery and Syrian marquetry in the form of mother-of-pearl-inlaid wooden boxes, chessboards and furniture.

At the hostel, Ed fixed punctures while I sewed a patch onto his trousers, sacrificing fabric from a pocket for the repair. As on any long journey, considerable time had to be spent maintaining equipment. We went through our kit, checking and repacking everything, cleaning the bikes, cleaning the stove, washing pans and dishes that had only been given a cursory rinse while on the move, washing clothes, hanging sleeping bags out to air. I had a shirt made up by a men's tailors in the main thoroughfare of the souk. It was long-sleeved, high-necked and long enough to cover my thighs but still allow movement for cycling. The sun was starting to feel hotter every day and I needed to prepare for the desert. In a few weeks the shirt would be bleached pale.

Earthly and Heavenly Pleasures in Damascus

At the Great Mosque (Umayyad Mosque) we sat on the floor of the vast courtyard in the shade, backs against cool marble, watching the steady stream of people coming to pray or to socialise. The polished white marble floor reflected the glare of the sun, a mirror to the double colonnade of Corinthian and Umayyad pillars joined by horseshoe arches.

There had been a house of worship on this site since the Iron Age. The Arameans honoured Hadad, the god of rain, here, and the Romans made offerings to Jupiter. Under Byzantine rule it was a Christian cathedral and became a Muslim site of worship as well after the conquest of Damascus in 634 by Abu Bakr, father-in-law of the Prophet Muhammad. Both faiths worshipped here at the shrine of John the Baptist, which remains on the site to this day, now encased in marble and positioned behind gold grating and green glass in a vast, carpeted prayer hall.

The current mosque began to take shape in the early eighth century, under the sixth Umayyad caliph, al-Walid. Its buildings still glimmer with remnants of the world's most expansive gold mosaic, depicting leafy trees, rushing rivers, decorative pavilions and fortress cities with a strong Byzantine influence; no humans or animals are represented, as dictated by Islamic tradition. These scenes were a vision of Qur'anic paradise for the desert-weary traveller and also perhaps, scholars have argued, a stylised map representing the key wonders of the Umayyad world, of which Damascus was the first capital. The Umayyad dynasty was the first great Muslim dynasty and its empire extended from Spain to Central Asia and India.

Gold glittered in the courtyard as well, where the Dome of the Treasury, an octagonal structure standing high atop more Corinthian columns, showed on one of its sides a mosaic image of a citadel beneath date palms overhanging a blue pool, framed by panels of scrolling acanthus leaves.

The Umayyads eventually lost control of their earthly paradise. They ruled like the old Arab kings, they were settled people rigid in their habits, opulent in their means and out of touch with the people of the Badiyah. In 750 the more austere Abbasids arrived from the east, from Khorasan in Central Asia, across the desert we were about to traverse in the opposite direction. The Abbasids turned their back on Syria and transferred the centre of Islam eastwards, to Baghdad, with eyes both on China and the desert.

In the Great Courtyard, people were sitting as we were, relaxing or chatting, sometimes at prayer. Most of the women were dressed in black, as I was, enveloped in an abaya rented at the entrance. At the fountain a man was washing his feet in preparation for prayer. It was a timeless scene not dissimilar to the one described by exiled Damascene poet Nizar Qabbani in 'Damascus, What Are You Doing to Me?':

I enter the courtyard of the Umayyad Mosque
And greet everyone in it
Corner to ... corner
Tile to ... tile
Dove to ... dove
I wander in the gardens of Kufi script
And pluck beautiful flowers of God's words
And hear with my eye the voice of the mosaics
And the music of agate prayer beads

I noticed a man looking at me and quickly glancing away. When I checked again, he was still staring. He was tanned and had dark hair and sunglasses. Paranoia about the security services welled up inside me. I looked again. He seemed familiar somehow. Was he a tourist or a local? He was staring at me. He took his sunglasses off.

'Rob!' I stifled a shout.

'Oh, it is you, Helen! I didn't recognise you in that ... erm ...' He flapped a hand at my headscarf and abaya. 'I didn't want to stare, especially here.'

I was impressed he had recognised me at all.

Rob had been a friend at university. He was taking time out from working in the City of London to go backpacking. We tumbled over accounts of our respective circumstances and travels of the last five years, amazed that, by some very strange chance, the threads of our lives had crossed again, here, at this very moment, in the courtyard of the Great Mosque. Was this an experience enjoyed by many travellers through the centuries, I wondered, travellers throughout the ages inevitably gravitating to the mighty oasis city of Damascus?

10
THE VALUE OF WATER

The cities dissolve, and the earth is a cart loaded with dust
Only poetry knows how to pair itself to this space.
Adonis, trans. Khaled Mattawa, from 'Desert', in Selected Poems

Water was going to be an issue from now on. In the Damascus hostel we had met a Korean couple who'd cycled from Korea to Syria via China and Central Asia, our first encounter with travellers coming from the east. We'd sat together, cross-legged on a cushioned platform in the hostel courtyard, drinking tea deep into the night and poring over maps. They warned us that there was very little water on the 250-kilometre desert stretch between the outskirts of Damascus and Palmyra.

It was ten in the morning and the day was already hot. We had spent the last two hours navigating the urban sprawl of Damascus. It was always harder to find our way out of a town than into it and we'd ended up hugging the side of a narrow road through industrial wasteland. Lorries piled with coal were having to slow right down to squeeze past each other. A group of builders crowded around us as we stopped at a junction to ask for advice, double- and triple-checking that the information was correct by pointing down all of the roads and asking if it was the way to Tadmor, the name that Syrians use for Palmyra.

Eventually, the concrete and scrubland of the suburbs thinned out and the volume of traffic decreased. By midday we'd reached the town of Ad Dumayr, though there didn't seem to be anyone much about. We pulled up at a roadside shop to replenish our supplies and, unusually, a woman was standing behind the counter when I entered. She tugged her headscarf as she saw me approach and smiled, looking confused. As I examined some tins and the array of bottled water, she called into the back and a man appeared.

It was the kind of shop where you had to ask for things from behind the counter. I pointed to two five-litre plastic cans of water, two litre-cartons of pomegranate juice, a packet of toilet paper, two big bags of flatbread and two tins of butter beans in tomato sauce. Ed and I then sat under the shop porch, drinking the juice as hydration for the desert ahead and dipping torn-up bread into one of the tins of beans.

We set off again, carrying fifteen litres of water in all. The Koreans had said there was a police checkpoint around halfway to Palmyra where we might be able to pick up more water if needed, but if a headwind hit we could be considerably slower than the two days we were reckoning it would take us to reach the oasis town. I cycled off behind Ed, conscious of the extra water sloshing behind me, accentuating any wobbles. Loaded with around twenty kilograms of kit and food, the bike never felt light, but at that moment it felt particularly heavy.

The road rounded a steep hillock, sending me into a sweat and causing me to worry that the desert might not be as flat as I had hoped, but then it opened out before us, an expanse of apricot-coloured earth glowing in the sunshine. A light, warm wind blew behind us and we descended gently. My pedals turned easily and my bike now felt satisfyingly stable and solid. We cycled two abreast, dropping back for the occasional vehicle to pass us. I was surprised at how little traffic there was. A few civilian buses overtook us, full of men wearing military combat uniform. Conscripts, perhaps?

Finding cover for camping was going to be a challenge. Mahmoud's uncle in Aleppo had warned us to be careful further north of Palmyra at night. 'There are bandits in this area. In the day, no problem, but take care at night. Camp with the Bedu, they are good people.'

'Do you believe al-Qaeda is in Syria?' I'd asked him.

'Oh yes, in the desert, but inside a long way – everyone knows they are there. Camp with the Bedu and you will be safe,' he'd reiterated.

There was little doubt that on this road, unlike on the network of roads around the Dead Cities and Krak des Chevaliers, everyone would know exactly where we were heading.

At around four we pulled off the road at a lay-by. The twin tracks of vehicles, slightly paler than the surrounding ground because the sparse shrubs did not grow on them, criss-crossed towards a solitary cluster of buildings or tents in the emptiness. Below us in the middle distance were a few long buildings and a line of mound-shaped houses. Some sort of traditional house, I thought vaguely, fishing out my mini-binoculars for a closer inspection.

'Just look at that view,' Ed said, munching on a piece of chocolate as he tried to capture the scene with his camera.

With my binoculars I scanned the scrubby earth and the grey tent of a Bedouin encampment with a 4x4 and motorbike parked next to it. A herd of sheep was scattered nearby. I looked up at the nearby building and immediately snapped my binoculars down.

'You better put your camera away now,' I said to Ed. 'That's a military base.'

In those few seconds I'd seen a line of tanks under camouflage netting and a helicopter, its rotor blades draped as if under a spider's web. Without binoculars they'd looked just like mounds of earth.

Ed zoomed in on one of the photos he'd just taken, deleted them, just to be on the safe side, and put his camera away. I buried my binoculars in my bar bag. I often worried that border guards might take me for a spy, not accepting wildlife watching as a legitimate pastime.

As I was rifling through my pannier for a chocolate bar, I heard the crunch of a car drawing up. A man with highly mirrored sunglasses and a white open-necked shirt got out. The light seemed to glare off him.

'Hello,' he said, walking over to us and flashing a laminated badge.

'Salam,' we replied. My heart was beating fast as Ed moved forwards to shake his hand. I could smell the scent of lemon cologne.

'Why are you here?' He asked the question I had been expecting.

'We are tourists. We are going to Palmyra – Tadmor.' I swept my hand out over the expanse of sand and rock and added innocently, 'It's very beautiful here.'

'Yes. Yes.' He tipped his chin up. 'Please show me your camera.'

Ed picked it out of the bar bag and handed it to him.

'Turn it on. Show me the photos.'

'The desert,' Ed said as he clicked open the first shot, 'is very beautiful here. We are tourists from Scotland—'

'Yes. Delete, please.'

'Okay.'

'Next.'

'Delete, please. Next.'

And on it went.

I glanced around us. There was no other traffic on the road. The military base was quite a long way away and I had seen no road leading to it. Where had he come from?

'The mosque in Damascus,' Ed was saying.

'Okay. Stop,' the man replied. 'It is not allowed to stop here. On this road. You understand?' And with that he headed back to his car.

'Okay. Shukran. Salam,' Ed said.

The man opened the car door and then paused. 'Welcome to Syria.'

His car was quite a way down the road before Ed and I looked at each other. Was he secret police, we wondered, thinking of the pizza-shop owner we'd met in Austria. 'My country is very safe, you know. Nothing will happen to tourist because everywhere there are policemen.'

The angle of the sun was low now, and the shadows of the rocks and shrubs were lengthening. We pedalled on. About an hour later, I could feel my bladder pressing. I scanned the verge. There was little cover and enough traffic for me not to want to pee in the open. I spotted a low drainage channel under the road, hurried down the embankment and shuffled into its darkness, picking my way through the sheep droppings. A vehicle rumbled overhead, its engine cut out and then there were voices. I peered out as soon as I could to see a group of men in khaki fatigues and trainers standing beside Ed and the bicycles. A khaki minivan was parked by the road containing further khaki-clad passengers. I could feel their eyes on me as I emerged.

One of the men was examining Ed's camera. 'Here …?' he said.

'North of Damascus. Desert.'

'Delete.'

Ed flicked through some more photos. I was trying to visualise what we'd photographed and hoped he wouldn't come to any of us camping in the desert.

'This?'

'Bedu. Near Homs.'

The men laughed and I knew they were looking at the picture of the boys with the donkey.

'Delete?' Ed offered.

'No. Okay.' The man waved the others back into the van. 'No photo. No stop.' He got into the driver's seat and said something into a radio.

'Do you think people are driving up and down this road just to watch us?' I said once they'd gone. 'I'm sure that van passed us a while ago.'

The shadows of our bikes were spindly when we set off again. My stomach growled; I'd hoped to stuff a couple of biscuits after my toilet break.

Fifteen kilometres later and the desert now stretched out into the dusk. It was difficult to tell what lay below the road now, in the direction where the military base had been. A star was pricking the clear sky ahead, which still had traces of deep blue in it.

We kept pedalling. Neither of us wanted to stop.

A car passed us. For a moment its lights blinded me and I then watched it move away from us across the desert, red tail lights shrinking and the headlights throwing a short beam ahead of it. It took a long time for them to shrink and disappear. There was a stationary speck of light up ahead and the car had seemed to move right into it shortly before it went out of view. Could that be the checkpoint?

We had few rules, but one was never to cycle at night as the risks of being hit by a car were so much higher. Today, though, the balance of risk was different. We had not discussed it, but we'd both decided not to stop until we found out what those lights up ahead were.

I squinted into the darkness, willing them to get closer.

After another half an hour, we could hear the sound of truck engines and people shouting. A policeman waved us down at the side of the road. He flicked through our passports and asked where we were going. To our surprise, once we'd answered 'Palmyra', he simply nodded and waved us on into the floodlit darkness.

The hulks of lorries were waiting in a siding by the junction. From here the road split, one branch heading east for two hundred kilometres across the desert to the Iraqi border, the other turning northeast for Palmyra, 140 kilometres away. We cycled round the siding slowly, giving us the chance to size it up for camping. Groups of men were standing talking by a lorry that had its wheel off. Others were helping a lorry reverse into place. There was a building nearby that looked like it could be a truck stop. As we cycled up to it, I could hear men shouting at each other on the veranda. The door opened, throwing a beam of light out and a man staggered down the steps and into the darkness towards us.

'Keep going,' I said to Ed, startling the man, who had not noticed us.

We did another loop, past a big road sign for Baghdad, some eight hundred kilometres away, and decided to head back to the police checkpoint and ask if we could camp there. The low building had a patch of fenced ground around it and we both agreed that there'd been something comforting about the policeman's disinterest in us.

The same policeman was still on duty. We asked him if we could set up our tent, motioning to the space by the police station. I was expecting to have to explain why we there in the middle of the desert without somewhere to stay and to then be taken into the police station to explain it all over again to his superior. But without so much as a furrow of the brow, he immediately said, 'Come,' as if us turning up on our bicycles was the most normal thing in the world.

He called another policeman over as he led us round to the back of the house. We were directed to a space under a pair of olive trees and they helped us peg the tent out. We worked quickly as we talked to them about where we were from.

'You have children?' our saviour asked.

We shook our heads.

'Well, maybe tonight! Syrian children!' He slapped Ed on the back.

Someone brought us a pot of tea with two glasses and once they had seen that we needed no help they excused themselves, saying that they had work, and pointed at the police station to indicate that we were welcome to join them later. We tiptoed into the station an hour later, once we'd eaten, hoping to be able to deliver our thanks. Through an open door into a bare dorm we saw that our guard was on a bunk snoring, so we left the teapot with someone else. Much later, we woke up to hear him calling, 'Ed! Helen!' outside the tent and knew that we were being summoned inside for dinner. We lay still, pretending to be asleep.

As soon as dawn broke, we rose, shivering as we put on clammy clothes, and stopped to thank the policeman, who was at the roadside again. He waved cheerfully, wishing us good luck. Yet again, I was impressed by how hospitality in Syria was always given unquestioningly, by people of all creeds, and how nothing was expected in return.

We had debated asking for water at the police station, but they were so busy and we were not sure if they would have access to a large supply of water anyhow, so we bought some bottled water at the checkpoint café. We were about to learn more about the value of water in this area.

The sun's rays began to warm us and we stopped to take off our gilets. Soon a hot breeze was blowing at our backs, pushing us along. A white Land Rover with 'UN' painted on its side passed us. Were its passengers on holiday from a posting in Iraq, I wondered – on a trip to Palmyra, perhaps? The US and allied forces were still sorting out the aftermath of the invasion of Iraq following the September 11 attacks. Saddam Hussein, the Iraqi despot who had orchestrated genocidal campaigns against hundreds of thousands of Kurdish Iraqis and other ethnic minorities, had been toppled and executed, but the claims led by George W. Bush and Tony Blair that his brutal dictatorship had links to al-Qaeda and that he had been hiding weapons of mass destruction had turned out to be false. Conflict continued as insurgencies opposed the coalition forces and post-invasion Iraqi government. Ironically, the ashes of destruction would turn out to be the ideal environment for culturing extremism, giving seed to the al-Qaeda-supported Islamic State of Iraq, which would go on to become ISIS.

We knew the aftermath of 9/11 had had a significant impact on Western tourism to Syria, but there was no evidence of unrest in Syria at that time. The Land Rover seemed rather incongruous here, new and shiny against the scruffy backdrop of the desert. Otherwise, there was little traffic and we were able to cycle along two abreast, enjoying the gentle breeze. Soon, though, the sun's heat intensified and the air distorted into a haze above the black tarmac ahead. We were rising gently, up onto a plateau of rock and thorns. There was no sign of human habitation.

A dark shadow wobbled in the haze ahead.

As we drew closer, we could see a large herd of sheep grazing to either side. A man stood in the middle of the road, his hand aloft, holding something long and rectangular. He was clearly signalling for us to stop. My heart quickened. Out here, with no one else around, it was hard not to feel vulnerable. I rarely had this feeling while we were on the move, but being asked to stop in the desert always set me on edge.

The man was dressed in a dark dishdasha beneath a dark cloak. His red-and-white shemagh was tied behind his head, leaving his weathered face exposed. His feet were in cracked plastic clogs. He was holding a dirty plastic bottle in his hand.

'Salam alaykum.' Ed offered his hand first.

'Salam alaykum.' The man stood looking at us.

We smiled.

'Awa,' he said.

When we did not respond, he jerked his chin in the direction of the back of my bike and held up the water bottle.

'Awa.'

He wanted water.

I lifted one of the three 1.5-litre plastic bottles from the back of my bike and handed it to Ed, who passed it over his handlebars. We were a long way from anywhere and as we had not been asked for anything in Syria, I imagined he must be pretty desperate. We had plenty of water in reserve.

The man nodded and stood staring at us. For a moment we stared back.

We had not gone ten minutes further when we saw another flock of brown and black sheep, their fleeces matted into dreadlocks with dust, and a few goats. Two boys who had been crouching by the roadside jumped up and raced into the middle of the road, flagging us down. The sheep surged around us. One of the boys threw a pebble at a goat that was making for my front pannier. It thwacked with force against its flank and the animal bleated and bolted, colliding with another goat.

The boys stood squinting at us. 'Awa,' the larger one said, holding his thumb up to his mouth.

Ed handed them a bottle. I expected them to keep it, but they simply took turns to drink from it, a few mouthfuls each, then handed it back.

'Do you have a bottle?' Ed asked.

The older one ducked back to a bundle lying by a thorn bush, retrieving an empty, battered Coke bottle. Ed knelt on the road and carefully filled it from our water bladder. A few precious drops rolled in the dust.

'Do you want a biscuit?' I said, offering an Oreo from my bar bag.

The boys hesitated and then took one each. They screwed up their faces when they put them in their mouths but politely ate the rest. Then they came up to our bikes, running their fingers over brake cables and handlebars. Ed let them have a go ringing his bell and showed them how the brakes worked. We were about to leave when the younger one, who'd not said anything yet, smiled at me and, as if suddenly remembering the words, said, 'Money. Money.'

The other one shot him a glance.

We pretended we'd not heard and waved and cycled off.

We now had about five litres of water left between us, so we were going to have to be careful. I looked at my watch. It was 9.00am and the sun was scorching. I had already drunk a litre and a half of water that morning and my mouth was dry. I felt sweaty and Ed had a tideline of sweat on the back of his shirt. I decided to stash some of the bottles inside my panniers, out of sight. Uncharitable perhaps, but we had no way of knowing if we'd get to Palmyra that night or if the wind might whip up and slow us down again. It was probably another seventy kilometres to Palmyra; at best we would be there by nightfall.

I had noticed how much more water we seemed to need to drink than people we'd met in Syria. At Mahmoud's house a single cup of water had been handed round between everyone before dinner. A small glass of tea seemed to be what kept everyone going. It was rude to drink more than three, so we generally only accepted two unless a third was really pushed on us, but even three glasses of tea would amount to little more than three hundred millilitres of tannin-rich liquid.

Half an hour later we were asked for water for a third time. Two men blocked the middle of the road. We poured about half a litre into their bottle and continued. It was a strange experience to be asked for something in this country, when we were so used to it being the other way round, and it was difficult to say whether they were grateful or not. Did they realise how much effort cycling took or did they just see us as equivalents to the people that passed them in cars?

The previous night one of the policemen had asked us how long it had taken us to get to the junction. He was shocked to hear that it had taken us all day from Damascus to do what should have been a couple of hours in a car. This unfamiliarity with how much slower we were than a car was actually a comfort; when locals saw us cycling in remote areas, it almost certainly didn't occur to them that we wouldn't reach a town by nightfall. We felt less vulnerable knowing this.

By mid-morning we'd arrived at the settlement of al-Basiri. It was a one-house town, but the house was a shop and we went inside and bought some more commercially bottled water. The cost per bottle was higher than it had been in Damascus. It was quite clear that being poor here would mean that you would not be able to afford water. We agreed to carry extra from now on. We were also especially careful when we were in people's houses not to drink more than the people around us.

The wind was still behind us and, with the terrain now sloping gently away, we cycled along with ease on the empty road, the desert stretching out around us. Days when the wind, road and weather conditions worked in unison to create perfect cycling conditions were rare, and this was one of them. It felt good to be on the move.

The road began to climb alongside a steep escarpment. There were shouts as a group of teenaged boys waved to us from the top of the cliffs. We came to the summit and suddenly the desert oasis of Palmyra opened out below us.

11
THE CHILDREN OF PALMYRA

At the beginning, the language of the desert
was grass blooming against the wall of wind,
tall palms swaying in the season of seeding
and cinders carried by air
to the blue welcome of warm sand.
She was our first fountain, our mother,
who held us, then gave us away
to the age of waiting cities.

al-Munsif al-Wahaybi, trans. Salma Khadra Jayyusi and Naomi Shihab Nye,
from 'Desert', in Salma Khadra Jayyusi (ed.) *Modern Arabic Poetry*

A long colonnade of pillars caught the evening sun, stretched across a vast area scattered with tumbled blocks and flocks of sheep accompanied by Bedu herders. To the south, Palmyra's oasis was a sea of green palm fronds among crumbling walls fringing the modern township, while behind us a bowl of dark crags encircled the Valley of Tombs spiked with tall, pyramid-roofed towers. On an isolated mountain to the north, the ruined fort of Qalaat Shirkuh stood sentinel.

A minaret's loudspeaker crackled to life, leading in long and wailing repeats of 'Allahu akbar (God is great)'; others soon joined. We sat in the setting sun watching the shepherds and tourists moving between the ruins. A camel with a tourist on its back was being led along the colonnade by a man in a white dishdasha.

Palmyra, or Tadmor, is one of the greatest sites of the ancient world, an oasis city of date, olive and pomegranate orchards fed by an underground spring. There has been settlement here for at least five thousand years. Palmyra became a strategic midway staging post between the Mediterranean and the cultivated regions of the Euphrates, a desert short cut to the more obvious route, which looped around the Fertile Crescent to the north, skirting the uplands of Turkey, but had become dangerous in the first century BC when the territories of the Seleucid Kingdom were coming under Roman control. An Arab coalition was formed to secure an alternative trading route between Homs and Tadmor, and this flourished under the Roman Empire, fuelled by the Roman upper class's appetite for the exotic. Most of the trade between the Mediterranean and the east came this way, including to and from India via the Persian Gulf, and in and out of Central Asia and China. Its success depended on both the ability of Arab rulers to control desert tribes and the maintenance of good relationships with the Parthian Empire to the east in modern-day Iran. Palmyra became a sort of neutral trading zone where goods from the two powers could be exchanged.

Power struggles from within began to weaken Rome, enabling the Palmyrenes to become increasingly independent. A local noble, Odainat, defeated the army of the Sasanian Empire, which had by now succeeded the Parthian Empire. As a reward, in 256 the Roman emperor Valerian placed all of the Roman forces in the region under his command. Odainat was assassinated, possibly by his wife Zenobia, who took over the city in the name of her young son and then proceeded to expand her empire, gaining control of Syria, Palestine and part of Egypt. The Romans struck back, with Zenobia eventually fleeing across the desert on a camel, only to be captured at the Euphrates in 272.

This defeat marked the decline of Palmyra's prosperity. Its traders were no longer trusted and the city survived largely as a military outpost until in 634 it fell to the Muslim armies of Khalid ibn al-Walid, paving the way for it to become the capital of the Umayyad dynasty. Al-Walid set off from the north of modern-day Iraq and probably captured Palmyra *en route* to his victory in Damascus. This involved a waterless six-day march across the desert. His men had no water bladders, so he forced his camels to drink water, then bound their mouths shut so they could not eat and slaughtered one each day in order that his men could drink the water in their stomachs.

As soon as we had descended from the ruins into the town, we were surrounded by a mob of touts trying to offer us hotel places. It was clear that Palmyra's proximity to war-ravaged Iraq had caused a sharp fall in tourism. Fending them off, we headed for the campsite, which was situated behind the famous ruined Temple of Bel. Birds chattered and palm fronds rustled as we wheeled our bicycles past a handful of German caravans. Later we would have a shower and walk into town for ful, kebabs and pomegranate juice, but first we drank all the remaining water. We had cycled two hundred kilometres in the last two days and were elated to have passed this desert test.

At first I thought the boy picking his way across the broken rocks of the Valley of Tombs towards us was another beggar. Over the past two days we'd spent in Palmyra, we'd met children in the ruins who had tried to extract money from us by volunteering to pose for pictures. A girl of around eight, dressed in an orange sequined tunic, had surprised me by putting an arm around me and asking for a photo. There was also the chubby-faced boy we'd met on the battlements of Qalaat Shirkuh. He was all dressed up in a red-and-white scarf and sand-coloured dishdasha, clearly for the benefit of tourists like us as few boys wore traditional garb. Having failed to persuade us to take him on as a guide, he asked to look through my binoculars. I stood hoping he wouldn't drop them over the parapet, but he scanned the desert below us and called out, pointing, that he had found his father's herd of sheep. He wrapped the cord carefully round the binoculars as he handed them back. We gave both children a tiny amount of money and chocolate; it was a surprise to be asked for anything here and anyhow they were nice kids.

But the boy in the Valley of Tombs was after an English lesson, and we were only too happy to oblige. He clambered over the last band of rock, schoolbook in hand, and sat down next to us.

'My name is Hassan. Do you speak English?' He pointed at a sentence in his book and looked up at me.

'That says: "I went to the cinema with my sister."'

'Siinema,' he repeated, then scribbled something down next to the word and flicked forwards a few pages.

'That says: "patient". It means not minding to wait.'

'Pay ... shunt.' He wrote some more. 'Pay ... shunt – this means what?'

'It means not minding to wait,' I said again. 'You know ... well, what example can I give? If you tell your friend to meet you at three o'clock and you arrive and he's not here, then if you are happy to sit and wait for him, that means you are patient.'

He nodded. Once he'd run out of questions, we asked him about his family. He was the youngest of four brothers and had two older sisters. He was sixteen.

'Are you married?' he asked us.

'Yes. For two years. And you,' Ed teased him, 'when will you get married?'

'I must wait for my older brothers,' he said. 'My parents maybe only have money for the first two.'

This was the second time I had heard this that day. A worker on the campsite had told us that he was unmarried because he was the youngest.

'And you have a girlfriend?' I asked Hassan, still teasing.

He shook his head. 'It is not like that for us.'

I nodded, feeling guilty.

'Do you mind if I ask a question?' he said after a pause. The colour had risen to his cheeks.

'Go on,' I encouraged. People occasionally asked us whether it was true that sex outside marriage was acceptable in Europe and I suspected Hassan was about to ask that too.

'How many girlfriends do you have?' he said, turning to Ed.

Ed laughed. 'Just one and she is my wife.'

'Yes, but do you not also have some girlfriends? This is normal in Europe.'

'You mean now, at the same time as my wife?'

'Yes.' Hassan seemed unperturbed that I was half a metre away.

'No. I know you can have many wives, but we don't do that in Europe. It is only really acceptable to have one partner, one wife.'

Hassan looked confused.

'Or girlfriend,' I added. 'Ed had some girlfriends before me and I had some boyfriends before him, but it is only considered right to have one at a time. Generally anyway,' I mumbled, not sure I had enough insight into the finer points of the ethical non-monogamy movement to explain that here.

'But I see tourist men from German and France coming with many girlfriends here.'

'Really, are you sure?'

'Yes.'

It took a moment for the penny to drop.

'You mean you have seen men travelling with groups of women?'

'Yes. They are their girlfriend.'

I laughed. 'No, they are probably just friends.'

He looked confused again.

In a country where women even ate separately from men they were not related to, it wasn't hard to imagine how strange it would seem to see a group of male and female backpackers laughing and joking together in the ruins, the girls with uncovered heads and in tight clothes.

'In our culture,' I said, 'it is fine for men and women to go out together or travel together. It does not mean anything.' As soon as I said this, I could picture my mother's raised eyebrows – a different generation's response. 'For example, maybe sitting in a restaurant for a coffee or going to the cinema.' There weren't many cafés in rural Syria. In the cities, yes, but even then not many with women in them. 'This does not mean they are ... well ... you know ... girlfriend and boyfriend.'

'It does not mean they are having sex,' Ed added helpfully.

'You know,' I continued, 'you might see some European or American movies where this happens, but it is not generally like that for normal people.'

I recalled walking into the internet café in Palmyra to see a man openly watching a porn video with a blond girl bobbing up and down. However, even the sitcom *Friends* would appear pretty raunchy by local standards. I was starting to see where Hassan's confusion came in.

We wandered back from the ruins into town and watched a man we'd spoken to earlier coax a female tourist onto the back of his camel. He'd encouraged us to take a picture as he posed, reclining on top of his camel, one arm crooked behind his head, sunglasses balanced on gelled hair. The camel's name was Casanova, he told us. Once the woman was seated behind him, the camel man let out a guttural cry and they raced off at full tilt. She clung on to him tight and, unlike brave Zenobia, her screams echoed down the colonnade.

'Good trick,' Ed said.

12
TO RAQQA

Gone are they the lost camps, light flittings, long
sojournings in Miná, in Gháula, Riján left how desolate.
Lost are they. Rayyán lies lorn with its white torrent beds,
scored in lines like writing left by flood water.
Tent-floors smooth, forsaken, bare of all that dwelt in them,
years how long, the war-months, months too of peace-pleasures.
Spots made sweet with spring-rains fresh-spilt from the
Zodiac, showers from clouds down-shaken, wind-wracks
and thunder-clouds;
Clouds how wild of night-time, clouds of the dawn
darkening, clouds of the red sunset, – all speak the
name of her.

Labid, trans. Lady Anne Blunt, from 'Mu'allaqa', in Marlé Hammond (ed.),
Arabic Poems

On our third morning in Palmyra, we were woken by the sound of the wind. We lay next to each other in the tent, listening to the rattling of the canvas. Outside, the palm fronds jostled and the air was grey and full of drizzle. We had five days left on our Syrian visas, so we planned to leave that morning. We intended to head east along the road to Deir ez-Zor before turning northwards for around eighty kilometres on a track across the desert that would take us to Raqqa on the banks of the Euphrates. Raqqa was within a day's cycle of the Turkish border and we thought it might take us three days to get there. We would attempt to camp at the ruins of Resafa, reasoning that there might be Bedu there.

We set off into the easterly wind with reluctance. By noon, we had been slogging into a headwind for two hours and had only covered sixteen kilometres. We stopped for a break and some water, turning our faces away from the driving dust and rain, which were mixing to mud in the air.

'This is bollocks,' Ed said, chewing a date.

I nodded despondently. I felt exhausted, as if the past two days of sightseeing and resting had been of no benefit.

He took another date and scanned the map. 'I think we should turn back,' he said after a while. 'There's just no point.'

I nodded again.

'At this rate we're going to be camping by the road thirty kilometres out of Palmyra, just using up water and food supplies.'

Neither of us mentioned al-Qaeda or bandits.

We packed away our snacks, turned around and were back at the campsite in town in under an hour.

Mohammed, the campsite manager, had a fire going in the porch and ordered his flunky, a small man with a lazy eye, to make way for me so that I could sit next to him. They both had woolly scarves wrapped around their heads like bandages, thick socks in their slip-on sandals and leather jackets drawn in close. Ed had to make do with the seat at a distance, despite my attempt to move.

'You should stay in our Bedu tent.' Mohammed gestured at the dripping awning of a square construction that was scattered with pillows and looked like it was better designed for shading tourists from the sun.

The assistant served us all tea, lifting the pot high as he poured, so that the stream of tea released steam into the damp air.

'Yes, stay inside with us. No problem. Like Bedu family.'

I shot a sideways glance at Ed. 'I think we will camp again tonight.'

The rain had eased a little, so Ed got up to go and put up the tent. 'No point in you getting wet again,' he said, 'if you're okay here on your own?'

I nodded, running the gauntlet for the sake of warmth.

'I also do Bedouin massage,' Mohammed said once Ed was out of earshot. 'Very traditional. Very good. Last summer many lady tourist liked.'

'Not for me, thank you, but I will ask my husband if he is interested.' I smiled.

A car drew up, providing me with the excuse to offer the prime seat to the new arrivals. More tea was ordered and I sat watching the flickering flames, listening to a flow of Arabic, and wondered how many ladies had opted for the desert spa treatments on offer.

Two hours out of Palmyra, on our second attempt at leaving, we stopped to check the map and realised that we'd forgotten to fill up our bottle of petrol, which was now only about 20 per cent full. In our concern about water, we'd neglected to think about fuel for the stove. A quick inventory of our supplies was not reassuring. Without the addition of rice, rice that needed petrol to cook it, we would be operating on a much narrower error margin, and we wouldn't have nearly enough flatbread to feed us both for the three days it might take us to reach the Euphrates. The empty expanse of the desert, with its many confusing dirt tracks seemingly coming from and heading to nowhere, was a daunting prospect. Once again, I wished we had a real map.

We pulled into a truck stop at the junction, explaining our predicament to the young men staffing it, but they had no petrol to sell us. Two cups of tea later, however, and one of them offered to ride his motorbike the ten kilometres to the next town to fill up our bottle. We accepted and gave him a fairly generous tip. That we needed petrol for our pedal bicycles was perplexing to everyone, but then foreigners were always strange people. We were taken from the plastic-chaired restaurant to the cushioned and heated back room for further tea while we waited. The desert wind howled outside.

Conscious that we now had just four more days left on our Syrian visas, we politely refused offers of overnight accommodation and pedalled off once more, hoping that as the road swung to the north the headwind would become a crosswind and might even push us along a bit.

As the day drew on and we began thinking about a place to stay for the night, we debated whether or not it would be fine to camp on our own. The conversation with Mahmoud's uncle in that smoke-filled room back in Aleppo played again and again in my mind.

'There are bandits in this area. In the day, no problem, but take care at night. Camp with the Bedu, they are good people.'

'Do you believe al-Qaeda is in Syria?'

'Oh yes, in the desert, but inside a long way – everyone knows they are there. Camp with the Bedu and you will be fine.'

Was it genuine advice or given for dramatic effect?

Osama bin Laden, the Saudi-born, now stateless leader of the global terror brand al-Qaeda, orchestrator of the 9/11 attacks, was at large somewhere. This was despite an almost decade-long effort led by the US to find him. He was rumoured still to be hiding out in the mountains of Afghanistan, or maybe in Pakistan, but could he actually be here, in the Syrian desert, perhaps even running training camps hereabouts?

Eventually, we came to a spot that looked hopeful. Two long, low black rectangular tents were positioned closer than normal to the road, guarding a small substation. The dogs began to bark as Ed walked closer. A man emerged and came towards him, then swept his arm out across the patch in front of his tent. We would be able to camp there.

As we set up our tent at a polite distance, a girl in an orange sequinned dress and a red-and-white shemagh came over and set a teapot and two glasses at our feet before fleeing wordlessly up onto a small hillock from where she watched us while pretending to watch her goats. When we were done, we returned the teapot. Our host held open the heavy fabric of the tent door and beckoned us in.

Shoes off, and we were in a low, carpeted room. The girl who'd brought us tea, no more than twelve years old, held her baby sister while two young boys played on the carpet. The man introduced us to his wife, who looked to be in her twenties. A clattering of dishes could be heard from the other room. 'Wife number two,' he explained. He had five children and was paid to guard the plant next door at night. He tapped a bit of electricity from it via a cable strung across the desert.

We made small talk, sipped tea, and after half an hour excused ourselves before we drank too much tea made with their precious water supply. The stars were sharing the sky with a gibbous moon, our tent a small dark shape under a vast dark dome. One of the dogs barked.

I woke with my tongue stuck to my mouth. Water. There wasn't even any dew on the ground – the day would be hot. The girl was already up, guarding both us and her goats again, shemagh still fluttering in the wind. We waved to her as we cycled off. There was no sign of anyone else, and we did not feel the need to disturb them. She waved back.

The road climbed into an area of wadis, to a higher plateau where deep channels appeared to have been carved by water, in some cases flowing across the road, except everything was bone dry. The wind was hot and dry, but it was blowing across us now at least. We stopped to sip some water, looking from the rim of the road across a barren hillside which undulated away into nothingness.

A car pulled up. A blacked-out window descended and a man leant out. There was a waft of cool breeze from the air con. He wore a starched white dishdasha, the white shemagh more commonly seen in Saudi Arabia, and dark sunglasses.

'Salam,' we said.

'Salam. Agua.' He pointed at Ed's water bottle. 'Agua.' He pointed again.

Taken aback, Ed handed it over. Like me, he was expecting to be offered water rather than be asked for it.

The man swigged from it before handing it inside to a second male passenger and then to a young boy who was sitting astride the gearstick. I tried to let my face remain impassive as I visualised the contents of the water bottle disappearing. We only had two litres left between us and it was hot.

The man nodded and the car sped off into the desert. We waved. Goodwill in case they decided to come back.

'Cheeky beggars.'

We were both unnerved.

Out here it would be hard to refuse anyone anything. Did they genuinely need water? Was it a test? Did they not realise how slow we were? Did they not care?

It was not until hours later that fields began to appear out of the desert, a thin sprinkling of green shoots hardly visible against the bare ground. Mud houses were dotted across the horizon. A family waved and shouted from a house a distance from the road. We waved back, ringing our bells, decided against stopping and then immediately regretted it.

Anyhow, at the next village we were caught. As we cycled past a house, a small girl dressed in purple rushed out. I screeched to a stop, panicking that the lorry which had come up behind me would not see her. It rumbled by as she danced excitedly by my bicycle. A large crowd of adults and children materialised and before we knew it our bikes were parked in her family's courtyard and we were sipping scorching hot tea, seated on plastic chairs.

The man of the house was elderly and his wife was swathed in black with an indigo mark of the Bedu tattooed on her forehead and chin. She sat on her haunches off to one side with her daughter-in-law, Fatima, who was wearing a deep purple abaya and matching headscarf. There was a second daughter-in-law, Hatidge, thinner and smaller and the mother of the little girl I'd met first. A portly man in a shiny suit was introduced to us as the headmaster of the primary school. He was clearly the guest of honour and led on interrogating us about our journey. When he heard Ed was a teacher, he urged us to come and visit him at the school on our way past the next day.

In the evening, I sat with the women in the room belonging to Hatidge. The children were asleep in the corner, tucked in with blankets. Hatidge pointed at a pastel photograph on the wall and passed her hands over her face. Her husband was dead. She told me she was remarried now, to his brother. She was wife number two. Fatima's situation seemed little happier. She was married to the youngest son, a young man, who had enquired earnestly and politely about our journey, but they'd not had any children yet, even after two years. She looked sad. She took me to her room to show me her things – a large white wardrobe, dressing table and a futon covered in white satin. They looked out of place in that house, a house that didn't have a toilet, not even an outdoor squat, as I'd discovered when Fatima had walked me out to the middle of the muddy field behind the house. Her defiant motion as she told me that these items were hers made it clear that she felt she had married down and she despised the family.

'And we have not had children,' she said again, taking my hand.

'Will he marry another?'

'No.' She shook her head. 'He does not want.'

'Good,' I said and squeezed her hand back.

She looked me in the eyes and shook her head at my naivety. 'My mother-in-law …' She jerked her chin towards the next room. I had heard the elderly woman scolding her and Hatidge as they scuttled around the house.

We spent the night on a deep mattress which was rolled out in Fatima's room. She and her husband lay in the next bed. At bedtime we held back, confused at this unorthodox arrangement. I had sat on the floor of the kitchen with the women, peeling potatoes for dinner, but when the food was ready they had not eaten with us, so how could it be that we would share a room? They got into bed fully dressed, then whispered like a couple in love. I wriggled out of my clothes only once I was under the heavy quilt in the darkness and wondered if everyone in Syria slept fully dressed and whether love would be strong enough to overcome the mother-in-law's desires for a grandchild. I kissed Ed goodnight very lightly, trying to make not a sound, and then we both lay awake for a long hour, sweating, thirsty and needing the loo but resisting the urge to move even an inch lest they think we were up to something aberrant.

We reached the ruins of Resafa early the next morning. The site of this abandoned city is mentioned in the Old Testament:

> *Did the gods of the nations that were destroyed by my predecessors deliver them – the gods of Gozan, Harran, Rezeph and the people of Eden who were in Tel Assar?*
>
> **(2 Kings 19:12)**

After Zenobia and the return of Palmyra to the Romans, Resafa became an important frontier fortress against the continuing Sasanian threat from the east. Later it became a centre of pilgrimage in honour of the Roman soldier Sergius, who was martyred there sometime between 305 and 313 when his refusal to worship at the altar of Jupiter revealed him to be a Christian. He and his fellow Christian, Bacchus, were dressed in women's clothing, chained and paraded around their town. Bacchus was beaten to death and Sergius was tortured and transported to Resafa, where he was eventually executed. In 313 the Roman emperor Constantine converted to Christianity and this new state religion soon dominated the empire. Syria, of course, already had a rich Christian tradition going back to the missions of St Paul after Jesus's death, but after the official adoption of Christianity, Christian buildings and sites of worship were able to proliferate, churches like those we had visited at Serjilla in the Dead Cities and the monastery of Mar Musa. Resafa became the second most important pilgrimage site after Jerusalem.

We wandered the basilica built in his name and then retreated to the delicious underground cool of the vast vaulted Byzantine cisterns.

They were once capable of holding fifteen thousand cubic metres of water, enough to sustain the city – by then renamed Sergiopolis – during drought or siege. The chambers were bone dry and echoed as we walked. There was no soul around, no tourists or anyone to buy a ticket from, only the wind and the desert sand.

Under the religiously tolerant Umayyads, the site flourished, even becoming the favoured city of the last great Umayyad caliph, Hisham (724–43). He built some palaces, and a mosque was maintained alongside the basilica. These suffered at the hands of the succeeding Abbasids, who emanated originally from Khorasan (eastern Iran and Central Asia) and would go on to build their own mighty empire, presiding over a great intellectual and scientific movement. Their focus was on the east, however, and Syria, no longer seen as strategically important, was neglected. A Christian population continued to worship at Resafa until the ousting of the Crusaders by the Mamluks.

Our next stop was Lake Assad, created by a dam on the Euphrates, which we intended to cross at Qalaat Jaabr. Our map had an enticing picture of this castle, which was situated by the turquoise lake, a favoured picnic spot for locals, complete with boat rides. As we cycled, we discussed how we were looking forward to a camping spot on the shore, a discreet (and in my case fully clothed) swim, and perhaps some cooked food at a waterside stand.

We reached the junction at midday, and the straggling town of al-Mansura. Honouring the promise we'd made at Fatima's house the day before, we tracked down the school to pay our respects to the headmaster. As the gates opened, we were mobbed by a gang of excitable children on their lunch break. A rock flew across the courtyard and two teachers with batons raised them threateningly, shouting hard. We were quickly ushered into a small office to enjoy the luxury of an instant cappuccino as we sat awkwardly on plastic chairs, feeling dusty and dirty in the presence of the headmaster, again in a shiny suit and with two of his teachers similarly attired.

We had sourced two heavy boxes of baklava, oozing with sugar syrup, at a local bakery. One for Fatima and Hatidge's family and one for the headmaster. He seemed perplexed at our request to deliver one with an accompanying note as a gift to the family. Perhaps we had insulted him with the suggestion that he should run errands to a poor family for us. Perhaps he had really only been with the family to chase up absences. We were glad to escape back onto the dusty road.

The weather turned very quickly, the wind suddenly strong from the west and the sky a deep orange. Sand and dirt and plastic bags careered across our path. We wrapped our faces against the blast and made headway at a frustrating five kilometres an hour. Only when we'd got halfway to Qalaat Jaabr did we accept that we'd have to give up on our dream of the turquoise lake. We had just two days remaining on our Syrian visas and to reach Turkey the following day meant we'd have to head east now, rather than go up to Lake Assad. We turned tail and, in the mounting storm, raced back to al-Mansura and out beyond it, to where we could meet another crossing point to the border. Pushed by the wind, we were now racing along at thirty-five kilometres an hour, dodging flying branches and whirling bags.

The wind would blow us out of Syria. To Raqqa that evening, the desert storm carrying us in a cloud of city dust and dirt past concrete tower blocks, a giant statue of the president's father Hafez al-Assad and yet more tower blocks. We found a room for the night in the grubby Hotel Tourism and did battle with the manager for some hot water to wash away the grime. There was desert sand in every cranny of our belongings. We headed back out into the wind to find something to eat. We found ourselves at a busy roundabout with a clock tower, crowded with yellow taxis and men whose dishdashas were flapping in the breeze under their leather jackets. There was a big jostle at one stand, with customers coming away with something wrapped in flatbread. We were ushered to the front of the queue and ordered two of the same. A mound of grey mince was piled from a hotplate onto the bread. Glancing down to my right, I saw a giant plastic bin overflowing with cracked sheep skulls. We ate hurriedly before squeamishness could get the better of hunger and retreated to the hotel, where mice kept us awake most of the night.

Had I known what was soon to unfold in Raqqa, I might have paid more attention to the city. Within four years, Raqqa would become the capital of the Islamic State caliphate. Following the suppression of protests against the al-Assad regime in 2011, only a year after we left Syria, and as the casualty counts rose, thousands of people left embattled cities like

Aleppo, Homs and Idlib and arrived in Raqqa. By March 2013 the Free Syrian Army as well as Islamist rebel forces, including the al-Qaeda-linked al-Nusra Front, controlled the city. The Hafez al-Assad statute was toppled, and briefly, Raqqa self-declared as the first liberated city in Syria.

Immediately, rifts emerged between the secular Free Syrian Army and the al-Nusra Front. A small group of new fighters carrying black flags appeared and stepped into the void. Fighters from the al-Nusra Front began to switch sides aligning with the new radicals, Islamic State. By 2014 Islamic State had complete control of the city. It was a social media machine. Its propaganda videos featured executions, beheadings, *Grand Theft Auto*-style chase and dispatch sequences and glamorised battle scenes – like a movie or a computer game but so very real. It declared Raqqa the capital of a new caliphate and spun other adverts, straining to show the dusty city in its best light, with pictures of children in a playground and a doctor with a British accent praising the modern medical services.

Soon, thousands of foreign fighters from countries across Arabia, Central Asia, Russia, Europe and North America were flocking to this new 'paradise'; estimates suggest as many as forty thousand. This included British-born fifteen-year-old Shamima Begum, who was lured to Raqqa along with two teenaged friends and where, ten days after arriving, she was married to a twenty-one-year-old Dutch-born Islamic convert.

The Islamic caliphate was anything but a paradise. Human rights atrocities in the territory controlled by the Islamic State are some of the worst since those committed in Nazi Germany, including systematic murder, torture, slavery and rape, and the large-scale ethnic cleansing of religious minorities, particularly the Yazidi but also Christians, Shia Muslims and non-Sunni Muslim groups across both northern Syria and Iraq. The clock tower roundabout where we had eaten dinner became a site of public beheadings. Torture, rape and execution were used to repress dissent. News was suppressed and internet traffic monitored. A group of citizen journalists under the name 'Raqqa is being slaughtered silently' secretly and heroically filmed atrocities and posted them on Facebook for the world to see. IS hunted them down, torturing and executing them and their families.

IS control of large tracts of Syria and Iraq galvanised intervention, including air strikes by a US coalition, and by June 2017 Raqqa remained the only major Syrian city fully under IS control. A bloody battle was led on the ground by the Syrian Democratic Forces, a coalition of groups opposed to both Assad and IS and backed by the US and its allies. This group included the YPJ, an all-female, predominantly Kurdish militia who fought alongside male YPG and other groups to liberate the city. The US bombardment of Raqqa in support took a heavy toll, with Amnesty International estimating that 1600 civilians might have been killed during the coalition air strikes and that by the end, 270,000 of the pre-war 300,000 inhabitants had fled the city. After the liberation of Raqqa, the region, constituted as the Autonomous Administration of North and East Syria (or Rojova), held out against the Syrian government until Assad's fall.

Father Paolo, whom we'd met at Mar Musa, had been ejected from Syria by the government for having written a letter pleading for a peaceful democratic transition, but in 2013 he returned to 'liberated' Raqqa in the hope of brokering a peace dialogue with the Islamists. He was kidnapped and possibly executed by Islamic State, although as I write this twelve years later, a five-million-dollar reward is still being offered by the US government for information about his fate. The Temple of Bel at Palmyra, which had survived 1500 years since Zenobia's rule, including the invasion of the Mongols, was blown up by IS fighters.

It is the normal people I think about most. Caught in the crossfire or forced to pick a side. No one could possibly have remained unscathed. When I think about Raqqa, I think about the desert to the south. I think about a small Bedu girl who is wearing an orange sequined dress. She is on a sand dune watching two travellers who have arrived on bicycles from a long way away. A man and woman with red faces and strange clothes. She places a pot of tea and two glasses outside their tent and then runs away, unsure if she should be scared or not. She is now watching them, pretending not to, and is guarding her goats. Her red-and-white shemagh flutters in the hot desert breeze.

Eastern Turkey

 March 2010

Tea and Grit

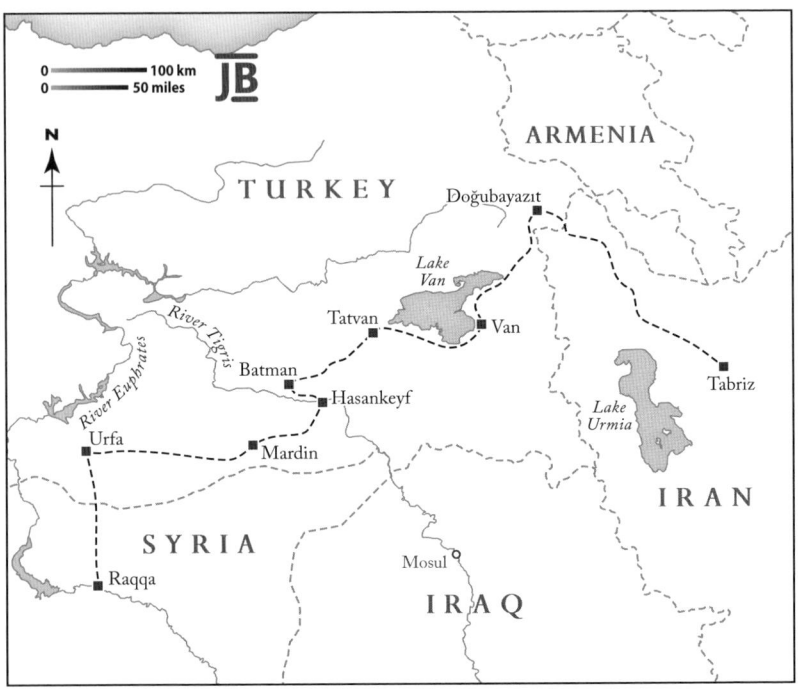

13
EASTWARDS

Outwards onto the steppe
The world stretches with the blue sky
You and me, both of us.
We are young, still young as the morning
And our smile has the look of a truant's

Gülten Akın, trans. Monika Carbe and Helen Watson, from
'Winterreise/Winter Journey' on www.lyrikline.org

'Hello, hello, helloooooooo ... Please come back!'

A man waved and shouted to us from outside a house where he was sitting with a group.

We waved back.

'Helloooooooo!'

He jumped up and, gesticulating madly, ran down the road after us. I turned round to look, waved politely, wobbled ... and fell into an irrigation ditch. Our fate was sealed. We'd crossed the border into Turkey at Akçakale less than half an hour ago and hadn't wanted to stop yet. But it was 6pm already, so we'd be staying the night in this Arab village in the Turkish borderlands no matter what.

Our bikes were taken off us and leant against the wall, plastic chairs were offered, tea was brought out and we recounted our story. Ahmet spoke in a torrent of English, Turkish and exuberant mime. It was impossible not to be sucked in by his enthusiasm. He was slim and good-looking and his eyes seemed to be constantly sparkling with one scheme or another. After a while he took us up the road to his house. His wife Hadije was plump and, at thirty-three, almost certainly younger than him. She embraced me, clucking maternally, and scolded Ahmet for not bringing us sooner. She had the air of a woman who was used to her husband's hare-brained schemes.

Ed was taken to the school where Ahmet was a caretaker, while I sat with Hadije as she sewed, first ripping pieces of emerald chiffon into panels, then stitching them together on her sewing machine. These were the finishing touches to a lined salwar kameez for an aunt. She worked quickly and used no ruler or pattern to guide her. We peeled potatoes for dinner, sitting on the floor in the kitchen around a large aluminium pan taken down from a high stack on a kitchen shelf. The house had running water, which came via a pump shared by a block of houses on the way to the communal toilet. A jug for use in the toilet was left by the pump and filled up on the way there.

Ahmet and Ed arrived back and at Ahmet's insistence I was made to wear one of Hadije's dresses. I tried to get her to put me in one of her less beautiful ones, but she was having none of that, so I ended up in a floor-length purple sequined dress with matching under-trousers, buttoned cuffs and a heavy leather belt around my waist. I clutched the fabric high above the dirt as I negotiated the muddy paths of the village in her flip-flops.

All the women in the village wore matching large, square lilac headscarves, some embroidered with white thread in geometric or floral patterns, some with the addition of white sequins. Hadije showed me how to twist one end and drape it over my shoulder and once I got it right the bystanders whooped with delight. Hadije now deemed my outfit complete and sent me on my way with Ed.

Our tour included the graveyard, where Ahmet said a prayer for his brother, explaining that, 'Musselman are buried with the face turned to the side, not like the Hueristan (Christians). This way the face is always turned to Mecca.' The graves had low head and feet posts of white stone. We trekked across the fields to visit his mother, her face tattooed with a line of indigo ink dots on her forehead and an X on her chin, her eyes black with kohl. Then on to the girls' school, where a call on Ahmet's mobile from Hadije sent us hurrying back home for food.

'My wife, she does not bleed anymore,' Ahmet announced after a tasty dinner of fried potatoes and chickpea stew accompanied by bowls of yogurt and wafer-thin bread, eaten sitting on the floor.

Shocked at his indiscretion, we feigned incomprehension, but Ahmet persisted. He mimed cutting himself so that we couldn't fail to understand that he was talking about periods. Hadije looked unperturbed. Perhaps it was a frequent topic of conversation. Perhaps it was surprising to them that we did not ask why they had no children, a question we'd been asked continuously in Syria.

Ahmet asked if we could send him some medicine for her from the UK. My heart sank. Had they seen a doctor, I asked? They had, even going all the way to Ankara, but the pills had not helped. We explained that any drugs in the UK would have to be prescribed, that there might be any number of reasons for infertility, and that infertility treatment in Britain was very expensive and would not guarantee a positive outcome. We were out of our depths and floundering, not wanting to offer false hope. I had seen a very good doctor in Ankara a few weeks earlier, for stomach problems that had turned out to be the return of the irritable bowel syndrome that had plagued me during my early twenties. The Ankara doctor took my concerns seriously, sent me for a barrage of tests and told me to minimise my bread intake and eat more yogurt. It turned out to be good advice. I told Ahmet with some certainty that there was no reason why the doctors in the UK would be any better.

Ahmet said that he got angry about this sometimes and hit Hadije. Embarrassment flashed across Hadije's face. To my relief, Ed said very firmly, 'No, that is never right,' and Ahmet hung his head in embarrassment. I felt pity and a deep sense of unease at his honesty and was at a loss as to what to say.

Ahmet and Ed went out for the evening, to visit an uncle, and Hadije immediately insisted that I should have a bath. She boiled up hot water in a gas boiler, spread a PVC tablecloth on the kitchen floor and set a large shallow aluminium basin in the middle. Then she fastidiously checked over the house, yanking every chink in the curtains closed against the eyes of opportunistic peeping Toms.

I stripped off, glad that a hammam in Ankara had prepared me for the un-British nudity, and crouched inside the large basin as Hadije poured jugs of hot water over me while I washed myself. She scrubbed my back vigorously with a mitt. After all the dust and exhaustion of our departure from Syria, I felt as if I was being baptised into a new country.

That night, she and I slept on mattresses next to each other in the living room – Ed, Ahmet and Ahmet's brother being billeted in another room. Hadije put a Turkish soap opera on the TV. It felt like a sleepover.

In the morning, Ahmet had religion on his mind. We'd spent the evening discussing the prophets, me grateful that my church youth group knowledge had given us a topic of conversation.

'Ibrahim.'
'Abraham.'
'Yusuf.'
'Josef.'
'Dawud.'
'David.
'Ayyub.'
I wracked my brains. 'Job!'

We recited the prophets in tandem, me trying to twist the sound into something recognisable. 'Sulayman (Solomon), Harun (Aaron), Yunus (Jonas), al-Yasa (Elijah)' – the prophets of the Abrahamic religions of Islam, Judaism and Christianity or the people of 'the Kitab (the Book)'. People in Syria had often reminded us of this too. And of course there was prophet Isa (Jesus), recognised by only two religions; and another, Muhammad, recognised by just the one.

After a breakfast of fried eggs, Ahmet took us back across the field to his mother's house. She was sitting in a small room cross-legged, back to the wall, prayer beads in hand, and we joined her on the floor. I sensed he had a mission in mind and it soon became clear that he wanted us to add the final prophet to our list. He begged us to recite after him: 'La illaha illa 'llah , Muhammad rasuulu-llah'

'What does it mean, Ahmet?' I said, knowing full well that this was the shahadah or declaration of faith. *There is no god but Allah. Muhammad is the messenger of Allah.*

He dropped his gaze to the ground. 'A special blessing. It will mean so much to me if you both say it.'

We declined with good humour, hoping that his mother would not be offended, but agreeing after much cajoling to recite the first half of the phrase once. We were touched that he considered our souls worth saving. His mother smiled good-naturedly; she had clearly expected this and like us perhaps considered that conversion by subterfuge would probably not be accepted on high.

We finally tore ourselves away at lunchtime, waving furiously until we had pedalled out of sight. We posted photographs of our stay as soon as we got to Urfa and while we were still in Turkey we would occasionally receive phone calls from Ahmet, checking that we were okay.

The next leg of the journey had been playing on our minds. The eastern, predominantly Kurdish region of Turkey continued to be politically tense because of Kurdish separatist movements active there, and we'd also read numerous online accounts from cyclists of ferocious Kangal shepherd dogs and stone-throwing children. The Islamic Republic of Iran loomed on its mountainous eastern frontier, but we were still swithering as to whether to go into Iran or not. Weeks earlier, in a hostel in western Turkey, we'd met a backpacker from Tehran, Farid, who had plied us with single-malt whisky and told us not to got to Iran because of 'our terrible government' and especially because of the recent crackdown on protesters. Protests were ongoing, and a foreigner had recently been arrested in association with them. We'd also heard stories of a German cyclist couple who'd been held in Iran for days on suspicion of spying simply because they were carrying a GPS. Our encounter with Assad's security forces in the desert near Palmyra had shaken us, making us acutely aware of how we too could easily be viewed with suspicion. Thank goodness we'd decided for that very reason to rely on paper maps and to carry nothing more hi-tech than pay-as-you-go mobiles.

Our current plan was to cross out of eastern Turkey into the far western corner of Iran, pick up visas for Azerbaijan in Tabriz, make a swift northerly exit from Iran into Azerbaijan and then take a ship across the Caspian Sea to Turkmenistan. That way we would be in Iran for just a brief stint and would avoid a committed crossing of its northern reaches, which might take a month or so. If we got cold feet about going into Iran altogether, an alternative option would be to head further north in Turkey and cross into Georgia and from there into Azerbaijan; this would avoid Iran completely but risked exposing us to seriously bad weather. The road along Turkey's southern border with Iraq was said to be closed to tourists and so was not in contention.

There were many variables and we frequently debated the pros and cons of the different routes while in the saddle or at rest. The continuing uncertainty was sapping our morale. The only obvious next step then was to get to Lake Van, high in the mountains in the far east of Turkey, from where our two possible onward routes diverged: north to Georgia or east to Iran. We could reassess when we got there. Lake Van was around five hundred kilometres from Ahmet and Hadije's village; we estimated it would take us about a week to get there.

Urfa (Şanlıurfa) also had an Arabic feel. Violet-scarfed women sorted through clothes in the pazar while men in baggy pants smoked and played dominoes and chess in the open courtyards of its teahouses. Waiters strode purposefully between the low tables and cushioned benches, their metal trays rattling with tulip glasses of tea and dishes piled high with sugar cubes. Elderly men, some also sporting lilac headscarves twisted in the Arabic way around the head, white beards flowing from wrinkled jaws, crouched on their haunches in the ubiquitous pose of the Arab world, demonstrating an ease and balance that put us twenty-something chair-users to shame. One of them started chatting to us, urging us to visit the sacred carp in the pool at the mosque of Halil-Ür Rahman. We took his advice later in the day and found the carp to be multitudinous and portly, luxuriating in a pool fringed by an Umayyad colonnade. Legend has it that Abraham was born in the cave beside this pool and that this was also where his nemesis, Nimrod, cast him into the fire as punishment for having fallen in love with Nimrod's daughter. God, however, turned the fire to water and the logs into sacred carp, which thenceforth should never be harmed.

I spent the next day painstakingly updating our trip blog in a slow internet café while Ed ran repairs on the bikes. A bad blowout to his back tyre on the way to Urfa meant that we required a new spare and the bikes needed cleaning and oiling after the dust of the desert. We had landed in a hotel also occupied by two Italian cyclists, Luca and Mateo, brown as nuts, with wild beards and long hair, who had cycled through the deep snow in central Turkey to reach Urfa, justifying our detour via Syria. They'd camped in some deserted ruins in the mountains above Urfa a few days previously and had been woken by a platoon of Turkish soldiers pointing rifles in their faces. Local villagers had reported them, assuming from their beards that they were terrorists.

To get to Van we had to first head east along the Syrian border towards Mardin before then turning northwards and crossing the mountains of eastern Turkey, which we hoped by now would be in a spring thaw. Our departure from Urfa did not go well. We had set off in the morning, the road east crossing the plains of the upper Euphrates. The air was humid. Here and there we passed women in bright headscarves bent low in the fields, tending to spring crops. Trucks rumbled by and the road undulated gently. But despite the pleasant change from desert to green pastures, we were feeling low. We'd had a late start because of a flat rear tyre, finding the right road out of town had been a challenge, and we were cycling into a headwind. Worse, by mid-morning Ed was feeling unwell.

I am sure that someone somewhere has written that you've not truly become an international cycle-tourer until you have shat yourself. Loose bowels and uphill pedal straining is a bad combination. I stood at a distance, guarding the bicycles while Ed hurried far enough off the road so as not to offend passing motorists. We would have to turn back to Urfa now, I thought glumly, not so easy after having psyched ourselves for this final section of Turkey. Suddenly all the time-wasting in Syria seemed like a bad idea. There was a definite feeling of spring in the air, which meant that soon it would be hot, not a pleasant prospect with the deserts of Iran and Central Asia up ahead in the haze.

Had we been going too slowly? I was sitting on the kerb deep in thought, hoping that Ed was okay, when I glanced up to see a man on a motorbike pulling off the road towards me. His head was wrapped in a shemagh. The motor choked to a stop and he called out to me. I nodded, avoiding eye contact.

The man hooked his little fingers together in the sign that meant marriage – or 'union'. He tilted his chin back, eyebrows raised, and twisted his hand palm down to palm. The sign that meant, 'So what's the deal with you?'

I got to my feet and pointed at the man standing in the field with his trousers round his ankles. 'Zawj. (Husband.)'

Understandably, perhaps, Motorbike Man seemed unimpressed. He repeated the locking-finger sign.

'La. Hayir. Zawj,' I said, repeating no in both Arabic and Turkish so as to be totally clear, pointing again to Ed, who was midway through switching underpants.

Motorbike Man lit a cigarette and stood next to me, staring at Ed, who was unaware of what was happening. I inched away from him and fiddled with my sunglasses, hoping that he would go away. He put his hand out, demanding the glasses.

'Hayir,' I said firmly, shaking my head, not sure what I would do if he asked a second time.

He did not. The cigarette was flicked away and the motorbike swept off in a cloud of dust.

Back in Urfa again, Ed lay in a hotel bed while I tried to entertain myself. Wandering the streets on my own gave me a new view of the city. Men sidled up to me in internet cafés and stared at me in the street. I was glad when a couple approached and spoke to me in German. They were Turkish emigrants on holiday back to their home town. They warned me that I should be careful in this part of Turkey – 'it's not Bodrum or Istanbul' – but relaxed when I told them I'd cycled from the west of Turkey and through Syria to get here. 'Then you know what it is like and you will be fine,' they said, following up immediately with an invitation to stay in their village some distance from Urfa. They were disappointed by my regretful decline. As I watched them hurry off into the evening gloom, I imagined the cultural adjustments they'd have had to make in Germany and wished I had been able to say yes, speak German with them for the evening and show them that a Westerner was capable of dropping the cautious, stand-offish attitude to strangers.

14

BANDIT COUNTRY

The street doesn't ask, Where are you now? And where are you
headed, you crazy girl?
The street isn't unjust and commanding.
It doesn't know terror.
Nothing of the street looks like men and
Nothing of men looks like the streets.

Kajal Ahmad, trans. Mewan Nahro and Alana Marie
Levinson-LaBrosse, from 'In the Country of Terror I Love
the Streets More Than Men' on poetrysociety.org

We had checked the Foreign and Commonwealth Office (FCO) travel advice in an internet café in Urfa. Most of Turkey was painted green, but the southeast was a patchwork of orange and red splodges. Orange denoted 'advise against all but essential travel', while red warned 'advise against all travel'. The reason given was the presence of armed groups hiding out in the mountains. These were members of the Kurdistan Workers' Party, the PKK. The PKK was designated a terrorist organisation by Turkey, the US and the EU; although the label was disputed by some analysts and organisations, who believed that the PKK no longer engaged in organised terrorist activities or systemically targeted civilians.

The PKK was formed out of growing discontent over the suppression of Kurdish people and the erosion of their rights. The existence of Kurds in Turkey had long been denied as part of a drive by the state for cultural homogenisation, with 'Mountain Turk' or 'Eastern Turk' being the state's preferred terms for the ethnic minority which actually comprises the dominant population of the southeast; even the words 'Kurd' and 'Kurdistan' (land of the Kurds) were banned. Following the military coup of 1980, using the Kurdish language in public or private life became illegal.

The PKK aimed to secure autonomy and improved rights for the Kurdish people. In 1984 it launched a full-scale uprising, which continued through the 2000s and included launching terrorist attacks on civilians, suicide bombings and the targeting of schoolteachers. Many lives were lost. Following the capture in 1999 of the PKK's leader in exile, Abdullah Öcalan, the PKK, under Öcalan's guidance, announced an intention to seek a peaceful solution. A ceasefire lasted until 2004. Another ceasefire had been announced a few months before we started our trip and was still in place, although the PKK had claimed responsibility for an attack near the Black Sea in December.

The towns that were marked in red on the FCO map were Diyarbakır and Siirt; there was a route that weaved between them via Batman, which was orange. We reasoned that the risk to ourselves was likely to be minimal since the conflict was internal and the Western position on the Kurdish cause was complex. On the one hand the PKK was a proscribed terrorist group in the UK, as in many Western countries; on the other hand, UK backing for the Kurdish cause in Iraq since the first Gulf War was relevant and had been a source of positive comment from Kurds we'd met in Syria.

Two days from Urfa, having cycled across the Mesopotamian plains, we were pleased to see the foothills of the Taurus mountains appear in the afternoon haze. We were deep into spring. The sun had an intense heat and women were in the fields everywhere, tending to sprouting green crops. Such a difference from the bitter Mediterranean coast two months before. The city of Mardin was a steep upwards slog, perched high on the hillside overlooking the plain.

The following day we were traversing a completely new landscape of terraced fields. The trees were splashes of white and pink blossom on the hillside. As we were passing through the town of Midyat, I looked up and suddenly noticed that what I had, at a distance, taken for a minaret of honey-coloured stone rising above the jumbled rooftops, was in fact a slender church tower topped with a cross. Then I rounded a corner to see a group of women shoppers walking along the pavement, in jeans and fitted jumpers and not wearing headscarves. Midyat and the villages on the surrounding hillside are in an area known as Tur Abdin, once a stronghold of Syriac Christianity and home to the biggest population of Christians in Turkey outside of Istanbul. It is a region with a tragic history. In 1915 Ottoman forces and some Kurdish tribes orchestrated the mass slaughter and deportation of Assyrian and Syriac Christians in Tur Abdin and across the rest of southeastern Anatolia as well as in Persia's Azerbaijan province. This massacre came to be known as the Sayfo or

Sword genocide. Together with the Armenia genocide, which occurred at the same time, it resulted in the deaths of perhaps 1.5 million people, mass deportations to camps in Aleppo and Deir ez-Zor in the Syrian desert, and forced conversions. The genocide laid the foundations for the ethnonationalist state of Turkey that Atatürk would then take forward.

We camped hidden from the road on a high plateau and watched the sun set on the neighbouring hillside. In the morning we were woken by an ancient tractor working the rocky ground of what turned out to be a field. A gently spoken old man with scars on his leathery face and an empty eye socket came over to speak to us before going off to gather firewood from spindly bushes. Later we passed more old men ploughing the fields with donkeys and wooden ploughs or handheld wooden hoes.

We descended through narrow gorges lined with blossoming trees to a plain at Gercüş. A headwind picked up and we struggled into the settlement of Hasankeyf, which was perched atop sheer, honey-coloured cliffs at a strategic crossing point at a bend in the River Tigris. For thousands of years the peoples of the many civilisations of the Fertile Crescent had lived there. It had been at the Roman frontier with the Persians. It had been a Byzantine bishopric. It came under Muslim control during the Umayyad and Abbasid caliphates and became a critical trading post on the Silk Road in the twelfth and thirteenth centuries under the Artukid and Ayyubid kings. There had probably been a wooden bridge of sorts there since at least Roman times, but the Artukids in approximately 1150 set about building what was likely the largest bridge span in the world at the time.

We stopped for shish kebabs overlooking the river. As we chewed on the slices of fatty lamb, charred to perfection by a man wafting the coal of a grill and then wrapped in bread with raw onion and tomato, we watched the silted olive-coloured waters of the Tigris flow by between banks flushing with the bright green shoots of spring. The Artukids' bridge had been two hundred metres long, and the ruins of its two vast piles, which had supported a central arch forty metres across, were still visible in the middle of the river. The bridge had proved to be a clever investment, for Hasankeyf went on to control the trade from Diyarbakır all the way down the Tigris to Mosul (in current-day Iraq) as well as north to south along the route that we were taking from the Euphrates to Lake

Van in the far east. With the wealth that flooded in, palaces and mosques were built, including the cylindrical brick minaret of the El Rizk Mosque, still balanced at the edge of the cliff.

A merchant visiting from Venice in 1507 noted in awe that the arch of the bridge was 'so wide and lofty that a vessel of three hundred tons, with all its sails set, can pass under it; and in truth, many a time when I have been standing on it and looking down into the river, the great height has made me shudder'. The explorer and archaeologist Gertrude Bell was not so lucky. By the time she got there in April 1911, the bridge was gone and she was stranded, the current being too strong for her rafts or for the horses to swim across the river. Two days later, the waters had subsided a little, but her horses were still reluctant to cross and some had to be tied to the raft. Her photographs show a tiny laden raft with horses struggling to hold their heads above the rushing torrent.

We clambered up the steep limestone hillside, which was pockmarked with caves, many of them inhabited. Some had been extended by further chiselling into the rock, others were built out with bricks of the same honey colour and had wooden doors for chicken coops. Little has been written by travellers about the caves, and Bell apparently did not mention them, but, as with the rock dwellings in Cappadocia in central Turkey, they have been lived in for generations.

We stayed there until quite late in the day, finding more and more hidden dwellings, then stood once again overlooking the Tigris as we ate another piping-hot kebab from the stall. It seemed to be sports day as a large group of children including girls in layers of tracksuit and hijab ran past us in the spring sunshine.

'This will be gone soon,' the stall owner told us, sweeping his hand out across the vista.

'Under the water. The will of the government to help all the Turkish peoples.' He laughed.

Construction of the giant Ilısu Dam downstream on the border with Iraq was underway, with a plan to relocate seventy thousand people, including all of the five thousand inhabitants of Hasankeyf, to purpose-built settlements. Most of the villagers were Kurds like himself, the stall owner told us. Decades of conflict between the PKK and the government had led to depopulation of the area, with many of the remaining Syriacs and Armenians fleeing to Europe. The government said the dam, part of the huge Southeastern Anatolia Project intended to improve irrigation and generate hydro-electricity, was proof it was not ignoring the southeast of Turkey and would bring prosperity and create ten thousand jobs. Others claimed the dam would have impacts downstream: on the ecology of the Mesopotamian Marshes and water security across the region.

Across the river from the village we found a perfect camping spot, surrounded by ruins and with a great view of the village and the many grave slots carved into the steep rock face. We set up our tent next to a large circular brick mausoleum glazed with lapis and turquoise tiles that had been built for Zeynel Bey, the son of a fifteenth-century ruler of Hasankeyf.

Despite a lot of national and international resistance, in 2020, while the world was in the grip of the Covid-19 pandemic, the constructed dam shut its gates and floodwaters gradually submerged the town.

We woke to a clear, calm day and reached the town of Batman by lunchtime. A sullen old woman in the first shop we went into insisted that we owed her thirty liras for the small pile of items that we had heaped on the counter. We left in disgust and went into a second shop to be charged ten liras for the same pile, but not before the son of the first owner came to remonstrate with us for refusing to pay. While Ed was guarding our bike by the second shop, a teenaged boy begged 'Money! Money!' and flicked his pocketknife aggressively. On the way out of town another boy on a bike raced to pedal alongside us, shouting 'Money! Money!' in reply to our greeting. We laughed in unison and pointed at his bicycle, which was a new kids' mountain bike with not so much as a mark on the paintwork. We were not tempted to hang around in Batman.

The landscape changed again. We skirted a high plateau fringed by sparsely vegetated hillocks with the profile of sand dunes, giving the impression that we were by the coast, not almost a thousand metres above sea level. For the first time, snowy peaks became visible in the distance. We sat on plastic chairs against the suntrap wall of a petrol-station forecourt, being served a succession of cups of scorching tea by the owner and workers. They sat with us and told us they were a Turk, a Turkish Kurd, an Armenian Christian and an Iranian Kurd. 'Dost (friends),' they said.

The owner asked excitedly if since we were from the United Kingdom we could speak to his son in Germany. Grateful that my childhood in

Switzerland meant that I could, I was instantly connected to Hamburg via his mobile. I sat staring out across a green landscape to snow-capped peaks as we greeted each other.

'What do you think of Turkey?' the chemical engineer's voice crackled down the phone in perfect German.

'We like it very much. Please tell your father that many people have been very kind to us here. Travellers are made very welcome. How do you like living in Germany?'

There was a pause. 'I am very grateful to work here.'

I suddenly felt the vast distance his voice was travelling, a distance I could picture exactly: back down the mountains and to the coast, to Greece and Albania, the mountainous jumble of the Balkans, then the Danube, the Rhine. I was overwhelmed by a feeling of loneliness from him. Since the 1960s, thousands of people from Turkey have moved to Germany to work under the Gastarbeiter (guest-worker) schemes. Many people head to the lands of opportunity to improve their lives and support family back home, but at what personal cost?

Having moved countries as a child, I understand the toll that migration exacts. The belonging to nowhere and everywhere. It is imprinted on multiple generations of my family. My grandfather migrated from Switzerland to the UK prior to the Second World War. His father moved the family to set up a factory manufacturing, as it so happens, ribbons made of silk. Silk had been traded into our Swiss home town of Basel from the east since the sixteenth century when Protestant refugees from the European silk-weaving capital of Lyon in France, fleeing from persecution by Catholics, took shelter in the Reformation city, bringing their trade with them. However, in the early twentieth century, the UK imposed tariffs on imported textiles, which was a big blow to the family firm, which counted Britain as its biggest market, and my great-grandfather was dispatched to set up a factory in the Midlands. Our family history recounts that my great-grandfather, upon arriving in England, 'soon spoke English like a native' and that my grandfather was told not to speak Swiss-German lest he be taken for a Nazi. Facts that have, to some degree, cost me my ancestral Swiss identity as I never spoke Swiss-German to him nor do I speak it with my own father. The really Swiss side of the family know us as 'die Englander'.

I have met many men and women who spend most of their adult lives working away from their family, sometimes leaving partners and also children with grandparents back home in remote villages in Turkey, North Africa, Nepal, Pakistan, India or the Levant to go and find their fortunes in Europe or the affluent oil nations of the Middle East. They send money home and perhaps make an annual visit if they are lucky. They are often stoical and lonely, and when they return they are irrevocably changed. Many are playing roles upon which the economic prosperity of the West is deeply reliant.

Not knowing what else to say, I bade him farewell and handed the phone back to his eager father.

'My son. Engineer.' He beamed.

I asked him if he had ever visited Germany. He shook his head.

The road continued ever upwards, passing through strung-out villages. At nightfall we camped behind a clump of trees in a steep pasture by the roadside. Flat space was becoming hard to find. A group of small boys appeared over the brow of the hill above us.

'Bang, bang, bang!' They pointed pistol-shaped fingers at us. 'Bang, bang!' And then the familiar refrain: 'Money! Money!'

Eventually the bandits came out of hiding, and after a long explanation, most of which we could not understand, it became clear they were after protection money. There were men with guns in the hills, they said, pointing finger pistols at each other's heads to ensure we had got the point.

We offered them biscuits instead, which they accepted suspiciously, showed them the stove, on which a pot of tea was bubbling, and talked them through the parts of the bicycles. One of them kicked a wheel rim aggressively but was shut up by a stern word from Ed and a slap from a fellow bandit. They couldn't decide whether they liked us or hated us. A ride on the bikes, one sitting high on the seat while the others pushed him through the long grass, helped to build the truce. They were cheeky and over-exuberant and I could see that Ed was poised to sprint off and rescue my bike if necessary. It was always my bike, as it was small enough for children. They tried some more lines about protection money.

'No problem. Bang, bang!' Ed pointed to our tent.

They nodded, taking this at face value.

As the light failed, we heard a woman calling. The bandits scarpered for supper, leaving us to a dinner of pasta, tinned dolma (stuffed vine leaves) and black olives and a discussion about how much they knew about the men hiding with guns in the hills. We were on edge because of the FCO advisory. The encounters in Batman had felt more hostile than anything we had witnessed recently. Other cyclists' reports of having been stoned by small children were also playing on our mind. Had it not been for the welcoming encounter earlier in the afternoon we might have been more tense. We were determined to hold our nerve, knowing that a little trust went a long way when meeting those that were on the fence about us.

There were no visits from bandits that night nor in the morning.

The sound of the kettle lid rattling woke me from a deep sleep. I lay on my back in my sleeping bag looking out at the sky from the tent porch as Ed crouched in the entrance, clattering with breakfast. I ran a mental inventory. As strange as it seemed, I was in a tent somewhere in a field in the east of Turkey. I barely knew where, and, I thought vaguely, if real bandits did appear then nor would anyone back home. The days themselves were often so full of physical and mental challenges that they gave little time to reflect. I smiled and then reached into my sleeping bag to try and find the bra I had been keeping warm overnight.

The road continued to get higher. In sections it was unsurfaced and lorries churned up big clouds of dust as they rumbled past us. We cycled with our faces covered. There were more villages, and sometimes children ran out shouting 'Money! Money!' One small boy, his training clearly incomplete, shouted 'Monkey! Monkey!' Another boy, standing with a group of men, issued the same call and was cuffed around the ear.

On a steep stretch of road we heard a cry and then a gang of kids poured onto the road ahead. Three of them bent down to the ground. 'They have stones,' I said to Ed as I passed him.

I always went first so that Ed could see what was happening, be ready to react. At ten metres' distance, I looked up at the group and waved with a cheery 'Salam', heart thumping. Always best to hang out the peace flag early. Black eyes stared out of a line of small-boy faces. I was pedalling uphill at walking pace and scanned the expressions as I passed. They wore the same look of mistrust, aggression and curiosity as last night's lads. There were hands in pockets and held behind backs. 'Hello. Salam.' I smiled and nodded again. They jostled each other, jeering. One called out 'Hello!' I heard Ed calling the same greeting behind. I pedalled on, not daring to look back, expecting the clank of a stone on my bike, or, worse, the back of my head. None came.

Shortly before the turn-off to Siirt we passed a military patrol with a tank and a large gun. We stopped for lunch soon after and sat on the edge of a bridge. A lorry pulled up alongside us and three men got out, carrying small stools and a table. They set up a backgammon board and sat in the sun, playing and eating lunch for half an hour. Later we cycled past a lorry driver who was praying in the sunshine on a prayer mat in a lay-by next to his truck.

On, up and higher, through small villages where we saw only men and all of them stared at us. A café owner called 'Chai! Chai'! to us from a truck stop and his two workers hurried round, making us glasses of tea, for which he then refused payment. Later, in Baykan, another town busy only with men, we drank sweet Nescafé in a dingy café, the proprietor having assumed that as Europeans we would prefer that over tea. We didn't want to contradict him in front of our audience, who were smoking and glancing over at us, listening to everything that was said despite the blare of the TV. This was not a place that women normally entered and I tugged my Buff neckband up over my head as soon as I took my cycle helmet off, as I always had in rural Syria, feeling more comfortable if my hair was covered.

All day, the road followed an ever-narrowing gorge upwards. As it grew dark, we became increasingly concerned about finding a campsite. A spot in a small field penned in by fences woven from sticks seemed like our best chance, so Ed approached a man at the bottom of the garden on the road opposite. I could see the man thinking it over. He gestured for Ed to follow him back along the road to a low concrete building and, before I knew it, many hands were helping us push our bikes up a driveway and unloading our panniers into a small room. We had been given a room in the local health centre for the night.

We laid out our camping mats on the concrete and cooked up pasta and soup on a small table, sitting in our down jackets. Night had fallen and it was bitterly cold. Judging by the scales and blood-pressure-reading equipment, we were in an appointment room. After our dinner, we headed outside and crossed the veranda to the health workers' living room.

'There are girls up in the mountains as young as twelve who we help,' Anna said. 'We helped one with twins. It is far too young to be married and to have children. It is a burden on their bodies.'

Our hosts were a married couple from the west of Turkey who had met because they were both placed here and now had a one-year-old daughter, who was entertaining us all as she played on the floor in front of the wood-burning stove. I sat sipping tea and eating biscuits, sweating and wishing I had not donned all my thermals after dinner.

'Healthcare here is very basic. Three of us look after this whole valley. We travel to see people if they need help.'

Anna and her husband spent most of their time on midwifery and health education. I sensed this world they had found themselves in was almost as alien to them as it was to us. Among the sympathy and the enthusiasm to improve living standards there was also embarrassment that this was going on within their own country. The legal age of marriage was officially eighteen in Turkey, Anna was at pains to point out.

The following morning we carried on climbing, initially towards the town of Bitlis. It was cold and dusty and icy splatters of rain stung our faces. We wrapped up well and pushed on as trucks squeezed past. The road was squashed to a narrow ribbon between a tributary of the Tigris and the steep sides of the valley.

For some time we had been noticing a lot of plastic rubbish caught up along the riverbank. Plastic rubbish, especially nappies with their teal tabs, were a ubiquitous feature of Turkey's roadsides, but the problem was noticeably worse here. The reason became clear when we crested a col to find a vast rubbish dump flowing down from the road into the valley below. As we watched, a truck reversed off the road and tipped out its load, rubbish bags spiralling down the hillside. A raven squawked and I peered over the edge to see a figure prodding the mass of debris with a stick, traversing the steep slope through a curtain of sleet, the grey river rushing below. We turned downhill towards Baykan, whose rubbish dump we had presumably met, and braced ourselves against the icy wind.

The town was a jumble of badly built tower blocks and full of people who were tightly bundled up against the foul weather. There were stacks of firewood lined up outside the shops on the high street. At a small café we warmed up with a giant bowl of lentil and mint soup and hunks of white bread. The rain was starting to turn to slush and we were determined to make it to Tatvan on the edge of Lake Van by nightfall in case the road was cut off. We struggled on up the steep road out of town, almost blinded by the wet snowflakes. Past a college boarding house with students rushing between buildings, where a girl in make-up and no headscarf returned my wave shyly; later, an old woman waved with great energy from the wooden balcony of her house. Then up and up, onto an exposed plateau ringed by snowy peaks.

Hard snowflakes were now whipping our faces. We passed two khan (caravanserai), one of them restored into a sprawling complex with domed roofs that suggested there had once been an extensive bathhouse. It was now a museum but was shut for the winter. The other, little more than a pile of crumbling rock, was gathering drifts of snow. In their sixteenth-century heyday these khans would have been vital refuges on this treacherous mountain pass for travellers on the Silk Road. I longed for hot water and would have given anything to lie on a hot slab of marble with an attendant scrubbing my back.

We hurried on in the gloom, across the watershed. A deserted dual carriageway sloped away to the horizon. There was no hint of the lake in the white air, but a large sign suspended over the road announced 'Tatvan, Van and Iran'. IRAN!

It was brutally cold and snow was driving so thickly through the half-light that we could barely see the mighty Lake Van even when we reached Tatvan on its shores. Ed cowered in the shelter of a shop porch with the bikes while I, shivering and soaking under my waterproofs, made enquiries for a hotel. Eventually I picked my way through dirty, slush-filled back roads to Hotel Tatvan. The receptionist waved me inside and to my relief immediately settled on a good price. I ran back to Ed, barely able to feel my frozen feet, to fetch the bikes and start the endless process of traipsing our multiple panniers through the lobby and up the stairs. We stashed the bikes in the coal shed, then stripped off our sodden clothes, hanging them in every available space in the room, before defrosting under a gloriously hot shower. There is nothing like the blessing of hot water after a long day, and thankfully this water was very hot. It was needed too. It had been five days since we last washed.

It was pitch-dark by the time our stomachs forced us to put on our remaining dry clothes and wet boots and venture back out into the snow. At a workers' café specialising in menu deals we celebrated having made it this far into eastern Turkey by wolfing down a giant meal of soup, saucy İskender kebab, tomato and cucumber salad, pide (Turkish pizza) and baklava, all with metal jugs of frothy ayran, Turkey's cold, salty yogurt drink, which was churned in a machine in the café. Followed, of course, by hot, sweet tea.

15
PREPARE TO FIGHT

Live securely as you wish;
The palace heights are safe enough.
With pleasures flooding day and night,
The smooth proves sweeter than the rough.
But when your breath begins to clog
In sharp contractions of your lungs,
Then know for certain, my dear sire,
Your life was vain as idle tongues.

Abu'l Atahiya, trans. James Kritzeck, from 'Vanity: To Harun al-Rashid', in Suheil Bushrui and James M. Malarkey (eds.), *Desert Song of the Night*

We woke to more snow and a bitter wind and sat having a big breakfast omelette in Hotel Tatvan's dining room, discussing the route options again. Would we go to Iran or not? We had the correct visas, having applied for them months ago in Athens, with me purchasing a headscarf specially and making sure to dress conservatively for the embassy, mindful that other cyclists had been denied visas for turning up in Lycra.

Option A was to head north up to Turkey's border with Georgia, bypassing Armenia immediately to our east, since long-standing hostilities between Turkey and Armenia meant that the border was closed to us. We could then apply for Azerbaijani visas in the Georgian capital, Tbilisi, head southeast to Azerbaijan and on to the Caspian Sea at Baku. Points against this option were the need to traverse further mountain ranges in the snow, the logistics (and likely wait) involved in organising the Azerbaijani visa in Georgia and then the Turkmen visa in Azerbaijan. The five-day transit visa across Turkmenistan started on a fixed date, but the ferry across the Caspian Sea from Baku to Turkmenistan was notoriously unreliable and apparently had no fixed timetable. Rumour had it that you needed to be ready at a moment's notice, waiting in limbo for a captain and crew to appear or sober up, or for the weather to be right, making the visa restrictions particularly tricky to manage.

Option B was to cross the entire width of northern Iran, from west to east, skirting the southern shores of the Caspian Sea, covering around 1500 kilometres from Tabriz to Tehran and then on to Mashhad near the Turkmen border. For reasons we'd raked over countless times, spending a month or so on bikes in Iran was an unnerving prospect, so this option was currently not a serious contender.

Option C, the one we'd come up with in Urfa, still seemed like the better alternative. This would see us spending only a very limited period in Iran. From Lake Van we would cycle east to Tabriz in Iran and apply there for an Azerbaijani visa, which we understood from internet forums to be a straightforward process. After a few days, we would then be able head north, leaving Iran via Azerbaijan. While in Iran we would travel only by bus, transporting our bicycles rather than riding them. Crossing the desert to Palmyra in Syria had shown us that we could become an obvious target for security services on long, empty roads.

We could still change our minds if necessary, but by now I was weary of all the decision-making, which felt like a giant game of chess.

Two days later we set off for Van in sunshine. The snow had melted and Lake Van gleamed a cobalt blue under a clear spring sky. The 450-metre-deep lake, which was formed by subsidence in the fault line that runs through Turkey, has no outlet, which makes it saline and alkaline, so it rarely freezes despite being at 1640 metres above sea level. The inhospitable waters are home to only two species of fish – together with, if Armenian legends are to be believed, the Lake Van monster. The white peaks of Nemrut and Süphan gleamed from the northern shores, a striking contrast against the blue. A bitter wind blew down the lake, but the sun sent out a radiant heat. We climbed up and along the lake's southern shoreline, sometimes enjoying views of the lake, at other times veering inland through forested valleys.

A lorry was parked up ahead of us and the driver waved us over with calls of 'Chai!' Hassan had the kettle on a stove by the side of his lorry and in no time a table and two chairs materialised from the depths of his truck. White cheese, bread, honeycomb and olives were pulled out of a side compartment and despite our protestations breakfast was served. The vast tub of honeycomb was dished out generously and we were forced to take second servings. He accepted some of our Milka chocolate in return.

'Iran,' Hassan said, pointing to the honey as he explained that he drove milk from Iran to Turkey for a living.

We relaxed in the warm sunlight, sheltered from the wind, and talked about journeys. Hassan was returning from Tehran to Diyarbakır, where his wife and two children were waiting at home. Diyarbakır had the best apricots, he said, which is what he trucked in the summer. Now it was milk. We told him about our journey, attempting to recite a list of the country names in our pigeon Turkish: 'Eescotcha, Ingiltere, Hollanda, Almanya, Fransa, Eeswitzera, Yugoslavya ... Bosna, Yunanistan, Türkiye, Suriye, Türkiye.'

He nodded along, interested but not surprised. Only lorry drivers ever really seemed to understand the reality of our journey.

That night we camped in a field below the raised road. Icy stars shone brightly through clear sky and we cooked dinner lying inside our sleeping bags and wearing our down jackets. The thermometer on Ed's wristwatch read minus 15°C, the altitude two thousand metres.

In the morning, the sound of barking had us scrambling out of the tent in concern. We found sheep grazing all around us and two seven-year-old shepherd boys in front of our door. One of them was wearing a once red Mickey Mouse sweatshirt and they were both dwarfed by long, wooden staffs. A low growl came from the field behind and two mighty hounds raced toward us. Staffs were raised with threatening decisiveness by the small boys and the dogs froze and slunk behind them. My heart was pounding in my ears. The dogs were tall, muscular and shaggy grey-blond. Whether they were Kangal shepherd dogs or the closely related Kurdish Pishdar, I didn't know, but all the dogs that we saw had the same massive builds and toothy jaws and looked unnervingly like wolves.

We grinned a nervous 'Hello'. The boys giggled, fidgeting and unsure what to do. The older one picked up a stone from the ground and threw it over the top of a straying sheep to keep it in check, but the herd was on the move. A loud whistle from the bigger boy and they raced away, dogs bounding on ahead.

We breakfasted listening to ever more distant barks and bleats punctuated by the occasional whistle. The sun was out, but the air was icy and when I went to do the washing-up in the small stream at the bottom of the field I could barely touch the water before my hands started aching in agony. Our water bottles had frozen to blocks.

By mid-morning we were properly warm again, the sunshine now blissful as it seeped through my shirt and penetrated my skin. In a village over the other side of a pass a group of women and men who were sitting drinking tea in a bare orchard by the roadside waved us over. The mother sat cross-legged with ease, layers of dresses folded over her knees and a white headscarf with a crochet trim on her head. She held my hand and smiled as she loaded a large spoonful of sugar into every cup of tea she passed to me. Her talkative, intelligent and beautiful daughter, Leila, who'd learnt English at college in Van, addressed Ed and me directly and bossed her younger brother around while her father and grandfather, a haji, looked on in doting disbelief. 'Take her with you,' the grandfather said to me at one point. 'Come and visit us again,' they urged when we left. Later, as I sat on the shores of Lake Van looking out to the picture-perfect island of Akdamar with its pink-stoned tenth-century cathedral complementing the green spring grass and cerulean lake, I wished I'd been able to ask Leila more about school and whether or not there were plans for her to get married. I hoped not for a while.

Reaching Van a day later felt like coming into a metropolis. The city buzzed with traffic, and people were out on the streets until late, frequenting pizza, baked potato and kebab joints. Women were visible at last and wearing every variety of dress, from short skirts and leggings to swathes of black. Van was famous for its breakfasts and the following morning we selected one of the many cafés and sat down to plates of honeycomb, clotted cream, cream cheese with herbs, olives, boiled eggs, fresh flatbread and of course black tea.

At Van Kalesi we scrambled over the castle ruins in the freezing wind, meeting Iranian tourists and young men hawking bottles of fizzy drink. Later, we sat in one of the city's parks, drinking tea brought to us by a tea seller and being watched by crowds of small boys and even the occasional girl as Ed fixed our bikes. One boy with his own bike observed us keenly and then came to us red-faced, his chain in two pieces. He'd obviously attempted to split the chain as he watched Ed change his own. Ed mended it for him in front of a crowd of goggle-eyed boys and then a man came over to thank him.

'I have twelve children, but two of them are dead,' the farmer, Cessim, said.

I looked around at the ten little faces of his family, who were watching us drink our tea as we sprawled in an ungainly fashion on a pile of cushions, and offered my condolences.

Cessim raised his hands. 'It is the way of Allah,' he said. His wife looked far too young and sprightly to have given birth to a dozen kids.

We were a hundred kilometres from Van and just as the day was drawing to a close Cessim had asked us if we wanted to camp in his field. The road had taken us along the east of the shore of Lake Van before turning north and climbing once again. Nowhere that we had stopped had we felt particularly welcome. Men stared at us in the petrol station and as we cycled through villages. No one said anything hostile, but hardly anyone approached us either. I had taken to keeping my head covered with my Buff neckband. It was nice to be at the cosy hearth of a home again, with a host who was the proud head of his family.

As so often on our trip, I wished I could play the guitar for Cessim and his kids or had some other skill I could deploy to entertain our hosts. We were always acutely aware that most of the families we stayed with would probably have met few if any foreigners before and so we felt obliged to put on a good show. We did this by chatting about our trip and families, showing photos from home and trying to engage with our hosts' lives if we were invited to do so. Not all tourists felt like we did, though. We met some travellers who'd become so complacent about staying in people's houses that they complained about being pestered too much by children when they were reading!

Once conversation had been exhausted for the evening, we retreated to our tent to cook supper, now in possession of four eggs and some tiny beaded slippers that I had made the mistake of admiring on one of Cessim's smiley little granddaughters. Despite my vehement protestations, the slippers were taken off the girl and given to me – for my first child, Cessim said with a grin.

The kids crowded round our tent excitedly in the morning as we packed up, and we took photos of them posing with our bikes and wearing our cycle helmets. Cessim asked Ed if he had vodka in his water bottle. When Ed responded that it was water, Cessim slapped him on the back, said, 'Good. Strong Kurdish man,' and, turning his back to the children, mimed that vodka caused impotence. We had seen blue pills on sale at truck stops and someone had told us that fecundity was the main weapon the Kurdish population had against the Turks.

We breakfasted on bread and goat's cheese while the kids got ready to go to school. Cessim said he was happy for his daughters to go to school until they developed breasts (more miming), after which point it 'caused problems'. I got the impression that he would have liked his daughters to be educated but feared the reaction from other men.

The road crossed a plain, distant peaks marking the Iranian border, then narrowed in a valley whose fields of volcanic rock covered in moss made me think of Iceland. We climbed and eventually found ourselves in a barren landscape with patches of snow dotted across the steep slopes. A barbed-wire fence with watchtowers appeared to our right. We were skirting the Iranian border. I stopped regularly, exhausted, my mind churning with concerns about the next stage of our journey, and kept on falling behind Ed, which irritated me. 'I'm always having to keep up, that's why I'm so worn out. I'm always at my limit if I'm keeping up,' I muttered to myself as I forced my aching thighs to carry on pushing.

It was bitterly cold at the 2644-metre Tendürek Pass. The wind blew strong and flurries of snow plagued us. We could endure it just long enough to stuff a couple of squares of chocolate and drink some tea from the thermos before fleeing down the other side. The snow clouds stayed away and a vast flat green valley bathed in golden sunshine opened out in front of us. Beyond, the dark flanks of a mountain rose into a snowy conical peak. Mount Ararat. I could almost see Noah's Ark balanced precariously on its summit.

There were shepherd camps dotted across the rolling flanks of the mountain as we descended. Herders were out with their flocks. Three vast Kangal dogs with collars of metal spikes growled at us fiercely, blocking our road, guarding a large flock on a bend. We sidled past them. The scruffy shepherd boys stared and made no effort to recall them.

Then, as we passed through another cluster of houses, a ferocious bark went up. I looked up at the hillside to see a pack of grey beasts pouring down the slope towards us.

'S***!' was all I could shout at Ed, who was in front. I could see from the dogs' trajectory that they were going to hit the road between the two of us. I screamed as loud as I could as I bent down to scrabble for stones as the pack drew closer. To continue cycling would be to risk them taking me down, bikes in motion and feet moving on pedals being particularly stimulating to dogs.

Ed had stopped up ahead and was also gathering ammunition. Any second, I expected a shout from one of the houses above to recall the pack. None came. I was still screaming when I heard the furious beeping of a lorry behind me. The lorry was crawling downhill, horn blasting, and a volley of stones was flying out from the passenger side. The pack altered course and charged towards the lorry behind me. I glanced over my shoulder to see one of the dogs launch itself at the wheel arch. I let go of my brakes and sped downhill. 'GO!' I yelled as Ed did the same.

Five minutes later, the lorry rumbled up behind us, having shaken off the hounds. It remained on our tail until we were well away from the village and then overtook to our grateful waves.

Once in the valley, we stopped to collect ourselves, get our breath back and stop shaking. I felt high and empty on adrenaline, fear giving way to aggression. We hunted for thick sticks in a field as we exchanged accounts of long teeth, barbed collars and saviour truck drivers. Back on our bikes, we were now armed and ready, sticks laid across our panniers. One thing was clear, we needed to be prepared to fight. The usual tactic of stopping abruptly and raising an imaginary stone in threat was not going to work on these monsters. They were obviously trained to protect their owners at any cost – from wolves and, perhaps more likely, from the Turkish army too.

In the next village we were ready. As the pack of dogs swept towards us, we whipped out our sticks and screamed. The dogs kept coming, then stopped dead in their tracks as a shout rose. I looked behind me to see two soldiers leaping out of an armoured vehicle with rifles trained on the dogs. We waved weakly as the dogs slunk off and the military disappeared down the road.

'If you kill a Kurd's dog you will be in big trouble. They might kill you,' a young Kurdish mountain guide told us that evening in the border town of Doğubayazıt.

We'd met him and his friend outside a gun shop on the main road and had walked around the town with them, ending up having dinner together in a kebab house they recommended. We were shown to the family section, which was busy, the first restaurant we'd seen in weeks to have women and children in it. Everyone swivelled to look at us as we came in. Waiters were taking it in turns to pray in a tiny space behind the handwashing sink near the counter. There was a watercolour of the Kaaba in Mecca on the wall.

We spent a pleasant time over dinner discussing mountaineering options with the guides. They offered us the opportunity to climb Ararat, buy beers and (shared in a hushed whisper) procure us pork sausages 'like Germany'. We were seriously tempted to stop for a week to try Ararat. They were talkative and open and it was good to be able to have an in-depth conversation. Towards the end of dinner our hosts excused themselves and we stood up to bid them farewell. They kissed Ed. Then one of the men took my hand and kissed me on both cheeks. The café fell silent instantly. My face flushed as all the diners' eyes bored into me. The men hurried out and the babble in the café started up again.

Apoplectic with rage, I sat stabbing baklava with a teaspoon in front of Ed, who was confused.

'Fine if this was France, but this is not f***ing France.'

'Yes, okay, but I'm sure they've met lots of tourists from all sorts of places.'

'I've just spent months covering up and wearing a headscarf.'

'It's confusing for them too.'

'I've spent months being told by men that women should not cycle or go to school. Going to houses where men and women eat separately. Cycling though villages where we don't see a single woman. Being told what NICE GIRLS do.'

'Are you maybe overreacting?' Ed said helpfully.

'You saw the response from everyone else in here. That was clearly a public insult. Or he got a kick out of it. They're from here, not the west of Turkey – it's not like they didn't know what the reaction would be.'

'Maybe they want things to change.'

'That's not going to help, is it, though? Literally everyone looked at me. They clearly think I'm a whore. And you didn't react at all.'

'What did you want me to do – start a fight?'

He had a point, but the argument continued when we got back to the hotel. I was hollow, still fuelled by adrenaline from the fight with the dogs, exhausted from all the deciphering of strangers' behaviour, and anxious about the next stage of the trip.

Marital relations were still frosty the following day as we stood on the promontory above the restored ruins of the Ottoman-built seventeenth-century Ishak Pasha Palace, gazing out over the wide valley below. The wind cut me to the core, but although a dull sky had drained the colour from the landscape, the scene was fairy-tale beautiful. A lost valley, ringed by a shadowy mountain and dominated by the vast volcanic cone of Mount Ararat. A stone palace with a dome and a needlepoint minaret marking the frontier to a new world. I squeezed Ed's hand. Iran was beckoning.

Tea and Grit

Iran

 April 2010

Tea and Grit

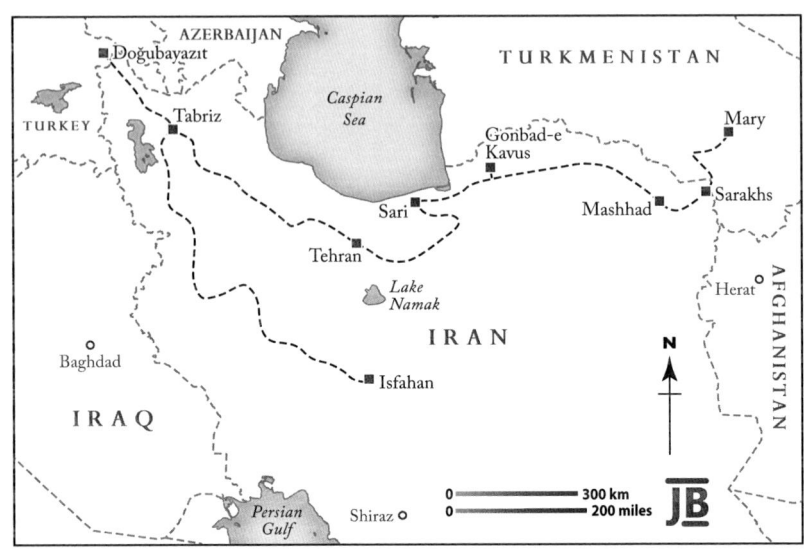

16
ALL THAT DOWNHILL WASTED

Beyond this window, the night quivers, and the earth once again halts its spin.
From beyond this window, the eyes of the unknown are on you and me.
Forugh Farrokhzad, trans. Sholeh Wolpé, from 'The Wind Will Blow Us
Away', in Sholeh Wolpé (ed.), *Sin: Selected Poems of Forugh Farrokhzad*

The next day, I was plunged into a dark mood again after a phone call with family. My father's anxious voice, painfully distant down the phone, asked me outright not to cross the border into Iran. To his enormous credit, since I'd turned eighteen he had never given me a direct request like that, and he would only give me one other, also on this journey. I put the phone down and lay on the bed in the hotel room in tears. I hated causing worry or hurt to the people I loved.

I understood very well what worry meant. I was someone who thought about death – mine and other people's – almost to the point of obsession. I would wait anxiously for Ed to return home from a day of ice climbing. I would fret incessantly about the health of my grandparents, to whom I was close. Rationally, I knew where this fear came from. As a teenager, I'd experienced the untimely death of three young people. My cousin, who was born with a rare genetic condition, died at the age of two. My friend's older brother, who had diabetes, went to sleep one day and did not wake up. A good friend at university fell to his death while rock-climbing. The bereavements shook me and left me all too aware that unforeseen disasters did happen. Existential anxiety had sat heavily on my left-hand shoulder ever since, but over on my right-hand was the drive to live every day as if it could be my last, to see as much as I could of the dazzling tapestry of life. I have found this duality to be a common trait in people who are driven to push beyond what are considered the 'normal' boundaries of adventure, even though they are often described as reckless. In the most unpleasant circumstances – during sandstorms, snowstorms or while enduring unwanted male attention – my thoughts always centred on how to get to the next point of safety, ideally one with a warm shower and a good meal. There was nothing appealing about returning to Edinburgh. The excitement and challenge of a great journey, so long held in my mind while cycling the streets of Edinburgh on my commute into work, had far too strong a hold on me. I was in agreement with the great Edinburgh writer Robert Louis Stevenson:

> *I travel not to go anywhere but to go. I travel for travel's sake. The great affair is to move, to feel the needs and hitches of our life more nearly; to come down off this feather-bed of civilisation, and find the globe granite underfoot and strewn with cutting flints.*

But how would I cope if my child, partner, parent or brother cycled off around the world without me there to keep an eye on them? I knew I was the worst kind of hypocrite and felt guilty about it.

The trip odometer counted round to ten thousand kilometres before we got to the Iranian border and we stopped in the chill wind to rig a photograph of ourselves, peaks foreshortening into the distance. The sky was grey and the mountains monochrome. Ten thousand kilometres and Iran in the same day – it felt like a true watershed. My stomach was in a tight knot of fear and excitement, and the hope of reaching China seemed further away than ever. Iran, Azerbaijan, the Caspian Sea and Central Asia felt like insurmountable barriers.

At a derelict, end-of-the world petrol station where we'd stopped to use the loo, the elderly owner offered us tea from the wood-fired range in his dark kitchen. Given that the price of petrol in Turkey was approximately twice that across the border, it seemed unlikely he ever had much trade. At our departure he shook Ed's hand with exaggerated solemnity, wishing us good luck, our final goodbye to Turkey. Great, even the Turks think we're foolhardy, I thought glumly.

There was a huddle of people waiting when we got to the border at Bazargan. I donned my obligatory headscarf, a khaki colour. I was already wearing a thigh-length tunic over my baggy cycling trousers and a down jacket over the top. Some women were adjusting their headscarves by a seating area of plastic chairs, while a long queue of men snaked through the customs hall.

As we were queuing, an official walked along the line and picked us out. We feared we were about to be hauled in for questions as to why we were cycling and what we were doing here, but in fact he directed us to an English-speaking guide who steered us through immigration. The guide explained, almost apologetically, that the British government insisted that Iranian nationals coming to the UK be fingerprinted, so they therefore had to take ours. This was a recent development and an honour reserved for US and British travellers, although, unlike us Brits, Americans were not allowed to enter Iran without a minder.

Our visas were stamped and our dollars exchanged for rial, and then we were directed to another small booth. I was again expecting an interview, but instead a man jumped up from behind the desk, pumped Ed's hand and began to pull out tourist maps and leaflets from a faded display, launching into a lengthy explanation about what we should see. We smiled and nodded politely, expressing vague surprise and enthusiasm about everything that was thrust in front of us. The ancient ruins of Persepolis, 'older than your Roman Empire'; the desert city of Yazd with its 'Fire Temple of the ancient Zoroastrian religion before Islam'; the mosques of Mashhad, a 'very special holy place, so wonderful for honeymoon'; the blue domes of Isfahan; and, more emphatically, since we thought it was wise and safe to be complimentary about the capital, the tower blocks of Tehran. He seemed to be fishing for reasons to detain us for further conversation.

'It is strange we have so few tourists – you are the first in a week. The government is trying to make more visits from people like you. Yes, you are very welcome. We have a big tourism expansion plan. One million per year, the government says.'

'How strange,' we said, 'when there is so much beauty to see in this country.'

'Yes, this is how I feel also,' he said a little sadly.

I felt sorry for him, waiting in vain for tourists who, like us, would be on edge and keen to get away from the border post as quickly as possible lest they be wrong-footed in front of an official. I certainly didn't want to dally under the bearded, be-robed and be-turbaned portraits of the supreme leaders that hung above his desk. Was he subtly trying to mine us for information to pass on to the security services, trying to get us to reveal something of concern in our plans or background?

We walked out into the cold air of Iran on the other side. I took a deep breath. We were in!

For a moment I had a strange sense of anticlimax. Where was the interrogation about our route and purpose? The stern warning about the headscarf law, not spreading satanical Western ideas or speaking against the government? The admonition that traversing the country by bicycle was madness? I snapped out of my foolishness. The reality of relations between Iran and the West was stark. There had been no formal diplomatic ties between the US and Iran since the 1980s, and Britain's diplomatic relations, although in an 'on' phase, were, as we would discover, limited. The Islamic Revolution of 1979, during which the last of the Iranian royals, the Pahlavi dynasty, were overthrown, kick-started the current phase, although as with everywhere across the region, international tensions had a far longer history.

The Pahlavis had taken over from the previous royals in a 1921 coup supported by the British and had in 1953 strengthened their position by means of another coup, also supported by Britain, with the US. At the heart of it were oil and Cold War politics. The West-backed shah, Mohammad Reza Pahlavi, started on an ambitious plan of modernisation and reform, 'the White Revolution', which included abolishing feudalisms, nationalising key resources, and improving literacy and women's rights. In 1936 his wife and daughter appeared unveiled and in Western dress, the first female royals ever to do so, as he announced the banning of the hijab. The message was clear: the veil was backwards and being unveiled was modern. Perhaps predictably, there was outrage both from the religiously devout and from those who objected to women being told what to do. Some women simply stayed indoors for years, and some middle-class women adopted the most conservative form of black chador in protest and solidarity. The biggest critic was Ayatollah Khomeini, who denounced the shah as a 'wretched, miserable man' in cahoots with the US, the 'Great Satan', and was promptly exiled. When Khomeini returned in 1979, having co-ordinated a revolution from Paris, five million people lined the streets of Tehran to welcome him. While in exile he had promised democracy, but he now immediately set about establishing a Shia theocracy, reversing the reforms, crushing any opposition and establishing a totalitarian state characterised from an international perspective by an anti-Western, anti-Israel, anti-Sunni stance.

The Iranian government, abetted by its military secret service, the Islamic Revolutionary Guard Corps, has an utterly appalling human rights record. In 2010 Ayatollah Khomeini was long dead, but his legacy lived on under the second Supreme Leader, Ayatollah Khamenei. Months before our arrival in Iran there had been the biggest protests since the revolution after incumbent president Mahmoud Ahmadinejad declared a victory in an election purported by the opposition to be rigged. The Iranian Green Movement or Persian Spring, which, like the subsequent Arab Spring movements elsewhere, organised itself with the help of the then new social-media platform Twitter, was crushed. Arrests, the torture and murder of prisoners, and a crackdown on the media and internet access followed. What had been publicised heavily in the West was that a French master's student was in prison, accused of having taken photographs of the protests.

We stopped on the far side of the border to eat bread rolls and cheese in the small town of Bazargan. Wind blew dead leaves along the road as we sat on a park bench watching a few cars heading back towards Turkey. In a nearby public bin someone had discarded a half-drunk bottle of rum, presumably inadvertently and illegally transported across the border.

We were on a gentle downhill with the wind at our backs most of the way to Maku, which we reached in the mid-afternoon, just as the rain started to descend in sheets. We were tempted to carry on towards Tabriz but agreed to keep to our plan of sticking to public transport so as to maintain a low profile. This meant finding a hotel in Maku and travelling to Tabriz by bus the following day. Once the rain had abated, we ventured out. I put on my manteau, a long, raincoat-style jacket, and a silk headscarf, both bought in Van, and we followed a muddy path up to some ruins. Families were barbecuing in the shelter of the dramatic cliffs and a few young men wandered around smoking, but, reassuringly, no one took any notice of us.

We woke at five to catch the first bus to Tabriz, so that we could get to the Azerbaijani Embassy before it shut. My heart sank as we loaded our bikes on. Were we giving up too easily? I propped my eyes open and peered through the morning gloom at mountainsides and empty valleys as the bus raced down and down to Tabriz. All that downhill wasted! Ed was asleep next to me. I struggled not to nod off too, not wanting to miss anything. One of the best things about cycling was that every portion of the journey was undertaken consciously; there was no dozing on the train, sleeping fitfully on a night bus or, worse, snoozing on an aeroplane, only to wake up somewhere completely different.

Our time in Tabriz was a whirl of activity. Our plan was to put in our visa applications at the Azerbaijani Embassy the morning we arrived, leave our bikes in a hotel for three days while we took the bus to the famed city of Isfahan, come back to Tabriz, collect our visas and then take another bus straight to the Azerbaijani border crossing at Astara, on the Caspian Sea, about three hundred kilometres to the east.

The embassy was shut, however. Its security guard invited us into his booth as he phoned through to double-check. It would be open the following day. We headed back into town by bus, me riding in the women's section at the back, Ed at the front. On the street near our hotel we bought boiled potatoes and boiled eggs cooked on a small circular charcoal stove by a blind man. He wrapped them into a flatbread with salt and we took our stodgy and highly satisfying picnic to a bench in the park. Some students sidled up to practise their English and then paid for our tea from a tea vendor. We bought roasted beets, which were juicy, starchy and sweet, from another elderly stallholder.

We'd arrived in Tabriz at Nowruz, the Iranian New Year, the country's most important festival, which celebrates the start of spring and has its roots in Zoroastrianism. The festival is celebrated on or around 21 March according to the Gregorian calendar, at the spring equinox, which is also the start of the Persian and Zoroastrian new year. Iran uses three different calendars – Persian, Muslim and Zoroastrian – and newspapers print all three dates. We had effectively arrived at the Iranian equivalent of Christmastime; the public holiday would last two weeks.

A roundabout near the park was decked out with a huge Nowruz haftseen, the traditional ceremonial table of Iran. This one came complete with a giant plastic apple, symbolising beauty, and mega-sized bright green wheat sprouts, symbolising rebirth. There were also plastic eggs, candles, goldfish, tulips and hyacinths. Vendors on street corners were selling goldfish in plastic bags, presumably so that people could add the real thing to their own haftseen tables at home. Traditionally the table includes seven symbolic items whose names start with the letter 'س', pronounced 'seen'. Nowruz is celebrated across the Persian world, including in Central Asia and by Kurds in Iraq, Turkey and Syria. Although we'd been in Tatvan on the twenty-first, we had seen no sign of the festival. A Kurd we'd asked there had denied that the festival was celebrated, perhaps suspecting us of being informants, since the festival has strong political connotations in Turkey.

We were standing watching couples posing for photographs in front of the roundabout's table when we turned round to find four men in Lycra standing behind us. They were Canadian-Iranian cycle-tourers, back home for the Nowruz holiday and about to catch the bus along the road we'd taken and go cycle-touring in Syria. We babbled excitedly. There was so much information to exchange as we all had valuable route details for each other. We met later, the men now transformed in jeans, tight T-shirts and cologne, and roamed the dark streets together in search of a shashlik joint. We crowded on to tiny tables, eating the grilled meat and drinking glasses of the salted yogurt drink doogh, which is like the Turkish ayran but perhaps a little thinner and is often served over ice and laced with dried mint, while chatting at high speed. The other male customers, in shirts and jackets, were clearly listening in and watching us. I felt quite self-conscious being in the company of five men, although our new friends were deliberately indifferent to the curiosity they were stirring up.

'Tabriz is a very traditional town, much more so than Tehran,' one of them said dismissively.

'Where did you get your headscarf from?' another asked me. 'How did you know you needed to wear one?'

I wasn't brave enough to tell him about the prominent instructions in my guidebook, which noted that Iran was the only country in the world that required all women, even non-Muslims, to wear a headscarf. It was reputed that even in Saudi Arabia Christian women could technically go without a headscarf so long as they wore an abaya. I also did not mention having watched a lot of videos online so that I knew how to tie them in Syrian, Turkish and Iranian styles and blend in when needed.

'Anyway, I'm used to it. I also wore one sometimes in Syria—'

'Syrians are Arabs,' he cut in. 'They are very different to us. We are Persians.'

I did not add that I knew that Iran did in fact have a small Arab minority on the Persian Gulf, the Bandari Arabs, who were Sunni and whose women wore metal face masks instead of the face veil. Nor that the

Arabs adamantly called it the Arabian Gulf. The Arab Umayyads occupied Persia and converted its inhabitants from Zoroastrianism (in the main) to Islam (in the main), but it was never made *Arab*. The Arabic script was adopted, and Arabic was used for administration, but Farsi, the Persian language, survived. Much later, in 1010, Persian was fully revived by the poet Ferdowsi, Persia's Shakespeare, through the epic poem *Shahnameh*. Under the Abbasids many Persian bureaucrats actually ran the empire in Arab lands, spreading Persian influence widely. However, despite this and the relatively brief reign of the Umayyads, the Arabs have never been forgiven.

The Iranian fashion in 2010 was to wear a square headscarf folded into a triangle. Women often wore it far back on the head with a section of fringe showing. 'It's disgraceful that they don't give them to you for free at the border if you have to wear one!' another of the men declared. I wasn't sure I'd have wanted to walk about in a free headscarf issued by the Islamic Republic, given how much care the women I'd met so far took over their appearance. Gone were the baggy trousers, heavy layers and crocheted headscarves worn by the village women of eastern Turkey; here it was all heels, heavy make-up, drainpipe jeans, French-style raincoats and Audrey Hepburn- and Elizabeth Taylor-style headscarves.

We took a taxi across town to a large park with an island of cafés floating in a big pool. The lights of the city sparkled in the water and stretched off into the distance as we sat among holidaymakers enjoying the last few days of Nowruz and talked about cycle-touring.

The Azerbaijani Embassy was still shut the following morning, but the remarkably obliging guard rang through again and said that they would fast-track our visas on the Monday morning. We left, full of doubt but with no other option than to hope they would issue our visas within one day. We only had that day before our Azerbaijani letter of invitation expired.

I can't quite remember how the man in a battered white Paykan car persuaded us to let him drive us back into the town centre. Faraj spoke good English and was excited to practise with us. We drove to the bazaar and sat in a dingy café eating a breakfast of fried eggs and tea. Some of the old men at nearby tables chipped in with the odd question in Farsi, which Faraj translated. He had gone into the café first to ask permission of the owner and customers for me to eat there. Faraj was a serious man in his mid-thirties; unmarried. Ed and I both sensed he was unhappy.

Later, he insisted on showing us the mosque and we sat together on the carpeted floor talking before he excused himself to go and pray, prostrating in a demarcated square of carpet. Women were filing into a curtained-off area and more men gathered on the carpet. I looked up at the dome of the mosque, listening to the mumbling of prayers and taking stock of just how far we had come in cultural terms. Our first entrance to a mosque had been in Sarajevo, where a plastic walkway was rolled out over the carpet at specific times so that non-Muslim tourists could walk in with their shoes on, as if it would have been an offence to ask us to take them off. In Aleppo and Damascus we had also entered as tourists, on those occasions leaving our shoes at the door and me hiring a chador. Now for the first time we began to see the workings of everyday mosques, places where people gathered for worship but also to socialise.

Faraj gifted Ed a turbah, a small clay disc which Shia place on the ground in front of them during prayer so they can touch their foreheads to it when prostrating. The disc symbolises the earth and some contain earth from the Kaaba at Mecca. This practice is, however, despised by the Sunnis, who say that Muhammad never carried a clay disc with him. Back at our hotel room, I noticed that a disc had been provided for us along with a prayer mat.

The overnight bus to Isfahan rushed through the darkness of the desert, stopping occasionally at tatty, floodlit service stations. I was uncomfortably hot in my headscarf and manteau, daring only to undo a few buttons and loosen the scarf from under my chin once I was sure everyone was asleep.

'Isfahan is half the world' – or, more poetically in Persian, 'Esfahan, nesf-é jahan' – was a moniker that lived up to its promise. The great Shia Safavid ruler Shah Abbas I (1588–1629) made Isfahan his capital and began a huge programme of town planning that transformed the city into one of the largest and richest in the world. Bigger than London, it was known as a centre of wealth to his contemporary, the English playwright William Shakespeare, who wrote in *Twelfth Night*: 'I will not give my part of this sport for a pension of thousands to be paid from the Sophy' – 'the Sophy' being the Safavid, Shah Abbas.

Now, for the first time since Syria, the air was warm and there was a light spring breeze. We strolled across the Maidan-e Naqsh-e Jahan (Image of the World Square), the turquoise of the domes and arches that framed the vast space resolving as we drew closer into complex, swirling mosaics. Families occupied every inch of the grass lawns that the shah had used for polo matches, sitting on picnic blankets filled with plates of food, thermoses and qalyan (water pipes). Some women were swathed from head to toe in black or patterned chadors, others were barefooted, their high heels kicked off next to them and their scarves falling loosely over the backs of their heads.

A young girl in a chador struggled to master an oversized bicycle on the marble courtyard beneath the entrance (iwan) of the Shah Mosque. Its honeycomb vaulting spanned two minarets, every inch tiled in mosaic. White Qur'anic calligraphy ran up and around the door frame against a deep-blue ground and spiralled around each minaret. Repeating floral motifs decorated every other free surface in seven colours: two shades of blue, green, yellow, pale pink, black and white, with the dominant impression being of turquoise.

We sat on a bench watching the girl take turns on the bike with her younger brother as the evening light glowed on the patterned soft-pink dome of the smaller Sheikh Lotfollah Mosque. The girl's chador was tied in a knot under her armpits and the end billowed behind her as she wobbled furiously. I fretted it might get tangled in the spokes. She was the first girl I had seen on a bike since Greece. Her grandmother, heavily swathed in black and deeply wrinkled, came over and pressed some sweets into my hand when the family got up to leave at dusk. The floodlit buildings and archways shimmered in the square's central pool.

A maid brought a laden tray to our hotel room door in the morning and we breakfasted on our balcony in the sunshine, savouring the warm ovals of bread, which were like a thin, corrugated naan, a vast improvement on the industrially yeasted loaves of Turkey, served with white cheese and carrot jam.

Fortified, we returned to the Shah Mosque to spend time marvelling at the patterning on the domes and vaulted interior. A sore neck was the price you paid for a trip to Isfahan. We roamed between the Sheikh Lotfollah Mosque, the Friday Mosque, the Grand Bazaar, the Ali Qapu Palace and the Chahar Bagh Madrasa (Theology School). A man with dreadlocks approached us in the square. I could not remember the last time I'd seen a man with long hair or any sort of unusual haircut. The many barbers we'd seen along the way in Turkey, Syria and Iran specialised in short back and sides and cut-throat-razor shaving. Beards being the preserve of 'mullahs, terrorists and Afghans', as our Italian cycle-touring friends had told us in Urfa.

Dreadlock Man glanced around before speaking. 'You are welcome to Iran,' he said. 'My religion is Zoroastrian. This is the true and ancient religion of Iran. Please remember this.' And with that he hurried on, before we had a chance to ask him anything.

We took tea with the carpet dealers who had their wares hung up in the shaded arcade of Naqsh-e Jahan Square. 'They will be keen to make a sale,' a passer-by had remarked when we paused to look at a huge, shimmering silk rug with a pattern that mimicked the kaleidoscope of vegetative and arabesque designs inside the dome of the Sheikh Lotfollah Mosque. The mighty Shah Abbas was also responsible for supercharging the Persian rug industry. He set up royal rug factories all over Iran and especially in Isfahan, and by establishing his capital in Isfahan he effectively rerouted the Silk Road so that his empire would enjoy a trading monopoly. 'It is Nowruz, the start of the year. The first sale can make a year of good or bad luck for the seller.'

As soon as we entered the shop, which was lined wall to wall with carpets, the seller had us sit down while an assistant brought tea.

'We're just looking,' I warned him.

'Yes, no problem. Looking only, but maybe you will like something. No problem you can use your credit cards here. No embargo. We have friends in Qatar.'

We joked that unless his carpets could fly us to China we would have to pass as we didn't have the space on our bikes.

'Don't be angry with me, but I don't believe in God.' Mina gave me a sideways glance from under her black headscarf as we walked together through Isfahan's botanical gardens, by the river. She'd already told me she only wore the conservative black head-covering for college. 'I was told off by a policeman the other day for not covering my head enough – at Nowruz of all times!' She lowered her voice and added, 'There are some very bad people here.'

A decade later and I would recall Mina's words with acute sadness. In 2022, Iran would be rocked by protests when Mahsa Amini, a twenty-two-year-old Kurdish woman, was arrested by morality police for wearing 'improper hijab' and subsequently died, likely following a beating in police custody. Outrage sparked demonstrations across Iran and a brief flurry of international interest. The crackdown that followed was swift and harsh.

Mina and her friend Armin, a male classmate who seemed attentive to her, had invited us to drink tea with them in one of the open-air teahouses overlooking the river. In Isfahan the tea was less bitter than in Turkey and came with slightly chewy lumps of cardamom-scented sugar. Armin held one of the lumps in his mouth while sipping tea through it. Armin and Mina had just had an English class and were delighted to have stumbled upon some foreigners to practise with. I also got the impression that being with us was giving them legitimate cover for spending time together.

We had still not learnt that it was going to be totally impossible for us to pay for anything, so we suggested, in the hope that we'd be able to reciprocate for the tea they'd bought us, that we all go to a biryani place for lunch. We sat down to mounds of fried, spiced lamb mince on flatbread. Armin fetched us all doogh, while Mina talked about her family and the course in biology that she was taking in Mumbai. She was only back for the Nowruz holidays. She whispered to me that there was an Indian boy there that she liked. Her mother was a teacher and wanted to meet us, she said. When we explained that we were taking the bus back to Tabriz that evening, she made us agree to let her mother drive us to the bus station.

Mina's mother arrived in a cream car, a dark scarf covering her entire hairline. Her eyes were blue and her eyebrows pale, in contrast to Mina's thick, shaped ones, and I realised that she was probably blond. 'My mother wants me to tell you that she does not always wear this full scarf, but she has just come from college.' This was her way of letting us know that she was not a conservative.

In her class, Mina's mother had a Christian pupil and a Jewish pupil. 'Christians and Jews are even allowed to drink alcohol and have their wedding parties with men and women together,' Mina was quick to point out. Many of the Iranians we met were, like Mina, deeply concerned that we should not consider them bigoted. There are an estimated ten thousand Jews and 150,000 Christians in Iran, but conversion from Islam to either of those faiths is punishable by death. The groups have reserved seats in parliament (three for Christians, one for Jews and one for Zoroastrians), but they also suffer discrimination and are subject to intense scrutiny of an order beyond what the general populace have to endure, which is already extreme.

'Do you like Rico?' Mina called out from the front of the car as she fiddled with the tape deck.

'Ah, Enrique Iglesias!' We laughed as the familiar music blared out.

We sped along the dual carriageway as two black headscarves bobbed in the front, singing 'I can be your hero'.

In the years that followed, I would get occasional messages from Mina asking me if I knew of any eligible men. The Indian prospect had not worked out. 'He was not a good man, but don't worry, he did not touch me,' Mina wrote, keen to impress on me that she was a *nice girl.*

The bus station was packed with people travelling back home after Nowruz with piles of luggage and large picnics for the long journey. As I watched the outskirts of Isfahan dissolve into the desert, I mulled over how brave Mina had been to tell me about her atheism and to defy the hijab laws. What would I do, I asked myself?

'Going to Azerbaijan might be more hassle than it's worth,' Ed piped up, once the bus was properly on the move and the noise of the engine made it less likely that our conversation would be eavesdropped on.

I had been thinking the same. Iran had seemed absolutely fine so far. More than fine, in fact. Not only had we enjoyed some generous hospitality, we'd also received less attention on the streets of Iran than we had the previous month in Syria and eastern Turkey. Perhaps Iranians were more subtle, but I felt we were exciting less curiosity. If the secret police were keeping tabs on us – I told myself that it was best to assume they would be – then we had seen no sign of them yet.

What I did not tell Ed was that I did not want to be a coward. That I needed to try to understand what it took to live here as a woman.

We decided that our plans would change and that on reaching Tabriz we would take the bus to Tehran, apply for our Turkmen visas there and then cycle the remaining thousand kilometres to the Turkmen border – a more manageable version of our previously discounted Option B. We had three weeks left on our Iranian visas, which should give us just enough time.

I wriggled out of my manteau in the humid darkness and placed it over myself. Yes, Iran was different to Syria. There, I had worn my headscarf voluntarily, to fit in, and perhaps to keep me safe. Here, I was constantly worried about breaking the law. A strange landscape of desert and tiny mud villages whizzed past. I caught glimpses of camels and then the ruins of a khan flitted by in the sodium glow of the motorway lights.

17
FREEDOM TO RIDE

I still dream
of my red bicycle
on the green shore of summer

            Azita Ghahreman, trans. Dick Davis, from 'Alleys in a Far-Off Land', in Dick Davis (ed.), *The Mirror of My Heart*

Tehran crawled with people and glared with lights in the darkness. Motorbikes, taxis and cars shoved their way around a roundabout encircling the vast Azadi (Freedom) Tower to the sound of near-continuous beeping. The tower looked like the legs and lower torso of a giant space rocket transported from the set of a 1970s sci-fi movie. It was lit up in neon Islamic green. It is, in fact, made of white marble and was installed by the shah in 1971 to commemorate the 2500-year anniversary of the Persian empire. The celebrations for that anniversary were extraordinarily lavish – a vast tent city was erected in the empire's ancient capital of Persepolis, where six hundred international royals and heads of state were then entertained at the largest and longest banquet in modern history, with fifty thousand European songbirds released so as to provide 'cheer' to the desert. The festivities were so lavish, in fact, that the enormous cost angered many normal Iranians, already aggrieved that the country had not made the economic progress the shah had promised. This played into the hands of the revolutionaries wanting to discredit the shah's regime. When the revolution came, the tower, which at that point was named after the shah, was the focus of many demonstrations. It is still a key protest site today.

We had been dumped off the bus from Tabriz on the western edge of town and were now cycling in full neon vests, hugging the kerb, trying to avoid being mown down as we headed for our cheap hotel in a whole other part of town. Pedestrians seemed to jump off the high pavements at random and weave their way through the traffic at crossroads. People called greetings to us as we pedalled. Somehow we made it.

A vast queue of people filled the steps up to the tiny hatch at the Turkmen Embassy, including a small throng of assembled foreigners. We duly completed the forms we were given and then hunted out the requisite photocopies, photos and dollar bills in a rush to submit everything before the embassy closed for the day.

The man behind the desk took my forms and shut the hatch. I waited for five minutes. The hatch reopened. 'Okay.' He moved to shut it again.

'MASHHAD?' I shouted desperately, which was where we wanted to pick up the visas.

'Okay, okay. Mashhad.' The hatch snapped shut.

God willing, inshallah, our visas would be waiting at the Turkmen Embassy closest to the border.

We took a metro to Tehran's former US Embassy to see the infamous anti-American murals. During the revolution, US Embassy staff were held captive here for 444 days by students who stormed the embassy. They were tortured and treated inhumanely. The event marked the end of US–Iranian diplomatic relations. Some of the murals had been painted over, but the Statue of Liberty with a bare skull and an American hand crushing the globe remained. The regime now organised annual flag-burning ceremonies in nearby streets, and the embassy has since 2017 become a museum to the 'Den of Espionage'.

We hurried by, heads down, giving the murals just a quick glance, not wanting to risk photography or attract attention. A stream of regular-looking commuters came towards us. A lady with a hairsprayed fringe and patent-leather handbag paused in front of us and shook her head at the mural. We slunk off. We had been treated so kindly so far and I was sorry if the commuters assumed we thought the murals reflected their personal views.

Later that evening it became clear that the average Iranian was quite enamoured of the 'Great Satan' USA. After scouring the streets for a decent restaurant or falafel stall, we were reluctantly forced to eat in Boof, an American-style burger joint. We sat under the neon strip lights, eating from plastic trays strewn with burger wrappers, imitation McFries, plastic sachets of tomato ketchup and *real* Coca-Cola. Iran seemed to lack the street vendors that were ubiquitous in Turkey and Syria and ironically was the country with the most Americanised fast food we had been in since the UK.

We paid for our date with the devil. I woke to hear Ed throwing up in the bathroom the next morning. Feeling fine myself, I left him in bed and nipped out to the bakery that sold large ovals of corrugated flatbread.

I was just starting to slather hunks of it with carrot jam when yet more retching echoed through the courtyard. I rushed upstairs to find Ed on the floor, shaking violently. His temperature was high.

I hunted through our medical kit until I found the photocopied pages of an emergency medical textbook a friend who was an international mountain guide had given us. These had an invaluable cheat sheet which told you what symptoms to match with what antibiotic. It had already been useful on a couple of occasions, notably in eastern Turkey, and we'd christened it the 'Good S***ting Guide'. It read:

Rapid-onset – Diarrhoea – Vomiting – Fever – No blood
Diagnosis: Salmonella
Treat with Ciprofloxacin or Trimethoprim

I held vigil for the next hour with a mounting sense of panic as Ed continued to be violently sick. There was no chance he would keep any pills down. As I tried to think through worst-case scenarios and a possible course of action, I flicked through our guidebook to the page about consular assistance.

The British Embassy has limited ability to help but can assist with … hospital visits

With shaking hands I punched the number for the embassy into my mobile phone. The holding message gave contact details for the out-of-hours service. Finally I was connected.

I explained Ed's situation as briefly as I could.

'Do you have travel insurance?' snapped the embassy woman in reply.

'Yes, of course, but I was wondering if you had a list of hospitals that might accept an arrangement with foreign insurers.' We had entered Iran with 2500 US dollars, more than enough to live on, but I was seriously worried we might not have enough to pay a large bill if a hospital trip was needed.

'No, I can't help you. Contact your insurers. Goodbye.'

I blinked at the silent mobile phone in my hand, confused. So much for medical assistance.

I punched in the number for our insurers, who promised access to a 24-hour, 365-days-a-year medical phone line from anywhere in the world. The dial tone seemed to be echoing down the line from another universe.

'Where are you?'

'Iran.'

A pause. 'Can you spell that for me?'

'I-R-A-N,' I replied with an exasperated rush of air.

'Hmm.' Another pause. 'I am gonna have to speak to our Middle East office.'

'Can you not just put me through?'

'Nah, the office is in Doha and it's a Friday, innit. Middle East. Shut. Muslim weekend and all that.'

No s***. I killed the call.

Ed was vomiting again, and shaking, and his breathing was shallow and fast. I knew this might be more serious than something that would just require a couple of days of sticking it out.

The hotel receptionist came to the open doorway of the room.

'Hospital?' I asked.

He nodded and within moments I heard him phoning from downstairs.

The sirens blared as the ambulance bumped its way across town. The paramedic ripped open a packet of sterile needles and jabbed a drip into Ed's arm. Ed was ashen grey and still shaking violently. Tears started to roll down my cheeks as thoughts of phone calls to his parents flashed through my mind. The paramedic looked over to me from where he was trying to hook the drip above Ed's head. 'Okay,' he said, nodding kindly at me.

The hospital was clean and spartan. Ed lay on a trolley in a large male ward while nurses and doctors milled around him. Every patient had a relative of the same sex with them and I realised it was probably a breach of etiquette to be accompanying my husband. A nurse hurried me out of the ward at one point, when the doctor came to see a patient next to Ed.

Had Ed been drinking alcohol, the doctor asked? Perhaps because a foreign tourist had died recently after drinking counterfeit alcohol, or perhaps because it was a common issue. A young man was admitted screaming and in a state of high excitement to the bed next to Ed. A hard-edged silence descended over the staff, who studiously ignored him, other than when administering drugs, as he vomited and ranted. He lay

Waylaid for the first cup of tea, shortly after crossing into Syria.

Camped at the Roman ruins of Apamea, Syria, the morning after getting lost and accepting a lift in the dark.

Inside the monastery of Mar Musa, Syria, home to a community that promoted interfaith dialogue founded by Father Paolo Dall'Oglio. The frescoes date from as early as 1058.

Invited for tea with Bedouin boys near Homs. The fact that we had photographed these boys and their donkey caused hilarity among the security services who inspected our camera later in the journey.

Casanova the camel and owner by the Monumental Arch and section colonnade in Palmyra, Syria. The arch was built in the third century and was dynamited by ISIS in 2015 along with much of the site.

Cycling desert roads, Syria.

Staying with a Syrian family. Ed wearing a shemagh offered by our host.

Staying with a Turkish family near Urfa. Lilac scarves were commonly worn in this region of Turkey. Our hosts often seemed to delight in dressing us in local clothing, and although I found this initially embarrassing, I became more than happy to provide some entertainment value in return for the kind hospitality we received.

Hasankeyf, Turkey. The town was completely submerged in 2020 by the damming of the River Tigris.

Me getting a sore neck looking up at Isfahan's stunning seventeenth–eighteenth-century Chahar Bagh Madrasa (Theology School), Iran, open to visitors on a rare day over Nowruz. I could fill a whole book with pictures of Isfahan and encourage readers to look up pictures of Maidan-e Naqsh-e Jahan (Image of the World Square).

One of many wonderful groups of Iranians who stopped us for photos and gave us hospitality.

The strange rocket-like tomb tower at Gonbad-e Kavus, built 1006, praised by Robert Byron in *The Road to Oxiana* as one of the most significant buildings in the world. I can't say I thought it beautiful at the time, but it has an oddly magnetic quality.

Stopped by women in Turkmenistan.

Picnic with Uzbek workers after crossing the border from Turkmenistan, vodka making its first appearance alongside tea and non (bread).

Cycling into Bukhara with the Kalon Mosque in the background. The minaret was built in 1122 and Genghis Khan spared it when he razed the city.

Holding a special non bread baked for us by Halim the baker. He explained that non was sacred and should never be placed upside down or on the bare floor or cut with a knife.

Bikes with Central Asia's tallest Lenin statue at Khujand (formerly Leninabad).

Lunch with a Tajik family. In Central Asia tea was always offered with bread and something sweet, in this case white mulberries and wrapped sweets, which were one of the few items on sale in the small shops we passed.

Camping above the river Panj, opposite Afghanistan. Our mysterious night-time camping companions appeared on the cliffs out of shot to the left.

Ed fixing yet another puncture on my twenty-eighth birthday before we reached Kalaikhum. We sustained over fifty punctures on the journey (most of which are not reported as it would make for very dull reading!).

Tajik demining operatives. The day we camped with them, they had retrieved the personal effects from a herder who had walked into a minefield a few years earlier.

Stopped by girls in the Wakhan Valley.

Pushing bikes through deep gravel for days out of the Wakhan Valley towards the Pamir Highway. Afghanistan in the background.

Celebratory photo after reaching the Chinese border!

contorted on his bed, wrapping his drip around his thin forearm in a way that made me cringe.

'Turn over. You're going to pull that out,' I ordered after I couldn't stand to watch him any longer.

The man moaned in response.

'You don't want to pull that out by mistake,' I said again, slightly less sternly.

He turned over and nodded vaguely. 'Thank you. There are bad people here.'

'That drip will make you feel much better.'

Had he drunk bad alcohol, or was he coming off heroin or something else?

A male relative turned up later to collect him and thanked me.

Three hours later, once Ed had improved, I sat in the café gingerly eating the only thing on the menu: a sandwich containing a processed pink sausage that looked and tasted just like pork. The tea was thick with tannins that stuck to my mouth and caffeine that sent my heart racing, doing little to calm my frayed nerves.

I went outside for a breather, to a courtyard set back from the street. The sun was shining and there was the constant sound of traffic honking. I sat on a bench and watched a succession of people walking along the pavement to the hospital entrance. An elderly woman, bony shoulders jutting from under her chador, was having her wheelchair lifted over a crack in the pavement by two broad-backed young men in tight T-shirts while a middle-aged woman in voluminous dark purple chiffon, carrying shopping bags on each arm, directed them. A man in the orange boiler suit of a street cleaner swung past on crutches while his friend spoke into a mobile.

There was a kiosk beside me selling things that might be needed by frazzled relatives or as gifts for the sick – fizzy drinks, cigarettes, crisps, magazines, plastic flowers – and an old man with a thin, lined face, dark trousers and a dark sports jacket was sitting on the bench next to it. There was a cage with a budgerigar beside him. I'd seen many caged birds like this for sale on the street, but surely this was not intended as a hospital gift?

As I was watching the splash of green and yellow hop around its cage, a woman carrying a shopping bag containing a giant watermelon and another stuffed with oranges stopped in front of the man. He reached inside the cage and gently fished out the bird. There was a plastic box full of wafer-thin rectangles of coloured paper next to him, and he held the bird over it. It pecked a few times and then lifted a slip of pink paper in its beak. The man unhooked the piece of paper and handed it to the woman, who unfolded it, glanced at it and then put it into her manteau pocket. The man gave the bird a seed.

Seeing me watching, the woman said something to him and nodded at me. He gestured that I should come over. I hesitated, but they both beckoned.

'Hafez,' he said as I stood in front of him.

The bird bobbed its head, this time pulling out a whole clump of green, yellow and pink slips. His handler unhooked them and carefully pushed them back into the pile with his tanned fingers. On the second peck, a single yellow slip was brought up and then handed to me.

The sun shone through the fragile paper as I unfolded it and peered at the couplet of flowing Persian text. I gave it to the woman to read, who looked confused and then alarmed. Realising that she would be no help, the old man called out to a man in a white coat who was passing.

'Doctora! Doctora!'

The man, who was clearly in a hurry, drew to a halt, deferential to the elderly soothsayer.

'Do you speak English?' the doctor asked me in a Canadian accent. 'You know, this is our famous poet Hafez. He comes from Shiraz.'

A fourteenth-century writer of mystical poetry, Hafez is so beloved by Iranians that it's claimed most households have a copy of his complete works, his *Divan* (or *Diwan*), next to the Qur'an. I had heard that randomly selecting a verse was a way of fortune telling, akin to the way the Chinese use the I Ching, and said as much to the doctor.

'This is superstition. You Westerners might find it strange, or maybe it is like your horoscope, but some Iranians love this. It is just superstition. I am a doctor, of course.' He laughed, as if a little embarrassed.

'Oh, I am a scientist too,' I said. 'Don't worry!'

He nodded, then furrowed his brow at the paper.

'How can I translate …? "The road, it is full of trouble …"' He raised his eyebrows. 'No, maybe "The road, it is full of trouble … to the eye of reason" or I should say maybe "science". He gave a small smile. '"The world and everything in it is without stability."'

I must have looked worried or maybe it was the hospital tea giving me the shakes. The woman patted my arm.

'Well,' he said, 'that is Hafez. Maybe it's superstition or maybe not. Anyway, good luck with your visit to Iran.' He hurried off.

The woman pressed two oranges from her shopping bag into my hand as if to compensate for my ill fortune.

Ed was discharged in the late afternoon, after the hospital had run multiple tests. These included an electrocardiogram, an ultrasound and, most concerningly, a chest X-ray. A nurse ordered me sternly to wipe away the ultrasound gel once she had finished examining Ed's abdomen on her monitor.

With every test, my fears that we would be unable to pay for all of this mounted. I held my breath as I queued at the payment desk with a flimsy yellow chitty of the same colour and consistency as the soothsayer's omen but this time with Persian numbers hand-scrawled on it; numbers that I could not interpret. At the desk, a man typed out the figures for me on a calculator. The number he held up was 354,000. I did a double take, counted out the rial and held them up to him to confirm that I had understood the number of zeros correctly. He took the money and gave me a receipt. The total fee came to just over thirty-five US dollars.

The three girls next to us were giggling and clearly talking about us. They were sitting, legs tucked under them, on a daybed in a dark teahouse in Tehran's Park-e Shahr. The park was a haven from Tehran's tooting traffic and we were spending a lazy morning there on a bench, while Ed recuperated.

We had sought out the teahouse for a lunch of dizi, lamb stew with bread, which we'd read was traditional teahouse and truck-stop fare. The expression on the waiter's face implied that he thought it far too basic for tourists, but we persevered anyway, batting off the offer of a sandwich or a dreaded burger. The stew arrived in a bowl together with a second bowl and a wooden pestle.

'I think you should put the bread in there.' One of the girls addressed Ed and pointed to the bowl that he was not using.

Like many women in Tehran, all three of them were wearing fashionably narrow-fitting tunics over slim-legged jeans, headscarves draped elegantly over coiffed hair.

There was more giggling.

'Are you married?'

'Yes.'

'Your wife is very beautiful, but my friend was hoping …' More giggles, and her friend punched her in the leg.

We chatted further, answering the direct questions which we were used to now.

'What do you think about Iran?'

'What do you think of Iranians?'

'Do people in Europe and America think we are terrorists?'

It was striking how many times we were asked that question.

'No, but you are right that unfortunately our media does not carry many positive stories about Iran. We don't think you are all terrorists.'

The girls discussed further among themselves. One of them had a diamond embedded in her tooth.

'Can we ask you another question about things that are allowed in your country but forbidden here?'

'Do you mean like alcohol?' I was also thinking about parties and extramarital sex.

'No, we know about that. Er … is it true that you eat the meat of the pig?'

'Yes.' I braced myself, remembering Aleppo Mahmoud's disgust and disbelief at this and how earnestly he had explained to us that pigs carried many diseases such as swine flu.

'Ahh.' She sighed. 'We hear it is so very delicious. What does it taste like? Please do tell us.'

So as not to challenge Ed's health too much, we decided to take the bus to Sari, northeast of Tehran, and to cycle the remaining nine hundred kilometres to the Turkmen border from there. That proved to be a good decision. The Sari road wound over a mountain pass, its narrow lanes choked with traffic that squeezed past our bus as we trundled uphill in the hot spring sunshine. We stepped off the bus to be mobbed by all sorts of people, including a fellow passenger called Sadeq, who wanted us to visit him when we reached Gonbad-e Kavus, further to the east; a policeman who insisted we follow him to a hotel he wanted us to check in to; and, most rewardingly, a couple of Iranian mountaineering enthusiasts, Rezza and Nazanin, who were keen to meet up with us that evening.

Rezza and Nazanin were in their early twenties, married and living in a room in his parents' house. We started the evening at their house, where we looked at mountaineering photographs, Nazanin hiking through snow in a knee-length shirt and black headscarf, her chador hitched up around her waist. They showed us a film of a female mountaineer climbing the steep snow slopes of Mount Damavand in puffy down jacket, ice axe and crampons. The dormant volcano is, at 5609 metres, the highest mountain in Iran. The film then cut to a studio interview of the same woman swathed in a chador.

They drove us to a viewpoint over the city and we sat eating take-away burgers on a picnic blanket in the dark. I was sorry it was not the weekend and that we could not stay on and go into the hills together. I have chosen to spend a good deal of my free time as an adult in the mountains and I understood how they offered Nazanin an escape from restrictions on the valley floor. Even in Europe, it's mostly men who go into remote places, and I couldn't help wondering how much harder it would be to make that choice in Iran. Nazanin did it, and I respected her deeply for that. There were other striking role models too: women like Leila Esfandyari, a microbiologist and climber who was to die on Gasherbrum 2 in the Karakoram in 2011; Parvaneh Kazemi, a maths teacher and mountaineer who has ascended multiple big Himalayan peaks, including making an ascent of Everest and Lhotse in the same week in 2012; and Afsaneh Hesamifard, a medical doctor, the first Iranian woman to climb K2 in 2022.

For me, remote places have always provided a great freedom from the gendered expectations of dress and behaviour imposed on us in the built environment. The freedom to choose how we dress is everything, and yet it is also worth remembering that the clothes we are forced to wear, or perhaps choose to wear, are meaningless and that generalisations about people based on their appearance reveals only our own blind spots.

Nature is also a great leveller. It is amazing how a storm can cut through bluff and bluster. The mountain ridge is where success often amounts to the capacity to endure hardship, the mental resolve to keep going, the ability to problem solve. It is not necessarily just about brute strength or the willingness to take risks. Mountaineering clubs can be intimidating places, full of crass jokes and backslapping and men barely turning away from you to pee, but they are often also populated by exceptionally talented and thoughtful men. I have experienced far worse sexism from men in the office environment, from men who have convinced themselves that they are better than they are but are less good at their job than I am, men that I could outpace along the high street, let alone up a mountain.

I was about to put my commitment to being a woman of the outdoors to the test once more. There were going to be no more buses till we got to the Turkmen border. The manteau and silk headscarf, which had allowed me to blend in relatively well, at least at a distance, were replaced with a baggy tunic and the khaki cotton headscarf I'd worn in Syria, which could go under my helmet. The tunic was definitely not my favourite item. It had a sort of tartan print and could well have been a pyjama top. Strangely, apart from endless manteaux and chadors, there was nothing that resembled modest sportswear for sale in Iran, nothing like a salwar kameez, which might have been practical. Perhaps because women mostly shed the compulsory outer layers as soon as they got into the house.

Unappealing clothing notwithstanding, it was exhilarating to be back in the saddle again. At the end of our first day's ride out of Sari, we camped next to the Caspian Sea in a municipal park at Bander-e Gaz. We had heard about these free campsites but had not seen one before. Each pitch consisted of a small, raised, brightly painted wrought-iron pavilion in which the Iranian families all around us had erected dome-shaped tents, the sort that required no pegs. We spent quite a while stringing out our tunnel tent between the balustrades and propping it up with bikes and panniers, much to the amusement of everyone else.

There was a cold wind coming off the water and I felt clammy and salty from a day's sweating in the sunshine. I pulled out my down jacket and added a second headscarf to the first, then heated up cans of Iranian-style baked beans to eat with flatbread and boiled some water for tea. As the sun set, the pier lights came on, casting reflections on the water. A loud orchestra of croaking frogs serenaded us from the rushes. It was good to be camping again.

It was also good to be by the sea again, even if only for a few more hours. In the morning we cycled out along the pier and gazed at the Caspian, as grey as the sky, with low clouds cloaking a ridge of mountains in the distance. Cheerily painted boats and pedalos were tied up along the length of the pier and rickety-looking tea-drinking platforms were set at intervals along its edge.

The landscape was now flat, covered with fields in which the first apple-green shoots of spring were poking out of muddy earth. The air was still and warm and a haze gathered at the horizon. The road was quiet and we made light work of it at twenty kilometres per hour, passing through Bandar-e Torkaman and then leaving the Caspian behind us. Many women were now dressed in floor-length dresses instead of manteaux or chadors. On their heads they wore large, patterned scarves in aubergines, maroons, golds and dark greens, like the shawls favoured by Russian grandmas, the corners hanging down their backs in triangles. Occasionally I glimpsed a face with the high cheekbones and Asiatic eyes of a Mongolian. We were close to the Turkmen border and would be paralleling it for the next six hundred kilometres.

At Aqqala we stopped to picnic in a park in the middle of a roundabout. I blinked and focused again on the figures up ahead, which for all the world looked to have the bulk and wobble of cycle-tourers. The silhouettes coming into focus turned out to be Luca and Mateo, the Italian cyclists we'd met in Urfa, by now even more tanned and beardy, clearly not concerned that the smoothed-jawed Iranians might take them for terrorists as the Turks had.

The four of us attempted to set up camp that evening by a reservoir but were found by a large woman called Maryam who insisted we pitch our tents in front of her small farmstead surrounded by fields. Our arrival attracted a gaggle of neighbours. We dined on mounds of rice and chicken with helpings of yogurt, Maryam, unusually, eating with us while the other women retreated.

'My second husband is a Sunni,' she told me. 'A truck driver.' She explained also that he washed his feet with water as well as his hands and face before praying, miming scrubbing between her toes and wrinkling her nose. She thought it was odd that he did that rather than symbolically pass his hand over the tops of his feet like she did as a Shia.

Some of Maryam's male neighbours burst into song and had Ed, Luca and Mateo up dancing. When everyone was together again, Luca and Mateo showed a video they'd shot while I'd been sitting with the women as dinner was prepared. I shifted uncomfortably as we watched a close-up clip of one of the young women milking a cow, her fingers running up and down the teats. I could sense tension around us and faces looked unimpressed as the young milker coloured and fled the room. I was surprised at our companions being oblivious to the offence they were causing. Then they played another clip. Did they not understand that many Iranians objected to women being photographed or filmed? Was it really necessary to bring along so much technology? They were always videoing everything and spent a long time in the evening downloading videos on to a laptop that they had with them.

Later, when I spoke to Luca and Mateo, I realised that they rarely had the opportunity to speak to women on their travels. Theirs were stories of being served from behind hatches, staying in a man's flat who was keeping a mistress, and drinking moonshine with dubious companions. Ed and I were lucky that, as a couple, we were often more easily accepted into family life, even though Ed himself had rarely spoken to any women directly since entering Syria.

Maryam grabbed my hand towards the end of the evening, when we were sitting just as the women again, and demanded that I take a photo of her with the other girls, so that I could remember them. They adjusted themselves, she drawing her chador up over her head so that the black cloth fell open across both shoulders, accentuating her high cheekbones, the girls pushing their headscarves far back. They had already made me remove mine, saying that it was not necessary for me as a Christian.

'You photo okay.' Maryam squeezed my arm as she shook her head towards the room where the men were sitting.

18
TELL THEM ABOUT THE REAL IRAN

Forget not when dear friend to friend returned,
Forget not days gone by, forget them not!
My mouth has tasted bitterness, and learnt
To drink the envenomed cup of mortal lot;
Forget not when a sweeter draught was mine,
Loud rose the songs of them that drank that wine—
Forget them not!

Hafez, trans. Gertrude Bell, from 'Diwan 35', in
Poems from the Divan of Hafiz

Sadeq, who had ridden the bus with us from Tehran to Sari, had insisted that we phone him when we reached his home town of Gonbad-e Kavus. Ed and I debated whether to do so or not, knowing full well that he would lavish hospitality on us, but we also knew that news would quickly circulate that foreign cyclists were in town and we didn't want to offend him by not calling. There was no debate, however, as to where in town we should meet Sadeq. It had to be the eponymous Gonbad-e Kavus Tower, lauded by the famous twentieth-century British travel writer Robert Byron and, at fifty-five metres high, impossible to miss, standing tall on a hillock and soaring into the dull afternoon sky.

Close up, the coffee-coloured brick tower looked more like a Victorian space rocket than a relic dating back to 1006, its shaft a ten-pointed star with the inner points rounded off, and topped with a conical roof. It had aged well, the tiny bricks fitting together perfectly, and staring up at its hollow interior was dizzying, like being at the bottom of a huge well. The tower was built by King Kavus, a ruler of home-grown dynasty the Ziyarid, as his tomb, and apparently a glass coffin containing his body once hung suspended inside the shaft. Robert Byron, an architecture buff who made an art form of talking down great sights, claimed that it was seeing a photograph of Gonbad-e Kavus that inspired his journey to Persia. He was not disappointed, writing in *The Road to Oxiana*:

Superlatives applied by travellers to objects which they have seen, but most people have not, are generally suspect; I know it, having been guilty of them. But rereading this diary two years later, in as different an environment as possible (Pekin), I still hold the opinion I formed before going to Persia, and confirmed that evening on the steppe: that the Gumbad-i-Kabus ranks with the great buildings of the world.

One of the photographs that Byron took in April 1934 depicts the tower alone on its hillock, seen from a distance away on the steppe, with two yurts in the foreground. The area around the tower was now neatly landscaped with paved walkways running between grass lawns, interspersed with cypress and palm trees and a forest of street lighting. Beds of yellow, white and blue pansies were offset by brightly painted red and yellow benches.

The tower was striking, and its geometry mysterious, but I was not sure I loved it. Perhaps I dismissed it too easily because of a prejudice about the need for big men to erect large monuments to themselves. Or perhaps the mystery had been dampened by that careful landscaping. Later, however, I found myself revisiting in my mind's eye a strange lighthouse standing sentinel on the edge of the Central Asian steppe.

Sadeq arrived and we all posed for pictures under the tower. An engineer, he was currently doing military service in Tehran but was on leave to visit his sister. At a small café where he'd worked as a child, we drank thick hot chocolate, a beverage I'd not encountered since Greece and a treat which he clearly thought appropriate for Westerners, seeking our approval anxiously after the first sip. We left our bikes so that we could take a taxi to a decorative shrine-tomb on the outskirts of town, the site of the former capital of Jorjan. The shrine was said to have been erected in honour of an eighteen-year-old martyr who launched a failed uprising of the people of Khorasan against the Umayyads. Every inch of it was tiled in blue, turquoise, yellow and white – the inner and outer walls and archways of the porticoed courtyard, the outsides of the minarets and the small domed mosque – in both vegetative and Kufic designs (decorative Arabic calligraphy). Inside the mosque, as is the custom with Shia shrines, the dome was tiled in mirrors to reflect the divine light of God.

When we re-emerged to retrieve our shoes from the huge pile at the door, a man was filming at the entrance to the mosque, using a hulking black video camera mounted on a tripod. I tensed, hoping he would not spot us, and bent down with my face turned away from him as I laced up my boots. I was in my manteau and hoped it would serve as cover. For the umpteenth time, I cursed not having slip-on shoes as I hurried away with my shoelaces still undone. Moments later the man had spotted Ed and, urged on by Sadeq, we were directed to stand together in front of a large brown foam microphone. I tugged self-consciously at my headscarf lest I have 'bad hijab' on TV.

'Is it a documentary about the mosque?' I asked Sadeq, hopeful that as infidels we might end up on the cutting-room floor.

'No, it is for the news. Tonight! You will be famous in Golestan!' The camera operator beamed.

Mercifully, he was satisfied with an enthusiastic description of touristic Iran and of course of the wonderful people of Gonbad-e Kavus, and it was over quickly. Ed and I had, by unspoken consensus, both omitted to mention our mode of transport, keen to remain as anonymous as possible once back in our cycling gear.

We reached the town of Galikesh at dusk and were directed to a park where we'd be able to camp. The park's janitor identified a spot, but while we were unloading our bikes he pulled out his phone and, shortly after, two men in baggy suits appeared. My heart sank. Had Golestan News24 really caught up with us? Had our answers offended the state and were we about to be questioned?

We beamed at the suits. Ed did a round of handshakes. We enthused again, and quite genuinely, about the touristic beauty and hospitality of Iran. They gestured that we should follow them. Concluding that we had little choice, we loaded the panniers back onto the bikes and wheeled them back the way we had come, led by one of the suits, the other speaking animatedly into his phone. The janitor trailed behind us.

We all came to a halt at the bottom of a set of steps up to a building that looked distinctly governmental. There was a collective moment of hesitation. I pointed to the dirt on the bikes, mock horror on my face, hoping that they would change their minds and decide it would be too much trouble to bring us inside after all, but the janitor was directed to run up and get help. Three further men appeared and our bikes were carried up the steps fully laden, with much grunting.

We entered a dingy set of offices with whitewashed brick walls, a shiny tiled floor and harsh strip lighting. The national flag hung on a pole, a tricolour – green for unity, white for peace, red for the blood of martyrs – with the takbir 'Allahu akbar (God is great)' repeated in Kufic script to either side of the white band and in the centre the stylised name of Allah in the shape of a tulip or crossed scimitars (the national emblem of Iran). This had replaced the shah's lion and sun after the revolution on the order of Ayatollah Khomeini. The latter stared down at us with cold indifference from a large portrait on the wall.

A big man with grey stubble, tinted glasses and a navy suit jacket greeted us. His paunch overhung his belted khaki trousers and gold rings gleamed on thick fingers.

Ed did another considered round of handshakes, labouring over the full names of all of the assembled party. We did more general beaming and exclamations about the beauty of Iran.

We were directed to sit down. The big man ordered a younger man to translate. We explained the detail of our trip carefully. Starting at the beginning and taking a long time to list, in what I hoped might prove to be slightly tiresome details, the stopping points on the whole trip. Perhaps they would leave us be once we ran out of mutually intelligible topics of conversation.

That chance was lost when the local English teacher arrived. He was thin, with salt-and-pepper hair, a black seventies moustache and darting eyes. He fired questions at Ed. Ed started again at the beginning and then began to answer questions about his profession.

'What teacher?'

'Secondary. Geography.'

There was some conferring in Farsi and Big Man Mr Kabiri, who I had decided had to be the town mayor, spoke on his phone again.

We sat there smiling. Ed showed some of the men pictures on his camera. Tea was brought in. We were in for the long haul. It was unclear what was going to happen next and I still hoped that after some further niceties we would be released back to the Eden of the park campsite.

Mr Kabiri stood up and gestured that we were to follow him to the back of his office. Expecting the interview proper to start now that the pleasantries were over, I blinked as we stepped into a kitchen diner with a vase of plastic flowers on the table. There was a bedroom coming off it.

He grinned at our surprised faces. We would be spending the night here, he said. They would leave us in peace for half an hour and then return. I sat on the bed and took a deep breath as I listened to the sound of footsteps leaving the building.

Big Man Mr Kabiri returned with his fourteen-year-old son and arms full of chicken kebabs and rice in take-away cartons. There were pickles and commercial bottles of fizzy doogh and delicious packets of olives marinated in walnuts and pomegranate molasses. The janitor appeared again, weighed down with an enormous basket of fruit.

They would come back at eight with breakfast and he would like us to stay on Thursday and Friday. We protested weakly and then more forcefully, but it was all rebuffed with a wave of a chubby hand. Resistance was quite clearly useless.

The following day we were subjected to what's best described as a voluntary abduction led by the jocular Mr Kabiri and the stern teacher, Mr Moghaddam. We were taken first to the boys' school, where I was asked to wait outside with a female member of staff while Ed spent a lesson with the class. Mr Moghaddam explained to me that my headscarf was a little immodest for the boys. I duly tugged the slippery fabric forwards over my forehead and the female staff member, who was swathed in a chador, gave me an embarrassed glance. I remembered Mina's mother in Isfahan apologising for her austere attire because she was a teacher. State institutions, it seemed, required more than just abiding by the letter of the law. I thought back to Nazanin and her mountaineering ladies in chadors. If you wanted to get on with the really subversive business of feminism, get ahead in a male-dominated world, perhaps even get to the top, then the chador and religiosity might, paradoxically to us, provide the perfect cover.

On to a second breakfast at Mr Kabiri's house, where we were served fried eggs and introduced to a grumpy toddler who had been circumcised the day before. Circumcision is almost universal for Muslim boys and often carried out before the age of two. Mr Kabiri proudly showed Ed gory pictures of the event on his phone. Ed explained that circumcision was not normally conducted in Britain for boys who were not Muslim or Jewish. Mr Kabiri laughed heartily and gave Ed a big backslap when the penny dropped that he was uncircumcised. 'Like baby.' He wiped away a tear of laughter before passing a pale-looking Ed yet another photo of the procedure.

Mr Moghaddam and his wife, Zara, who was also a teacher, and their two studious daughters picked us up and took us on a picnic and then back to their house to watch their holiday videos of a trip to India, Mr Moghaddam interrogating us on the finer points of English grammar, which, to his obvious dismay, we were hopeless at answering. We then attended a lesson at the girls' school, where we were installed with a lot of ceremony on plastic-covered armchairs at the front of the class. Mr Kabiri gave a speech. Mr Moghaddam gave a speech. We were quizzed by a group of teenagers with excellent English. A sea of fresh faces haloed by black.

'What is the national food of Scotland?'

'Why did you come to Iran?'

'What do you think of the hijab?'

'You are all very beautiful ...' I said, and then hesitated.

'Yes, but do you think it should be the law to wear the hijab?' a girl in the front row pushed.

'I would prefer it to be a choice,' I said, looking her straight in the eyes, 'but I understand that as a visitor to your country I must follow your law.'

I think about that answer a lot, recalling the comment by Shirin Ebadi, Iran's first Nobel Peace laureate, that 'cultural relativism is nothing but an excuse to violate human rights'.

A different line of questioning was introduced brightly by Mr Moghaddam.

Once outside, we were interviewed for a local paper, Mr Moghaddam translating and, I suspected, vetting our response.

Back at his house, we found that Zara had prepared the famous Iranian dish ghormeh sabzi for dinner – lamb stew in a sauce of dried lime and herbs. There were mounds of rice with a perfect tadikh, the moreish crust made by cooking the rice at the bottom of the pan with butter and discs of potato. More fresh herbs. Pickles. Yogurt and doogh.

They checked that we were happy to eat all together sitting on the floor and we batted away any suggestion of us needing to eat in private or to sit at their dining table. 'We have this,' Mr Moghaddam explained, gesturing to a flashy glass table with tall chairs at the end of their large living room, 'but it is so much more comfortable to sit on the floor.' He did indeed look more relaxed at last, now that he was sitting cross-legged on the carpet in his socks, open-necked shirt and no tie.

After dinner, Zara invited me to sit with her in a side room. She took my hand once she had finished pouring me a cup of tea. 'You know it is very difficult here,' she said.

I nodded and squeezed her hand, not sure if she meant Iran in general or the rural areas she had been brought to by her husband. She was originally from the city.

'I can't speak to any men. Even if I see my brother-in-law on the street, it is impossible for me to acknowledge him. I can only socialise with male blood relatives and my husband.'

I squeezed her hand again as I simply did not know what to say. For me to suggest that things might change seemed ludicrous. Trapped and stifled, that's how I inferred women must feel. That was how I felt, even after a few months. Constantly having to edit a version of themselves for the outside world.

'I would like to show you my hair,' she said suddenly, and began unpinning the black headscarf which completely covered her hairline. I felt a small shock as she lifted her scarf away. Her face was completely transformed by the beautiful thick grey wavy hair that framed her grey eyes. I understood in that moment what it might feel like to be a man who, never knowing what the hair of the women surrounding him in daily life looked like, got to see this for the first time.

We were not allowed to relax for too long. Mr Kabiri turned up and announced we were going to a wedding. We drove into the countryside for an hour, with the setting sun. From the way Mr Kabiri talked about the wedding host, a Mr Tabrizi, the man was clearly a big cheese. The boss or maybe the boss's boss. He was holding a pre-wedding party for his niece, whose wedding was going to be the next day. He was keen to meet us foreigners and could not be refused.

It was pitch-black by the time we pulled up to a large house with a floodlit veranda in the middle of nowhere. I could see no other lights. A slim, middle-aged man in jeans and an open-necked shirt came out as soon as we got out of the car and strode down the steps to shake both our hands.

'Hello. Welcome,' Mr Ahmadi said in a mid-Atlantic accent.

Mr Kabiri greeted him and after what seemed like a brief interrogation from our host took his leave and walked back to his car.

'Have they been treating you well?' Mr Ahmadi said as he held the front door open, letting a blast of music out into the night air and waving us inside.

We fell over each other to express our gratitude.

'Good,' he said. 'You know, people from these village areas are kind but not always that sophisticated.'

'They have been kind,' I said, suddenly feeling hurt on their account. 'Very kind. And Mr Moghaddam's wife is a wonderful cook.'

As soon as we entered the house, I understood why Mr Kabiri was waiting in the car. The living room was a disco and three bare-headed young women in short dresses were dancing while aunties in hijabs sat gossiping and the men stood at the kitchen bar drinking beer. Beer! Almost immediately, two of the girls pulled me onto the dance floor and tugged at my headscarf and manteau, ordering me to take them off.

A few songs in, I extracted myself and finished the round of introductions. A male cousin who had flown in from Canada especially for the wedding poured me and Ed double shots of single-malt whisky that he had smuggled into the country. He told us about wild parties where everyone drove far out into the desert, camped under the stars and drank moonshine. About hymenoplasty operations to 'put back' virginity. About how the engaged couple, both university students, had had to pretend for two years that they were not seeing each other.

As 'Bad Romance' by Lady Gaga came over the stereo, the bride-to-be and Mr Ahmadi's niece pulled me up to dance with them again. Bad romance – how apt, I thought, for a country obsessed with bad hijab.

I danced, infected by their hedonism and perhaps their heroic ability to endure this nonsensical female oppression, no longer caring that I had bad headscarf hair, that my clothes were dowdy or that the morality police were likely lurking in the bushes. Perhaps the single malt helped – it was months since I'd had a drink.

'When you go home,' one of the teenaged girls shouted, 'you must tell them Iran is like this. You must tell them that it is not all chadors and mullahs and terrorists. You must tell them we like this. This is the real Iran. Promise me you will.'

We sang together about kissing in the sand and horror and love and criminals.

We were begged to come to the full wedding the next day, but we explained that we were on a visa deadline. Neither of us wanted to gatecrash their real wedding and we had nothing we could possibly wear for it. But as with so many invitations in Iran, we worried that we'd caused offence by turning it down.

Mr Kabiri was waiting outside in the dark to drive us back at two in the morning.

'Promise to tell everyone what it is like in Iran. Promise,' Mr Ahmadi's niece reminded me, hugging me as I left, diamond-studded earrings glittering in the moonlight.

The next day we were firm with Mr Kabiri that we had to leave. We were plied with breakfast and then when we were definitely clear that we were leaving, loaded with fruit, chocolate and nuts and presented with a commemorative plaque 'From the people of Golestan', the land of flowers and, as we would soon learn, one of Iran's most lush provinces. I was given a vial of perfume in a box with, inexplicably to me, a picture of the Grand Ayatollah on it. We took rounds of photographs and Ed let everyone try his fully laden bike, Mr Kabiri wobbling worryingly and looking delighted in Ed's bike helmet. We eventually set off at eleven, though this was not to be our final goodbye. Mr Kabiri had insisted that we join him and his friends for a picnic lunch further up the road.

19

MEETINGS IN LEOPARD COUNTRY

Like a leopard
he emerged
from the bushes
with Genghis Khan's smile on his lips

Sara Mohammadi-Ardehali, trans. Dick Davis, from
'Meeting', in Dick Davis (ed.), *The Mirror of My Heart*

The road began to rise and oak forest appeared. We were on the fringes of Iran's Golestan National Park, the Golestan Jungle. The jungle is actually a remnant of a large, temperate, broad-leafed forest that today stretches in an arc along the southern coast of the Caspian Sea and the northern slopes of the Alborz mountains. It was once home to the now extinct Caspian tiger and is still home to leopards, wolves and bears.

A steady flow of traffic chugged past us as, for the first time since Turkey, we really felt the effort in our thighs, our heavy panniers pulling us back. As we climbed, we started to receive concerned phone calls from Mr Kabiri. Where were we? Were we okay? An hour later, he slowed alongside us in a beige Paykan, waving and shouting encouragement from the window, before the car sped off. It took us another hour still of grinding up a steep gorge to reach the designated picnic spot. My head was pounding with exhaustion and I stopped to swallow two paracetamols, feeling uncharitable about being harassed.

The picnic area was in dappled light under oriental beech trees and the smell of shashlik greeted us. There were mounds of salad, piles of bread, and a profusion of plastic bags, cool boxes and picnic-ware. The women sat at one tablecloth and the men at another. We were given a tour of the visitor centre and made to admire the stuffed, cross-eyed Persian leopards. Iran is their global stronghold, but fewer than a thousand are thought to be left in the wild. Like so many wild cat species, they can now live only in remote places because of hunting, poisoning and human development of their habitats.

There was more climbing the following morning, with sixty kilometres of energy-sapping gradient, made worse by a strengthening headwind. We emerged from the forest onto a high, arid plateau where yellow and red poppies dotted the dry ground, then continued our ascent to 1350 metres. At the crest of the hill we met a motorcyclist who was pushing his bike. Pleased to be able to do someone else a favour, we emptied our stove bottle into his tank. He seemed pleased, although somewhat dejected that he'd not met us earlier. From here it was a steep downhill into farmland. We stopped at the next petrol station and were immediately gifted a litre of petrol by the man working the pump.

The hot, forceful headwind continued into the next day too. With Mashhad now about three hundred kilometres east of us, we pedalled on stoically, through fertile valleys and gullies, greeted by countless enthusiastic families, presumably still on their Nowruz holidays, flagging us down on the road, having overtaken us earlier, and presenting us with oranges, bananas, flatbread or sweets. By mid-afternoon I was carrying three rounds of bread and a couple of kilos of fruit. At one point a car overtook us, then reversed back towards us, drew level and continued alongside us. A man leant out of the window and passed Ed a glass of tea. Once Ed was finished, the glass was refilled and passed to me. Tour de France, Iranian style.

Late that afternoon, a battered white saloon car began crawling alongside us, its family of occupants hanging out of the windows as we sweated up another hill, photographing us and gesturing for us to stop. Any cyclist will know that there is nothing worse than having to break momentum on a hill. The sun was searing through the back of my sweat-soaked shirt, my thighs were straining, and the smell of the exhaust from the car was choking. My focus slipped and my irritation levels rose. 'Don't they understand how hard this is!' I muttered to myself. Eventually we gave in and stopped and I felt guilty when after the obligatory photo session we were presented with sweets and issued with an invitation to stay when we reached Mashhad.

Soon after, a flash car screeched to a halt and a young man who spoke good English jumped out of the passenger's seat. He had just done his first parachute jump over the national park and was alight with the crazed joy of having survived it. He was excited to have found some fellow adventurers in us. Ed posed for photos with him, the setting sun burning the desert orange behind them. Next were an elderly man and a glamorous girl in another expensive-looking car. The man, owner of a local salt factory, presented us with his card. 'You must come stay at our house,' he said instantly. 'It would be an honour.' We were disappointed to discover that his house was forty kilometres away, too far to make that night. Our last encounter of the day was with a lone man in a suit. We greeted him, by now fully expecting to be welcomed to Iran or offered something from his boot, but instead he launched into a series of questions about us, in a tone that was more insistent than friendly. I was on guard. An invitation to come and stay with him was issued, which we declined politely, and he did not reissue it.

We camped that night in a gravel pit, hidden from the road. As the wind battered the rain against the canvas of the tent and we shovelled down soggy rice with a tin of olives, I imagined sitting cross-legged on a deep carpet in the salt factory owner's luxurious house, in front of a mound of steamed rice and lamb stew.

Had that last guy been secret police, we wondered?

I hopped out of the tent under the cover of darkness to have a pee. The wind was howling and car headlights were moving in the distance. Back inside, all I could hear was the rain on the canvas. There would be no possibility of catching the crunch of boots on gravel.

In the dark, all unknown places look unfriendly and threatening. The wind had changed direction, blowing at our backs now instead of slowing our progress. Our legs turned the pedals easily. The flow of traffic had increased again since passing through the town of Shirvan. Lorries rumbled by at regular intervals, but there was a decent hard shoulder to cycle on. As darkness fell, we found we'd been blown to the outskirts of an unmapped village. We had been cycling at well over thirty kilometres per hour for the last three hours and, seduced by the ease of travel, had not come to a decision about where to camp. A park twenty kilometres back would have been ideal, but it had seemed too soon to stop. Another passable spot later on had to be discounted because we'd forgotten to fill up with water so had to push on to the next service station.

We pulled off at a truck lay-by and examined the map under the sickly glow of the sodium lights. Dust and rubbish whirled past in the unrelenting wind. We crossed the road through an underpass and asked at a shop whose windows were illuminating a scrubby patch of wasteland whether they would mind us camping in front of them. The man who came outside to talk to us was confused by our presence and even more so when we gesticulated that we needed to camp. He eventually understood but shook his head. We retreated. It was impossible to blame him for refusing our bizarre request.

Just when it seemed we had no option but to push on along the dual carriageway, a young man emerged from an alley, came to an abrupt stop, hesitated for a moment, and then walked purposefully towards us.

'Salam,' we said.

'Salam.' A young, open face flashed a wide smile. He beckoned. 'Come.'

Within moments we were wheeling our bikes along a bumpy alleyway behind him. Blank walls gave way to a solid iron door, which opened into a courtyard.

'You stay here.'

We parked our bikes and were ushered indoors. There was a rustle of gathering chadors as women retreated. An older man stood up to welcome us, only a faint trace of surprise and questioning in his expression. After the introductions, there was an embarrassed silence bridged only by the background sound of the television. I looked around the room, which was carpeted in red machine-made city rugs and scattered with large cushions. On the walls was a painting of a dark bearded saint in a green turban, handsome and pensive, surrounded by a halo of pastel roses. Ali, Muhammad's son-in-law, revered noble warrior and the Shias' usurped rightful caliph. There was no furniture other than a display cabinet of crockery upon which stood a jar of plastic flowers and a statue of a camel.

The women were collecting cooking utensils behind the kitchen counter and smiled shyly at me before ducking down to take their place on the floor, out of sight behind the counter. Soon our host had phoned a male friend and an English teacher was brought in to fill the gap. He was just married and explained that his wife might be angry that he'd been dragged away, but he was glad to meet us. I imagined her having prepared one of their first dinners together for him. He left before ours was served.

I joined the women in the kitchen – mother, daughter-in-law and teenage daughter – while they grated potato and then fried it into cakes. When dinner was ready, the men waved me over, but I asked to stay with the women. The men protested, but the women took my side, pleased that I wanted to sit with them.

After we had eaten from the same plate, the extra food forced upon the men, I got out my photograph collection and showed the ladies my pictures of friends and family back home, and, always popular, the photos of our wedding. Then the daughter-in-law produced her mobile phone from within a fold of her chador and started to flick through a set of photos to show me. Picture after picture of romantic pastel images of couples walking along the beach at sunset, women entering the sea in bikinis or rolling in the sand, then a bare-breasted woman under a waterfall and another equally naked one under some palms. I tried to not register surprise as the girl nodded to me again – 'You like?' – as she had for every shot.

Did she fantasise about the lifestyle presented in the images that she had downloaded from the internet or which had perhaps been sent by a friend? Did she imagine that was how I spent my time back in the UK? Frolicking naked under a waterfall rather than clutching a hot-water bottle in pyjamas watching TV while the rain battered the single glazing? I'd come to realise that people saw Western culture through narrow filters, most of which seemed to revolve around fashion and pornography, with the boundaries between the two confusingly blurred and not self-evident.

The photograph I have to remember them by was taken in their courtyard the following morning, Ed standing with the men to one side of the bikes and the women standing with me, patterned chadors pulled tightly around manteaux, the wind off the steppe tugging at them, me in cycle helmet and headscarf, a long tunic over my trousers and a waterproof jacket on top, looking only slightly less wrapped up.

20

Money Laundering

I shall roll up the carpet of life when I see,
Thy dear face again and shall cease to be
For self will be lost in that rapture, and all
The threads of my thought from my hand will fall

Jami, trans. Frederick Hadland Davis, from 'Self Dies in Love', in *The Persian Mystics: Jami*

I knelt on a Persian rug, ironing dollar bills. The midday call to prayer crackled from the loudspeaker of the mosque as wafts of hot steam rose through the languid air to meet my face. I worked the point of the iron across a crumpled White House, then placed the note under the guidebook and took another. The creases weren't coming out easily. Water drops fizzled on the iron's metal plate and rolled off onto the next note, dispersing into damp stains. I muttered and ironed back and forth over them. As the patches faded, the corners of the note began to curl.

We had reached Mashhad three days ago. The desert had suddenly given way to the urban sprawl of Iran's second-largest city, bristling with concrete arteries along which the traffic roared and tooted. We spent more than an hour circling the city, desperately trying to avoid getting sucked into the network of underpasses that crossed under the shrine of Imam Reza, the holiest place in Shia Islam, mausoleum of the eighth imam of Twelver Shias and the biggest mosque in the world by area. Twelvers, the largest group of the Shia, believe that there are twelve imams who are the spiritual and political successors to the Prophet Muhammad, starting with Ali and ending with Imam al-Mahdi, who since 874 has lived in occultation (hidden) and will reappear only at the end of time. As such, Imam Reza is a major place of pilgrimage, welcoming 25 million pilgrims and honeymooners every year from across the Muslim world – including, some time back, our mountaineering friends Rezza and Nazanin.

So far, however, the city had seemed to us like a hot, concrete nightmare and noticeably more conservative than Tehran, with most women in chadors. We paused to consult the map yet again and an elderly lady came out of a shop bearing iced lollies for us, before disappearing into a car clutching three more for her passengers. Exhausted, we stopped in a park only to be approached by two young men who were dishevelled and smelt strongly of marijuana. When we eventually arrived at the budget hotel listed in our guidebook, we were grateful to wheel our bicycles into a courtyard, take our shoes off and sit on a carpeted balcony drinking tea.

Mahdi was a carpet dealer and the room I was ironing in was covered in a hotchpotch of tribal rugs coloured in shades of mulberry and pomegranate. The smaller, more intricate pieces were hung on the walls: a naive scene with two girls and chickens either side of a central tree; a beige panel featuring four stick sheep set in a lattice border. There was another huge pile of rugs in the corner, patterned borders protruding from the layers. Mahdi had unrolled each of them that morning, sending out the smell of dust and lanolin into the room as he described their special features. 'Typical armband design from Turkmenistan ... The red background is popular in Europe, but the Russians prefer blues and greens. A Kordish (Kurdish) carpet – see the deep pile? – but it is unusual for a tribal piece as it has a central medallion ... See, this one has the tree of life and those symbols are for good luck. This rug is for prayer. Look, the name of Allah ...' He talked continuously as he flattened them out on top of one another.

There were prayer rugs, saddlebags for horses or motorbikes, jug-shaped salt bags, tasselled spoon bags for storing small items, larger 'joval' bags for clothing. Kurdish rugs with stylised animals and people, even one with a man wearing a tie, and rugs with the Zoroastrian motif of the boteh, the 'eternal flame', that gave rise to the paisley pattern so common in Europe. Most were woven from sheep's wool and coloured with natural dyes made from indigo, walnut husks, madder and saffron. Wedding rugs often had a central field of undyed coffee-coloured camel hair containing the hopes of a bride-to-be, goats for wealth and birds denoting the number of children. Most of his Iranian customers, Mahdi said, preferred new, synthetic, machine-made carpets over these traditional, handwoven ones, considering the tribal rugs uncouth. He showed me a prayer rug depicting the tower of Gonbad-e Kavus in the central field and another with the hand of Fatima 'in the place where hands would go'. 'That should not be hung on a wall,' he said, 'and I would like to sell it to someone who will use it. It should be placed on the floor facing Mecca and rolled up when not in use.'

There were war rugs too, showing tanks, helicopters, aeroplanes or Kalashnikovs in repeating patterns, or scenes of battles in Afghanistan.

'They are just made by poor people and they weave what they see,' he said, shaking his head. And then more brightly, 'But big market in Europe and USA. There are special collectors.'

He purchased the rugs from nomads who brought specially made pieces or antique tribal heirlooms with them across the desert from Herat in Afghanistan, Ashgabat in Turkmenistan or Yazd in Iran to fund their pilgrimages to the shrine of Imam Reza. In the seventies he had driven vanloads to Switzerland with his wife, selling them to high-paying collectors in Zurich and Geneva. That was in a different era. Since the revolution, Iran had been placed under a raft of sanctions by Western governments in response to the Iranian government providing training, finance, weapons and safe havens for non-state militant actors such as Hezbollah in Lebanon and Hamas in Gaza, and because of Iran's uranium enrichment programme. Iran was in fact the most sanctioned country in the world until Russia invaded Ukraine in 2022. The effect of sanctions on the Iranian economy had been dire. Mahdi was now taking a tourism diploma at college and ran a homestay for the few Western backpackers that still ventured across Iran.

I could hear the clatter of pans upstairs, which meant we would soon be sitting down to lunch together on the shaded balcony laid with rugs, Mahdi's wife Masoumeh flitting barefoot between us and the kitchen to bring rice, fesenjoon (chicken cooked in a sauce of pomegranates and walnuts) and homemade yogurt. We had been at the homestay three days, our longest stay anywhere since Tehran.

I finished ironing the last note, re-knotted my headscarf to stop it from slipping forward and then pulled the pile out from under the guidebook to start another round of ironing. We had been told the dollar bills needed to be crisp and printed after 1996. These notes had travelled with us from the UK, rolled up and sewn into my sports bra, carried on sweaty mountain days and through soaking rainstorms. With trade embargoes making it next to impossible to access Western banking facilities of any kind in Iran, it would not be easy to get better ones. Mahdi had once had to temporarily bankroll a Dutch tourist who'd turned up in Iran expecting to use his credit card and then had to go all the way to Tehran so that his embassy could bail him out.

'Dollar!' a voice barked from a hatch in the wall of the Turkmen Embassy later that afternoon.

I peered into the dark to see a shirted arm moving the slips of paper we had just handed in around on a desk. A crowd of men pushed behind us, trying to see in.

'Dollar!' the voice barked again, sounding impatient.

We counted the dollar bills out from between the pages of our guidebook and the Iranian lorry drivers queuing behind us pressed round curiously as Ed handed over 150 dollars to pay for our visas. The hatch slammed shut and we continued standing in the searing sunshine. A five-day transit was the only visa the xenophobic regime of Turkmenistan issued for travellers, unless they were able to pay for an expensive tour guide, who would anyway probably not take kindly to us cycling. It was the only way we could cross into Uzbekistan and eventually China, other routes being barred due to war in Afghanistan.

'Nyet.' Two bills landed back on our side of the hatch, rejected.

Ed handed over our spares. Also quickly rejected. The lorry drivers shook their heads in sympathy.

We'd seen this before and knew that the official might get bored at any moment and simply tell us to come back next week, by which time our Iranian visas would have expired. Out of sight of the hatch, I placed the dollar bills between my hands and breathed on them, firmly flattening the notes out even more.

'Da ...' I'd duped him with the first.

'... Nyet.' The second was rejected.

'Spasibo. Please,' Ed begged.

Suddenly a stranger's hand reached over Ed's shoulder and placed a crisp fifty-dollar bill on the desk. I looked round to see a suited man snapping shut a briefcase lined with pristine bills, just as another hand from inside Turkmen soil grabbed the note. I thrust my limp fifty toward our saviour, but he just waved his hand dismissively.

We now had a few days to unwind before we needed to arrive at the Turkmen border on 26 April, when the window for our five-day transit visa opened.

I enjoyed regaining a sense of domesticity cooking with Masoumeh. She showed me how to make the rice with the tadikh crust in the way we had been served it by Zara at Mr Moghaddam's home in Golestan. She began by heating a generous amount of oil in a pan, to which she added slices of potato, then lightly sprinkled on layer after layer of freshly boiled al dente rice, put the lid on and cooked it on the lowest heat for an hour. This was the normal way to make rice in Iran. I cringed inwardly at the alternately soggy, al dente or burnt stuff I managed to produce on the ferocious flame of our camp stove.

Masoumeh made five litres of yogurt a day for the family, incubating the heated cow's milk in a heavy saucepan wrapped in a blanket. Milk was rationed by the government, but she told me that the daily milk queue was a good place to make enquiries about potential matches for one's children. In fact, given the restrictions on mixed-sex mingling, it was one of the only places for matchmaking.

One afternoon, Masoumeh lent me a chador and Mahdi showed Ed and me where to get the bus for the shrine of Imam Reza. 'You know it's terrible,' Mahdi said, looking me up and down as we stood at the bus stop, 'that women have to wear this. They can't easily do anything with their hands.' The chador is a simple length of cloth which has to be clasped shut with a hand or even bitten together between the teeth, something that I had noticed older women doing in particular. 'Their children can't recognise them in public. Imagine every woman looking the same if you are a lost child! Mammy! Mammy! Everyone the same in black! You know it is also so difficult for them when they have their period – so hot.'

I sat at the back of the bus with other ladies. The lunchtime call to prayer started midway through the journey and everyone turned in their seats to face Mecca and said their prayers. Ed and I then queued at the separate male and female entrances to the outer walls of the mosque complex, which had airport-style security. Clutching my chador tightly, I passed through without remark, but Ed, clearly a tourist in his cobalt-blue hiking jacket, was pulled aside and we were then directed to the Islamic Relations Office, where we were allocated a guide, a serious young woman. 'I am so glad you wore black,' she said to me in a kindly way after we had introduced ourselves. 'It is really so much better.' We followed her through the outer marble courtyards, smooth surfaces reflecting the hot sun. It was not busy, just a gentle ebb and flow of honeymoon couples, men dressed in their best suits or starched dishdashas, and people wheeling the elderly.

British travellers Robert Byron, in May 1934, and Colin Thubron, in the early 2000s, both obtained entry to the inner courtyard (illegally) despite their non-Muslim status. We had to content ourselves with mere glimpses of the turquoise domes and golden minarets beyond the cordon. Byron, who had painted his beard and adopted the dress of a lower-middle-class Persian man, described the inner Mosque of Gohar Shad as one of the four great buildings of Persia, along with the tower of Gonbad-e Kavus, and Isfahan's Friday and Sheikh Lotfollah mosques, all of which we had also visited. He felt the beauty of the tile work was only surpassed on the minarets of Herat.

Thubron, who arrived during a festival crush on the birthday of the twelfth imam, was swept along into the inner sanctum. He described how:

all its arcades and iwans, its open sanctuaries, shone in a mist of porcelain tiles. Its minarets were dusted with dark diamonds enclosing white script or blossoms, set in pale brick. Inside the iwans, the stalactites clustered in a scalloped density of aquamarine and white. New colours – mustard and rich damson – burnt under the vaults. And over all the spandrels a translucent foliage swarmed into golden blooms or a rain of milky flowers. In the court's centre, half obscured by pilgrims, a marble pool and fountain stirred. And along the roofline, in deep, continuous frieze, ran a bramble of magnificent script.

The rest of us non-Muslims have to make do with snippets of YouTube videos shot by Muslim tourists inside, footage of Muslims from across the world gathering in the vast courtyard in socked feet, clasping at the grilles of the tomb of Imam Reza under a ceiling of a thousand mirrors, the golden domes and minarets shimmering in the polished marble floor.

I was starting to feel faint in the bright sun. The midday heat radiating from the white marble was burning my face and sweat was pooling under the manteau and headscarf that I was wearing beneath the chador. Our guide gifted us each a large packet of postcards depicting close-ups of the magnificent frescoes forbidden to our eyes and we were seen safely through the exit.

We wrote and posted all the postcards, and, finally succumbing to the purchase of souvenirs, bought some rugs from Mahdi and sent those home too. One of them depicted four girls in bright high heels and knee-length dresses in a garden containing goats, peacocks and the tree of life. 'I love the fact they are wearing these modern dresses,' said Mahdi, cackling, before adding sternly, 'You must not put that on the floor either, because, see, the name of Allah is written up here.'

21

WOMAN, LIFE, FREEDOM

I could be wearing all the clouds in the world
and they'd still throw a cloak over my shoulders

Granaz Moussavi, trans. Dick Davis, from 'The Blue Headscarf's Words', in Dick Davis (ed.), *The Mirror of My Heart*

There was a concerning headwind blowing straight from Turkmenistan and the day was hot. By lunchtime we had covered seventy kilometres from Mashhad and rested in the shade of a bridge to escape the blazing sun. We stopped again later on, in a lay-by, and saw an enormous camel spider with meaty, hairy legs that had been squashed dead by the side of the road. It was the diameter of a side plate. I wondered if the Turkmen desert would be full of them and after that became much more watchful about what was on the ground and carefully tapped out my boots every morning.

The steppe was beautiful, though, allowing space to think. Crumbling cliffs in bands of pink and yellow sand. Sparse green vegetation dotted with poppies. An eagle soared above us on the lookout for ground squirrels, which had burrows dug into the sandy earth and were gathered in clusters of four or five, taking it in turns to keep watch. Hoopoe, with their black-and-white-striped wings, pecked at the ground, sandy crests bobbing, a sight unchanged since at least the ninth century, as described in a ghazal (trans. Paul Smith, in *Selected Poems*) by the great Persian-speaking poet Rudaki.

It was close to Sarakhs that I saw a hoopoe …
Whose small song to the clouds was reaching.
That one was wearing a little coat I observed
That was made up of such different colouring.
O you old world, so ugly, and so mixed-up …
Before you staggered and awed, I am standing.

We passed an encampment of six low grey and tan canvas tents in the soft folds of a low cliff, white jerrycans and blue water butts scattered around its perimeter, a large tripod for cooking, parked motorcycles and dogs scuffing in the dirt. A man lifted his arm in greeting from behind one of the tents.

As the afternoon drew to a close, the road steepened, heading over the brow of a line of cliffs. We dropped over the other side and took a dirt track to a platform overlooking the valley. The light was soft and the night warm. We pitched our tents on the baked earth between tussocks of thorn and grass. I primed the stove. Masoumeh had given us slices of kookoo sabzi for the journey and I munched on one, enjoying the fresh taste of the herbs in the omelette and the contrast with the sweetness of the raisins and slight bitterness of the walnuts as I cooked up much less inspiring dried pasta. The light intensified on the pink bands of rock as the sun began to set. There was the sound of birds chirruping.

We had now been in Iran for twenty-seven days and we would reach the border post at Sarakhs tomorrow, in time for an early departure the next day. A month ago, I had stood in icy wind at the ruined Ishak Pasha Palace in eastern Turkey, looking out to Mount Ararat and the Iranian border with a cold dread about what would come next. A month ago, my father had begged me not to cross the border to Iran and although it had hurt me to disregard his pleas, I had gone anyway. I had been communicating via occasional text messages to my mother since, not particularly unusual, but I could feel my father's silence stretching across the mountains and desert behind me.

Had the risk been justified? It was impossible to tell. Being a tourist in Iran had been exhausting, overwhelming and life-affirming – the way that good travel should be. We had seen a tiny slice of this complex nation. I wanted to stay longer. A month had been too short. Of course I wanted to see 2500-year-old Persepolis and to visit the Zoroastrian Fire Temples of Yazd and Hafez's tomb in Shiraz. I wanted to go back to Isfahan, which has undoubtedly the most beautiful public square on earth. I wanted to eat more, I thought, as I took another bite of kookoo sabzi! The disastrous Boof burger aside, the food, especially in the houses of people who'd hosted us, had been the best I'd eaten ever. Chicken fesenjoon, ghormeh sabzi, and the rice … The hospitality had been all-enveloping. Iranians were hospitable, curious, insistent, proud, Muslim not Arab (mostly), modern not American. Full of contradictions.

I wanted to understand more. Particularly about the lives of the women I had met and about what it took to live under the restrictions. Endure was a word I kept coming back to. So many of the women we had met were highly educated – Iran had the highest female university attendance in the Middle East and female literacy rates in the young were almost 100 per cent. So many were learning English despite it being unlikely they would ever travel abroad. They faced enormous legal and cultural restrictions. The legal age of marriage for girls was still thirteen.

Sitting in people's houses, there was more I would have liked to have asked the men as well as the women, but I was not brave enough. In part because of a genuine concern about the eyes and ears of the state being everywhere, and especially because of what careless talk might do to the Iranians we had contact with; in part because it seemed cruel to explore topics that I had little experience of and only false hopes to offer; in part because of not wanting to cause offence to our hosts. The choice to travel abroad, the choice to date instead of being chosen by a man from the milk queue, the choice to ride a bike … There was so much open to me that was not open to many of the women of Iran.

When Mahsa Amini died in custody a decade later, in 2022, after being arrested by the morality police for bad hijab, the protestors who took to the streets across Iran chanted 'Jin, Jiyan, Azidi', Woman, Life, Freedom. Opinion polls suggested the vast majority of Iranians opposed the compulsory hijab. The world's media was briefly outraged and Western female politicians and celebrities spoke out in solidarity. The message of the protests was clear: without female liberty, everyone's liberty suffers.

Travel to Iran made me a feminist. I hadn't thought of myself as a feminist until then. I returned to the UK thinking that women's rights were a problem mainly in far-off places, but having spent the decade and a half since our trip building a career in the UK, I've realised that this is far from true. The UK still has some considerable way to go. Even so, there is simply no comparison with what women in Iran and many other places have to endure, something I wish we Western feminists would remember in solidarity a little more often.

The moon and the stars had replaced the light in the sky. I sat there a little longer on my last night in Iran, wondering if I would come back; hoping I would come back.

Tea and Grit

TURKMENISTAN

 APRIL 2010

Tea and Grit

22

TURKMENITRANSIT: ACROSS THE KARAKUM DESERT

Imagine that you were set up to travel the world on a horse as fast as the wind.
(...)
If you happen to be in the desert and cannot find any shade,
Imagine you found shade in the Garden of Eden.

Magtymguly Pyragy, trans. Zohra Meredova, from 'Imagine', in Paul Michael Taylor (ed.) *Magtymguly: Poems from Turkmenistan*

'Not need this!' the border guard barked at me, plucking at a corner of my headscarf.

After a month of having a safety blanket to hide behind, I felt self-conscious lowering it in front of the assembled crowd of male Iranian truck drivers. The guard had a black bun scraped back high on her head and wore a calf-length skirt suit in heavy khaki material. Buttons and medals gleamed on her tightly jacketed and ample bosom. She called out orders to a male guard as she marched up to us, high heels clacking on the concrete floor, pointing at our bicycles, which we had wheeled inside the border office. We'd been waiting a long time behind the queue of drivers, trying to look entirely unbothered, even though I could feel the sand of the Karakum Desert running through a giant egg timer. We had five days to cycle 550 kilometres to the Uzbek border. Five days that were turning into four and a half.

'What this?'

'Chader. Palatka. Camping. Tent.' Ed mimed a triangle with his hand, offering up the word in Turkish and Russian, and started to open the bag.

'This?'

'Clothing.' Ed yanked at his shirt, mimed putting on a jumper and then helpfully pulled out his sweat-stained spare shirt.

'No. Okay.' She looked visibly disgusted. One could never be too helpful with border guards. 'You cycle from UK?' She rolled her eyes.

A strange phenomenon had started. Cycle-tourers and other overlanders on motorbikes and in campervans probably made up the majority of the handful of tourists here. Few others would have reason to transit Turkmenistan.

'Any medicines?'

'No.' A quick lie to protect our personal cargo of antibiotics.

The Iranian truck drivers who'd helped us negotiate our way through the crossing were looking on in amusement.

'Okay, you go,' she said, batting us away like a minor annoyance as we scrabbled to re-hook panniers onto our bicycles.

'Spasibo,' I said, giving her a big smile.

'Welcome to Turkmenistan, lady.' She smiled back, showing a complete row of gold teeth.

We started pedalling westwards on a dusty road and soon the headscarf was back on, covering not just my hair but my mouth as well. Our route would continue west for around twenty kilometres before dog-legging back east to the main road, which would ultimately swing northwards for five hundred kilometres across the Karakum Desert to the border with Uzbekistan. We had heard rumours of a short cut from other cyclists, but a scout around a dilapidated row of buildings at the likely area of the junction revealed no obvious track leading due north. The night before, we'd sat in the motel at Sarakhs and weighed the risk of wasting time on a potentially slow, sandy or thorny dirt track against the forty-kilometre detour and committed to the latter unless the way was obvious. There was no room for time-wasting errors, especially because the wind strength and direction could make the difference between doing thirty-five kilometres per hour and walking.

The wind was in our faces now and we were only doing nine kilometres per hour, one of us tucked in behind the other. The land was flat and shrubby and the sky grey. Irrigation ditches lined with poplars followed the road and led off at right angles, alongside dry fields of cotton plants.

We were soon led across the Karakum Canal, one of the longest canals in the world, built to carry the waters of the Amu Darya across the desert and to the criss-cross of irrigation channels that feeds the cottonfields. Constructed in the 1950s during USSR rule, the 1400-kilometre canal runs the length of Turkmenistan and is responsible in part for the disastrous shrinking and toxification of the Aral Sea. The Amu Darya and the Syr Darya, further north, both rise in the high mountains of Central

Asia and flow down to what was formerly the fourth-largest lake in the world. The Aral Sea once measured 68,000 square kilometres, but it began to shrink after irrigation projects on both tributaries were used to feed cotton fields in Turkmenistan, Uzbekistan and Kazakhstan. By the time we visited Turkmenistan, the sea had split into multiple smaller lakes and was now just 10 per cent of its original size. This left two major fishing ports high and dry and resulted in the disappearance of numerous species and mostly likely the extinction of the Syr Darya shovelnose sturgeon. The draining has caused salt concentrations in the lake to increase, and toxic dust storms of salt and accumulated pesticides from the cotton production threaten human health. The Central Asian cotton fields are some of the biggest producers in the world and forced child labour has been used extensively.

We slowed down for two soldiers who stood at a booth next to the empty road. They inspected our passports and then pointed at Ed's watch expectantly. While Ed patiently showed them some of the settings (without removing it from his wrist), I casually rooted around in my bar bag, happening across a packet of biscuits (which was offered but refused) and some cigarettes (which were accepted). We had bought a packet from a street seller on the Iranian side of the border for just such an encounter. They lit up and continued to eye the watch, but when we stood beaming dumbly at them they waved us on.

Occasional trucks passed us and we saw a few people working in the fields, but otherwise we were on our own. I pushed down hard in the pedals, against the wind, and told myself that we had never planned to cross the Karakum Desert by bike and that if we only made it the first two hundred kilometres or so to the train station at Mary, then so be it. What went unspoken between us, though, was that this was a test. This was about proving to ourselves that we could do it.

Part of me regretted that we would miss out on the capital of Ashgabat, famed for being the sterile showcase of Turkmenistan's megalomaniac dictator Niyazov, who died in 2006. We wouldn't get to see the twelve-metre-high gold statue of Niyazov on top of the Arch of Neutrality that followed the sun as it revolved, and nor would we try out the Walk of Health, a concrete stairway that ran for thirty-seven kilometres along treeless mountains around the city and which it was compulsory for all government officials to hike once a year. But I knew that I would regret not doing the long ride across the desert more. I wanted to approach Bukhara in Uzbekistan the hard way, like the many traders on the Silk Road who for millennia had driven their caravans across the desert.

We came to a strung-out row of houses on the road and stopped to ask a group for directions. I wheeled my bike towards them, slightly intimidated, and was soon surrounded by a crowd of brightly dressed women. Perhaps it was the relief after the muted colours of Iran, but Turkmen women seemed to dress in one of the most beautiful ways I'd seen. They wore long dresses in black, brown, blue, maroon or dark green, with embroidered necklines. Their headscarves, generally with paisley-style (boteh) patterns in brighter greens, golds, burgundies or purples, were somehow bound into stiff cones that sat far back on their heads. Over this they would sometimes wear secondary scarves wrapped so loosely over their heads as to make it look as if their hair was piled high at the back, framing their faces like halos.

A small woman in a large green headscarf with deep lines in her tanned face grabbed me and pressed me to her bosom. Gold teeth gleamed as she spoke to me, seemingly casting a blessing over me. I tried out my first rudimentary phrases of Turkmen, a language akin to Turkish. A younger woman handed me a bag of cakes, which turned out to be a sort of dried gingerbread. We would buy it in bulk when we found it – good fuel for our desert crossing. The women assembled themselves around me, happy enough for Ed to take a photograph.

In the end we found the turn-off easily because, just as we reached it, one of the Iranian truck drivers from the border overtook us and beeped and pointed as he turned off down the dusty road, a last greeting from Iran.

The light was starting to fade, but there was no sign of the fields giving way to better camping territory. At each side of the road there was an irrigation ditch that could only occasionally be crossed by a wooden plank and anyhow the heavy soil beyond was not a particularly inviting prospect. The ground was covered in a thin white sheen; whether that was dried salt or pesticide residue we weren't sure.

In the end we camped among some poplars in a dip at the edge of the road, reasoning that it would soon be dark and no passing truck would notice us. Normally we would have been concerned about camping in such an exposed place, but we had little choice. In the night, I was startled awake by the sound of a car drawing up close by, its headlights dazzling us through the tent. My heart pounded as Ed scrambled out in his pants and shouted 'Zdrastvuytye!' – Russian for 'Hello!' – over the noise of the engine. A loud squawk was heard and the man who had chosen to take his pee stop next to our tent shot back to his car and screeched away. We laughed about his likely tale of a pale and naked ghost emerging from the darkness!

The following days followed a similar pattern. Dawn would break cool and dewy, alleviating our clamminess a little. Days of hard cycling in the heat and no washing meant that, like the ground, we were permanently covered in a layer of salt topped with grease, dirt and suncream. If we had enough water, we would treat ourselves to a heated pan with some flakes of soap in it and use a small corner of a trek towel that I had sewn into flannels to wipe away some of the worst grime. Breakfast consisted of yesterday's flatbread, called 'non' in Turkmenistan. This was heavy but good when fresh. It was round and had a rim like a plate and was decorated with different designs of whorls and interlocking circles made up of small dots. The tool that made these designs was called a durtlik, or bosma, and apart from letting the steam escape it also stamped the baker's unique pattern on the bread. Durtlik were in fact often made from recycled bicycle spokes. I loved this bread, but it quickly went stale. Every morning, we rehydrated broken chunks in hot chicken stock, making a sort of breakfast porridge, which became surprisingly palatable, perhaps because of our constant loss of salt.

Food was a big issue. We set off at eight and tried to do at least forty kilometres before stopping. The morning's task was to find food and water before it was time for lunch. We would pull up at a truck stop with tapchan (tea beds) built out by the canal and shaded by trees, but there was no time to sit and rest, just to buy dried biscuits, bread, macaroni and water. We were not going to take chances with any local sources. The only water we could see was in the network of brown canals over which the long drops were placed, so our bikes wobbled with five little cans strapped to the back. We had left the comforts of Iran: truck-stop toilets no longer provided water for washing and only if you were lucky would there be a bucket of torn-up school jotters or scraps of fabric for loo paper.

As the morning drew on, the heat rose and the winds picked up. Despite having changed direction from the first day, we were soon cycling into a headwind again, one behind the other, with Ed cycling at the front for twenty minutes and then me taking over for ten; we found that this was the fastest rhythm, as I tired more quickly. The need for efficiency left no room for pride. When the wind was at its strongest and we were only managing eight kilometres an hour we'd reduce Ed's time at the front to ten minutes and mine to five. At the end of my stint, I would be desperate to hand over and feel the resistance on the pedals slacken. Our faces burnt in the sun. We passed women, working in the cotton fields, hunched down, with their entire faces swathed in bright cloth, only their eyes showing.

On the second day we reached the town of Mary close to lunchtime. The quality of the road surface began to improve and suddenly we were in a smart town with tree-lined streets and gleaming buildings. On every street, groups of women, faces completely covered and wearing dayglo vests over their dresses, brushed the streets, bent low, with brooms. At first I thought they were convicts. A group of girls in emerald silk dresses walked down the street carrying schoolbooks, wearing the most beautiful school uniform, which of course was the colour of the national flag. A band of red carpet with five different gul (medallion) designs representing the major tribes of Turkmenistan runs down the left-hand side of the green flag. Just to the right sits the crescent moon of Islam and five stars for the five pillars. The Turkmen consider themselves a nomadic people and practise a Sunni faith blended with animist beliefs.

Occasionally, we'd see an expensively and scantily dressed Russian-looking woman tottering along the street or stepping out of a blacked-out 4x4. The town itself seemed lifeless. There was a shiny five-star hotel, a library and a museum but not a single eatery or roadside stall was apparent. We stopped at an open-air market where women were hawking piles of cheese, vegetables and packed goods. A large lady in a voluminous purple shift hurried to a house door just behind the market to get us bread, and a girl with an emerald headscarf knotted round her neck and matching green eyes packed our grocery bags. When she smiled at me, I just managed to hide my surprise at the gold teeth shining out from her beautiful young face. I asked if I could take a photo with her, which she agreed to delightedly, hugging me tight and complaining how short she was in comparison to my average European height. In order to look 'better' for the photo, she took off her beautiful scarf.

We cycled long after the sun had set, past people walking home from the fields. Few seemed to have a private vehicle here and there was not the usual swarm of two- and three- wheeled beasts on the road at dusk. We camped at the edge of a cotton field and the moon rose as we cooked while wearing mosquito nets. In the morning two elderly brothers found us. They brought us a wheel of non and sat on their haunches talking to us over breakfast as their donkey grazed by a tree. When they grasped that we had come from 'Angliya', they shook their heads and looked solemn, telling us that they were sorry about all the problems in our country. Press freedom in Turkmenistan is one of the most restricted in the world, on a par with North Korea, and we wondered what disaster stories about the West were being emphasised in order to ensure the populace knew how lucky they were to live in Turkmenistan.

Crops gave way to bare sand, the headwind persisted and the temperature rose. There was no shade for lunch save a tiny patch under a tamarisk bush that we wedged ourselves under. After bread with sun-heated and fizzing cottage cheese, I dozed for ten minutes, waking up feeling worse than before.

Towards the end of the day we came to a small, dusty town with a chaikhana, a teahouse. While we drank tea and bottles of Turkmen Coke, the lady offered us a visitors' book which was full of entries from other cyclists. Not so surprising, because with the road to Pakistan closed except to those with a military escort, due to the insecurity in Afghanistan in the aftermath of the US–Coalition invasion, this dusty road was one of the main – if not the main – highways linking Europe and Turkey to China. That evening, when the light had gone milky and a hint of cool had crept into the air, I blinked and, yes, there was a cyclist, all Lycra and skinny tyres, wobbling out of the haze towards us, closely followed by a car. We stopped and shouted hello as he passed us, head down, earphones in, the car crawling two metres behind him. Barely a nod of acknowledgement as he raced past, on some sort of mission, perhaps. Unbelievable!

We wheeled our bikes off into the sand dunes, away from the headlights of any trucks that might pass in the night, and sat out late, enjoying the cool air. Later we lay on a million grains of sand looking up at a million stars. My back and limbs ached. I squeezed Ed's hand in the darkness, glad that we had each other and that we were not in a hurry.

It was another hot, windy day. The never-ending desert was punctuated by occasional Bactrian camels grazing on shrubs at the side of the road. Often, I wondered if I was really doing this at all – could I really be cycling across the desert, passing camels? A blacked-out 4x4 slowed and wound down its windows. The driver was gesticulating excitedly and we stopped to speak to him and his teenaged children. A half-drunk bottle of ice-cold Coke was handed out for us to take a swig from and I could feel the cool breeze of the air conditioning from inside the car. We were given a bottle of water before they drove off, which was a godsend as we'd been worrying about how long it would be until the next stop.

At a checkpoint, women swarmed around us, selling trinkets including small, handmade felt camels. I was negotiating over two of them, unable to understand if the women were asking for dollars or manat, when a suited man with a briefcase came up to the stall and bought them for me. The camel hung from my handlebars, swaying in the deserts of Central Asia, reminding me of how generous the people of Turkmenistan had been.

We spent our final night in Turkmenistan in Turkmenabat, another anachronistically gleaming city, where polished tower blocks, deserted triple carriageways and blacked-out people carriers emerged from the dust. We found a room tucked away in an ageing tower block and had just enough energy to gulp down a thin bowl of lamb stew provided by the statuesque dezhurnaya (floor lady). I had a cold wash in a vast bathtub and imagined how many legions of civil servants posted here from Moscow, St Petersburg or the outer reaches of the USSR would have done likewise over the years, trying to cool down and escape the blinding sun. I told myself that I should be taking advantage of the water supply to wash our sweat-encrusted clothes but instead collapsed into a deep sleep on threadbare cotton sheets.

Uzbekistan

 May 2010

Tea and Grit

23

UNDER THE SHADE OF A MULBERRY TREE

All is as it is supposed to be:
There is happiness now, be happy.

Rudaki, trans. Sassan Tabatabai, from 'Destiny's door', in Sassan Tabatabai (ed.), *Father of Persian Verse: Rudaki and his Poetry*

To cross the wide, muddy, fast-flowing Amu Darya we had to negotiate a series of loosely connected metal plates on floats with gaps between them big enough to swallow a bike tyre. The bridge was wide enough for two vehicles, but lorries in both directions drove on the upstream side to avoid tipping it over. We cycled slowly over the smooth plates, which wobbled with each oncoming vehicle. Forty kilometres on – twenty-five more than was shown on our map – we crossed the border into Uzbekistan.

An hour or so later, a large group of men picnicking under the trees waved us over. We sat shoeless on a big blanket and were offered the remains of a lamb stew scented with coriander from blue-and-white-painted crockery bowls. The men all wore doppi, the boxlike hats of the Uzbek, in a sun-faded black fabric with white embroidery in scrolls or paisley patterns. They greeted us with robust shakes of their leathery hands, grinned at us with gappy smiles punctuated by gold teeth and served us green, not black, tea, in smaller bowls of the same blue and white. An empty vodka bottle lay among the pile of cooking utensils.

Scrubland gradually gave way to fields interspersed by small copses of willow and poplar and villages started to appear. Irrigation channels of thick, stagnant water ran through the baked clay at regular intervals. At a small shop we stopped to resupply and came away with biscuits, eggs and bread, and bottles of luminous yellow fizzy drink in place of water. The acrid taste of sweeteners made it barely drinkable despite our thirst. Water would continue to be a problem.

We camped that night in the courtyard of a wayside chaikhana, the kindly owners bustling with our bags and helping us to pitch our tent. We were immensely relieved to have met them just as night was falling.

The husband poured water from a jug over our hands so that we could wash them before we sat down to dinner, a practical and touching gesture we had encountered many times in areas without mains water. We ate dumplings in a delicious broth speckled with dill and fresh coriander. I could feel the salty liquid surging into my parched system and chased it down with bowl after bowl of green tea. Only later did I realise that the handwashing jug – and the kettle too, I feared – had been filled from the same brown irrigation ditch over which the toilet hung.

As in Turkmenistan, this was land where cotton was literally sucking the water away, much of it evaporating in open irrigation systems before it even reached the crops. Also as in Turkmenistan, the fields were covered in a crust of white residue.

Everywhere now, men wore Uzbek hats and women wore a loose version of the salwar kameez: short-sleeved tunics over baggy trousers gathered at the ankle. Most were in a local style of ikat or abra fabric, where the warp threads had been tied and dyed in different colours along their lengths, producing when woven a fabric of geometrical patterns that bled into each other in the colours of the rainbow. Small headscarves were knotted behind the head in a style similar to that of the Roma people of Europe. Gold teeth flashed from virtually every smile.

When we stopped for lunch on a bench the following day, for the first time in months a woman addressed us in public. She was with a small, tubby girl with a shorn head who kept on running away and had to be recalled as we spoke. Girls everywhere seemed to have their hair cut short when they were young. The small girl was scared of us and did not appreciate her mother's insistence that we take their photograph. In the photo a beautiful woman in a purple headscarf smiles a gold smile as her daughter tugs urgently at her arm.

Bukhara was at the crossroads of two major branches of the Silk Road, one coming from Kabul and Balkh in Afghanistan in the southeast and crossing northwest to Khiva and then the Caspian Sea; the other, the one we had travelled, running southwest–northeast, from Mashhad and Iran to Kashgar in China. Silk, obtained from the cocoons of the larvae of the mulberry silkworm, was made in China thousands of years BC and kept a closely guarded secret. In 105 BC a Chinese emperor sent emissaries to the Parthian ruler of Persia and a few decades later the Persians unfurled silk banners at their battle against the Romans at Carrhae (Harran), near Urfa in modern-day Turkey. We had visited the site with its beehive mud dwellings two months earlier, an ancient trading capital of the Fertile Crescent that predated the Roman era by thousands of years, perhaps all the way back to the twenty-fifth century BC. It was said that the sight of the silk banners fluttering in the breeze intimidated the Romans into fleeing, precipitating one of their greatest military defeats.

Defeat notwithstanding, silk would soon become hugely popular in Rome – so popular, in fact, that attempts were made to ban the cool but scandalously contour-revealing fabric. The Romans' thirst for luxury was insatiable and the Silk Road would bring them and successive civilisations of the West many more goods in addition to silk. Over the centuries exports included porcelain, paper, gunpowder, jade, rhubarb and medicines from China; cashmere, sandalwood, cotton cloth and cane sugar from India; rubies and lapis lazuli from Afghanistan; silver from Tibet; horses from Central Asia; roses and tulips from Turkey; pistachios, dates and walnuts from Persia; and frankincense and myrrh from Arabia. In return, bronze, glass, wool and linen were traded from the West.

In 965 a Jewish merchant from Spain reported that dirhams struck in Samarkand in 914 were in circulation at Mainz market on the Rhine. Also being traded there were spices that came from India: pepper, ginger, cloves, costus (a spice made from the root of Himalayan thistles) and galangal. Routes went north too, where fur was bought and sold in vast quantities.

People were traded as well – slaves, acrobats, musician and mercenaries – and so were ideas. Mystics and men of religion spread Buddhism from India west to Turkmenistan, Zoroastrianism east from Persia to India, and Christianity east to China. And, of course, from the seventh century onwards, Islam spread from Arabia in all directions, with the Abbasid caliphs from their stronghold in Baghdad controlling trade along the Silk Road from Sicily to Afghanistan up to 1258.

Bukhara had been the religious and cultural heart of the semi-autonomous Samanid dynasty in the ninth and tenth centuries and its madrasas nurtured some of the greats of the Islamic world. These included Ibn Sina, known in English as Avicenna, the philosopher-medic who when he was just sixteen healed the ruler of Bukhara and went on to write the *Canon*, the principal medical text of the medieval era and European medicine right up until 1650. The city was also home to Ibn Sina's great rival, al-Biruni, a polymath astronomer, and to Ferdowsi, the Shakespeare of Persian literature and author of the epic *Shahnameh*.

In 1220 Genghis Khan razed Bukhara to the ground, but by the sixteenth century it was flourishing again as the capital of the Bukhara khanate, with three hundred mosques, a vast market, many caravanserais, and madrasas able to teach ten thousand students.

On the suburban approach it was difficult to conjure up anything of the reputation the fortress city once held as we cycled past lines of dreary flats in grey and pistachio, and orange dogs roaming the dried-up communal gardens. The setting sun fell on the ancient fortress walls of the Ark as we arrived, lengthening the shadows of the wooden staves that poked at right angles from its vast mud-brick flanks, apparently a way to regulate the humidity. The Ark had been the seat of Bukhara's fearsome emirs, including Nasrullah Khan, who had obtained his throne in 1827 by executing his brothers and twenty-eight other relatives and went on to behead two British agents attempting to negotiate a friendship treaty.

The area in front of the city walls was deserted and swept clean. We stopped to buy what looked like yogurt-coated peanuts from a toothless woman sitting cross-legged against the fortress wall. She had piles of them arranged in plastic bags at her feet, packets of cigarettes and a stack of fizzy drinks. She adjusted her white headscarf, draping the ends over her purple dress, and then insisted we photograph her, charging us for the privilege. The white balls were indeed a sort of dried yogurt; solid and chalky, they tasted rancid to us.

Inside the old city we came to the Kalon Minaret, constructed from honey-coloured bricks arranged in alternating bands of geometric shapes and diamond patterns. It has stood since 1122 and so impressed Genghis Khan that he ordered it to be spared when he raided the city; he clearly had a penchant for grand towers (or saw their strategic use) as he also had Gonbad-e Kavus saved. Throughout the centuries the Kalon Minaret was used for adhan, in this holiest of Central Asian cities, as a strategic lookout, and for executing criminals, giving it the name 'the Tower of Death'. A royal wife who'd fallen out of favour allegedly survived her death sentence by wearing all of her skirts to slow her drop. Craning my neck to scan the forty-six metres of tower, I thought this unlikely.

As in Isfahan, blue-domed mosques and blue-tiled madrasas filled the old city. There were wonderfully breezy passages through covered, domed bazaars. Stallholders packed the otherwise empty streets with tourist trinkets. Vivid silk scarves and silk carpets shimmered from the roofs of alleyways. Suzani, brightly embroidered wall hangings that had once been dowry pieces, were stacked in piles in the madrasas, red pomegranates on a white background a typical Bukhara design. Blue- and green-painted ceramics lined the pavements in well-ordered displays as European tourists, mainly middle-aged and French, snapped photographs and ambled past in ergonomic travelling shoes and bumbags. Uzbek families were tourists too. The women of one family – a mother and three daughters all dressed in matching pink, green and purple ikat – lined up for photos in front of the brick minaret. A little later I watched as a group of teenaged boys in skullcaps, blue shirts and flannel trousers jostled each other on the front steps of the cobalt, turquoise and ochre-tiled pishtaq entrance gate of the Nadir Devanbegi Madrasah, originally built as a lodge for itinerant Sufi mystics in 1620. Two jade birds with snow-white wings and twisting tail feathers hung frozen in flight on the arches above the boisterous boys while a portly teacher in a suit directed them to stand in formation.

A flat-capped youth on a rickety bicycle led us through a warren of narrow passages between tightly packed two-storey buildings towards the promise of a guesthouse. It was good to be out of the blazing sun, but we were in the guts of the old town now, far from the sanitised alleyways of the bazaars. We navigated our bikes round pot-holes and pools of murky liquid and rotten vegetables as the smell of baked urine infused the air and electricity cables criss-crossed above our heads. Heavy wooden doors adorned with brass studs and door knockers were carved with geometric patterns of stars or, highlighting Buddhist links, swastika designs.

We came to a halt at a solid metal gate and passed through it into a low stone passageway in which a battered, boxy cream Lada was parked.

A small flight of steps led up to a raised, enclosed courtyard in the middle of which a vast mulberry tree was shedding its berries. Piles of the white raspberry-shaped fruits were drying on plates and sheets, turning brownish in the sun. Rooms led directly off the courtyard and through the open doors I could see each had a mattress on the floor (and sheets that turned out to be of dubious cleanliness). The walls were decorated with niches carved from the thin wooden panelling and painted with geometric borders and stylised vases of flowers. I had seen these in one of Shah Abbas I's Isfahan palaces and, weeks later in China, I would spot a ripped-out panel of this type lying in the rubble in Kashgar's old town.

The guesthouse owner, Mobinjon, a wiry man with a small paunch hidden by an oversized leather jacket, slicked-back grey hair and a permanent aura of cigarette smoke, was busy dealing with some German tourists who were complaining about the lack of a bathroom. When they left to find another pension, he shook his head and then looked at us as if daring us to complain. 'Hammam is close by.' He jerked his head. 'Mobinjon good.'

We drank tea with him in the courtyard. Green tea in cracked, gilt-edged china bowls, sun-worn hands tremoring slightly as he twice poured the tea into the bowl and back into the pot, serving us on the third pouring. We were offered a tray with drying scraps of day-old non and sweets in bright wrappers as he lit up. He showed us his collection of sprinting medals. He had once run a hundred metres in 10.4 seconds – 'best fast man in Central Asia' – and had qualified for the 1980 Summer Olympics in Moscow, which were boycotted by the West because of the Soviet invasion of Afghanistan. An injury and a reciprocal USSR boycott of the 1984 Atlanta Games had put an end to his Olympic career. Later we saw Mobinjon taking tea in the courtyard with the local mayor, now in a suit jacket with his running medals pinned to it. The gate we had come in through was painted with the Olympic flame.

Mobinjon's grandfather had been a wealthy camel-caravan trader and the family had had to defend their 'bourgeois' home from the Bolsheviks in 1920. Once the Red Army had forced the emir, Alim Khan, to flee his lavish palace, they then raised a vast red flag atop the Kalon Minaret and proceeded to go door to door arresting merchants. Mobinjon's grandfather, who'd had to defend his caravans many a time on the road, refused to surrender. He threw the Red Army captain against the wall, a gunfight ensued, servants jumped to his defence, and eventually the grandfather was shot. Mobinjon's mother, fifteen years old at the time, vowed never to give in. She worked her way up the Soviet system to become a teacher and somehow managed to hang on to the house.

The house was truly worth hanging on to. It was magnificent. Encircling the courtyard was an upper balcony supported by carved poles in dark wood, similar to those of the emirs' eighteenth-century Bolo Haouz Mosque opposite the Ark. Its walkway was whitewashed and had stalactite combing and painted friezes of geometric bands and false windows dressed with floral designs in pistachio, blue and yellow. White doves cooed on the balcony and fluttered down to the courtyard, Mobinjon batting them away from the mulberries. Each of the rooms surrounding the courtyard had fretwork grilles in the wall to keep the air fresh.

That evening, I lay on my front in the ramshackle banya (public baths) while a stern masseuse dug her elbows into my back, twisted my arms above my shoulders and then placed her fingers between my toes before yanking them with a violent tug so that they all cracked. I had already scrubbed myself clean with scalding water. Ed received the same treatment. Together, we floated back to our guesthouse feeling deliciously clean, all our aches pummelled. The dusk air had cooled just enough for us not to break out in a sweat.

The most enjoyable thing about Bukhara was the chaikhanas. There were tapchan – tea beds – in leafy gardens everywhere: large raised wooden platforms, some of them ornately carved, generally the size of a double bed frame, with a railing to act as a backrest and thin mattresses so that diners could sit cross-legged and take tea and food on a cloth or low table. Here we would sit, in the dappled shade, eating laghman (a soup with thick noodles), shashlik (skewers of lamb), tomato and cucumber salad with piles of herbs and yogurt, and shorba (lamb broth). The tea was always green, served in large blue-and-white pots with ceramic or china piala (tea bowls). It made me feel calm. The fresh taste of coriander. The satisfying slurping of noodles. The hydrating salt broth. The astringency of green tea. The custom of pouring tea between the cup and the pot, a third cup always brought in case a guest arrived. The breaking of the rounds of non. The blessed value of shade and the continual presence of heat. The sense of being a tiny part of the traffic of the Silk Road, unceasing for centuries.

As we sat under the shade of a mulberry tree, tucking into a second round of noodles, for the first time it seemed to me that we had a realistic chance of crossing Central Asia and reaching China.

24

THE ROAD TO SAMARKAND

Till you have endured dire straits on that road,
Your soul is two-faced, though your form is one.
> **Sanai, trans. D. Pendlebury, from 'The Walled Garden of Truth', in Peter Washington (ed.),** *Persian Poems*

Ed was gone.

I blinked, trying to absorb it.

Ed was gone.

He had chased the man who'd threatened us with our dog-beating stick. Ripped in a swift move from the back of my bike. Ed's camera, money and mobile phone had been taken from his bar bag. The other men had run off.

Ed was gone.

I mentally put myself on the map: a dirt track running through a willow-lined cotton field. One day's cycle from Bukhara. At least one more day's cycle to Samarkand. Uzbekistan. More than ten thousand miles from home. Alone.

'ED!'

Where were the other men? I scanned up and down the track. Where was Ed? Which field? I started towards the drainage ditch and then thought better of it. Stay where you are. Stay with the bikes so that we can get away.

The men had come up to us while we were eating a late lunch under a tree. They were farmworkers drunk on vodka. We yielded to rounds of handshakes, but they had cracked a few too many jokes in Uzbek, so we started to pack up our tarp, flatbread and cottage cheese as casually as we could. Then, somehow, they were around us as we loaded up the bikes, us still keeping up polite banter. One hugged Ed in jest, and then – that old chestnut – moved in to hug me. I ducked away. A hand prevented Ed from opening his bar bag. Another pulled a handful of notes out of Ed's wallet, a third grabbed our dog-beating stick. Ed roared, 'WHERE IS MY CAMERA?' and they scarpered in all directions.

Another farmworker who had paused to watch the drama started up his tractor and disappeared. Ed raced away, stick in hand.

'Ed!'

I couldn't hear anything.

Then some crashing in the undergrowth and far up the path a figure appeared.

'ED!'

It was not Ed.

It dropped a dark object. Instinctively I raced towards it. The phone? And then ... THUD!

Pain radiated through my knee and wrist. I was face down in the grit.

F***! F***! F***! My foot had got caught in the ditch. I struggled up, tears welling. My leg wasn't working.

'ED!'

'It's alright. I'm here.' He stood next to me. 'I got the camera.'

I could sense someone behind one of the hedges. Neither of us wanted to risk another encounter by searching for the phone.

We were trembling as we got onto our bikes and pedalled off towards the main road, back to the safety of passing trucks and minibuses, craving to be absorbed into the anonymity of the flow of traffic.

We cycled in silence. Hearts pounding, then slowing. Thinking. My knee burnt and creaked with every pedal stroke. Five minutes later a battered green-and-white police car passed us and my heart started up again. 'Definitely not going to the police,' I said. We didn't want to be squeezed for money or questioned about why we were here. And I didn't want to be responsible for sending someone to an Uzbek prison – or worse. I'd read an Amnesty International report about people being tortured – boiled alive, even – in Uzbek prisons. Enough stories not to want to get involved with officials more than we could help.

We'd been carrying the stick – actually a long, heavy piece of wood – since eastern Turkey and our confrontation with the Kangal shepherd dogs, teeth bared, streaming down the hillside towards us, but we'd never used it. And now it had been used to threaten us. Not any more, though. The Turkish stick we'd carried across Iran and Turkmenistan was now lying in an Uzbek field and we did not replace it.

'I actually think the guy I chased was s***ting himself that I was going to beat the crap out of him, which is why he dropped the camera.'

'I'm not sure you should have run after them anyway.'

'Yeah, I know. Stupid reaction. F***ing stupid.'

There was always an edge of unpredictability when meeting groups of men like that. Sometimes it felt as if the atmosphere hung in the balance and we'd have to work hard to keep it from flipping in the wrong direction. In Serbia one time, at ten in the morning, a group of men in combat fatigues sitting on benches in a village flagged us down and made us drink shots of rakia and look at phone pictures of their machine guns. They were hunters, they said. 'We hunt many things here. Animals and people,' the scar-faced ringleader added darkly. We nodded with polite interest. Then in Albania, when we were attempting to cross from Berat to Gjirokastër over a pass on an appalling road, we accepted a lift and were taken to a small bar where I was left outside with the children while Ed was invited for five rounds of firewater and told stories about bandits on the road. An enthusiastic and increasingly drunk young man then insisted on driving us on to Gjirokastër. In Syria, at the edge of a refugee camp near Hama, we were stopped by a group of men who were drinking maté by the side of the road. It was clearly an unofficial checkpoint. Some of the men looked Arabic, some South American. The boss had a salt-and-pepper slick-back and lounged back on his plastic chair with his legs wide apart, dishdasha taut over them, Cuban heels visible under the hem, and smoke wafting over the collar of his leather jacket.

'Are you not afraid here?' he said, fixing me with piercing blue eyes.

'Why?' I replied. 'What is there to fear?'

There had been a few other incidents like that, where the threat of violence hung unspoken and there was a palpable sense of relief when the encounter came to an end, but this was the first time things had tipped over into actual violence. Our job was always to jolly the men along and extract ourselves as quickly as possible without creating an excuse for offence. Alcohol added a particular element of unpredictability.

A car slowed down and beeped next to us, and some hands reached out, flapping. For a moment I pulled closer into the kerb, alarmed, heart beating fast, expecting the worst. And then I saw the smiling faces of two women peering out of the grubby window and remembered to smile and wave back. 'I'm not going to let those men change anything,' I said out loud.

The landscape was flat, with clusters of villages strung out along the road. Most of the land was given over to farming, small green shoots struggling out of the cracked yellow earth. There were going to be few places to camp unless we managed to hide in a copse like the one we'd had lunch by. I shivered. There were certainly no towns big enough to have a hotel. We were definitely not keen on camping by the side of a field, ready to bump into workers, perhaps even the same ones, as they came home.

The sun was low and casting tall, wobbly bicycle shadows out into the fields beside us. In the distance the bright dots of headscarves showed that women were still out working. We were just debating whether to ask at the last farmhouse in town or strike out onto the treeless plain when a man stepped over a tiny bridge across the canal and signalled for us to stop. Within quarter of an hour we had set up our tent on the bare ground behind the house. The farmhand and his friend did not seem to feel the need to entertain us. They sat cross-legged on a tapchan in front of the house, finishing off a dinner of chicken as we cooked up pasta on the ground nearby. Just before it grew dark, a big man turned up in a car, accompanied by a plump wife and teenaged daughter. The women milked the cow that was tethered in the courtyard as we talked to the jolly farm owner. As soon as the milking was done and we had taken a few photographs at their bidding, they drove off again, leaving us to crawl into our tent in the half-light and listen to the howling of the dogs tethered to their posts.

Pain from my fall into the ditch radiated through my knee the next day. We discussed whether we might need to take the train or a bus but decided it would be less hassle to keep pedalling, however slowly. We sat having a breakfast of eggs in a café and were pestered by a woman who was drinking beer. It was 8am. At lunchtime we chose to sit on a grass verge in a dip below the road but were found by an old man who was drunk but friendly. This was a noticeable change from Iran, Turkey and Syria.

Later, we ate plov for the first time, served to us by the proprietor of a tiny café despite our insisting that we just wanted chai. Within minutes, a steaming mound of plov, two spoons and two small salads were set in front of us. As the second salad was set down, the proprietor adjusted his doppi and announced that no payment would be necessary. He leant back against the post of the kitchen door, sturdy arms crossed over his broad chest, to watch us eat and beamed at our compliments.

Plov, which is Uzbekistan's national dish, was available at many chaikhanas at lunchtime provided you arrived before it ran out. It was essentially a risotto, or in fact pilaff, that contained lamb and onion and often also shredded carrots, pumpkin and raisins. It was cooked in a vast paella-like vat. Generally the roasted lamb was shredded and placed on top, although the flavour of lamb pervaded the dish due to the large amounts of sheep-tail fat. From now on we'd find that sheep everywhere had enormous bottoms that flapped comically as they ran. They were bred especially for this delicacy. Once we became connoisseurs, the best plov, as far as we were concerned, was easy on the bottom fat and was instead served with half a boiled egg on top. For this, our first experience of plov, we were given a boiled egg and plenty of raisins. Our judgement may have been coloured by our rush of gratitude for this kind man, who was not just feeding us but also nourishing our slightly bruised souls with his hospitality, but I think by far the tastiest version we had was that first one. Later, in the High Pamirs, where food was scarce, I would often dream about this meal.

We camped in a farmyard where children brought us cherries and non. The next morning the tent was heavy with dew in the humid air. We packed up at sunrise and stopped at a chaikhana, the first customers of the day, where we sat outside watching trucks go past while we ate fried eggs, stale bread and tea. The spotty youth who served us tried to charge us a ridiculous amount for sugar, the equivalent of five dollars. We batted him away, laughing as if it were a joke, but felt surprisingly angry by this unusual attempt at extortion.

The fierce sun was high in the sky by the time we reached the town of Juma on the outskirts of Samarkand. The throng of motorbikes, bicycles and stubby Daewoo vans piling up at the side of a square signalled that there was a bazaar close by. We squeezed our bikes through the crowd and I went round the stalls buying lunch. Lines of women stood with fresh wheels of golden non, each stamped with their own pattern, the rest wrapped in blankets in a basket or a pram, resupplied by a teenaged boy pulling a trolley of hot bread behind his bicycle. There were grated pickled vegetables – carrot, cucumber, cabbage and pepper – scooped out from buckets, and bunches of spring onion, coriander, dill and parsley tied together to be sold with the white cottage-cheese-like suzma, a strained yogurt that we'd been eating regularly since entering Turkmenistan. And there were mounds of hot pastries filled with meat – samsa. I grew to love these opportunities to speak to the bazaar stallholders. Often they would offer me things to try, ask me where I was from and sometimes fight for my custom. I returned laden with a large picnic, stomach juices flowing, to find Ed surrounded by a crowd already munching a pastry given to him by a nearby stall owner.

We pushed our bikes back through the crowds and cycled along the road for as long as we could bear until we came to a shady orchard. Once we'd sated our hunger, we lay on the tarp, languid in the sweltering heat, drinking tea. I had bartered for tea bowls at a long line of ceramics purveyors in Bukhara and we used these for tea, keeping our camping mugs for soup.

Two children arrived from a neighbouring field. A tall girl of around eleven and her younger brother. She was dressed in traditional red and purple ikat, colours that would have looked completely out of place in the UK but here added sparkle to the dusty landscape. They approached us hesitantly and then stood at a distance examining our bicycles. Here, as in Syria, people had no compunction about touching our bikes, squeezing brakes, testing pedals, in a way which would generate suspicion in the UK. We feigned disinterest and continued talking together so as not to scare them away. Eventually, after a few sly glances to check that we did not mind, the girl started to help the boy up onto Ed's bicycle. Soon Ed went over and offered my smaller bicycle instead, and the two children took it in turns to push each other around wearing our sunglasses and bike helmets.

One of the few things that we could give back to people while on our trip was time and trust and respect. In these rural, out-of-the-way places villagers were likely to have few encounters with foreigners. It was down to us to be good ambassadors.

From its outskirts, Samarkand looked like a bomb had struck it. Everywhere, houses were being torn down and roads ripped up, the gaps filled with the skeletons of tower blocks. Dust and dirt whirled. Roadworks diverted us on to a convoluted route into the centre, full of beeping vehicles, and then suddenly we emerged from the concrete maze to find ourselves at the heart of Central Asia, in front of the Registan.

This was the epicentre of Timur's great empire, the public square at the heart of his famous capital, Samarkand, a repository of the immense riches and skilled artisans Timur (or Tamerlane) brought back from his conquests across the Muslim world, as, one by one, between 1383 and 1404, he forced Isfahan, the Volga, the Caucasus, Delhi, Baghdad and Aleppo under his control.

Timur claimed to be a descendant of Genghis Khan. Timur's own grandson, Ulugh Beg, was of a different mettle, not an impressive leader but an intellectual, a great mathematician, astronomer and all-round polymath who made it his mission to turn Samarkand into an unrivalled centre of learning. It was Ulugh Beg who had the first of the Registan's famous three madrasas – colleges – constructed. Clad in exquisite turquoise tiles, the fifteenth-century Ulugh Beg Madrasa carries a constellation of blue stars on its pishtaq, the rectangular frame around its arched opening, in honour of Ulugh Beg's passion for and expertise in astronomy. Ulugh Beg managed to discover calculation errors in the work of Ptolemy, whose figures had been used since the second century.

The madrasa on the opposite side of the Registan was built two hundred years later. This is the Sher-Dor, 'Possessing Lions', and is unusual in Islamic architecture for its tilework depicting two big cats. These have the mane of a lion but a tiger's pelage and may have been inspired by the Caspian tiger, which was still found along the Amu Darya as late as 1970. The tigers are chasing a pair of white spotted deer – possibly fallow deer.

Even more strangely, behind each tiger rises a sun bearing a human face with arched eyebrows and flared nostrils, reminiscent of Buddhist design. Sher-Dor's pishtaq is flanked by twin fluted domes in turquoise tilework, almost impossibly exotic.

Gazing up at this beautiful building, I felt as if we had landed in a fairy tale. The guidebook we'd used for planning our journey, the *Adventure Cycle-Touring Handbook*, had become a bible to us in the months prior to our departure, and inside it there was a photo of a fully laden tandem in front of the Registan. After two years of planning and 311 days on the road, we had cycled straight into the book.

We found our way to a B&B in a traditional house in the old Jewish quarter close to the Registan. The rooms were furnished with bright suzani on the walls and had carved wooden doors and painted ceiling beams. We had a delicious dinner in the hotel courtyard of manti (dumplings filled with lamb), laghman and salad in the company of a Danish ethnobotanist who was about to set out along the Wakhan Corridor in Afghanistan in search of a population who, living at such high altitude, reputedly made no use of plants and so relied entirely on their livestock for sustenance. He planned to continue southeast to the Tajik capital of Dushanbe and then head along the Pamir Highway up the Amu Darya and cross over to the Afghan Wakhan at a remote mountain border post. This part of Afghanistan was so isolated from the rest of the country that it was considered relatively safe.

'Surely they must use plants for something?' I said. 'Like herbal remedies or teas.'

'Exactly. I must disprove this theory.'

He was young, eccentric and determined and I imagined he would have an amazing adventure.

We stayed three nights to give my knee time to recover. In the Siyob bazaar we restocked with leathery brown but delicious dried apricots, walnuts, almonds, apricot kernels, blue raisins and Uzbek pistachios that were small and buttery. Vendors handed us samples to try, sometimes shelling them for us and squabbling over our custom. We purchased more pickled salads, similar to the ones we'd had on the way into Samarkand. We were constantly craving vegetables, since cooked food was generally lamb based. As I watched the seller scooping the pickles out of big plastic buckets, I wondered how hygienic it was. Predictably, we both got food poisoning the next day. I browsed the clothing section of the bazaar and purchased a cotton salwar kameez. The temperature seemed to be rising by the day so I left my jeans in the hotel for another traveller. Somewhat revived after a day of relative rest, we revisited the Registan in the warm night air, the setting sun glowing on the blue domes.

25
STALIN'S MAP

I was not here for hundreds years,
But nothing changed for ages here ...
In the same way the divine lyre
Pours bliss from the eternal crests.
Same are the waters and stars' throngs,
And endless bleakness of skies' domes,
And flying seeds in airy flows,
And mothers sing the same sweet songs.
Forget all troublesome and cruel –
It's safe – my dear Asian home ...
I'll come once more. Let fences blossom
And pools be clear ones and full.

Anna Akhmatova, trans. Yevgeny Bonver, 'The Moon in a Zenith', www.poetryloverspage.com

Uzbekistan was proving to be difficult for camping as every square inch of the country seemed to be a field, a canal or someone's farm. We had spent a lot of time worrying that we might get caught out by our lack of OVIR (Department of Foreign Travel and Exit) registration slips. Technically it was illegal not to register every night with the migration police. Mostly this could be done by a hotel, with the owner laboriously writing out a chitty. But for the many nights we'd spent camping, we had no registration slips. We had been carefully storing up the ones from Bukhara and Samarkand in the hope that the border guards would not feel the need to count them out, but we'd heard about people being fined for not having a complete record. We decided to try and cover the three hundred kilometres to the capital, Tashkent, in two days so that we'd only have to log one unregistered night in between.

We thought the road would be flat, busy and fairly fast, but by lunchtime on the first day it was ascending unexpectedly steeply over a band of mountains. As the plains slipped away and the farms thinned out, I felt the sheer joy of cycling being rekindled. There were beehives in the fields and roadside stalls every kilometre or so selling honey in shades of amber. We pulled up at one and selected a litre Coke bottle full of honey.

'Otkuda?' A balding middle-aged man got out of his pick-up to come and sell it to us, using Russian to ask us where we were from.

'Shotlandiya.'

'Shotlandiya. Da! William Wallace!'

I thought of the woad-painted, kilt-wearing, bare-buttocked, horse-mounted Mel Gibson playing William Wallace and roaring 'They may take our lives, but they will never take our freedom!' before they faced off the English at the Battle of Stirling Bridge and wondered if the honey seller had found in Wallace parallels with his country's own circumstances. Central Asia had received close attention from Stalin and the Soviet system, enduring a programme of forced collectivisation from 1928–40 intended to eliminate private property and terminate nomadic lifestyles. Tens of thousands of Central Asians were executed in the purges for having bourgeoise or Turkic attitudes.

We paid the three som for the honey, and the man gave us each a yogurt ball he called kurut. Since buying those rancid-tasting ones from the old lady under Bukhara's town wall, we'd seen them being sold everywhere, in different sizes. These were the size of a golf ball. We tried to refuse them, but to no avail.

'Pivo,' he said, circling his index finger and thumb and flicking the finger at the side of his throat in a way that almost looked aggressive.

'What?'

'Pivo!'

'Ah … pivo – beer!'

The man mimed chasing the yogurt ball with a swig. We learnt over time that this flicking motion was the Central Asian gesture for having a drink. Presumably because the vodka stung your throat. He meant that the kurut was a good bar snack.

I gave my yogurt ball, already going sticky in my sweaty palm, a cautionary and hopeful lick once we were down the road and out of sight. It was just as grim, leaving a rancid and slightly chalky taste in the mouth. Guiltily, I lobbed mine into a field.

By late afternoon we had covered about 140 kilometres and were now descending, rapidly at first and then gently, to the fertile plains of the Syr

Darya. The Syr Darya rose in the Tian Shan mountains in Kyrgyzstan to the east of us and flowed north-northwest to the Aral Sea. Like the Amu Darya, its waters had been diverted for Soviet farming projects. The road was carrying us swiftly along with a stream of lorries, buses, Ladas, heavily laden donkeys, and people cycling with bags of flour balanced on the back. At one point, as we were taking a break in a lay-by, a car full of boisterous, drunk youths got out and rushed up to us with two rounds of bread for the journey.

We were now close to the Kazakh border, the road having to kink around a bulge of Kazakhstan and then skirt it to reach the Uzbek capital, which sat right on the edge of Kazakhstan. The part of the map we were cycling across was a nest of wiggling land borders drawn by Stalin so as to keep dangerous 'Pan-Islamic' or 'Pan-Turkic' ideas at bay by exploiting the rich tapestry of religious, ethnic and tribal allegiances that characterised the region. Here there were, broadly speaking, pastoralist Kazakhs on the steppe, mountain-herding Kyrgyz, valley-farming Uzbeks, desert-dwelling Turkmen, all of Turkic descent, and Persian Tajiks, also farmers, each with their own clan or tribal sub-groupings. There were also other minorities, including Jews, who played a central role in Bukhara's trading success, and the Mughat, Central Asian gypsies. An astonishing 1924 different nations were created to accommodate all these subdivisions, each with their own sanitised and to some extent invented national, historical and linguistic identity, identities from which the role of Islam was excised. Some say that Stalin himself drew the boundaries for these numerous pockets of different groups, each with claims to the land. Presumably thinking that only a strong central government like the USSR would then be capable of keeping such a mess in check.

A man in the toothpaste-green uniform of the police waved us down at some barriers. A battered toothpaste-green car was parked at the side.

'Where are you from?' he barked, eyeing with suspicion our passports' front-cover inscriptions, which helpfully spelled out the options as 'European Union The United Kingdom of Great Britain and Northern Ireland'. 'Irelanda?'

'Inglistan,' we answered in our cowardly way, unwilling to introduce complexities and so risk being detained for longer. I could hear William

Wallace groaning all the way from his execution place at the Tower of London.

'Where will you sleep?'

I could see Ed calculating if the response would be accepted. 'Tashkent.'

'Okay. Cigarette?' he asked, fixing me with a stare of crystal blue eyes that reminded me of a Polish friend.

I wondered what journey the Uzbek guard's genes had taken across Eurasia. The USSR had not only attempted to impose order in Central Asia through confusing land boundaries, it had also shipped around peoples to exert control. Any kulaks ('wealthy' peasants) who resisted collectivisation in the west were moved to Siberia or Central Asia. Millions of people with Soviet Greek, Finnish, German or Polish backgrounds were deported east, due to concerns about allegiances with their home nations. Hundreds of thousands of Crimean Tatars were deported en masse to Central Asia as punishment for alleged collaboration with the Nazis during the Second World War, and about half a million Soviet Koreans were also moved into Central Asia after the war to 'stem the infiltration of Japanese espionage'; it was often their ancestors who sold the pickled salads, which bore a resemblance to kimchi, in the bazaars.

I shook my head apologetically at the guard. I had run out of cigarettes.

The flow of traffic had virtually stopped now and there were no houses lining the highway, just the occasional road going off at right angles into flat fields and farmsteads. The light was beginning to fade. We cycled on quickly, worrying about the lack of camping opportunities. Once we were out of sight of the checkpoint, we made sure no one was watching us and turned off onto a road that was raised above the level of the fields. There was no one around to ask and no spare ground, but we were getting desperate.

A donkey appeared on the road ahead, followed by a figure. Ed pedalled off towards them and by the time I arrived a man was shouting down to a woman feeding chickens in the farm below. We wheeled our bikes down the flat verge while the owners debated where we should camp, in the end opting for a place behind a barn that was not visible from the road.

They didn't seem that happy about us being there. We struggled with the tent pegs in the baked ground and then I put on the tea, hoping that us having set up camp would make it harder for them to change their minds.

A while later, the man returned with his wife, whose matronly folds were enveloped in a tent-like velour shift. She sported a heavy black monobrow, emphasised by kohl, a sign of beauty in Uzbekistan, and smiled with a complete row of gold teeth. They posed the usual questions – 'Where are you from? What is your name?' – and then she disappeared into the house and came back with a bowl of yogurt.

'Cigarette?' the husband asked, returning a while later with a friend as I sat cooking, a rare request for something from our hosts in the last months. 'Pivo?' The same flick of the throat.

'Very sorry. No cigarettes. No pivo.'

They walked off into a field, presumably to have a drink at someone's house, and we did not see them again. We left the yogurt bowl full of biscuits in the morning.

We slept abysmally. A tethered dog barked incessantly for the first part of the night and then a storm started. We had pitched the tent using only three pegs in the hard-baked ground, which, as on so many farmsteads, seemed to have been deliberately compacted to give a smooth surface. The wet canvas buckled and flapped in the wind, which had switched from southwest to north-northeast. There'd be a headwind tomorrow.

By seven in the morning we were off again, under clear skies, muscles aching and heads full of sleep. The road was now choked with lorries and buses, its surface deep in grit. We struggled against the unforgiving wind. The dull pain of menstrual cramps began radiating through my abdomen, so we stopped again at 10.30am, having only covered thirty kilometres, and I slept for two hours in a painkiller-induced doze under a tree.

I found a suitable bush behind which to do battle with my menstrual cup. We were long into a tampon-free zone, since apparently in this region of the world there were cultural objections to women touching parts of their own body. Since Turkey, all I'd been able to find were sanitary towels of alarming bulk, so thank goodness I'd persevered with the menstrual cup. Needless to say, periods were not the riding-your-bike-in-the-sunshine-with-the-wind-in-your-hair experience conveyed by the sanitary-product adverts of the nineties. I am grateful to have been born in a tampon oasis and for having a mother who put a packet of junior tampons in my hand and told me to persevere. Taboos around menstruation and lack of access to menstrual products and appropriate toilet facilities remain significant barriers to girls' schooling and sports education globally.

It was 4pm and we were still ninety-one kilometres from Tashkent when the rain descended thick and heavy as if wrung from a steaming bath-house towel. The drops rolled and bounced, brown with dust, then joined to form a muddy channel. We stopped at a roadside chaikhana and sat under the porch on a tapchan, drinking tea and eating fortifying bowls of laghman as the rain battered down outside. Frustration at having to stop so close to Tashkent was tempered by the chance to sit down, eat and rest. Dusk fell and the downpour continued unabated, so we gladly took up the invitation to bed down right where we were, on the raised cushioned platform at the chaikhana. It was always far better, anyhow, to approach a big city in the morning, or at least not at the end of a long day when your energy was completely sapped. As you got closer, the traffic would begin to swell, and there would be side roads and junctions requiring map stops and enquiries, leading to niggling doubts as to whether you'd gone wrong. All these things put immense pressure on the exhausted brain. When you were at that stage of exhaustion, it was much easier to keep cycling than to stop and think about a junction.

Duly arrived in Tashkent, we headed for the Chinese Embassy to buy our Chinese visas. We now had five days before our Uzbek visas expired. From Tashkent, our plan was to head southeast to the Fergana Valley and then on to the Kyrgyz border at Osh. From Osh, you could theoretically reach China in a matter of days by heading south to Sary-Tash and then on to the border post at Irkeshtam, but we planned to spend at least two months in Kyrgyzstan and wanted to do a longer route. Once inside Kyrgyzstan, we would head for Jalal-Abad, then cycle north and east over the Fergana Range to Kochkor via the high alpine lake Song-Kol. The lake was home to yurt-dwelling herders and rumoured to be one of Central Asia's loveliest spots. We planned to include a few weeks of trekking around there, away from the bikes. After that, we would make for Naryn and the Torugart Pass to China.

Everyone in the queue was tense. People were being let in two by two. There were rumours that the Central Asian embassies were not issuing visas to China easily, and no one wanted their plans to be thwarted. A straw-haired Belgian backpacker in baseball shorts, vest top and flip-flops was complaining loudly about his embassy experiences so far. 'They said it would take fourteen days minimum to issue a transit visa … That is so long … I asked them if they could speed it up, but they said no. I'm going to go back now though and try with more money.' Ed and I glanced at each other in relief when another applicant resumed their place in the queue between us and him. I didn't want to be applying alongside a foreigner trying to pick a fight and who'd given no thought to how his appearance might be perceived by officials. From what I'd seen in the Islamic world, men never revealed their legs or upper arms (and boys rarely) and were generally neatly turned out.

Eventually, ten minutes before closing, we were let in. With trembling hands, we rushed to fill in the visa forms. We had already decided on our strategy. We would focus on our long-term plan to visit the far east, Beijing, Shanghai and Hong Kong, as even mentioning the troubled Xinjiang region at the border of China's far west could be problematic, let alone raising the possibility that we might cycle across it. We smiled as we handed over the forms to the young woman behind the desk.

'There is a big problem,' she said as she scanned them.

My heart sank.

'You want dual-entry visa for China? Hong Kong need separate visa.'

'Oh, very sorry, we did not understand this. We will miss out Hong Kong and just go to Beijing and Shanghai instead.'

'Are you sure? You not need Hong Kong?' She looked at us, confused.

We smiled naively. I kicked myself for having such poor knowledge of the geopolitical consequences of our own imperial history.

'Okay, come back tomorrow.'

Downtown Tashkent was all wide boulevards of concrete, marble and glass. Blacked-out vehicles zoomed up to traffic lights and twiggy Russian and Korean women tottered along the streets behind expensive sunglasses. A gang of women in green scrubs and face masks were polishing the History Museum of the People of Uzbekistan, standing at the top of the steps, running feather dusters over the exterior. How or whether they would polish the upper storeys was not clear. The pavements too were spotless, being swept continuously, and vehicles with flashing lights sprayed water on the roads to keep the dust down in the heat of the afternoon. An army of people were paid to scrub the desert dust from every corner of the city centre, as if there was a need to deny the existence of the cracked, salt-crusted earth that characterised the rest of the country. Was this a directive straight from the top, I wondered? From President Islam Karimov himself, the man who had declared Uzbekistan independent during the break-up of the USSR and now had an iron grip on the country, banning opponents from standing in elections, severely restricting freedom of religious expression, and treating any dissenting protestors with bloody heavy-handedness.

Cycling back from the embassy, we got hopelessly lost and stopped to ask directions from a man standing beside a black Land Rover with green diplomatic plates. He seemed unwilling to engage at first, answering warily in a thick French accent, but eventually he relaxed and helped us out. The two blond children strapped into the back of his vehicle peered curiously at us. Mindful that the British ambassador, Craig Murray, had been removed from post a few years previously for speaking out about human-rights abuses, as detailed in his book *Murder in Samarkand*, I imagined that life as an embassy official would be fraught with tension.

Early next morning, as I was sitting reading on the tapchan in our hostel courtyard, the door of one of the lower rooms opened quietly. The argumentative Belgian backpacker emerged in boxer shorts and bare feet and hurriedly ushered out a slender East Asian girl in platforms and a short white cotton dress.

26
ONCE BITTEN...

Who comes to a spring thirsty
and sees the moon reflected in it?
Rumi, trans. Coleman Barks, 'Unfold Your Own Myth', in *The Essential Rumi*

By the afternoon we were travelling on an undulating track through fields of wheat splattered red with poppies. The sun was high and hot again, but as we rode a breeze began to gather. It was good to be free of the city. Although I had enjoyed walking the streets and crammed bazaars of Bukhara and Samarkand, I was looking forward to getting out of the intensively farmed lowlands, with their hemmed-in feeling, humidity and ever-present dust, and to be heading up into the high mountains. Three more nights and then we would be in Kyrgyzstan, which in my mind was a land of chocolate-box blue sky, bubbling mountain streams and white peaks. 'Then,' I said to myself, as ridiculous as that sounds when you are actually on a prolonged holiday, 'we can relax a bit.'

Shortly after entering Kyrgyzstan there would be the option of visiting the idyllic-sounding village of Arslanbob, which was famed for its walnut groves and cherry harvest. One could apparently overnight in homestays through Kyrgyzstan's well-developed ecotourism scheme. I imagined snoozing on a tapchan under dappled shade for a few days while we planned some expeditions on foot into the higher mountains. Little did I know, as I cycled alongside Ed, our shadows lengthening, that it would be months before that sort of rest would be possible.

Meanwhile, however, we were still in Uzbekistan, now approaching the town of Angren, where small bread stalls lined the road. Piles of hot non were placed in baskets under a blanket, with one round and shiny wheel displayed on top. We stopped to buy a couple from a young woman, who giggled and called into the house behind her as we dismounted. I handed over some tatty notes as a group gathered.

'Come, come!' An athletic young man with a skullcap, a wide smile and a dusting of flour on his jeans beckoned us through a gate and into a courtyard with a tapchan. At one end under a roof, there was a large wood-fired oven, black with charcoal and built from earth. 'Tandoor,' Halim said.

I peered at the glowing bed of charcoal, the heat singeing my eyebrows. Halim picked up a long wooden paddle and loosened a wheel of bread. Inside a small hut, two men were working at a bench covered in flour, a long row of shaped mounds of dough by each of them. They offered us their wrists, apologising that they could not shake our hands. Back outside, Halim was loosening rounds onto a large pile of bread. He rolled up his sleeves, exposing muscular forearms, and began bare-handed to slap a new batch of dough onto the roof of the tandoor, reaching deep inside with his whole body. Once all the dough was put to bake, two extra wheels of hot bread were dumped in my arms and he broke a third, offering us pieces.

'Good,' he said, chewing thoughtfully, then called to the two men, who were taking it in turns to pour water from a jug for handwashing. They beckoned to Ed and set off through the gate, returning with our bikes. It seemed we were staying the night.

We spent the evening visiting Halim's brother and Russian wife and laughing at their breakdancing toddler over a couple of shots of vodka and manti. Back at Halim's, we were treated to a mound of plov cooked by his sister, the stallholder, each of us eating with a spoon from the corner of the plate. We sat on the floor and Halim said a prayer and then broke a wheel of bread, passing his cupped hands in front of his face, saying 'Amin', then giving us each a piece with his right hand. The formality of this sent a small shock of recognition through me – was this the living embodiment of the stylised ritual that had become incorporated into Christianity's Holy Communion? 'And as they did eat, Jesus took bread, and blessed, and broke it, and gave to them, and said, Take, eat: this is my body,' Mark writes of the Last Supper (14:22). I had always assumed that the breaking of the bread was a ritual that had been conducted specifically for this occasion, when instead it was perhaps an adaptation of a common pre-dinner rite.

Halim explained that non should never be placed upside down or on the floor or cut with a knife. Every crumb was swept up carefully at the end of the meal, and the old bread put out for the birds. Bread was never treated casually in the Arab, Persian or Turkic regions we had passed through – remnants were always tidied away and old bread was often hung out for dedicated roadside bread-waste collections – but in Central Asia this respect seemed even more developed. Likely it was ancient, dating back to the invention of agriculture. Bread also has an important role in Zoroastrianism, where it is used in ritual offerings.

At 5.30am we woke to find Halim and his worker kneading and spinning soft mounds of proofed dough into plates and then stamping them with the bosma to create the patterns. He broke an elaborate flower-patterned loaf he had baked specially for our breakfast and we sat around a tablecloth on the floor and dipped the steaming pieces into homemade apricot jam and clotted cream.

I was sad to leave the gentle hospitality of Halim's family, but anxiety was starting to rise. I did not want any more distractions before reaching the border. We had to get into position by the evening so we could cross the next day.

The road ran uphill beside a reservoir then turned into switchbacks as the valley narrowed, a battered sign announcing a 17 per cent gradient. We climbed for ten kilometres, passing through two tunnels. My knee, the one that had been injured in the dog-stick incident, began to burn and ache with pain. We struggled up the 2268-metre Kamchik Pass alongside lorries whose protesting engines were belching acrid fumes in our faces and at the top were stopped by guards who demanded to see not only our papers but also our camera. They made Ed delete some photos of fossils we'd taken in the valley below. Fossils that were, Ed informed me with his geography teacher's knowledge, *Gigantoproductus*, a common brachiopod shellfish that lived in shallow, sandy seabeds and in this case had risen out of the closing Tethys Sea. We were crossing one of the outer ripples caused by the great shock wave, 100 million years ago, produced when the Indian subcontinent collided with Asia. This gave rise to the Himalayan plateau and, in its northwestern corner, to the range of mountains known as the Tian Shan, which was where we were headed. Of what significance the fossils were to national security was unclear.

We descended the other side slowly on a heavily rutted road through a scrubby, crenulated gully towards the Fergana Valley. The valley, which is at the head of the Syr Darya, is renowned for its fertile soil and is very densely populated, home to eight million people. It is Uzbekistan's fruit and cotton basket. The population are overwhelmingly ethnically Uzbek, unlike Samarkand and Bukhara, which are predominantly Tajik. We had heard talk that this was a more religiously conservative area and reputedly where most of Central Asia's Islamic extremists came from. Andijon, a town made famous because of a brutal crackdown by President Karimov in 2005 that left seven hundred protestors dead, would be our last staging post in the valley. After that we would cross to Osh, a town with a sizeable ethnic Uzbek population on the Kyrgyz side.

In order for the valley to belong to Uzbekistan at all, it looked like Stalin had taken a great ragged bite out of Kyrgyzstan. It was even more complicated than that. The Syr Darya ultimately flowed out of the Fergana Valley into the lowlands of Uzbekistan, but a narrowing section of the lower valley was claimed by a curling tendril of Tajikistan. The only entry to Fergana through Uzbekistan was over the Kamchik Pass and the narrow isthmus which surrounded it. There were also enclaves of Uzbekistan dotted within the Kyrgyz side of the valley, like puncture wounds from the bite.

We had descended quite a way and were checking our map near some houses at 6.30pm when a man came over to offer us a place to sleep for the night. We spoke with him and his wife for a while as we debated whether to push on and get closer to the border. Considering it wiser on our last night not to risk camping at the edge of a field, with its potential for drunken visitors, we accepted.

Their courtyard was lively with four small children and a wiry, yappy orange dog. We were ushered up a flight of metal stairs to the living room. I eyed the smallish dog warily on my way past as it snapped and jumped towards us, at one point having to be held back by one of the kids. My adrenaline surged. Since the experience in eastern Turkey, any barking set me on edge. We had seen few dogs in Iran or Central Asia so far. Dog saliva is considered to be impure in Islam and thus dogs are rarely kept as pets. There is a logic in this, as saliva is the route by which rabies is transmitted.

We sat together for tea on their carpeted living-room floor and I was relieved to note the dog was not allowed into the house. My knee was protesting at being bent into a cross-legged position and I was acutely aware of how sweaty and dishevelled I must look after the last two days. There was a perpetual humidity, even at night, and the air still seemed to be laden with salt and dust. Worried that my socked feet would not be smelling great, I excused myself to visit the squat toilet in the courtyard. I had a pair of fresh socks in my pocket and could do a quick change without inconveniencing our hosts by making it seem like I needed more complex washing facilities such as a bath. It was always tricky to anticipate domestic arrangements. We were rarely given any time for privacy and I didn't have the energy for anything other than polite conversation over supper this evening.

The steps down to the courtyard were in darkness and I felt my way along the metal railing slowly, wary of my aching knee. Because I had seen it on my way in, I knew where the toilet door was on the opposite side of the yard. I was halfway across the open space when there was a low growl followed by an immediate stinging pain on my knee. The dog had its teeth locked on to my kneecap.

I shouted and shook my leg out, freeing it on the second shake, and it ran away barking. The leg of my trousers had been torn.

'Once clinical symptoms appear, rabies is virtually 100 per cent fatal.' This statistic ran through my head as I hobbled back into the house and rolled up my trouser leg. Toothmarks were clearly visible on my kneecap. My mind began to fill with flashbacks from educational videos about rabid foxes that I'd been shown as a child growing up in what was then a rabies zone in Switzerland. This dog had seemed normal – but then it bit me completely unprovoked. It had come at me like a small, silent assassin in the darkness. Did that mean it was rabid?

The family was embarrassed and fussed round me, apologising for the damage to my trouser leg, which was their principal concern. Not wanting them to feel responsible, I repeatedly told them not to worry, while Ed fished out our first-aid kit, rinsed the wound with water and applied iodine disinfectant. The wife insisted on sitting next to me, patting my hand occasionally, while one of the daughters was charged with fetching a clean towel. I watched Ed with a detached and horrible clarity, knowing that we would not be going to Kyrgyzstan tomorrow. This was immediately followed by a rush of thoughts about alternative ways out.

Once my knee had been dressed, we sat on the floor with the family, eating with spoons from a big plate of macaroni with lamb mince and tomato. More cushions were proffered to support my leg. While Ed spoke to them about our journey, I nodded and smiled and chewed, my brain whirring. We had both had a full course of rabies inoculations at the travel clinic in Glasgow before our departure. The vaccination did not provide immediate protection against rabies, but it did simplify the treatment in the event of a bite. Everything I had read in preparation for the trip had advised that if bitten by a dog, the assumption should always be that it might carry rabies, and treatment should be sought IMMEDIATELY. The vaccination bought a bit more time, but it was still URGENT. 'Seek post-exposure treatment within five days' was the snappy phrase that went round my head. Was the dog really rabid though? Why hadn't it barked first – did that make the risk higher? It was a pet, not a stray – surely that reduced the risk? Could I carry on and get the vaccine in the Kyrgyz capital, Bishkek, in what might realistically be three to five days' time – or maybe less if we got a taxi?

We finally retired for the night, lying in our sleeping bags rolled out on mattresses on their living-room floor. We had a whispered conversation facing each other in the darkness. One way or the other, we both agreed, I needed a rabies booster vaccine. The risk might be marginal, but the potential consequences were great. I did not want to be cycling around with the sword of Damocles hanging over my head. I might be able to push thoughts away on the bike during the day, but then at night, lying in a tent on a remote mountain pass, I would be hyper-alert, wondering if every ache in my body was signalling certain death. I ran through what I could remember of the *Outdoor Medical Emergency Handbook: First Aid for Travelers, Backpackers and Adventurers*. I had tried to internalise relevant sections back in Glasgow, the straightforward clinical advice providing a diversion from having to trawl through scientific papers on an obscure aspect of evolutionary theory for my PhD thesis. It was all too clear now that I was not the useful kind of doctor. I had photocopied pages from the book but not the rabies section. I was sure the general advice for rabies ran something like: 'The first symptoms of rabies may be similar to the flu, including fever or headache … These symptoms may last for days. Symptoms then progress to anxiety, confusion, fear of water' (I was not quite sure why) 'and agitation … eventually death.' The early symptoms were discomfortingly generic, especially for a routine headache sufferer. In addition to this, in the current situation 'anxiety' seemed assured. So I needed the vaccine. The question was where?

Our first option would be to try to taxi it across the border into Kyrgyzstan and then on to the capital Bishkek. That was a long way over mountain passes. How easy would it be to find a van to take our bikes? Bishkek was also a complete unknown. Would it be safer instead to simply head back to Tashkent and seek treatment? In which case, should I return there alone, leaving Ed hereabouts with the bikes?

We finally went to sleep having agreed that it had to be Tashkent and that we'd decide whether to both go once we had found somewhere with a taxi rank and established if we could get ourselves as well as both bikes and eight pannier bags into the vehicle. It was just about feasible, assuming that there was a clinic with the vaccine, that we (or I) could do a dash there and back and still make it over the border tomorrow.

We left our host family after breakfast, without mentioning our plans, and had a rapid run downhill to the wide plain of the Fergana Valley. There was no sign in the morning haze of the mountains which fringed the valley. We crossed the Syr Darya and reached the settlement of Danghara, where we wasted time debating whether to visit the dilapidated health centre, with its peeling walls and rubbish drifting in an unkempt garden, finally deciding against it. There was no taxi rank in sight, so we pushed on to Kokand, where we were soon surrounded by a gaggle of taxi drivers confused at why we were leaving already, having only just arrived. We managed to negotiate a Daewoo minivan to take the two us and the bikes the two hundred kilometres back to Tashkent for forty dollars.

The van was hot and I looked despondently at the landscape slipping away from us. Alexander the Great reached the Fergana Valley in 329 BC and it became the most northeasterly point of the Macedonian Empire. For centuries this valley had been the border between empires and an important staging post on the Silk Road for goods and people travelling over the high passes from China, with the valley itself a centre of silk production. I wondered gloomily if it would also be the closest to China we would get on our journey. We were so near and yet we had seen nothing of the valley, nothing of Kokand apart from the chaotic and grubby transport hub at the bazaar, none of the many ancient madrasas and mosques promised by our guidebook. A guidebook that was currently useless. On our day of departure, I had ripped out the pages about Tashkent and handed them blithely to an incoming French cycle-tourer. Pages that also, it turned out, contained a map marking the recommended hospital.

For months our mobile phone had only been able to send text messages, so we borrowed the driver's mobile to phone the British Embassy help desk and got the name of a recommended clinic. I got through to the clinic eventually and was now waiting for a call back to confirm that they had stock of the vaccine and could see me. As we bumped along, I thought about the family we had left behind and how easy it was for us to extract ourselves by applying cash to the problem. The wife had revealed to me over breakfast that the dog had also bitten her. Caught off guard by the revelation, I had suggested, though not forcefully, that she see a doctor. It was unclear if the bite had been recent. Did two cases of biting make it more or less likely that the dog was rabid? Was it a story I was being told to make me feel better or them less responsible?

We arrived back in Tashkent at four, thirty minutes before my appointment. I switched into a taxi at a busy junction while Ed guided the van driver to the hostel. Then I was suddenly in the waiting room of the spotlessly clean Tashkent International Medical Clinic, with its sparkling windows, matching chairs and pot plants. I was called in exactly on time by a young male German doctor in an open-necked shirt and white jacket.

'You are lucky. As far as I know, we are the only clinic in Central Asia to stock the vaccine. Perhaps in Almaty, but certainly not in Bishkek or Dushanbe. Istanbul would be the only other viable option.'

They had to fly it in specially on 'cold chain', apparently, and sometimes had issues with the supply logistics. If I'd not had the pre-exposure immunisation course, I would certainly have had to go to Istanbul for the immunoglobulin, he told me. As it was, I would need not just one but two shots of the vaccine, with the second delivered in three days.

My heart sank. 'Do you know where I can get my visa extended for medical reasons?'

'I suggest that you don't mention that. It is likely to complicate the process if they know you have an urgent reason to stay.'

I watched him draw from the vial of vaccine and flick the bubbles from the syringe, feeling immensely grateful for my ability to buy medical treatment and health insurance. I made a second appointment for three days' time. Now we would need to figure out how to stay.

At the hostel, Ed was having dinner with a group of travellers, including the French cyclist who was in possession of our guidebook pages. I delivered the mixed news and was met immediately by a barrage of encouragement and lateral thinking. It felt good to be in the company of people who implicitly understood the problems we were now facing. I had made a bad error of judgement by texting my parents a garbled message shortly after the dog-biting incident, asking them for help finding the address of the health clinic. On receiving 'BITTEN BY DOG. MASSIVE PAIN. NEED RABIES VACCINE. CAN YOU TEXT NUMBER OF HOSPITAL IN TASHKENT', they had unsurprisingly assumed that the bite was very serious and I had been sent a string of messages urging us to return home. Guilt overwhelmed me and it felt good to be distracted by company.

The extension to our Uzbek visas required a long visit to a grey tower block containing the OVIR office. Eventually, the man on the desk agreed to call an English-speaking supervisor to help us. We had to purchase evidence that we were leaving Uzbekistan by air, which necessitated a trip to an internet café where we opted for a flight to the Kyrgyz capital, Bishkek. We then had to visit a bank to make the visa payments and get a form stamped, before returning to the office when it reopened in the afternoon. We had no intention of taking the flights, knowing that once the visas were issued, they would be accepted by any border crossing. By the end of the day, we had clocked up 334 dollars on flights and eighty dollars on visa extensions, on top of the 230 dollars on injections. We were worried about our dwindling funds and filed an insurance claim in the hope that it would come through quickly.

We returned to the hostel to find everyone staring at maps on the tapchan. Why so many people? The news was quickly shared. The border between Uzbekistan and Kyrgyzstan had been shut.

'Shut?' I repeated dumbly into the mass of babbling voices. 'Why?'

There was a roadblock at one of the enclaves, clashes, and talk of 'ethnic tensions'. The border between Andijon and Osh, it seemed, had been shut as a precaution. The other land borders between Uzbekistan and Kyrgyzstan were also currently in question, but there was little information. We did not know it at the time, but the whole region was about to descend into unrest, resulting in more than four hundred people dead and thousands of people fleeing the area. In 2020 Human Rights Watch was still calling on the Kyrgyz government to reopen investigations into possible human-rights abuses which occurred.

Although we did not know what was to come, it was clear that no route via Kyrgyzstan would be possible in the short-term. With our extended Uzbek visas, now due to run out in five days, we needed a Plan B. Over a pot of tea on the tapchan in the hostel courtyard, we pored over our maps. We discounted heading north via Kazakhstan. Neither of us fancied flat steppe in the summer heat. The only other option was to go south to Tajikistan and via the Pamir Highway. This road skirted the border with Afghanistan. It had been built by the Russians in the 1980s during their occupation. It was long and high and remote, staying above 3500 metres for more than four hundred kilometres. Obtaining food would be an issue. There would be lots of military checkpoints.

We set off to the Tajik Embassy the next day and, taking it as a good omen, were issued visas on the same day. The following day we went to seek an extension to our Kyrgyz visas, after a visit to the clinic for the second round of jabs. The Pamir Highway would take us the long way round: south, east and then north again to the remote Kyrgyz town of Sary-Tash, which was south of Osh, just across the Alay mountain range that formed the southern rim of the Fergana Valley. A day's cycle from there would take us to the Irkeshtam border into China. However, our Kyrgyz visas, which we had obtained in Ankara, would have run out in the month it would take us to cycle the Pamirs. After some negotiation, and another three days' delay, we received handwritten extension notes in our passports. There was a risk: if, by the time we got there, the Tajik–Kyrgyz border at the other end of the Pamir Highway was closed as well as the Uzbek–Kyrgyz borders, we would be stranded in one of Central Asia's most inaccessible regions with only days left on our visa. But it was a risk we were willing to take. Our next stop was now Dushanbe, Tajikistan's capital city, where we would stock up for the ride ahead and obtain the necessary local permits and visa extensions for the Pamirs.

Tea and Grit

Tajikistan: The Pamirs

 May – July 2010

Tea and Grit

27
PAMIR PREAMBLE

The great and almost only comfort about being a woman is that one can always pretend to be more stupid than one is and no one is surprised.
Freya Stark, *The Valleys of the Assassins: and Other Persian Travels*

An unvoiced tension spread between us. We were both concerned about further barriers materialising to block our departure from Uzbekistan and whether we had the fitness to take on the challenge of the Pamirs. And, inevitably, we had both suffered another bout of food poisoning, having frequented a wide assortment of food stalls during our prolonged stay in Tashkent.

Our first night back on the road came with strong winds and we woke to driving rain at 5.30. It was Ed's twenty-ninth birthday, but neither of us was in much of a mood to celebrate. Ed's camping mat had deflated in the night due to a puncture. I produced a small assortment of strictly useful presents obtained from the bazaar – a bag of sweets, a bar of milk chocolate, a pair of rip-off Curiosity Kindles, aka fake Calvin Klein boxer shorts, and two cotton handkerchiefs. We left at 7.30 and battled with heaving rain until ten, reaching the Oybek border post for Tajikistan at midday. Thankfully, our concerns that either our visa extensions or our lack of OVIR registrations would be picked up on came to nothing.

Once we were on the other side, the sun came out and our spirits lifted. We stopped in the shelter of an orchard to camp at 5pm and pitched our tent on grass containing sweet-smelling herbs. A shepherd boy came to speak to us and then returned with a huge pan of yogurt. We sat under the light of the moon eating until late.

The morning brought more heavy rain and after we'd packed up we waited it out under the trees, the shepherd boy joining us in companionable silence as we all gazed out at the downpour. We finally set off into a strong headwind, but the cycling was enjoyable, with mountain views on both sides, and by mid-afternoon we'd descended back to the Syr Darya and the lower Fergana Valley. We were now downstream of the section of river we'd crossed to get to Kokand on the morning of the dog-bite flight to

Tashkent. The river flowed with invitingly blue waters, triggering thoughts of swimming.

We took a break for lunch in the busy town of Khujand, which had once been the site of Alexandria Eschate (Furthest Alexandria), the most northeasterly military post in the Macedonian Empire. Under Soviet rule the town had been called Leninabad and we sat under an imposing statute of Lenin, his coat sweeping out behind him in an imaginary wind. The statue was reportedly the highest in Central Asia at twenty-seven metres.

Over the next two days we ascended the Shakhristan Pass (3378 metres), wild camping and passing through deep gorges with flat, fertile valley floors and stopping at chaikhanas for shashlik served with aromatic salads. Villages now had water pumps displaying the logos of international aid organisations and we were grateful to be able to fill up our own bottles after months of having to buy commercially bottled water. Tajikistan was by far the poorest of the post-Soviet stans. Independence had been declared in 1991 after the dissolution of the USSR, but the mountainous country had soon descended into civil war between multiple factions from different valleys. In the chaos, Russia stepped back in to control its old military posts – fifty or so of them – along the Afghan border. Against this backdrop there were droughts and failed harvests and Tajikistan plunged down the ranks to become one of the world's thirty poorest countries. A ceasefire had been declared in 1996, but the country was still catching up.

We washed our clothes in the river and dried them in the strong sun. The final ascent to the pass was long and steep on an appalling road surface which was even worse on the descent. We eased our way downhill, under high banks of dirty snow and past overturned lorries. The Fann mountain range, jagged teeth with white caps, stretched out against an azure sky.

We passed through the beautiful village of Ayni, a splash of green along a jade river, with tall poplars catching the sunlight and low houses clinging to pink crenulated hillsides. We collected a gaggle of children on bicycles, all tatty T-shirts and slip-on shoes, who pedalled furiously with us for over an hour, weaving, racing us and laughing. Two girls dressed in pink tunics, the younger one wearing a green fleece, the older a navy headscarf, showed us to a campsite in an orchard and brought us their school jotters to inspect. The river was the Zarafshan, nourisher of both

Samarkand and Bukhara to the west. It once joined the Amu Darya but now dissolves into the desert.

The road ascended again towards the Anzob Pass. We stopped for tea at a chaikhana, sitting in the shade of a balcony that overlooked a dry valley with green trees at the bottom. The sun was strong and I had badly burnt my fingers, which were exposed on my handlebars. The chaikhana was run by a lady whose seven-year-old son we entertained as we drank tea. Two donkeys were outside on the terrace and we laughed with him as the smaller one tried to mount the larger. I remembered the two Bedu boys with a donkey that we'd met crossing the desert in Syria and wondered why donkeys seemed to be universally the butt of jokes.

I struggled on in the afternoon, having to break regularly. I was breathing hard and it felt like only a thin trickle of energy was reaching my legs. The altitude was a new factor that I knew I would acclimatise to, but I had a nagging worry that I would not have it in me to tackle the Pamirs. As ever, Ed was forging on uphill, repeatedly having to stop for me. At three thousand metres we reached the entrance to the Anzob Tunnel, a dirty mouth drilled into the mountainside. Dark brown water poured out into the snow and gravel at its entrance. Fear rose in my stomach. We'd entered a similar tunnel in Bosnia, with a one-way system controlled by traffic lights, and had had to pedal for what seemed like aeons in a pit of darkness.

This time we flagged down an open-topped lorry and were loaded into the back with sheep. We bumped into the darkness at high speed, flinging ourselves onto our bicycles to stop them bashing around and hitting us and the sheep, which had crammed themselves in fright against the side of the truck. Diesel fumes hit the back of my throat. The roar was deafening and icy water splashed down onto us. I expected it to end soon, but we went on and on into the darkness. Panic began to swell inside me and tears started to pour down my face. Finally, after about five kilometres, we shot back out into the light. But the lorry carried on, down and down.

'Make him stop, please!' I shouted to Ed pathetically.

'How exactly?' he shouted back.

The lorry was clinging to a thin road with precipitous sides. It felt as if it could trip over at any moment, emptying two cyclists, their bicycles and five sheep into the abyss. Soon it became clear why the driver was cheating us out of the descent. We barrelled into and out of a series of smaller tunnels and at one point screeched to a halt and then inched our way past an oncoming lorry. We finally stopped around a thousand metres down the mountain. Ed paid the driver generously. I sat on the wet gravel cramming my mouth with sweets to try and ease the shakes.

We whizzed downhill in the sunshine to Dushanbe. Luxury holiday developments and a shiny presidential retreat became visible from the road on the approach. We found a B&B in the suburbs that had signs forbidding the watching of pornography and served a small, overpriced breakfast. We headed into town and paid for large bowls of kasha (buckwheat porridge) with cherry jam in a workers' café.

We had tasks to do in Dushanbe. We extended our visas and obtained GBAO permits to allow us to enter the Gorno-Badakhshan Autonomous Oblast, the far eastern part of Tajikistan that we would need to cross to reach the far northern border with Kyrgyzstan. The region is bordered by Afghanistan in the south and west and China in the east. We picked up a post restante parcel sent by my mother which contained an extra set of thermals for the cold. Ed gave the bikes an overhaul, replacing his front tyre and my rear brake cable. The wet grit on the way over the Shakhristan and Anzob passes had worn down brake pads, which also needed replacing. Now that we were back in mountain country, Ed was relieved to be able to replace his worn-out walking boots. We'd both cycled from Scotland in walking boots, which were protective, durable and warm both on and off the bikes. I'd replaced mine in Athens.

The most important task was food shopping. We planned to carry supplies for around twenty days, relying on only limited supplementation. At a supermarket we purchased twenty sachets of instant mashed potato. This would be a godsend since we were also concerned about access to fuel. We would have two litres of petrol for the stove but it would be a struggle to boil anything at high altitude, as the Silk Road traveller Marco Polo had noted in his *Travels* (though there is some dispute about whether he actually visited the Pamirs in person or depended on others' accounts):

For 12 days the course is along this elevated plain, which is named Pamer; and as during all that time you do not meet with any habitation, it is necessary to make provisions at the outset accordingly. So great is the height of the mountains, that no birds are to be seen near their summits; and however extraordinary it may be thought, it was affirmed, that from the keenness of the air, fires when lighted do not give the same heat as in lower situations, not produce the same effect in dressing victuals. After having performed this journey of 12 days, you still have 40 days to travel in the same direction over mountains and through valleys in perpetual succession, passing many rivers and desert tracts, without seeing any habitation or appearance of verdure.

I added a savoury porridge mix made from buckwheat, and dried macaroni to the basket plus a supply of vegetable stock powder for flavour and rehydration; I had tried never to be without this for the whole journey. Semolina, milk powder and sugar would have to form the basis of every breakfast, since semolina would cook quickly. Chinese super noodles would be our lunch. Dried fruit and biscuits for snacks. The menu was distinctly beige.

In Friendship Square we stopped in front of the statue of Ismoil Somoni, the tenth-century founder of the Samanid dynasty, which at the height of its power ruled an empire that stretched from Fergana to the Caspian Sea and had its capital in Bukhara. In 1999, on the 1100th anniversary of the Samanid empire, Somoni's statue had knocked Lenin off the plinth; and one of the country's highest peaks, formerly Peak Communism (7495 metres), now bore his name. A parade of children were marching and singing and waving flags to celebrate the Day of Children while a small crowd watched. Two policemen in stained shirts and scuffed shoes approached us and demanded twenty dollars for vodka. We laughed, pretending it was a joke, and they staggered away. There was heavy reference to corruption in our guidebook and I was worried that this was a sign of things to come at the many remote checkpoints which were promised along the high road.

We splashed our way through deep rivulets of dirty water, navigating roadworks and dense traffic as we headed east out of Dushanbe towards a road junction at Vahdat. From here it was theoretically 220 kilometres in a roughly easterly direction to Kalaikhum on the Panj river, which formed the border with Afghanistan and was the start of the Pamir Highway. However, a pair of Italian motorcyclists we'd crossed paths with in Dushanbe had warned us that a section of the 3252-metre Khaburabot Pass had collapsed in heavy rain. This necessitated a detour south and then north via Kulyab to where the map descended into a criss-cross of dashed lines marking minor roads. The motorcyclists had been wildly beardy and deeply tanned, with lips blistered from the sun and wind. They'd had to push their motorbikes for two whole days in the Pamirs. I wondered what we were letting ourselves in for.

We drew the route on the map that they had taken, to be sure we would remember it – crossing the Shurabad Pass southeast of Kulyab and descending to the Panj and the Afghan border about a hundred kilometres downstream of Kalaikhum. The distance markings were also missing from this part of the map, but the detour was probably an extra two hundred kilometres. We thought we might be in Kalaikhum in five to seven days' time.

The rain came on heavy that afternoon as we slogged up to an unnamed 1600-metre pass. We stopped at a police checkpoint and were waved inside. Five officials wearing military fatigues greeted us in turn, each inspecting our passports earnestly. We were offered tea and I felt they were stalling for a pretext to keep us longer; whether out of curiosity, boredom or something else, it was difficult to say. We became animated and cheery, extolling the virtues of Tajikistan as we explained our trip in painstaking detail. Once we'd been served tea, we offered each man a cigarette.

They were slight, young men with a mixture of Tajik and Mongol complexions, apart from one tall hulk of a man with close-set blue eyes who, since his vast frame was covered in khaki, I mentally christened 'Shrek'. Shrek had forearms the width of my thighs and the other men lowered their eyes in his presence. I studiously tried to avoid his gaze, which seemed to settle on me too often. He called Ed into his office and as I listened to him repeating the same round of questions again, I knew that my turn would be next. I gave Ed a hard stare as I was called to switch places with him.

Shrek pulled my passport out of my hand and thumbed it with thick fingers.

'Mush. Husband.' He jerked his head in the direction that Ed had just gone.

'Da.'

'Malenkiy? Baby?'

'Nyet.'

He stared at me. 'Problem? You need Russian baby? Strong man, strong baby.' He flexed his biceps and stared at me.

'No, thank you. Spasibo,' I said firmly. 'No baby.'

'Russian baby very strong.'

There was a silence. I could sense Ed straining to listen from next door.

Shrek stood up, walked through to the next room and said something in Russian. There was nervous laughter.

'Vodka?' He flicked the side of his throat and gestured at a half-drunk bottle sitting on one of the desks.

We declined, thanked them all for the tea, did a round of enthusiastic handshakes, gifted them a postcard of a bagpiper and said that unfortunately we had to be on our way. We rode hard downhill without stopping.

Two days later, having cycled over another 1500-metre pass high above the turquoise Nurek Reservoir and then descended to the sunny plains, we reached Kulyab, bathed in sweat and longing for shade. A bazaar was in progress and piles of fresh apricots, tomatoes, cucumbers, cherries and plums sat alongside buckets of cottage cheese and wheels of non. There were sacks of dried apricots, almonds, walnuts, raisins and mulberries, and a section where fifty-kilogram bags of flour stamped with the logos of the UNDP or other international aid agencies were lined up for sale. Did this black-market produce command a different price depending on its logo, I wondered?

We found a small hotel above a line of shops and were shown by a friendly floor lady to a clean room with brown and orange blankets and lace curtains. The owner turned up and scowled at us suspiciously, snatching away our passports 'for OVIR registration'. We sat in our room worrying and counting the minutes creeping by. I snacked on some raisins we'd bought in the bazaar and wrinkled my nose at the acrid taste. They must have been contaminated with diesel fumes, maybe while being transported into town on someone's farm wagon.

The hotel owner had been the first openly hostile person we had met in Tajikistan, and we sat on the bed questioning the sanity of allowing him to walk away with our documents and regretting not being able to get in the shower until he returned. An hour later he arrived back with two policeman. They came into our room and sat on our bed to question us, at one point calling on the assistance of a translator through the chunky receiver of the cream plastic telephone with a rotary dial. Eventually they seemed satisfied with the account of our journey and the excuses provided for our gaps in registration, leaving us to enjoy a shower and wash the salt from our clothes. We decided it would be best to keep a low profile and forego the bazaar, so we cooked pasta in our room, sitting at the open window.

We slept badly in the clammy heat and with the whine of mosquitoes. When we came to leave, the owner embraced Ed heartily and the floor lady and other staff lined up to wave us off. Perhaps relieved to get rid of troublesome foreigners.

28

GOODNIGHT FROM AFGHANISTAN

If you want to live, leave your banks
as a small stream enters the Oxus, miles wide
Or as cattle moving around a millstone
Suddenly circle to the top of a sphere

Rumi, trans. John Moyne and Coleman Barks, from
'Quatrains', in *Unseen Rain: Quatrains of Rumi*

I was slow that morning, toiling uphill in the unforgiving sun and breaking regularly to rest on my handlebars. I felt sluggish. Weighed down with weeks of food supplies and extra litres of water, my bicycle was extremely heavy. Ed, as always, was carrying much more than half of the weight of our kit, but there was rarely anything which would slow him down to my pace. He waited patiently for me at regular intervals, but I could sense the frustration, and my temper started to fray as my blood sugar slumped, leaving me hollow and shaky. My inner dialogue began a cycle of, 'I can't f***ing do this. I've been trying to keep up for the last ten thousand kilometres. It doesn't matter how hard I try, I'm always going to be holding us up,' as I trod down angrily on the pedals.

The road was unmetalled and we were slogging up a rutted uphill section near midday when a woman working the fields in an emerald salwar kameez and matching headscarf straightened up and waved us to a stop. Children clambered around us, small, grubby hands helping to wheel our bikes into their garden and prop them against a mud-brick veranda that looked out over their fields and across the valley. We fumbled with bootlaces in the porch and then crossed the threshold into a dark, cool room with wooden beams and pillars. My eyes adjusted to the gloom and I was suddenly gripped with confusion and fear. A baby, naked from the waist down, was strapped down to a crib, wailing. He was thin and his ribcage heaved with his screams. I stared in alarm. What was wrong with him? The strap looked barbaric.

Nasiba, our hostess, approached and, cooing gently, rocked him back and forth, batting a few flies away, then beckoned to me to sit. She undid the strap and picked him up, wrapping his bottom in a cloth. I noticed that the crib had a hole in it, under which was placed a dish – an alternative to nappies and a solution to having no spare hands or extra help while weeding the fields. Nasiba's daughters were still young and her husband, a lorry driver, was away, transporting apricots to Dushanbe and Tashkent.

She poured us tea, returning it twice to the pot and back into our bowls, and proffered brightly wrapped sweets and non, then served us a bowl of buttery potato soup from a pan which was bubbling on the stove. We sipped the deliciously hot broth and showed her and the children photographs from Scotland. It was the only time on the whole fifteen-month, fifteen-thousand-kilometre trip that we were invited into a house by a lone woman.

We laboured on upwards again and rested at 3pm in the shade of the only tree, crickets humming in the long grass and sweat pouring from our backs and into our eyes. By 5pm we'd reached the Shurabad Pass. We pitched the tent on some flat ground. Dark red lilies grew in the long grass. Cows came by, snuffling and nudging at the tent, and were followed by herders, who called out greetings from horseback before descending the mountainside on sure hooves. Large herds of black and brown sheep moved on green mountain ridges below us, and beyond that the sun set into the haze of the plains of Tajikistan. We cooked, steam billowing in the cooling air and rich evening sunlight, shivering as our damp shirts chilled, faces still burning from the sun. We slept well, despite distant rumblings of thunder.

In the morning, we traversed a high plateau and then dropped on a rough track through a twisting red gorge. As we rattled downhill, the view opened out over a wide river valley, flat bottomed and fertile, cut through by a deep gravel channel in which a braided river flowed. On the other side rose mountains of red rock covered in a velum of green vegetation and peaked with white caps. Afghanistan!

The river beneath us was the Panj, a main tributary of the mighty Amu Darya (classically known as the Oxus). Its ever-changing serpentine length formed the no man's land between Tajikistan and Afghanistan. From where we were, the Panj flowed southwest to Termez in Uzbekistan, where, having joined with the Vakhsh (which rose in Kyrgyzstan to the northeast), it became the Amu Darya and then the Uzbek–Afghan border boundary, continuing on to Turkmenabat in Turkmenistan, where we had crossed it six weeks ago. Our road now led north and then southeast, following the Panj as it contoured the Afghan province of Badakhshan. This was a remote corner of an inaccessible part of an inaccessible country.

I first heard about Afghanistan when I was five. It was 1987 and two small children turned up one morning at my kindergarten in Switzerland. Like me, they had arrived recently, but these kids had come with only their mother; their father was missing. They had fled across mountains from the war with the Russians. A few times a week, the three of us were taken out of class for extra German, and I sometimes went home with them to their grandparents' house. Their grandfather, a surgeon, spoke English to me, and their grandmother hugged me and cast Pashtun blessings across my head before retreating to the kitchen to produce grilled aubergines or tea or watermelon ice cream.

The war was to be to Communist Russia what Vietnam was to the USA, with fifteen thousand mostly conscripted Russian soldiers succumbing in remote mountain terrain to a never-ending wave of determined mujahideen freedom fighters supported by CIA cash, and a hundred Afghans dying for every Russian soldier killed. When the Russians eventually backed out after a decade, six million Afghans had fled the country, my school friends among them. In the 1990s, civil war descended. The mujahideen failed to keep control and a more organised, militarised and religious group arising from the Afghan refugee camps of Pakistan took over – the Taliban. My friend's mother had worn miniskirts in her youth in Kabul; now women had to wear the burqa. The Taliban had been giving refuge to the Saudi mujahideen and founder of global terror organisation al-Qaeda, Osama bin Laden, since 1996. He was the US's most wanted terrorist, but the Taliban had refused to give him up and the US and its allies were now nine years into the fight on this front in their war on terror. Bin Laden had still not been found and hundreds of US and British soldiers were being flown back home in coffins or maimed for life while insurgents stood their ground and normal Afghans continued to suffer. It had been one of the worst years for allied casualties, and support for the war, which had never been strong, was waning further.

Afghanistan was an 'advise against all travel' country on the FCO list. Although we knew this was a remote corner of the country, the only province that the Taliban had not taken control of and a region whose inhabitants still practised Ismaili Shia beliefs, regarded as heresy by the Taliban, we were nevertheless nervous to be so close to the border.

There was no sign of anyone on either the Tajik or Afghan side of the river. Only a lone Himalayan griffon with a white underside and black tail feathers thermalled in slow spirals above the steep, scrubby valley sides. We bumped downhill to eight hundred metres and came to a small cluster of houses with a shop. The shopkeeper, a plump man with a skullcap, shook his head when we tried to select some biscuits and sweets from his meagre array of produce, hustled us out of the shop, locked the door and led us to his house.

We ate lunch sitting cross-legged on his veranda overlooking the Panj. A group of young boys and men crowded around us on the cushioned platform, peering at our camera and asking us about our journey. The shopkeeper's brother had spent time working in Moscow and led the questioning. We were offered tea first, and dried white mulberries from a vast bowl. Our host broke the round of bread. His wife and daughter brought out a large bowl of lamb stew and yogurt and we all sat together. Ed and I were served the biggest pieces of meat. Large chunks were placed on the plate of the shopkeeper and his brother, and the broth and smaller pieces were distributed among the women and children. I chewed frantically on a rubbery kidney, forcing myself to swallow a large lump. Towards the end of the meal, I noticed that the men had not touched the biggest pieces of meat. Our host returned them to the bowl and, registering my glance, said, 'For the women and children.' He raised his cupped hands over his face saying 'Amin', the same gesture used by our Uzbek baker friend, Halim.

We thanked him for a delicious lunch and dared not raise the question of returning to the shop in case he gave us our purchases for free. We had another failed shopping attempt less than an hour later. A girl was selling old plastic water bottles of red juice by the side of the road. We handed over some som for one and undid the sticky lid, hoping it was cherry juice. It tasted acrid and, unsure if it was food or medicine, we left it prominently on a rock a few kilometres further on, in the hope someone else would make use of it.

We encountered our first set of border guards soon after. Two soldiers on patrol: one with a Kalashnikov, the other with a rocket-propelled grenade launcher. They told us the road was closed and seemed disappointed when we directed them to the GBAO permit stamp and the handwritten official flourishes added to it in our passport in Dushanbe. We had now entered Badakhshan, a region divided between the Gorno-Badakhshan Autonomous Region in the Tajikistan north and the Afghanistan Badakhshan Province in the south. Geographically, the area of Badakhshan essentially encompassed the watershed for the upper Panj river, with the series of side valleys that drained into it from high on the Pamir Plateau to the north and east, where we were heading, and the short rivers that fell from the steep wall of the Hindu Kush mountains to the south.

The Panj Valley narrowed, and there were no more villages. Only two trucks had passed us all afternoon and the only other sign of life had been a large citrine-coloured snake sunning itself on the hot gravel in the middle of the road. We had drawn up and wheeled our bikes slowly past it at a safe distance. A small path had appeared hours ago, clinging on to the cliffs on the Afghan side of the river, sometimes zigzagging up cliffs, sometimes squeezing right along the edge of the river, but we had seen no one on it. The shadows were starting to lengthen. It was time to find somewhere to camp. We paused, resting on our handlebars to look at the map and discuss options. There was little cover or flat ground, so we pushed on for another hour until we found a more suitable spot.

A small track headed up the mountainside from our road to what looked like an outcrop. Weary and hoping to find flat ground, we ditched the bikes behind a boulder and then clambered up the path, my knees protesting at the change in activity. We arrived at a tiny levelled area surrounded by a low wall – an old sniper's nest. The road lay beneath us, beyond the foaming brown torrent of the Panj, with Afghanistan a steep broken cliff-face beyond that. The footpath on the Afghan side still ran along above the river, deserted and in places merely a scratch across sheer rock. The combination of flat ground and cover from the road below meant no discussion was needed. We trotted back down the track and hurriedly pushed my and then Ed's bike up the steep incline together. As we left the road with Ed's bike, me shoving at the pannier rack from behind, I looked left and right along it – empty. There had not been a truck driver or anyone else since our encounter with the guards hours ago.

'There's a light on the Afghan side,' Ed said as we sat eating dinner in the tent porch half an hour later.

I put down my plastic bowl of mashed potatoes and stared hard through the evening gloom, to the opposite bank of the river, to where we thought there had been no one.

Hurriedly, I fished my binoculars from the tent pocket. A man in a pale salwar kameez was down by the rushing water. Two others were tending an orange glow on a flattish spot on the tiny path above him.

The men must have seen us. They must have arrived while we were busy cooking and we had not expected anyone to come along that empty improbable path at dusk. However, even had they wanted to, it would have been impossible to shout across the roar of the Panj which was whipping up a chilly breeze between us in the night air. I shivered, feeling suddenly exposed.

'Do you think they could be smuggling drugs?'

Ed voiced both our fears. Afghanistan was a major producer of heroin and growing it was a prime economic activity of Afghan Badakhshan. Sales of heroin were known to fuel the activities of the Taliban, and the Pamir Highway was one of the main conduits out to Western markets. Tajikistan was taking a cut and had been described to us as a narco-state, with drug-trafficking activities apparently permeating the country's economic and political systems. Heroin had supposedly been virtually non-existent there until the mid-1990s and the time of the civil war, but now around 30 per cent of the Tajik recorded gross domestic product was thought to come from the opiate industry.

Anxiously, we discussed if the men might be looking for a handover party and might have mistaken us for them. Crossing the torrent would be madness, though. How would you get across here? I looked again at the tumbling brown water that was being forced through the narrow gap in the cliff. They were less than two hundred metres away. I imagined a crossbow being fired over and packages being hauled across, then dismissed the thought as ridiculous. It was just very strange that they had stopped just there.

'Perhaps they are trying to leave?' I said, thinking of refugees and then, searching around, 'Or looking for Badakhshani rubies?'

Badakhshan was famous in antiquity for rubies, and its rubies were important Silk Road products.

'Or maybe they're just walking to another village?' Ed offered. 'Or collecting plants –mushrooms, perhaps?'

It seemed a bit dry for fungi.

We agreed that the Gore-Tex red of our mountaineering jackets, shining brighter than rubies in the gloaming, would have told them instantly we were not locals.

All we could do was sit and speculate over our mashed potato, now solidified into an unappealing cold lump in our camping bowl. We might as well have been watching from a sofa ten thousand miles away. Eventually all we could see was the fire and we knew they must be huddled close, perhaps cooking on the embers. Maybe they were cradling steaming bowls of tea, laughing at the madness of two tourists with bicycles. Maybe coming from a country at war, they had more existential things to think about and we were flattering ourselves that they cared.

Once in our down sleeping bags, we lay on our stomachs, propped up on our arms, and peered out into the darkness together. The rushing of the Panj was still creating a strong breeze. We could not resist sending one long flash on my head torch out across the dark void.

A moment later, a light came back from the other side. The unmistakable blue glow of a mobile phone's backlight signalled goodnight from Afghanistan.

29
No Room at the Inn

In Xanadu did Kubla Khan
A stately pleasure-dome decree:
Where Alph, the sacred river, ran
Through caverns measureless to man
Down to a sunless sea.
    Samuel Taylor Coleridge, from 'Kubla Khan', in *The Nation's Favourite Poems*

We woke at 4.30am with the intention of being on the road by seven. As we cooked an unappealing breakfast of semolina and powdered milk we could see two of the men from the previous night scrambling precariously above the path on the Afghan side of the Panj, tossing items to the third man below them. Small clouds of dust hung in the air above where the items had tumbled down the slope. I stood again watching them through binoculars, trying to discern what they could be doing. It did not have the look of path building, foraging, or an escape plan. Perhaps they were retrieving a cache of something? However, as is so often the way with the mysteries of the road, there was no neat denouement.

'I'm going with rubies,' I said to Ed, perhaps more in hope than anything else, before turning to my packing. As I knelt in the tent stuffing my sleeping bag away, I wished them a glittering haul and a rich man's return to their villages after a fair price and a slap-up meal in the bazaar of Mazar-i-Sharif.

Very aptly, in view of our night-time companions, the Persian poet Attar of Nishapur (1145–1221) wrote: 'You turn kindling into Badakhshani rubies'. These 'Balas' rubies (technically spinels) are also mentioned in the poetry of Dante and Chaucer, and the Black Prince's Ruby, which has been in British possession since 1367 and adorns the imperial state crown of the United Kingdom, is thought to have come out of the ground in Badakhshan.

There was limited time for romantic notions of finding treasure however, as more military checkpoints appeared along the next section of road – another pair of young men with RPG launchers. They had their names and their blood group written on tags on their oversized and untucked khaki shirts. I eyed their weapons anxiously, hoping their sloppy dressing did not translate into sloppy use of the safety catch, if indeed they were fitted on rocket launchers. The pair earnestly inspected our passports, the first studiously looking at my visa upside down and then handing it to the second, who did not turn it the right way up. Once the formalities were over, we offered them a cigarette and showed them some postcards of Scotland. They were bored and appreciated the diversion.

The sun was fierce and we stopped by a cool slab of rock under a tree and snoozed for a few hours. We were woken by shouts and could see small boys jumping into the river below us on the Tajik side. There were more further along. They were naked and stood up to wave as we approached. As we drew level, cries of alarm went up and they dived into the pool as one, laughing and whooping. The assumption at a distance was always that I would be a man. We eyed them jealously. Naked boys aside, this quiet stretch of the river looked inviting for a swim, but we had been warned that the banks often contained washed-out unexploded ordinance left over from the civil war of the nineties.

The gravel road turned to asphalt suddenly, with a sign declaring that it had been funded by Iran. We stopped at a water pump at the next village and were soon surrounded by a crowd of children. Some helped me to wash the pans we'd not had a chance to clean at breakfast. We politely turned down the offer of tea from a softly spoken young male English teacher, saying we had to push on, assuming that we would, as usual, be pressed repeatedly to accept. We instantly regretted it when he took us at our word, as it would have been nice to speak in more depth to someone. Before we parted, he said something to some of the children, who scampered off into their houses and returned with gifts. We left town with two litres of yogurt decanted into our camping pan, and a wheel of bread.

We camped above the Panj again that night, listening to its endless rushing and watching fireflies at dusk. There was a small scorpion hiding under our tent when we packed it up in the morning.

Now we were catching glimpses of life on the Afghan side. Clusters of low mud buildings clung to the side of the valley, set among terraced green and yellow fields. A woman in a cornflower-blue burka paralleled us on the path across the river. Later, a man in a turban was digging at a section of the path, tossing huge rocks down into the roaring torrent.

We sat down under a mulberry tree to eat some of its sweet white berries with packet cake in celebration of my twenty-eighth birthday. I was tired and looking forward to reaching Kalaikhum later that day. This would mark the point where we rejoined the Pamir Highway, following the detour recommended by the Italian motorbikers to avoid the collapsed section of road on the more direct route from Dushanbe. I was not that bothered about my birthday – I've never been one for big celebrations – but I needed a decent meal. There had been far too many bowls of semolina, super noodles and mashed potato in the last week. I also really wanted a shower. Ed showed me a photograph of a present that he had bought me and posted home in Dushanbe: small dolls dressed in Tajik clothing, male and female, tucked up in a bed together. I laughed, remembering seeing them at a small stand among secondhand mobile phones and piles of crockery in the TSUM department store in Dushanbe. We hugged each other, agreeing that a warm bed, a warm shower and a good meal would be the best present right now.

Shortly after we set off again, my bike took a puncture in the rear tyre. An hour later, the same tyre deflated once again. Ed thought it could be that my wheel rims were deteriorating. We were back at a narrow point in the river and I shivered a little in the shade of the gorge as I sorted through our repair kit, finding the tools to hand him. I rubbed the area of the puncture with sandpaper while Ed felt around the rims for shards of metal. Collapsed wheels at this point in the journey would mean we'd have to head back to Dushanbe on a truck – and that would be the end. Anxiety started to overshadow the birthday atmosphere.

A boy stopped to watch us while we were dealing with the bicycles and told us it was his birthday too. He was interested, sitting on his haunches while we did the repair job. Once it was over, we sat on the grass together and ate a bar of chocolate and the rest of the cake in celebration of a double birthday and a bike fixed.

Kalaikhum was at the junction of our road and the M41, which came in from the north and Dushanbe. At this point the Panj was forced into a narrow gorge and flowed fast, no longer brown but a milky jade colour with white foam. The surrounding cliffs were bare and looked like they were in a state of constant erosion. Houses protruded from the hillside a few metres above the river, some with balconies that overhung the water.

There were vines growing over covered terraces and roofs of corrugated iron. A bridge of steel girders linked Kalaikhum to the Afghan side of the river, which was perhaps twenty metres away. There was a roadblock in the middle of it. We knew from our guidebook that the border was not operational.

We stopped at the police checkpoint to be registered and were told that there was nowhere to stay in town but that there was a homestay a kilometre back the way we had come. Reluctantly, we cycled back to it, only for the owner to wave us away impatiently, saying that he wasn't open. Despondent, we returned to town again. I was hungry now, my appetite whetted by the anticipation of having reached Kalaikhum. The smell of baking non drifted on the breeze from some hidden courtyard. It was early afternoon and the sun was high and the heat oppressive. It was quiet. We asked the few people on the street in turn if they knew of anywhere to stay, but everyone shook their head. We had received so many invitations so far that it was surprising to get such an emphatic response.

We found a chaikhana at the entrance to the bridge with Afghanistan, with a balcony overlooking the river, and took up seats in the shade of the awning and ordered shorba. After an hour, we plucked up the courage to ask the owner if he took overnight guests, expecting him to offer us the option of camping on the terrace, or sleeping in the dining room, but he shook his head decisively. We sat slurping a second round of lamb broth and tea, listening to the river and debating whether to push on a further forty kilometres to the next place that might have accommodation. The promise of hot water on my birthday had taken hold in my imagination. I was going to wash my hair and my clothes. I was also feeling quite unwell now, my stomach having suddenly begun cramping. After some back and forth, we decided that there was no point in trying to push on in the vague hope of a shower. We would move on in due course, as the day drew in, and camp in a hidden spot close to town.

We let a second hour slip by and then a third, hoping that the restaurant owner would give in. It seemed to work as, towards the end of the third hour, a man turned up and offered us a place in his homestay. We followed him, fearing that it would be terrible, and were surprised to be led to a courtyard with numbered rooms leading off it. He showed us the toilet and a separate shower. By some miracle, the water was hot, and

I stood in the room, lit only by a narrow vent in the top of the door, as scalding water streamed over my skin. I scrubbed and scrubbed at it with a flannel, feeling muscles ease and tension lift, better than any spa. Why had no one in town told us about this hotel, I wondered? And why was no one else staying there?

We laid out our sleeping bags on soft mattresses with additional blankets for warmth. I was clean and warm and well fed and quickly drifted into a deep sleep. The sound of the river ever present as I rushed and tumbled down the torrent, heading backwards and backwards on a jumble of water, joining the Amu Darya, the Syr Darya, the Tigris, the Euphrates, the Danube, the Rhine to the North Sea and home.

On the edge of my subconscious I had become aware of the noise of people arriving in the night. Voices, footsteps, the sound of engines and vehicle doors shutting. The vague smell of cigarette smoke. I started awake about 3am, needing the toilet urgently, opened the door and stepped out into the courtyard. It was in gloom and it took me a few paces to register that the yard was packed with men. Some sitting cross-legged, some reclining. There was the glow of cigarettes, and the steam from bowls of tea caught the light flooding out from underneath the doors of the other rooms. Some of the men were dressed in Western-style clothing with skullcaps – Tajiks – but many others were wearing the oatmeal-coloured salwar kameez, waistcoats and mushroom-shaped hats (pakol) that identified them as unmistakably from Afghanistan.

The toilet was just metres from our room. Two men who were slumped against the wall, asleep, lifted their beards from their chests briefly as I slipped past. I crouched in the darkness, toes gripping the plastic toilet slippers, trying to pee quietly, too afraid to turn on the light, my sleep-fogged brain whirring into gear. The Afghans had clearly come across the bridge, which was why there'd been no room at the inn anywhere in town. But why?

When we woke at seven, the only evidence of the overnight guests was a pile of empty tea bowls. Whatever was being arranged had been done in secrecy, no doubt with border guards and perhaps a whole village being paid to sleep through it. This would not be the only evidence of the drug trade we'd see on our journey through the Pamirs.

30

MINEFIELDS IN THE GARDEN OF PARADISE

A Book of Verses underneath the Bough,
A Jug of Wine, a Loaf of Bread – and Thou
Beside me singing in the Wilderness –
Oh, Wilderness were Paradise enow!

Omar Khayyam, trans. Edward Fitzgerald, from 'The Rubaiyat', in Peter Washington (ed.), *Persian Poems*

The Panj was now taking us south again. The valley opened out a little and villages as well as orchards of apricot, cherry and mulberry occupied any flatter ground created by meanders or alluvial fans from tributaries on both sides of the river. We saw more traffic on the track on the Afghan side and were raced by children on bicycles for a stretch between two villages. They shouted and whooped and wobbled alongside us for ten minutes until we lost them at another bend. On the Tajik side, small children ran out to meet us every time we passed through a village, little hands helping to push us along and up hilly tracks.

In one village my heart skipped a beat when I saw a small red-headed girl in a green salwar kameez. Her skin was paler than that of her siblings, just as mine is, because we redheads carry a mutation in a gene called MC1R which disrupts the production of the pigment eumelanin. As we approached, I tried hard not to stare. She was the first redhead I'd seen since the boy working as a blacksmith in the souk in Aleppo.

A commonly held belief is that the people of the Pamirs are the descendants of Alexander the Great's army, which settled along not only the upper reaches of the Syr Darya in Fergana but also the Amu Darya and Panj. There has also been a great deal of Slavic Russian presence in the Pamirs since the beginning of the twentieth century. However, the Scythians were an Indo-European people who inhabited large areas of western China, Central Asia and Siberia from at least as early at 2000 BC and in 329 BC were fought, alongside the Sogdians, by Alexander the Great in his struggle to exert control over the Fergana and the Panj.

Ancient Chinese texts report that the peoples who did battle with the Greeks had blue eyes, fair skin and red beards. Much later, in the seventh century, the Buddhist traveller Xuanzang also noted that in this region people's eyes had a blueish-green tint. The people of the Pamirs today are therefore likely descendants of a once widely distributed population that has remained in inaccessible valleys, reasonably undisturbed by the successive waves of invaders and settlers into Central Asia, from the Persian Sogdians, the ancestors of the Tajiks who had their capital in Samarkand, to the Arabs of the Umayyad and the ructions created by the likes of the Abbasids, Genghis Khan and Tamerlane.

I could see liver spots on the girl's face already, even though she was only six or seven. I had been struggling to stop my skin from burning, particularly the upper parts of my hands and wrists. The tops of my fingers, exposed most of the day as they gripped my handlebars, were red raw. Would she have a shortened life because of melanoma? Why the paler skin coloration has survived within the population of the Pamirs is unclear, since it is deemed to bring negative consequences to populations south of the 45th parallel. Potentially, high, isolated mountain communities experience both sufficiently miserable weather and a lack of influx of other genes to replace these traits. Whatever the explanation, whether ancient or recent, I saw three other people with red hair on the Pamir Highway, and many people had lighter skin and hair tones, and blue, green or hazel eyes.

There was often fruit for sale now in plastic buckets along the road. Apricots and red cherries in large quantities. We paid a few som for a bucket of each, stuffing them into plastic bags on top of our panniers, and gorged ourselves on them. They were some of the most aromatic fruits I have tasted – and not just because our diet had lacked variety in the last few weeks. Especially the apricots, which were small and firm and carried a mouth-watering scent even before the first juicy, sweet-tart bite. I ate five, one after the other. DNA analysis has now also revealed to us that apricots were domesticated from the wild plant *Prunus armeniaca* growing in these remote valleys of Central Asia. Varieties arising from different populations were likely carried both west to the Mediterranean and east to China two to three thousand years ago.

In the heat of the late afternoon, on a section of river that was deserted, we left the bikes by the road and climbed up to a waterfall. We were completely hidden from the road beneath and there was no sign of life on the Afghan side, so we stripped naked and washed under the icy cascade. I gave myself an ice-cream headache rinsing soap out of my hair and stood shivering despite the strong sunlight as I dried myself off, one eye on the riverbank in case of observers.

In some ways it felt as if we had discovered a hidden Shangri-La. The little villages that we crossed seemed like miniature paradises, with their drystone-walled gardens, the tinkling of running water, the scent of apricots, red hibiscus bushes and running children. There was no litter and in contrast to the unforgiving cliffs of the valley the flatter areas seemed bursting with green life. On the Tajik side the houses were sometimes of mud but more often of painted brick with pitched tin roofs. On the Afghan side they were low, of brown mud and flat-roofed. Nevertheless, satellite dishes angled up into the gap of sky between the cliffs from villages on both sides of the valley.

Two small girls of perhaps six ran out to greet us from their garden and tugged our hands, leading us to the cushioned tapchan under a mulberry tree. They delighted in bringing us water from a jug to wash our hands. One ran off to get a tatty jotter and pencil to take our order at their 'café'. We asked for tea and it came with non and a dish of clotted cream. They looked confused when we attempted to pay and ran into the house.

An elderly man in a skullcap with a brightly embroidered band of red, yellow and blue shuffled out of the front door and cast a blessing over us, waving us on. Everyone stopped to talk to us on the road. A father in a similarly embroidered skullcap and his son, in a baseball cap, were coaxing a large herd of sheep and goats along a clifflike stretch of road. They waved us to a stop and asked that we take their picture, posing together with long wooden staffs in front of the mass of animals, which were setting to on the thistles and plants poking out of the dry rock.

The next request for a photo came from a group of small boys. They laughed and joked and ran around as we passed through their village but stood to attention in front of the camera, sticking their chests out, chins up, arms straight by their sides, faces serious, lined up like a mini ragtag band of soldiers in holey T-shirts. A truck driver stopped and opened up the back of his lorry, handing us six eggs from a massive stack nested in corrugated cardboard. That they were still intact on the bumpy road seemed all but impossible.

Nonetheless, there was always a reminder that despite the semblance of paradise, life in these valleys had been rocked by external forces. That evening we set up camp in a grove of willows outside the village of Togmany. The grass under the trees was soft and springy, and after pitching the tent we relaxed, stretched out on the ground by the camp stove, sipping tea and watching the sunset. The river had widened out here, no longer a rushing torrent but stilled into great pools between meandering banks of pale shale and grass. The motionless slate surface of the water mirrored the peaks on the Afghan side. Mountains the colour of iron ore were capped with a dusting of snow, their lower flanks steep fans of red and grey moraine spilling down to the river's edge.

As the rust rock glowed pink in the setting sun, I got on with dinner. I took the kettle across a shale bank and down to the water and filled it, the peaks wobbling as I sent ripples out. The air was starting to chill and it seemed still now, without the rushing of water that had been ever present over the last few days. I returned to the stove and boiled up a pan of water to mix with yet more mashed-potato powder, adding the rest of the slightly warm yogurt we'd been carrying since meeting the teacher. It would have to do.

I re-boiled the kettle for tea. Ed was writing his diary in the grass next to me. We sat watching the mountains as darkness fell and the stars came out. Thinking that we were unobserved, for the first time in days we dared to use our head torches as we were getting ready for bed. We walked down to the river again together to splash water on our faces and brush our teeth. Stars gleamed in the dark pool. Just as I was wriggling into my sleeping bag, we heard the sound of male voices calling out. Ed scrambled out of bed – it was always his job to greet strangers. I did not envy him having to be the first to confront the new arrivals in the darkness. Having people visit us at night was always nerve-wracking.

Two men appeared in the entrance to the tent. Ed went out to greet them and fished around in our bar bags for our passports. I knelt on my sleeping bag, watching them through the fly-net. I could see the glow of a cigarette and the smell of smoke wafted in on the breeze as I made out two young, clean-shaven faces, military shirts and the outline of Kalashnikovs slung over their shoulders. Ed was going through the usual round of answers about where we were from as I mentally prepped myself to have to pack up and move on, but after a short exchange the men continued their foot patrol, seemingly unperturbed by our accommodation arrangements. I lay back in bed, heart pounding, listening for footsteps retreating, unnerved that men with guns knew where we were staying the night.

We came to a minefield left over from the civil war of the nineties. A fading red sign painted on a boulder in Cyrillic script that we could not read appeared to be a warning. It listed the co-ordinates of the site. There were also small rocks that had been painted white and red placed across the ground. We surmised that these were demarking no-go zones on flat parts of the riverbank that would have otherwise been tempting picnicking or camping spots. The cliffs around us were pockmarked with bullet holes and as we cycled on we passed the rusting carcass of a tank, only its khaki frame left, stranded on its belly with missing caterpillar tracks and hollow window sockets.

Where were we going to sleep, I wondered? The ground continued to be littered with painted rocks. We'd cycled through many demarked areas months ago in Bosnia, where it had seemed that most of the county's verges had been mined during the conflict of the 1990s. The 'minefields' – actually often steep cliffs where undisturbed vegetation was growing rampantly – had been marked with red metal signs with white skull and crossbones: 'PAZI MINE!'. We had spent days camping on asphalt to ensure that there was no danger of being wrong and it looked like we might have to do the same on this stretch of the Pamir Highway. In which case, we'd need to find a lay-by that wasn't demarked with red-and-white rocks. We were in a narrow, twisting stretch of the valley again, so it didn't seem like there'd be anywhere suitable soon.

Thirty minutes later, we rounded a bend in the road and saw a line of white canvas tents on a flat piece of ground under the cliff. A large sign declared that it was a demining project supported by Swiss and German government funding.

We stopped to ask a man at the edge of the camp if he knew of somewhere nearby to pitch a tent. 'Here?' he said, waving us into the camp and directing us to a flat piece of ground demarcated by yet more white rocks.

We were invited into the mess tent, where we met a fourteen-strong team of Tajik demining operatives. They were mostly young men. Some of them wore skullcaps and some wore baseball caps and they all had royal-blue jackets emblazoned with the logo of the FSD, the Swiss foundation for demining. They had been taught by Swiss operatives and some of them had trained in other parts of the world, including Bosnia.

We sat down to eat from a vast communal metal dish of potatoes and lamb, which was delicious but extremely greasy, swimming in lamb fat and cotton seed oil, a cheap fat used for cooking in Central Asia. We tucked in hungrily, mopping up the juices with stale bread. They told us that they had found the identity document that day of a herder who had walked into a minefield a few years ago and was blown up. Until now it had been too dangerous to retrieve his body.

'You know, it is not always possible to go in and help people if they are injured,' one of the men said. 'He died slowly and no one could help him. The mines sometimes wash up on the riverbank. A young boy was killed this year because he found one.'

I shuddered, thinking of the boys we'd seen swimming in the river and my visit to the bank the previous evening. The route down had clearly been a path used by herders to take their livestock to drink, but …

'We have lots of problems with children following their goats in.'

We talked late about their work and the different devices designed to kill. I could not imagine volunteering for their job. In the morning, the whole team lined up outside the camp to wave us off. We took a group photo dwarfed by the cliff surrounding the narrow valley, sheer and devoid of life, blasted over millennia by the violent forces of the all-powerful river, the Panj Valley sneering at the ridiculousness of human ambitions to conquer it.

Khorog, capital of the Gorno-Badakhshan Autonomous Oblast, is sited at the confluence of the Gunt and the Panj. We reached it three days later, greeted by blue and red tin roofs strung out along either side of the Gunt, the town being crammed onto flat land between high valley sides and greened by lines of tall poplars and willows.

The Russians established a base here in 1886 during the period when boundary lines were being drawn between the Russian and British empires. From Khorog, the M41, the main Pamir Highway, headed away from the Panj, through the Gunt Valley, but our route would continue along the Panj, taking us south for a hundred kilometres until we reached the Wakhan Corridor, the panhandle which juts out to the east of Afghanistan and was the bizarre cartographic outcome of all that empire tussling. The corridor was drawn up in 1893, after an agreement between the British Raj and the Emir of Afghanistan. This narrow strip, in some places no more than seventeen kilometres wide, was intended to act as a safe buffer zone between the two empires. Its formation was the culmination of the period of espionage and land grabs known by the British as the Great Game and by the Russians as the Tournament of Shadows. Britain feared Russia's southward expansion would threaten India, and Afghanistan was caught in the middle.

The current British involvement in Afghanistan was, thus, far from its first. It was in fact the fourth time our troops had been sent onto Afghan soil. There had been three conflicts, in 1838–42, 1878–80 and 1919, in which Great Britain, from its base in British India, had sought to extend its control over neighbouring Afghanistan and so oppose Russian influence there. The British eventually signed a peace treaty acknowledging the independence of Afghanistan in 1919 and Afghanistan soon became one of the first states to recognise the Bolshevik Soviet government. A 'special relationship' evolved between the two governments, which lasted until the Soviet Union invaded in 1979.

It is said that the Russians were welcomed to Khorog when they arrived to stake their claim before the British did because the Pamiris who practised their Ismaili Shia religion had been heavily persecuted by their Sunni neighbours from the emirate of Bukhara (which eventually fell to the Russians in 1921) and Afghanistan. The Pamiris had survived for centuries by hiding in isolated valleys and practising their religion in secret. The Ismaili religion is said by the Pamiris to have been brought to the Wakhan in 1057 by the poet and Ismaili missionary Nasir-i Khusraw, who fled to Badakhshan under threat of death from the Sunni Seljuk rulers. The Pamirs are today home to the largest population of Ismailis in the world. They practise Nizari Ismailism, a branch of Shia Islam, focusing on the mystical path and nature of God. They agree with the Twelver Shia of Iran on the succession of the first six prophets but believe that the seventh is Isma'il ibn Ja'far (hence Ismailism). Ismailism has a strong connection with Sufism, which is a mystical expression of Islam that is found in both Shia and Sunni traditions.

Aside from Nasir-i Khusraw, many of the great poets, including Rab'eh, Rumi, Hafez, Sanai, Jami and Attar, are considered to be Sufi. Some argue that Sufism is just how Islam was expressed before more literalist and legalist strains of Islam like the Wahhabi movement originating from Saudi Arabia predominated. Today, Nizari Ismaili women are able to divorce and do not have to take the veil (so long as these rights are also upheld in national law). Polygamy is outlawed and equal opportunity in employment is encouraged.

The Russian influence on the region brought education and was arguably also welcomed (at least to some degree) due to the values Ismailism places on learning. It is likely that a willingness to play along with socialist atheism while continuing to practise their religion in secret, as they'd being doing for centuries, was a factor in minimising conflict with their occupiers. The area was now receiving massive investment by the Aga Khan IV, the Swiss-born leader of the Nizari branch of Ismaili Islam. We passed some new yellow housing blocks on the outskirts of town which were home to the University of Central Asia, established in 2000 under the Aga Khan Development Network.

We checked into a B&B with a wooden veranda and cushioned platforms where we spent time catching up with some other travellers including two Swiss couples who were also on bicycles. Friends Fabi and Denise were on a six-week holiday to Central Asia and were pretending to be brother and sister so as to avoid awkward questions. Boyfriend and girlfriend Ueli and Erika, on the other hand, were wearing wedding bands even though they weren't married. Ueli and Erika had cycled from Switzerland. The two couples had spent the last two weeks cycling together as a four. We all spent two frustrating days trying to get registered at the GBAO checkpoint, being told initially to come back the next day, only to be informed the next day that registration was not necessary until we reached Murgab. We had three long lunches with the Swiss at a café in town that served Pakistani food, the first hint that we were not far away, and Coca-Cola produced in Afghanistan, presumably a result of the recent invasion. We ate as much as we could, salivating over flavours like chilli, cumin and ginger that we'd not encountered for some time. Our companions were talkative and I got the impression that they were glad to have other people to speak to.

'What do you talk about when you're on the bike?' Erika asked me as we walked back to the hostel ahead of the others.

I was surprised by the question and did not really know what to answer. I'd never once struggled to think of conversation with Ed on the trip, or worried about it if we cycled in silence. When I thought about it, I was not sure what we discussed. We often talked about the people we'd met, comparing notes after being hosted at someone's house, where there was rarely any time to chat to each other. We talked about the road ahead and future plans and we joked a lot. We shared a sarcastic and fairly puerile sense of humour. We argued, mostly when I was physically exhausted or hungry, but I never got bored of being together. Erika told me that she now cycled with her earphones in for most of the day and that they saved conversation for the evening.

I could tell that she was angling for us to join them. 'I also feel so much safer in a bigger group,' she said. I sidestepped her hints. I was not keen to be in a bigger group. Not because I thought I wouldn't enjoy the company of other travellers – it was really good to meet people who had so much in common and had faced the same challenges – but I knew it would get in the way of our ability to encounter people who lived locally.

On departure day, we set off mid-morning and realised five kilometres out of town that we'd forgotten to fill up on petrol. We had used most of the half-litre in our small bottle, although we still had an untouched one-litre bottle from Dushanbe. Ed's temper was, uncharacteristically, fraying this morning. It had been his turn to be up in the night with food poisoning, overindulgence on curry no doubt the culprit, and we had set off late to allow him some extra time in bed. He didn't want to turn round and further delay the day, arguing that we'd be fine. I told him he was being over-optimistic and was adamant that we needed a full complement of supplies. We were going to be cycling at a higher altitude, up from two thousand to well over four thousand metres, and I was worried that we would burn through our supplies quicker than anticipated. I wanted to be sure we would have enough to get us to Murgab, high on the Pamir Plateau and the only significant town before we reached the Kyrgyz border approximately ten days away. Fuel meant food. I was always hungry and often hangry. I countered that I did not want to risk unnecessary marital disharmony if we had to ration food supplies, or, worse, tea, even more than we already did on the plateau. Normally Ed would have volunteered to cycle back to get the petrol. He always had more gas in his human tank than I did. But this time I said I would go.

Our mood did not improve as we cranked our pedals against a headwind that was tunnelling through the valley. I had my head down against the wind and suddenly heard the loud rumble of rock. I looked up to see a big cloud of dust falling off the steep cliff on the Afghan side of the river. We stopped to watch the dust clearing. Fifty metres downstream, a group of men in salwar kameez were sitting on yellow jerrycans under a makeshift stone shelter on the path, which ended abruptly at the cliff. A cable snaked out from them to the blast zone. There was another rumble and a further chunk of cliff collapsed into the river. They took up pickaxes and started to hack out the blasted section of path, giving us a cheery wave before setting to.

By mid-afternoon we should have covered much more than the forty-five kilometres we'd achieved. We stopped to eat some biscuits and discuss options. There were thermal hot springs marked on the map at Garm Chasma, a seven-kilometre detour up a side road near to where we were. We decided it would be worth it and I let myself imagine a campsite with a mountain view and a hot soak in a riverside pool. The road was steep and rutted and it was dusk by the time we reached what turned out to be a dilapidated complex of corrugated-metal buildings clinging to cliffs which had stalactites of luminous sulphurous deposit running down them. Groups of men were smoking and lounging outside on the concrete steps below a sanatorium, which had perhaps once been a cure resort for Soviet officials. One man had a bottle of beer in his hand. Ed approached them while I stood back with the bikes, examining the dirt and feeling on edge. I could hear laughter.

'It's men only,' Ed said once he'd returned.

We bumped back down the way we'd come. I felt nervous. The road to the spring was one-way, up a narrowing valley, and it was now obvious to the assembled audience where we were heading. The light was fading rapidly and we needed to find a space to camp as soon as possible. We were both thinking about minefields marked only by painted stones and how we needed to be sure not to miss them in the half-light.

We pulled off into a flat area behind some large boulders. The eggs we'd bought in Khorog had smashed in my pannier and I worked as quickly as I could in the dark to clean the mess off all of our other food supplies and salvage the remainder so we could have scrambled eggs for dinner. Night fell and I continued with a torch. A car drove up the road, its headlights reaching us long before the vehicle passed. I turned off my torch, waiting till it had gone, music and engine noise fading back into the stillness of the night.

After dinner, we lay in bed unable to sleep, on edge because of the location. Most nights, I fell asleep instantly and deeply. I was often at the edge of my energy reserves and sometimes it was all I could do to eat my dinner before I had to lie down, eyes closing like a doll. Ed had always been a much lighter sleeper, almost an insomniac. As a student, I would fall asleep and then realise that he had been up baking flapjacks at two in the morning, writing an inevitably late essay or reading climbing guides. I'd not noticed it at the start of our journey because I was used to him being awake, but I'd come to realise during the course of the trip that he was often on watch during the night. I'd begun to suspect that it was not just because he was the lighter sleeper but because he felt it was his job to face any enemies that might arrive in the night. At guesthouses, he would often therefore have a much greater need to sleep than I did. I'd not asked him about this, because neither of us really wanted to voice our fears about the darker possibilities of camping in remote places. Only after we'd returned to Scotland did he admit that he had slept with one eye open for much of the journey and often stayed up late, listening and watching me sleep.

This evening, however, even I was not going to sleep. The atmosphere at the springs had been unsavoury and I was unsettled. I told myself that now we had decided to camp here there was little point in worrying about it and that part of the anxiety was the anticipation of a long, nervous night, being on the alert for any sound. With the light of morning, it would all be better. Conscious that we were both straining to hear in the darkness, we started to talk to kill time, discussing the cyclists we'd met in Khorog and our plans for the next days. We joked about the latest bout of food poisoning and that it seemed we were either plagued by constipation or the reverse. We fell back on a game we'd started to play a few weeks ago, challenging each other to compose limericks, which were inevitably crude.

'Okay, I've got one,' Ed said.

'There once was a Western traveller called Ed,
With a foreskin as nature intend-Ed ... '

'Ha ha,' I said. 'Good one.'

'Iranians laughed till they cried,
Once they had surmised,
That he still had a c—'

There was a shaking of canvas and a man's voice.
I clutched Ed's arm.
'Salam alaykum!' Ed shouted loudly, scrambling up as I pulled a hat on low over my face.

I saw our cooking knife, a foldable Opinel hunting knife on which the blade could be fixed, in the tent pocket and quickly slipped it into my own. Not so much because I was planning on using it, but more because it might be seized by an opportunist.

My heart pounded.

Ed unzipped the entrance and shone his head torch straight into the face of a man who was crouching in the porch. He lurched backwards, startled by the glare of light, and Ed dropped the beam slightly.

I looked at his face and saw the sunken eyes of an addict.

The man tried Tajik and then Russian on us. The only word we could make out was 'antibiotica', which was repeated urgently.

Was is it really antibiotics he was after or did he want us to open up our medical kit to get a good look at what was in it? I was thinking about the powerful opioid tramadol we had for emergencies, our sets of sterile needles and other things he might be thinking of. Or maybe it was the only word for medicine he thought we might know.

A few moments later a second man arrived, clutching his stomach. His face was also thin and sunken.

'Antibiotica!' the first man shouted agitatedly at us as the second one lay in a foetal position on the ground outside our tent.

'Nyet doctor,' Ed said, shaking his head at the man.

I stared out into the darkness, looking for further moving shapes, wondering if there were others and if the men might be armed. Wondering if there was a danger they might become further agitated. Was this a bad trip, illness on top of their addiction or something else? A trap? A decoy?

'Khorog. Doctor.' Ed pointed back down the valley.

'Antibiotica!' the man shouted again.

If the man had a genuine need for antibiotics, then handing over paracetamol or something else reasonably innocuous could delay real treatment.

Both men were now lying in front of the entrance to our tent.

A car engine thrummed in the distance and suddenly I had the answer. I fumbled for my boots and head torch, then ran onto the road and flagged down the car, shouting 'Doctor!' and waving.

The car was blaring music and full of young men. I pointed at the light by the tent. 'Doctor!'

Two of the men leapt out and ran down with me.

When we reached the tent, I could see from their expressions that they had been expecting to help a tourist and not two local drug addicts. We emphasised that the men had to be taken to a doctor and eventually manged to persuade them to drive them to Khorog in the car. Ed gave them some som for the 'medical fees'. They headed down the valley, though I feared that the addicts might be kicked out further along the road.

We lay in our sleeping bags fully clothed, heartbeats returning to a normal pace but still on edge, waiting for any of the men to return, possibly having hatched a plan for how to rob us now that they knew we were here. I squeezed Ed's hand, ears straining into the darkness of the valley. It was easy to conjure demons out of the night and dawn was a long time coming.

31

PRAISE BE FOR A COMFORTABLE BED

O widely read, O globally travelled one (still earth-bound, still caught beneath the sky) what value would the spheres yet hold for you were you to catch a glimpse of hidden knowledge? Will your flesh luxuriate forever in the boons and blessings of the world? Why not for a little while enjoy as well the fruits of knowledge with the tongue of the Spirit? The dreamers' banquets cannot profit him; only the waking know the taste of gain and loss. What does the dreamer know of stars and turquoise domes, or things the Almighty brings to pass upon his dust sphere?

... Wake up

Nasir-i Khusraw, trans. Gholam-Reza Aavani and Peter Lamborn Wilson, from 'Divan', in *Forty Poems from the Divan*

The sun had risen on the horrors of the night and when light started to come into the sky we slept deeply. We got up at six, when the heat became too fierce on the canvas, and sat bleary-eyed on the grass in the bright morning, gazing across green pastures to the white-capped peaks. Two small girls in plastic sandals, holey leggings and woolly jumpers found us with their flock of lambs. They stood by the tent and watched me curiously as I worked the stove and made breakfast. They each lifted up a lamb, hugging the wriggling, curly-haired creatures tightly, almost as big as they were, proud to show them off to us.

We whizzed back down to the Panj. Mid-afternoon, we came across another thermal spring in a simple stone-lined pool by the side of the road. The area where the Pamirs meet the Hindu Kush is one of the most seismically active regions on earth, the Hindu Kush thrust up in response to collision with the older Pamir plateau. The Wakhan Corridor, which we were now entering, is where the two mountain ranges meet. The water in the spring was not hot but lukewarm and Ed sat in it in his underpants while I bathed my legs. I was not keen on stripping off in such a public location nor on exposing my skin to the cold wind that was still coursing down the valley despite the fierce sunshine.

That night, knowing that we were now in a region where landmines were not a danger, we camped on a wide shale plain by the river. We passed through the village of Ishkashim the next day, Badakhshan's only open border crossing with Afghanistan. As it was a Saturday, we were hoping to visit its market, reportedly the one time every week when traders from the Tajik and Afghan sides were able to meet and exchange goods on a shale bank of no man's land in the river. Disappointingly, the market was off that week, due to security concerns.

The valley had now opened out into a huge floodplain, alluvial fans spilling down side valleys to meet a blue-grey Panj. Finally, a wall of peaks stood ahead, a vast line of white teeth – the Hindu Kush. The sun was hot and we laboured past large fields of potatoes and wheat guarded by thick fences of thorns. Hoopoes were scattered across the fields in splashes of black and white and sandy, peachy orange. I stopped to watch one, smiling at the bobbing of its punky crest as it hopped about in pursuit of an unfortunate beetle. In Persian literature the hoopoe is a harbinger of good fortune and leads the lover to the beloved. In Attar of Nishapur's epic twelfth-century poem *The Conference of the Birds* the birds of the world gather to decide who is to be their sovereign, as they have none. The hoopoe, the wisest of them all, suggests that they should find the legendary simurgh, a wonderous, phoenix-like creature who we had seen depicted in jade and turquoise tiling with its twisty, flame-like tail feathers on Bukhara's Sufi madrasa. The hoopoe leads the birds, who all represent human faults, across seven valleys representing seven different stages of enlightenment. The journey is arduous and many birds give up or perish. Only thirty make it to the home of the simurgh, where the birds learn that they themselves are the simurgh. The mirror finally held up to the soul.

We stopped every now and again to entertain small children who ran out to meet us. A group of teenaged girls going for a stroll were delighted at encountering Ed and gigglingly insisted on a photograph. A nine-year-old girl invited us into her house for tea with her mother and toddler brother. She was learning English from a CD-ROM. The Aga Khan had said everyone should learn English, so that's what she was doing. She wanted to go to the USA to study medicine. She proudly showed us a letter another tourist had sent her.

Later that day, once the light had grown soft, a pink tinge crept into the white caps of the Hindu Kush. Now that the searing rays of the sun had vanished, the air had turned chilly and was rustling through the fields. Soon it would be cold and starry. We were down by the Panj, in search of a campsite on the shale floodplain, eyeing clumps of willow as potential cover, when a man found us. He had been out collecting firewood and had a large bundle on his shoulder.

'You come in my house.' It was not a question but a statement.

We smiled, knowing we had been rumbled and that there was no arguing with him. We picked our way back up the bank after him, crossing a tinkling irrigation ditch. He nodded in recognition when we reached our bikes, but there were no more words. We tailed him back along the road, pushing our heavily laden bicycles.

Dogs barked and children laughed excitedly as we drew up to the house and an old man appeared in the doorway. Blue eyes twinkled from a sun- and laughter-creased face beneath an embroidered skullcap.

'My father,' our guide said, and disappeared into the house. There was no additional sign from the son. No 'did you just invite them in for a cup of tea or are they staying the night?' look from the father.

'Salam. My name is Hassan,' the man said, taking Ed's hand.

Shoes off, and we were led along a corridor and into a large room with a raised platform around the edge. Light fell from a skylight set into a timber star of concentric squares, and five carved wooden pillars held up the roof.

We sat cross-legged around a low table on the platform with Hassan. The wall and the platform were carpeted in machined 'city' carpets of Persian design. Tea in a battered aluminium teapot was brought to us by his daughter and served in large crockery bowls. In a now familiar gesture, Hassan tore a wheel of dense brown non and placed pieces in front of us, to be eaten with apricot jam that was sweet and made with big chunks of aromatic fruit.

Hassan had learnt English because he had been called to do so by the Aga Khan. It was his religious duty. A large portrait of the leader hung on the wall. He told us that there were no mosques in the valley, rather that every Pamiri's house was a place of prayer, used for daily worship and also for marriage and funeral rites, secretive worship being the response of a persecuted people.

As in all Pamiri houses, the five wooden pillars connecting the platform to the ceiling represented the five members of Ali's family. Ali the cousin and son-in-law of the Prophet Muhammad, and in Shia but not in Sunni Islam his rightful successor. There was a pillar for Muhammad, one for Ali and one for Ali's wife, Bibi Fatima. The two pillars in front of the door represented Ali's sons Hassan and Husayn and were connected with a cross-beam signifying their brotherhood. The thirteen wooden beams on the ceiling related to the six prophets, Adam, Noah, Abraham, Moses, Jesus and Muhammad, and to the first seven imams of Ismailism. The cross-beam which joined the Hassan and Husayn pillars was carved with swastika and sun designs and above it was hung the mighty curling horns of a Marco Polo sheep, all of these being Zoroastrian symbols that predated Islam. The layout of traditional Pamiri houses is thought to go back over two thousand years, to the time when Zoroastrianism was the predominant religion of the civilisations of the Oxus, and the arrangement of the beams can also be related to Zoroastrianism's five major deities (Surush, Mehr, Anahita, Zamyod and Ozar), six geographic directions (East, West, North, South, Upper and Lower) and seven heavenly bodies (Sun, Moon, Saturn, Jupiter, Mars, Venus and Mercury), among many other symbolisms.

Other family members joined us on the platform. Hassan talked about the new bridge at Ishkashim, and the market, where, for the first time in years, Pamiris on either side of the Tajik–Afghan border could meet, trade and visit family. He talked about his second son, who worked in Russia, and his six grandchildren, who wandered in and out and peeked at us curiously. He asked us about the difficulty of cycling and our families. Our pictures from home were examined carefully, not least the living rooms with sofas in them, the different mountain scenes and the shots of people in sportswear.

We all shared a huge plate of Russian noodles laced with fresh herbs, each of us dipping our spoons in from our own side of the dish. When the last noodle had been forced on Ed, dinner was declared over. Hassan stretched out his upturned palms before lifting them and wiping them in one motion down in front of his face. We joined him, glad again that Halim the Uzbek baker had taught us the 'Amin'.

Beds were made up for us in an anteroom, which, from the fancy wardrobe and framed photographs, we suspected the wife of the son working in Russia had given up for us. Deep mattresses were covered with heavy quilts. Praise be for a comfortable bed, I thought, marvelling at how on earth we'd ended up here.

I slipped out to the loo for the last time and in the corridor my hand was caught by Nasiva, one of Hassan's granddaughters, who'd been waiting there in case I needed to venture outside. As we squatted next to each other in the darkness, she swept her hand across the night sky, which was littered with stars, as if to say 'Look!' Snow on the Hindu Kush across the broad valley gave out its own gleaming light. Water babbled, dogs barked in another village and everything else was still, Tajikistan and Afghanistan asleep. I blinked. Orion's Belt swam and merged into a blur behind a hot tear. I was overwhelmed. Somehow, deep in the constellation of my neural cells, I needed to store this moment, exactly like this, forever.

32
A Maze of Dashed Lines

Before long the tea cups had gone its rounds, infusing warmth into our frames, and a glow into our hearts, that made us, I dare say, happier than many a party who were at that moment quaffing their claret, and surrounded with all the luxuries of civilised life.

John Wood, *A Journey to the Source of the River Oxus*

The next section of road along the Wakhan deteriorated markedly, often turning into patches of deep gravel. We headed upwards for the following two days, struggling with the glaring sun, passing Zoroastrian shrines, their whitewashed walls decorated with the skulls of ibex and Marco Polo sheep, the skulls a symbol of purity. We camped on the roadside just outside Vrang after a horde of small children helped us to push our bikes up some steep bends in deep gravel at sunset. The next day we found a small roadside bath house at Shirin. Scalding-hot water bubbled in an indoor pool and we took it in turns to sit in the fierce sunshine on the stone steps outside the door as the other bathed. No one turned up and the road was empty. We rinsed our shirts and pants for the first time in days.

In the village of Langar we stopped at a chaikhana, trees rustling in a light breeze giving some relief from the sun. All they had to serve us with our bowls of tea was eggs and bread. When we visited the shop, there were only biscuits and sweets for sale, but we managed to find more petrol for the stove. We were burning through supplies more rapidly than expected, even given the altitude, which was now well over three thousand metres, probably because it was dirty fuel.

The chaikhana owner called on two small boys to take us on a twenty-minute walk up a steep mountainside to a huge natural pavement inscribed with petroglyphs. There were hundreds of ibex and people with drawn bows as well as Zoroastrian or Buddhist swastikas and Buddhist stupas. The site is one of the largest of fifty similar locations known in Gorno-Badakhshan and believed to date to around 1000 BC, to the time of the Scythians. The boys enthusiastically demonstrated how they added their own petroglyphs, bashing at the smooth rock face with a stone despite our protests.

The site was also a spectacular lookout across the confluence of the Pamir and Wakhan rivers, which together became the Panj and then flowed on to the great Amu Darya. Slivers of land patchworked with green and yellow fields fringed both the Tajik and the Afghan sides and between them stretched a vast braided shale plain, dark green bushes lining the more permanent channels. Sheer mountainsides of moraine sent rocks continually trickling into the river, and above them the peaks were white. We descended with the boys and then cycled on up switchbacks, forced to push our bikes through gravel and helped over a section by yet another band of children who we paid back with our newly acquired supply of sweets. We camped high above the Pamir river, looking back towards the confluence, the sunset casting a rich, warm yellow over Afghanistan. I could only agree with British explorer Charles Adolphus Murray, who travelled in the Pamirs in 1892–93 and noted that the colour of the land seemed to glow with a richness and clarity that was hard to describe.

On the Pamirs, I have often seen evening tints in the sky, the colours of which I do not believe that any landscape painter in the world could give a name to, and the after-glows, which would almost answer to our twilights in Europe as so exquisite in their refinement, that it were absolutely impossible to attempt to describe them.

We could not stop soaking it up and sat out late.

Further up the Pamir river but tantalisingly out of reach was Lake Zorkul, the long-sought and contested source of the Oxus. It is possible that Lake Zorkul was documented by Marco Polo, who reports finding a lake in his account of travelling up 'The Great River of Badakhshan', however the first confirmed European visitor to it was John Wood, in 1828. He was a thoughtful British officer who decided against naming it Lake Victoria after his queen, retaining the local name Zorkul, although Victoria was later used and is recorded in the 1895 'Agreement between the Governments of Great Britain and Russia with regard to the Spheres of Influence of the Two Countries in the Region of the Pamirs', one of the key treaties of the Great Game:

Her Britannic Majesty's Government engage that the territory lying within the British sphere of influence between the Hindu Kush and the line running from the east end of Lake Victoria to the Chinese frontier shall form part of the territory of the Ameer of Afghanistan, that it shall not be annexed to Great Britain, and that no military posts or forts shall be established in it.

China was not involved in these discussions and it would be 1963 before the Chinese boundary with what was by then Pakistan was agreed, and 2002 before agreement was reached between China and Tajikistan on the Pamir boundary – with the Chinese insertion of 'for the time being'.

Here we were in Tajikistan, camped only a few days' walk from the borders with Afghanistan, Pakistan and China, on a bulging overspill of the Eurasian land mass created when the pointy western corner of the Indian subcontinent ploughed into it forty million years ago. The borders in this knot of mountains still showed as a maze of dashed lines. They were remote, seemingly illogical and politically diaphanous, yet impermeable to travellers. We had come as far east as our permits would allow. Zorkul was out of bounds and there was no through route to China's Tashkurgan, a sparsely populated, ethnically Tajik part of western China. We would have to head 350 kilometres north and into Kyrgyzstan before crossing eastwards into China.

Francis Younghusband, Britain's infamous player in the Great Game, had been attempting to reach Zorkul in 1891 when, camped just over the other side of the Little Pamir at Boza-i-Gumbaz in the Wakhan, he met Capt. Mikhail Ionov, who claimed the territory as Russian and invited him politely, over dinner, to leave, in what was subsequently referred to as the Pamir Incident. At the same time, another British officer, Lt Davison, was arrested by Russians in the Alichur Valley (a little further ahead on our route).

The Pamir Incident caused outrage in Britain, with one lord comparing Boza-i-Gumbaz (which no one, not even the Foreign Office, had heard of) to Gibraltar. As John Wood astutely noted, it was bemusing why plain dwellers from all points of the compass continued to meddle in these high reaches of Eurasia.

A Maze of Dashed Lines

How strange and how interesting a group would be formed if an individual from each nation whose rivers have their first source in the Pamirs were to meet upon its summit; what varieties would there be in person, language and manners; what contrasts between the rough, untamed and fierce mountaineer and the more civilised and effeminate dweller of the plain.

What is striking about the Great Game in the Pamirs is how little time was spent physically 'occupying' territory that was demarcated in 1895, land that of course was and continues to be occupied by the people who actually make their lives there.

We pushed our bikes for all of the next day, upwards through deep drifts of gravel and rock. I attached a bungee from my belt to my seat post to help pull my bicycle upwards. The sun was fierce and there was no vegetation, so we put up the tent at midday to get some shade, snow-clad peaks taunting us with thoughts of ice. Eventually the road opened out to a high plateau, the mountains now set back and rolling, reminiscent sometimes of Iceland and sometimes of the Cairngorms. A pair of white griffon vultures circled above us, fat orange marmots whistled and scattered in our wake and we encountered black and shaggy yaks. The roadsides were littered with the horns of Marco Polo sheep. We camped on flat grass by an abandoned village. The water was silted and we filtered it through a T-shirt before boiling it to drink. The night was bitterly cold and we woke to find the canvas stiff with frost.

There were more marmots and two-humped Bactrian camels. We crossed paths with a couple from Budapest in a 4x4 and were able to ascertain that the border with Kyrgyzstan had reopened, at least for now. We reached the Khargush Pass (4344 metres) early afternoon, really only marked by the fact that the road then started to descend. A glorious gentle downhill! We bumped on through a wide, arid valley, set up camp by a lake on short sward studded with pale pink saxifrages and lay outside, enjoying some sunshine before the shadow stole over us and the warmth vanished. The pale disc of a waning gibbous moon hung in the dusky sky above needle-like cliffs as I got up to fill the kettle. In the half-light a white chalky deposit glowed at the edge of the water. I dipped my finger in and tasted salt. Thankfully we had just enough water for the evening and next morning.

We continued downwards, through the wide, dry valley, yellow rock stained with white salt, and eventually, detouring off the main road, on to the freshwater lake of Bulunkul. The wind blew fiercely and ice-cold across the lake's blue surface, despite the bright sunshine. We struggled on for the rest of the day up a terrible track to a campsite opposite the ruined caravanserai complex of Sumantash on the Alichur river. The river was too deep to cross, but I stood looking through binoculars, examining the domed roof and arched entrance, site of two decisive skirmishes, one in 1759 when the Chinese defeated the Muslim rulers of Kashgar and the second in 1892 when Capt. Ionov of the Pamir Incident killed a small group of Afghans, effectively ending the Afghan presence in the eastern Pamirs.

Once the mountains had become dark silhouettes against the stars, we tortured ourselves with thoughts of food. We lay on our backs in the tent, bodies aching, faces glowing from the day's sun and the pit in our stomachs only half full. As on most nights since leaving Dushanbe, we'd shared a Russian-made packet of dried mashed potato for dinner. Breakfast had been semolina with milk powder, lunch super noodles hydrated with fresh water from lake Bulunkul, and the rest of the time we'd been rationing stale biscuits. I was burning food like a candle. No sooner had I eaten something than my insatiable hunger returned. I was obsessing over the next snack and I was losing my temper easily as my blood sugar crashed, especially when having to get off and push my bicycle over difficult terrain.

'Real mashed potato with mustard,' I offered in a repeat of our favourite bedtime game.

'Chips,' Ed replied. 'French fries and British.'

'Boiled with butter.'

'Baked with beans and cheese – no, hang on, chilli and cheese.'

'Potato salad with mayonnaise.'

My exhausted mind drifted down the dusty roads we'd ridden and back ... To the Kyrgyz yak herders by Bulunkul who'd welcomed us in for salt-greasy yak-butter tea and thick double cream, which we'd restrained ourselves from eating more than a polite share of. To the small shops surrounded by green fields in the Wakhan Valley that sold little apart from dusty sweets, dried biscuits and the occasional onion. To the children who ran towards us with grubby handfuls of tart cherries, their faces stained pink. To the women who found us washing up at the river and insisted on filling our pans with fresh yogurt. To the truck stop on a hairpin bend where men hawked sackfuls of dried apricots and sweet almonds from orchards lower down the mountain. To the chaikhanas where we'd sat cross-legged on shaded tapchans eating kebabs with deliciously charred fat (my former vegetarianism now well and truly history), steaming bowls of laghman noodle broth and heaps of plov with carrots, raisins and lamb.

To the flatlands of Uzbekistan, where the bazaars of Samarkand and Bukhara shimmered in my mind's eye as gold-toothed grandmas dressed in bright ikat tunics sold mounds of cottage cheese, dill and coriander, cucumbers, tomatoes, vats of pickled carrot and cucumber and piles of lamb manti. To the ubiquitous non sellers, their bread round and golden, stamped with the baker's mark and stored lovingly beneath blankets in a pram. Back across the Turkmen desert to Iranian chicken fesenjoon, eaten with steaming rice on Mahdi's balcony carpeted with tribal rugs. And to ghormeh sabzi, lamb in herb sauce, made by Zara and her daughters in Golestan.

'Dauphinoise!'

'Colcannon.'

'Curly fries.'

'Crisps.'

I breakfasted in Syria, dipping bread into yogurt, and thyme and sesame za'atar. Wafer-thin lahmacun in Turkey, a pizza-like base covered in spiced lamb, eaten with a squeeze of lemon juice (my mouth watered) wrapped with a handful of coriander and washed down with a glass of salty yogurt ayran. In Gaziantep, I dreamed of rose-scented pistachio baklava accompanied by tulip glasses of sweet tea …

'ROAST!'

I started awake.

The next day in a small village we asked for a shop and eventually some girls found the shopkeeper for us, who opened up a disused lorry container revealing a treasure trove of Ukrainian caramel sweets, dried biscuits, eggs, noodles … and a CABBAGE!

That night I hungrily tucked into my mash with a mound of fried cabbage. The cabbage was unseasoned, oily and undercooked, but at least different and recognisably a fresh vegetable. We sat cross-legged in the tent entrance. The herder who had come to speak to us an hour ago, asking for us to take a photograph of him and his dogs, was now moving across the valley below with a flock of black yaks, tiny babies skittering after their mothers, his Kyrgyz white felt hat still visible. Yurts were dotted across the distance and the sun's final rays cast that rich yellow light from behind dark clouds, illuminating pools of green pasture on the valley floor and patches of deep red rock on the mountains above. Soon the stars would come out.

I shivered and took a sip of hot green tea. Another meal on the Silk Road to be remembered.

33
JUST KEEP PEDALLING

Oh, come, so that your picture be placed within my heart-
don't go to China for there they'll paint it just on silk!
Mir Dard, trans. Annemarie Schimmel, from 'Diwan-i Farsi', in Annemarie
Schimmel, *A Two-Colored Brocade: The Imagery of Persian Poetry*

I peered through the wrought-iron gates into China. A lone soldier stood on guard at the far end of the empty square beyond them, and, above, a huge red flag flapped slowly in the hot breeze, its five gold stars rolling. I gazed up at the unfamiliar mountains, folded layers of red and green sandstone.

We had crossed the Alichur Plain, taking another day from the fort at Sumuntash to reach the dusty settlement of Murgab. A cluster of low concrete buildings, shipping containers and the odd yurt. The white mass of the 7546-metre Muztag Ata in China in the far distance. The weather had turned bad and we made a false start out of Murgab, returning to a homestay for another night having battled for fifteen kilometres into an icy headwind. Our route now took us north and the following day we summited the Akbaytal Pass. The road skirted the barbed-wire border fence with China and I watched a Kyrgyz herder in a long padded coat and white felt cap following his yaks and their calves along the other side of the fence as I fought fatigue and hunger on the way up the pass. I had to push my bike up the last stretch of gravel, breathless, with my freezing face wrapped up, finally reaching the 4655-metre high point at 6pm.

We camped on the other side, in a hollow just below the pass. It was minus 15°C. The Swiss cyclists had also crossed over on the same day and we huddled together in one tent for dinner, sharing stories and chocolate, glad of company in the starless, freezing darkness at the end of the world. We all stayed together for two nights at a Kyrgyz homestay overlooking the vast black lake of Karakul, white massif behind, as the wind howled outside. Yaks roamed the rubble-strewn ground beyond our window and the wind whipped our faces raw with ice crystals when we ventured outside. We all slept on the floor of the same room and rested for most of a day, trying to keep warm in our sleeping bags. In the evening the owner's eight-year-old daughter, Jamila, her cheeks wind-burnt and her hair in two shiny black pigtails, gave us a concert performance with the help of her younger brother. They sang and danced to Chinese pop songs they'd spent a long time perfecting from the TV. Afterwards the owner put the generator on and screened a Russian romantic comedy that we fell asleep to.

The weather eased and another day saw us over the 4232-metre Uybolok Pass and on to a high blond grassland bathed in sunlight. The following day we rode over the Kyzylart Pass (4280 metres) and into Kyrgyzstan, then down and down through a red-rock valley fringed by white peaks into a lush green corner and the village of Sary-Tash. After a detour of forty-one days and 1433 kilometres we were now a mere two hundred kilometres south of the Kyrgyz town of Osh, the place we'd been heading for on the day of the dog-bite incident. White yurts were everywhere and we looked back at a great white wall of mountains – the Trans-Alay Range that fringed the Pamir plateau, which we had somehow slipped through. The 7134-metre-high Lenin Peak towered over the rest. The wind blew icy cold over our tent that night and starlight gleamed off the thick snowcaps.

'Are we really here at the border to China?' I felt suddenly afraid, but Ed, my travel companion of 340 days and husband of almost three years, squeezed my shoulder and grinned.

The border was shut for lunch; we would have to wait. We wheeled our bikes back towards the long line of waiting Kyrgyz trucks and rested in their shadow. Panniers off. Stove out. Tea on. I relaxed into our daily lunchtime routine. A truck driver wandered over to us and we chewed some of his sweets. He sipped tea from my camping mug, while I cupped a piala I'd bought in Bukhara. As he and Ed battled to exchange journey details in a mixture of Russian, Kyrgyz and English, I leant back against the truck's massive wheel and shut my eyes. I was glad we still had another

250 kilometres through the fringes of the Taklamakan Desert to reach China's westernmost city of Kashgar. At least two more days of cycling. Two more nights of camping. I did not want it to end.

The gates clanged open.

We hurriedly packed away our lunch. Then I swung a leg over the crossbar of my bicycle and pushed down on the pedals.

Just a few more strokes now. All you need to do to get to China is just keep pedalling, I thought for the last time as I passed through the gates.

Tea
A sip
A hundred journeys back in time
On roads of silk
Cross mountain passes
Rest weary legs
On shaded carpets
And grateful lift a bowl
Of amber to parched lips
Tasting salt and grit.
In just a sip.

Tea and Grit

The Long Return

34
ADRIFT WEST OF EAST

My mother said:
You will come back
When the apricot trees start to blossom,
When the birds sing their spring songs.
But you didn't come back.
Instead, all the swallows have returned

Aziz Isa Elkun, from 'You Did Not Return', in
Aziz Isa Elkun (ed.), *Uyghur Poems*

As any traveller will tell you, the process of coming home can be a long one. The relocation not only of the physical body but also of the mind.

China was immediately another world. There were now crenulated yellow hills of sandstone and felt yurts with crèches of baby camels penned within a criss-cross of sticks. We camped on a platform hidden above the road and victoriously watched veins of reddened stone appear in the hills during the glow of sunset.

'China! We've cycled to China!' we exclaimed, over and over, hugging each other and dancing around the camp stove that was boiling water for tea, bare feet on the warm rock.

We called my brother on my mobile phone, surprised to find it working again. As I hurried through the details of the last month, I wondered vaguely whether the Chinese security services would appreciate an unregistered mobile placing a call on their network in such a sensitive region. There were reports in the UK media about the Great Chinese Firewall of the internet and we knew that online surveillance was tight.

The only question the border guards had asked us was if we were carrying a laptop. They rooted though our panniers, wrinkling their noses at grubby clothes and half-washed camping pots, abandoning their search before they got to a lower layer containing out fat guidebook to China. Had they looked at it, they might have noticed that a page was missing. We had removed the picture of the Dalai Lama, other travellers having warned that the guidebook might be confiscated otherwise. The spiritual and political leader of the Tibetans had been living in exile as a refugee in India since 1959, following the annexation of Tibet by the People's Republic of China. The chatter from travellers was that it was now the Uyghur ethnic minority that the Chinese were most concerned about. We had entered the region of Xinjiang, the only area of China that was predominantly Muslim. This was not technically out of bounds to foreigners, but we had known in Tashkent that it would have been unwise to draw attention to our actually wanting to visit. However, that evening there was not a soul around – not Uyghur, not Han Chinese, not anyone.

In the morning we celebrated by washing in a bucket of water drawn from a silted stream, standing naked in the river in bright sunlight as we watched a herd of Bactrian camels walk the perfect tarmac surface. There were green poplars and deserted mud-brick villages that day. Then there was a touristic viewpoint and a busload of Han tourists from Beijing, all bumbags, trainers and baseball caps, kindly and enthusiastically shepherding us to have a photo with some faded plastic ibex, concerned that we had wasted time on photographing the other-worldly and beautiful hillside of banded rock. They had truly come from afar, Beijing being further east of Xinjiang than Aleppo was west. Then a town with row after row of identikit low yellow houses and a shaded chaikhana where we had tea and noodles. And suddenly on the road there was a woman in a short pink dress, leggings, a floppy hat and a face mask on a *bicycle*. She stared at me, confused by my jubilant waving. After her, there were lots of bicycles and mopeds.

The mountains stood further back from a shrubby gravel plain as we descended in a strong wind and camped by some tiny domed tombs, barely sleeping for fear the tent might be flattened by the wind, which had intensified and was now hot and violent. Then came a dual carriageway with big red lorries and choking fumes and more motorbikes. Huge swarms of them in towns, and people on the back carrying shopping and children; some even carrying their own drip high above their head, the cannula protruding from their other arm. And lots more bicycles. Everyone was wearing face masks for the dust and then when we got to Kashgar there were pharmacies with open doors revealing people sitting in rows, plugged into similar-looking drips, perhaps for rehydration or a general boost as it was so hot. A digital display above a shop read 45°C.

There were terrific walls of dust and noise and an enormous statue of Chairman Mao, his right hand raised as if about to pat the heads of visitors to the central square, long coat blowing in an eternal desert breeze, red flags hanging limply in the stifling heat on a line to either side of him. There were identical nankeen-beige tower blocks everywhere and signs on everything in impenetrable Chinese characters and sometimes English. 'Donotdrivetiredly'.

It was so hot, I could barely breathe, and there were people everywhere, some with sun umbrellas, men with their T-shirts pulled up to cool well-fed bellies beading in sweat, women in short sundresses and small children in shorts and vest tops. There were shopping malls and a KFC, but there were still lots of hats. There were the faded box hats for the Tajiks and Uzbeks and the felt caps of the Kyrgyz and the fine white skullcaps of the Hui and everywhere the pistachio silk box hats of the Uyghur. There were women in small gypsy headscarves or velour and gold-embroidered box hats wearing dresses and sleeves of all lengths and sometimes bright splashes of red, pink and gold silk atlas (Uyghur ikat).

By the wide Kashgar river there was a new promenade with lights and a landscaped walkway and great fountains cooling the air, a glass building with a curved roof like a mini Sydney Opera House, yellow plastic pedalos, and fixed plastic pagodas to provide shade. Across the slow water, cranes hovered over the skeletons of tower blocks going up.

Men in hats sat talking by the river at dusk, time-warped into this urban setting. There were so many different faces with features that seemed to hail in assorted combinations from Bukhara and Beijing, Lhasa and Lahore. Each person was a riddle of ancestry and testament to the fact that Kashgar, an oasis town on the crossroads between China and the Middle East, had within the last two thousand years been variously under the control of Chinese, Turkic, Mongol and Tibetan empires and hosted generations of traders on the Silk Road. It was currently the turn of the Han Chinese, who make up over 90 per cent of the population of the People's Republic of China.

Modernisation was everywhere. We stopped near our hostel, which was in an old 'Bukhara'-style house, to watch bulldozers flattening an area of abutting brick houses and narrow alleys while people in neighbouring houses looked on and sprayed water to keep the dust down. The mulberry trees that had once shaded inner courtyards were now stranded in a sea of rubble and living rooms had been ripped open to the elements, exposing the painted panel work and wooden beams. Residents were apparently being moved elsewhere, further out of the city to the newly built blocks of flats which had many storeys and lots of tiny windows and perhaps better sanitation and electric rather than natural air conditioning. Perhaps the move would be separating families who had lived alongside each other for generations. Perhaps deliberately.

On a hillock by a peaceful stretch of the river some parts of the old town were still relatively intact. A jumble of houses merged with the mud rock, their balconies and wooden walkways and rooftop terraces overlooked by chrome tower blocks, a hospital and a large Ferris wheel. There were mopeds parked by each rickety door off the narrow alleyway, peeling paint of sky blue and peach, donkeys with carts, and grocers snoozing in the shade of shopfronts displaying piles of cabbages, peppers, tomatoes, garlic and turnips with wilting tops. There were stalls with wheels of non and women sitting by shops with dusty mannequins wearing headscarves. In the oppressive midday heat, an elderly muezzin in a white turban stood atop the tiny balcony of a minaret and, hands cupped over his ears, sang out the adhan. We paused in the shade to listen. Heart-achingly beautiful. I took a deep breath of the hot air.

It was the Sunday market, which was still the domain of the men with hats. Sandalled feet risked crossing dust made liquid with the urine of animals to inspect rows of fat-bottomed sheep lined up for sale, their huge balls on display, watch men wrestle a bull onto the back of a flatbed truck by its tail or test-ride a horse or a Bactrian camel. Elderly men of any hat with deeply sun-wrinkled faces wore faded navy Mao suits, the middle-aged generally in shirts and suit trousers and the young in jeans and T-shirts. Women and children were in their Sunday best of sparkling atlas. There were stalls with gleaming Uyghur knives and others hung with carcasses of dead animals, the smell of meat and animal excrement stifling in the hot air.

We sat at a crowded stall shaded by a red awning. The chef, a tall man in a Uyghur hat with a deep scar on his cheek and a face that looked like it had as much Slavic as Turkic ancestry, had a long line of noodles strung out between his fingers that he was beating against the table. The dough was rolled and stretched and beaten into laghman noodles, thicker than the Uzbek type, boiled and refreshed and then placed in a bowl with ladles of chewy lamb and spicy tomato broth. Everyone held bowls up to their mouths and shovelled noodles in with disposable chopsticks and much slurping.

Tea bowls were filled with weak and tepid tea, drunk at this workers' stall without ceremony and in place of water. Now tea was everywhere and if we requested water it was always boiled, often weakly with tea leaves and sometimes tasting like dishwater. The story went that sometime around 2700 BC, the Chinese emperor Shennong was drinking a bowl of just-boiled water – having decreed that his subjects must boil water before drinking it – when a few leaves were blown into it from a nearby tree, changing the colour and taste. The emperor took a sip and was pleasantly surprised by its flavour and restorative properties; thus tea was invented.

One day as we were walking back to the hostel, we came past lots of parked cars decked out with pink plastic flowers and a band playing on the back of a pick-up. We stopped to watch what was clearly a bridal party and were pulled into a Uyghur wedding by the groom. It was being held in a hotel conference suite with plastic Grecian pillars, Louis XVI gilt and red brocade chairs and a man singing Uyghur pop songs into a microphone. The room was packed with men dancing in suits and silk box hats, children diving across the dance floor and women in sequinned dresses at tables piled up with half-eaten plates of pulou (plov), nang (non) and the gnawed ribs of cut watermelon. The female bridal party wore translucent white headscarves over bouffant hairdos in the style of Margaret Thatcher, topped with box hats in maroon velour and gold embroidery. The bride was in a Western-style dress of stark white embroidered tulle and a jacket of maroon, gold and green atlas. The groom wore a navy suit with a scarf of matching atlas tied over the jacket around his waist. The bride had a face that could have featured on the front of an Istanbul fashion magazine: porcelain skin, hazel eyes and wavy chestnut hair. Her eye make-up was smudged with tears and she looked exhausted. The wedding had been going for two days and had one more to go, in the village where they came from. It was not appropriate for her to look happy when she would be leaving her mother and father. Family photographs were taken and the couple did their first dance, standing apart from each other, arms out, shoulders rhythmically rotating, in a shuffle to the pop music. Everyone clapped and jigged along and a man with a video camera filmed the whole thing.

Later in the evening the groom pulled up a chair to our table. He spoke English and told us he worked selling atlas in the bazaar. His wife had not eaten in two days, as was the custom. They had met as students. He leant in and under cover of the loud music confided, 'You know there have been problems for us, since the protests in Ürümqi. The government is trying to stop us – our culture, our weddings.'

I glanced around the room of partygoers, none of whom looked like spies, but he was nervous about this exchange.

'It's important to us that you see this. My wife is very happy you are here.'

I looked across at her. She was gazing fixedly out across the busy room, as if she would rather be anywhere but there.

Having got to China, we were adrift, overwhelmed by the people, the heat and the noise. We compensated by eating and eating, to fill the calorie deficit left by the Pamirs, our stomachs now sucked into our ribs. Uyghur laghman in a restaurant with tapchans and wooden panelling; a lottery of Chinese dishes, our favourites being mapo tofu, spicy aubergine and rice; squeamishly steering away from buffets that displayed cuts of pig – ribs, trotters, snouts – seemingly cooked in a hundred ways, and curries in a Pakistani restaurant. We needed to rest, but traipsing round the town in the heat was exhausting. We were not sure what to do next.

In theory we could head south to Pakistan along the mighty Karakoram Highway, but a dam had broken after an earthquake and the road was currently cut. It would be too hot to cycle eastern routes, which skimmed either the northern or southern fringes of the Taklamakan Desert. We had arrived in Kashgar on 7 July and rumour had it that temperatures in the Taklamakan could reach well above 50°C in the summer. There were vast distances between towns and sandstorms could be lethal.

Ideally, we would have liked to cycle the 'back route to Lhasa', a ride of at least six weeks on dirt roads to the Tibetan capital, running high over the Tibetan plateau, past sacred Mount Kailash. It would be an enormous challenge, but doable. Tibetan pilgrims walked the route, prostrating on their hands and knees at every step, taking years. We knew of cyclists who had done it a few years earlier, but it was now compulsory to have a guide at all times. Mysteriously, we had noticed that our email accounts had both stopped working, despite being perfectly usable for the first week we were in Kashgar. Was it a coincidence that the day before we had mentioned in an email to our parents that we were thinking of heading to Tibet?

A group of Chinese cycle-tourers were packing up in our hostel one morning. They were four students from Beijing and had arrived by train to start their trip along that very same back route to Lhasa. 'You are so lucky,' I blurted out, 'that you are able to travel to Tibet.'

'Yes, we know,' one of the bespectacled youths replied as he sorted through at least fifty packets of instant noodles.

I eyed them up, thinking it would be a hungry journey.

'It is too dangerous for foreigners to go. The high mountains are not good for you,' his friend said, smiling at me.

'No, that's not the reason,' I said. 'We are not allowed to go without a guide to Tibet. We foreigners have to be accompanied for political reasons.'

'No. Everyone can go. It is because it is too dangerous for you,' a girl with pigtails explained to me earnestly. 'Foreigners cannot cope in the high mountains. The Chinese government must ensure you are safe.'

I wondered if they would make it. Their bicycles looked shiny, with cheap disc brakes and suspension that would likely malfunction and get gummed up with dirt, and their camping equipment was flimsy. No doubt they saw us as an equal liability, having heard horror stories about tourists flying into Lhasa, which, at 3656 metres is one of the highest cities in the world, and succumbing to altitude sickness. I briefly entertained the idea of asking if they would like to look after us so we could take the same route.

It turned out, however, that we were being watched. We went to a market with a group of travellers from the hostel. We had reunited with the Swiss and a French couple Nico and Sarah who had been in the hostel in Tashkent when we arrived back after the dog-bite incident. We all sat together on benches at a food stall. I had placed my bag on the floor beside my feet. My back was against the wall of the fabric awning. It seemed safe. I was suddenly aware, at the edge of my subconscious, of someone quickly brushing past the canvas on the other side. I looked down at my feet. My bar bag had disappeared. It contained not only my wallet and our only remaining mobile phone but also my passport.

We rushed back to the hostel to ask the English-speaking owner for help. The British Embassy was in Beijing, five days away by train, and how would I transit the country without ID?

The hostel owner was impassive. 'I think you don't need to worry. The police here, they are very good. I think they will find it for you. It is not uncommon for this to happen to foreigners. To my guests. There are many pickpockets around. You will certainly get your passport back.'

At the police station, a jovial police chief sitting behind a large wooden desk decreed that we should come back in the afternoon. 'I think we will have found your bag by then,' he said.

When we returned, my red bar bag was indeed waiting on his desk. The passport was there, and so was my wallet, with all the bank cards and around fifty dollars' worth of yuan. The phone was missing.

'It might be good,' the chief said, 'to give a reward to the person who was kind enough to hand in the bag.'

We would spend another two and a half months in China before it was time to go home. We took the train to Turpan deep in the Taklamakan, where the thermometer registered 47°C. There were no sleeping berths left and on the thirty-six-hour train journey we were put in a group of six seats with four Han Chinese students, three boys and a girl, who spoke good English. They were kind and curious and we shared food and talked and took turns to sleep on the seats next to the wall. One of the young men explained that the Chinese government looked after its ethnic minorities well and that in fact they had extra privileges. It was true that at this time minority groups including the Uyghurs were exempt from the one-child policy. I dared to ask him if he thought the one-child policy was an infringement of his personal rights.

'Ah,' he said with a small smile, pleased to have encountered this textbook case, 'that is a typically Western perspective. Here in China we do not think about what is best for the individual; we think about what is best for the people.'

We carried on to Lanzhou, this time crammed three-high into bunks, sharing with a mother and daughter and her baby. The chubby son was in split pants and was held out of the bunk and over the aisle when nature called, the Chinese attitude to the floor a marked contrast to that in the Islamic world.

We went in search of ethnically Tibetan areas outside the Autonomous Region, taking the bus to Labrang Monastery on the northeastern fringe of the plateau. Founded in 1709, this is Tibetan Buddhism's most important monastery town outside the Tibetan Autonomous Region. People surged round the building on their kora, a circular walk of devotion, chanting continuously: monks in burgundy robes and shaven heads, women carrying children tied to their backs with bright shawls, old ladies with two grey pigtails. They walked with purpose, giving the painted prayer wheels a good push as they passed, and then struck out for a line of prayer wheels set into the wall of the monastery. On the road between the café and the complex, people moved about on other business. Taxis and motorbikes passed. A man pushed a wooden cart piled with bread. Children crossed the road carrying schoolbooks. A monk spoke into his mobile. A Han Chinese tourist stood on the corner of the pavement watching pilgrims and passers-by through a telephoto lens.

We sat people-watching at the fourth-floor window of a café that overlooked the monastery. For three days I was transfixed by a young woman crawling the kora. Her face was beautiful, with high cheekbones blushed pink by the fierce Tibetan sun. She wore her hair in a thick braid and had heavy earrings of silver and coral. Leather, silver and turquoise belted her coat. She would place her hands together, drop to her knees, slide forward, prostrate in the dirt, stand, take one tiny step and then repeat. She wore large pads on her knees, like a skateboarder, and blocks of wood strapped to her hands. She was inching towards a vast prayer wheel set at one corner. The smell of burning yak butter wafted out. I had passed her, trying not to stare, and headed up the hill on the longer circuit, which took me clockwise around clumps of prayer flags, above gold and white chortens and red-roofed halls of the complex. By the time I descended, she had covered less than a hundred metres.

It was a further twenty-four hours by train to Xining on the edge of Amdo Tibet and in the region of Qinghai, where unsupervised travel was allowed. We were now with Sarah and Nico again, the French couple from Kashgar, and we buoyed each other along, cycling abreast on deserted roads undulating high into the Tibetan grasslands. We cycled across passes littered with chortens and spiders' webs of prayer flags, past countless camping spots with great grassy vistas, herds of yaks guarded by women with thick braids, patterned aprons and heavy earrings of silver, turquoise and coral, men in heavy coats and necklaces of huge coral and turquoise beads, and maroon-robed monks on motorbikes. The smell of burning yak butter drifted out from wayside shrines.

We stopped at wayside cafés to eat the Tibetan staple of tsampa (roasted barley flour mixed with tea) and drink yet more yak-butter tea. There were days when we barely knew where we were. Our map only marked major roads, and in one village the whole population turned out to stare at us. We sat in a tavern with twenty people pressing their faces to the window and more crowding into the doorway. A child sidled across the room, reached out to touch us and then ran away screeching when we spoke. Everyone else stared in silence. Otherwise, people were kind and curious but not effusive and we cycled for weeks carefree and glad not to be under constant scrutiny.

On 1 August we celebrated one year on the road and fifteen thousand kilometres of cycling on the same day. We were somewhere on an empty stretch between the towns of Zgengis and Mangra when the odometer clicked to fifteen thousand kilometres. Nico photographed us jumping for joy next to our bikes, and we sat on the grassy verge under the open sky and filtered silty water for tea. Then we carried on. There were no food treats for celebration. We were almost completely reliant on super noodles bought from tiny shops, or tsampa or noodle broth made in small wayside cafés. It was impossible to understand what to order and the tasty, postage-stamp-shaped noodles were served in broth so heavily laced with la (red chilli) and ma (anaesthetic Sichuan pepper), that it was often almost inedibly spicy to us. After one incident when we'd ordered big steaming bowls of broth only to have to walk away from them, apologising profusely to the confused tavern keeper, Ed lost his temper.

'This food is f***ing s***e.'

I was taken aback. He was rarely angry. He looked thin and drawn and he'd lacked energy the last few days, crawling into bed early. Worry welled up inside me, but I pushed it down.

A few days later, having eked out the packets of super noodles, we were victorious when in a larger town we found a restaurant serving less spicy dishes from the lowlands. It was crammed with Han diners and we recited the words for aubergine, tofu, vegetables and rice to the waiter and soon had a table laden with dishes. Rice! But Ed was picking at his unenthusiastically.

'You okay?' I said.

'Fine. Just guts again.'

Half an hour later, Ed said he would get a head start out of town. He had stomach pain. He would find a field, which was preferable to the restaurant's communal squat toilet; like many places we had encountered in China, this consisted of an open trough with no doors.

We three finished our lunch and packed the leftover rice into our pans. At the edge of town, we found Ed curled up in a field, almost unconscious.

'Pain,' he moaned as I knelt next to him in the mud.

Something was badly wrong. It was finally time to stop cycling.

We returned to the UK by aeroplane six weeks later. After a worry that it was appendicitis, a local hospital diagnosed a large kidney stone with the help of an ultrasound machine. The hospital was dirty and said it had no means to assist us. Grateful for the moral support of Nico and, particularly, Sarah, a qualified nurse, I orchestrated a lengthy extraction to Chengdu. We were, it turned out, not meant to be where we were and the fact that we were there meant that officials could neither allow us to stay nor allow us to leave. To complicate matters further, most roads out of the region had been closed. The monsoon rains had hit the eastern side of the Himalayan plateau and landslides had cut many of the exit routes. I spent a day in negotiations at the local governor's office, going round in circles, drinking bowl after bowl of green tea. An English-speaking Tibetan student was found to come and translate. He whispered to me at the end of the hours of negotiations that it had been the most exciting day of his life to meet a foreigner. He pressed a map of China with names in scrolling Tibetan script written on it into my arms on departure. I shook his hand hard, wishing I could hug him tight, and took photographs with him, but I could not share his excitement. Worry was consuming me.

I was not allowed to hire a taxi, but the officials did let me pay for an ambulance to transport us both to the airport in Songpan, a five-hour journey, from where we would fly to Chengdu. As we bumped along the road, I was anxiously watching Ed and taking stock as the wide Tibetan grassland whizzed by in bright sunshine. He was in serious pain. He had not been able to pee for the whole day. If the kidney stone was fully blocking the outward flow of urine, that could mean permanent kidney damage. At every rut in the road Ed groaned. A paramedic was accompanying us, wearing a stained white coat. Every half an hour or so, he would gesture to a syringe that he had loaded on a steel kidney tray on his lap and I would vehemently refuse. While Ed was still groaning, I knew he was still alive. I had no idea how much opiate the syringe was loaded with and I had not seen it come out of a sterile packet. I gritted my teeth and resolved to remain mean.

The ambulance gave an enormous jolt. Ed screamed. The paramedic shouted at the driver. As we drew to a stop, he started towards Ed, brandishing the syringe again.

'I NEED TO GET OUT!' Ed shouted and raised himself off the stretcher, pushing the paramedic away. The ambulance had come to a halt in a muddy pool. Yaks were grazing on the verge around us. Ed struggled his way to sitting again.

'Lie back down!' I ordered.

'GOT. TO. PISS. HELEN.'

'HE'S GOT TO GET OUT!' I shouted, as if saying it louder would help.

Ed gestured at his crotch as if unzipping himself. The paramedic opened the back door of the ambulance and we helped him out onto the grass. 'ARRRGGGGGGGGGGGGGGGGGGGGGGGGGGGGGGGGGGGG

GGGGGGGGGGGGGGG!' Ed said, emptying his bladder under the vast Tibetan sky onto a patch of edelweiss. A kidney stone landed somewhere. A grey yak and calf grunted confusedly at the doings of these strange visitors.

Ed slumped back against us and we bundled him back into the ambulance.

'Xiexie. Thank you.' I patted the paramedic's arm.

He nodded and gave me a grin.

The bumping continued, but the groaning was reduced. I reached out and squeezed Ed's clammy hand. It was limp, but he squeezed back weakly.

'Not sure what those yaks thought they were looking at.'

I gazed out of the window. It was so beautiful, the big blue sky. We were here together. It would be okay. It had to be.

My mind flitted back to something I had seen when I was following the policeman into the governor's office, distracted and anxious. A young Tibetan man was handcuffed to a post in the courtyard. He was sitting on a chair, naked from the chest up, and his muscular torso had large pink burn marks on it. A water hose was hung above him and water was running across his chest. He was in the shadows and I had only looked his way when I heard a moan. I drew to a halt in shock. What was I seeing? What was wrong? Had he tried to self-immolate? Was this rudimentary cold-water treatment or further punishment? He glanced up at me and I looked him straight in the eye. He moaned again. The police officer who had accompanied me from the hospital suddenly realised that I was not behind him and shouted for me to keep up, impatiently directing me up the steps to the governor's office.

I looked the handcuffed man in the eyes again.

'I am sorry …' My empty words trailed off into the void between us.

Then I hurried away to try and rescue the man I loved above all else.

35
THE MOVING GROUND

If one day the people should choose life
Fate is certain to respond.

…

The wind muttered between the ravines;
'When I aspire to a goal,
I ride my wishes, forgetting caution,
Face the wilderness, the rugged trails
And flaming days –
He who does not like scaling mountains
Will live eternally in pot-holes'

Abu al-Qasim al-Shabbi, trans. Lena Jayyusi and Naomi Shihab Nye, from
'The Will of Life', in Marlé Hammond (ed.), *Arabic Poems*

HIGHLANDS, SCOTLAND, JUNE 2025

However lengthy the journey, it is only possible to cover a tiny amount of ground. We cycled fifteen thousand kilometres to China, but we still didn't know what lay behind that fence two metres away from the line of the road we took. We didn't know anything of the people who were there five minutes before us, that town we didn't have time to visit, the festival we missed by one day. A journey is like a vanishingly fine thread of silk weaving its way from place to place, encounter to encounter. An inadequate transect of the beauty of it all.

Of course, the thread is also fragile because the world changes after the journey. There have been seismic changes in the region we cycled through, both literally and metaphorically, in the fifteen years since this journey took place. In October 2011 an enormous earthquake with an epicentre close to Cessim's family house that we camped outside near Lake Van killed more than 570 people, destroying thousands of homes. In February 2023 earthquakes with epicentres near Gaziantep, where we started our journey into Syria, left over 53,000 dead and over 1.5 million people homeless. It is always challenging to grasp numbers, and the reality of human lives that have changed. I find it so much easier to think of individual people, faces, gestures, a child's knitted booties, tea sipped together.

Unfortunately, the manmade catastrophes have been even worse. After a brutal crackdown in response to peaceful protests, thirteen years of civil war devastated Syria, killed around half a million people, caused fourteen million people to flee internationally and led to the internal displacement of 7.2 million people, creating a ripple effect of instability across most of the region we cycled through in 2010.

The person I most often think of is Manoor, my 'twin' from Idlib who spoke better English than the men, who had daughters she was hoping to send to university, who gifted me a nightdress so I could keep Ed interested on our arduous journey, who wrote a poem in my diary. I see her face swathed in a familiar maroon headscarf. She is lying on the ground in a dusty street. Dead. Bloody, her lower torso is blown off. Caught in a bomb blast from one faction or another. I can barely look when I stumble across the picture while scanning the morning news in my office before work. I force myself to look. Is it really Manoor?

I don't have a photograph to be sure. Tears run down my face. Could it be her? I have asked myself a thousand times in the past years. If she did live, then what challenges has she faced?

In many places where there has not been such direct upheaval, the response has been paranoia about similar events unfolding and an increasingly iron grip of government surveillance and control. Global news, phone banking, educational resources, Candy Crush, pornography – the internet brings the good, bad and banal to people everywhere. Today, however, governments can monitor activity more closely through the internet, CCTV, automatic-recognition technology and algorithms that mine the cacophony of communication for signals of concern. Travel along the Silk Road has taught me that in my world, the 'free world', we often only have a vague understanding of hard-won liberties. We become easily outraged and call for debate to be shut down, instead of defending core values of democracy, human rights and freedom of expression. We seem to be increasingly unfamiliar with the architecture of our own freedoms and are thus becoming blind to the fact that they are being eroded. We often look down in pity on those who are suffering and oppressed beyond our borders, imagining that we are other and hold all the answers. Instead, we should look up. Look up to learn what it means to be courageous, to resist, to endure, to have grit. In 2023 the Nobel Peace Prize was awarded to Iranian woman Narges Mohammadi for 'her fight against the oppression of women in Iran and her fight to promote human rights and freedom for all', twenty years after it was awarded to another Iranian women, Shirin Ebadi. In her acceptance speech, which was smuggled out of prison, Mohammadi said, 'I remember the unnamed and courageous women who have lived a life of resistance in various areas of relentless oppression.'

And we should look out to the horizon and far along the road, to ensure we understand the many possible versions of the future.

The war on terror has marked the whole adult life of my generation. We millennials first became conscious of politics from grainy footage of people knocking down the Berlin Wall and the supposed end of the Cold War – we became politically conscious in a world celebrating the ending of divisions. Then, the brink of adulthood after the 9/11 attacks, a new binary world order began with roots in the last. To this day, I cannot get out of my head the images of people falling, down and down, down the side of those twin towers. The silent footage of the planes absorbed by their glass flanks belying the violent smashing of windows and cracking of girders and the thousand-degree inferno. Burning beacons that would unleash decades of war. However, what has the West's desire for retribution in Iraq, Afghanistan and elsewhere achieved?

It was a suspicion about war-on-terror rhetoric that sent me off on the journey east and I am now sure it has not made the world a safer place. So few people in charge seem to have understood anything of the part of the world they have tried to control from inside office rooms and armoured tanks. Few have seen the lives of normal people, good people, people who want a quiet life, just people. Few have tried to understand how THEY are perceived.

I asked Ed the other day, as we were sitting at our kitchen table, what he thought the best thing about the journey was. He said without hesitation that it was good to have to deal with real decisions: where to sleep, what to eat, how to be safe. When I lay awake in the darkness of the night shelter in Glasgow, I knew that there was a terrible privilege in the choice of this. How can you choose to spend time and money, risk pain to family members, on a journey that others can only take smuggled in a lorry or a dinghy in desperation and fear? Perhaps I can make a case that, despite the fine thread of silk, travel to understand other people should not be a luxury but is, in some form at least, a necessity. To take tea. To cross thresholds. To exchange ideas. To understand what good we have done and what we might have got wrong. This dialogue across continents has produced some of the greatest human thought over thousands of years. Human culture is not made safe in the hamlet or farmstead or Edinburgh tenement, but is woven on the Silk Road. Like Attar of Nishapur's brave hoopoe who led the band of birds across the seven mountain passes, the journey and its encounters brings a mirror to the soul.

Humanity starts with a meeting.

From setting out. From opening the door.

36
Homecoming

I have learnt
to wander
on the border between
me and myself
without being a stranger
or tired.
I have not found my home
but I have learnt
to live
in my voice.

Rawia Morra, from 'Ghurba', in Nathalie Handal (ed.), *The Poetry of Arab Women*

GLASGOW, SCOTLAND, OCTOBER 2015

It was raining heavily as I drove home from the night shelter at dawn. The radio was turned up loud to keep me awake. A reporter was talking about the construction of a vast refugee camp built from shipping containers. He was broadcasting from the Turkish town of Kilis, triggering thoughts of cycling across the Syrian border on that warm spring day more than five years ago.

By the time I got to Edinburgh, the day was lighter, but rain was still lashing down. The news programme had moved on to other stories. Shaker Aamer, the last British resident to be held in Guantanamo Bay, had landed in the UK, having been detained for thirteen years without charge. A fifteen-year-old boy from Blackburn who'd plotted to behead police officers at an Anzac Day parade in Australia had been sentenced to life in prison. The Britain Stronger in Europe campaign had been launched in response to an impending referendum to leave the EU.

I pulled into work, the first person into the office, made a cup of green tea, sat down at my desk and prepared to open the report I was writing on how to improve a breeding programme for an endangered antelope species on the Arabian Peninsula. I enjoyed my occasional visits out there and the echoes of Bedouin hospitality in the gleaming, air-conditioned offices of the Gulf, but I was not sure that my recommendations were workable or that they would be listened to. The unit I'd joined was desperately short-staffed and I'd had lots of technical issues in the lab, so I was floundering with the analysis now. I missed the open road. And, although we were sharing a house and remained happily married, I missed Ed. We spent our days separately and our evenings were full of concerns about work.

I switched on my computer and the Karakum Desert blistered under a virtual sun on my screen. The figure cycling towards the horizon along a road flanked by sand and scrub was now waylaid by a band of desktop icons for documents that I had been too lazy to file –'Employ_satisfact_survey.doc', 'Conference_reg_Nov2013.pdf' and the like. They were gradually closing ranks to block my former self out of the picture. I thought glumly about the book I was trying to write about our journey, but then the war in Syria had happened and it all seemed so irrelevant. I felt powerless. I wanted to do something to help. The borders at Kilis and Akçakale loomed large in my mind's eye.

The following weekend I took the night train to London for a course run by Citizens UK on how to lead a campaign to rehouse fifty thousand Syrians through community resettlement. My fellow participants had come from as far afield as North Wales, the Scottish Highlands and Cornwall in England and were from a wide variety of professional backgrounds. Some of us had transnational heritage – the children of Jewish refugees from the Second World War; a Sudanese immigrant; a South African; me. The course was in the best tradition of church-hall-style meetings – there were uncomfortable chairs, the hall was freezing, there were lots of biscuits, egg mayonnaise sandwiches and vast mugs of milky tea, and everyone was passionate.

We were being taught how to form community networks and how to organise meetings with our local MPs. Part of our training included us each developing a story about how we'd come to be involved with the Refugee Resettlement campaign. Someone told of their grandmother arriving on a boat during the Second World War. Someone else told about growing up in apartheid South Africa. Another participant talked about tiny drowned Alan Kurdi being the same age as their son. We had to rehearse a short piece that we could use to introduce ourselves to MPs or other key stakeholders. I stood up and said:

'In 2010 I cycled to China via Syria. A lot of people told us not to go. We queued at the Turkish border with some trepidation and then crossed over into Syria. We had been cycling for maybe an hour when a group of six men jumped out in front of us, waving and shouting. My first thought was that we were about to be kidnapped. Instead, they asked us to sit with them and we drank tea together. This experience was repeated day after day when we were on the road. That is how I came to understand the power of a personal welcome and that is why I want to help with community sponsorship.'

May 2017

Two years later I stood at the door waiting, a knot of anxiety in my stomach. They were on their way. I checked my text messages. They had just left the hotel, where they had spent their first night in Scotland, together with all of the other Syrian refugees who had arrived through the resettlement scheme.

I looked around the tenement flat that we had rented for the family. There was a room with a double bed, two bedside tables and a wardrobe that was full of winter coats donated by our group members. There were two other bedrooms for children. All the beds had bright quilts on them. My colleague at work, a brusque Irish lady whom I found rather frightening, had surprised me by making them for me. The cot had been donated by one of our members. The cupboards were full of clothes for five-, seven- and eight-year-old girls, including piles of dresses and T-shirts and a sequined jumper with a cat on it that I suspected might be fought over and become a favourite. New packs of M&S pants. Toys. A cuddly animal for each bed.

British people are very good at donating things. I was worried that it might be too much, a bit overwhelming. I tried to think about what toys I had seen in houses on our travels. I couldn't think of any. A group of children by Krak des Chevaliers chasing hoops down the road at sunset.

Administration is a much harder sort of donation. Since I had attended the workshop, it had taken us almost two years to fully constitute ourselves as a group. Among us numbered doctors, a teacher (in the form of Ed), benefits workers, and tech experts who helped us embrace the app Trello for planning everything. We filled in the lengthy documentation, which required a resettlement plan and safeguarding policy. We had to raise funds for the family, given a kick-start by an extremely generous donor, set up bank accounts, attend a council training course and find translators. There had been endless meetings. Then suddenly our application was approved. We had a timeline. They were coming.

I stood at the door thinking about the long distance stretching back to war-torn Syria. Thinking about how different this house with its table and chairs was. No one we'd met in rural Syria had felt the need for a table. Thinking about how different life was here. Would it be possible for the family ever truly to *arrive* here, having been wrenched away? Every day would involve the need to make a hundred choices between the culture they had come from and the one they were arriving into.

I did not know the people that this flat would now belong to. I had seen their photographs and a short bio from the UNHCR that the Home Office said only two of us in the group could read and which had to be deleted as soon as we had read it. We were legally responsible for their resettlement for the next two years. I pinched myself; it seemed unlikely that we had got to this stage. This was a brand-new scheme. Canada had resettled thousands of people this way, but the UK had had nothing like it before. It would pave the way for the much simpler Homes for Ukraine scheme. There had been months of meetings and preparation. Meanwhile, millions were waiting elsewhere. Was the government getting ordinary citizens to do its job? There was a division in opinion. Well, I thought, at least some would be safe. At least I can do *something*.

The kitchen table was laden with food, a mix of British and Syrian dishes, cake and hummus, flatbread and biscuits.

My phone buzzed again.

'We are just getting out of the taxi,' my teammate texted me.

I heard footsteps and children's voices in the corridor. I took a deep breath.

'Welcome,' I said as I opened the door and hugged a beautiful young woman wearing a pink hijab and carrying a baby.

She smiled weakly. She looked like she had not slept in a long time. I shook her husband's hand.

Three girls, having in an instant removed their trainers, slipped over the threshold, past the family's suitcase, which was blocking the entrance, and between our legs. As we adults looked at each other, deciding what to say across a void of uncertainty, the girls ran along the corridor to their room, whooping as they spotted their beds.

Barrelling over the threshold, small travellers entering a new world.

Tea and Grit

Notes and Resources

Notes on the Chapter Epigraphs and Their Authors

My love of poetry comes from my mother and my paternal grandmother who read poems to me from a young age. Like so many British people I have grown up loving poems with orientalist themes like the wonderfully lyrical 'Kubla Khan' by Samuel Taylor Coleridge, 'Ozymadiaz' by Percy Bysshe Shelley and 'The Golden Road to Samarkand' by James Elroy Flecker. The first two poems were contained in a book published by the BBC in 1996 called *The Nation's Favourite Poems* that my grandmother gifted me for my fifteenth birthday and she would recite these poems, word perfect, even when aged ninety-two her memory for everything else was failing. Although the poetry by writers from Silk Road countries provided the inspiration for these famous English poems, much of the rich poetic heritage of the region is unknown in the anglophone world. Poetry is a fundamental lifeblood of Arabic, Turkic and Persian cultures. Poets are also often the only subversive voices of resistance left when oppression has silenced all else. It seemed appropriate then to feature a broad selection of historical and contemporary writers of both genders from across the region (and some with links to it) in the chapter epigraphs.

I give the voice of the wound
To the tongue of strangled bells,
To stone approaching from afar,
To aridity and the arid land,
To time borne on a stretcher of ice,
I kindle the fire of the wound.

Adonis, from 'The Wound', Adonis, trans. Khaled Mattawa, 'Desert', in *Selected Poems*

1: Mohsin Hamid (b. 1971) is a British Pakistani novelist. His novel *Exit West* is about a couple who are escaping war in an unnamed city and was written at the height of the Syrian refugee crisis.

Notes on the Chapter Epigraphs and Their Authors

2; 26; 28: Rumi (1207–73) is an enduringly popular poet who wrote in Persian, Arabic and Turkish. His influence has transcended national borders and ethnic divisions. He is the Persian Sufi poet most familiar to Western readers. Rumi was born in either Afghanistan or Tajikistan, lived in Samarkand until the Mongols invaded, fled to Iraq and then moved to Syria and finally to Konya in Turkey, where he founded the Mevlevi Order of whirling dervishes.

3: Nizar Qabbani (1923–98) was a highly influential poet and writer from Damascus, Syria. He mainly wrote about love, feminism, Arab nationalism and religion.

4: Fadwa Tuqan (1917–2003) was born in Nablus, Palestine. She is often considered to be one of the most avant-garde poets of the Arab world.

5: Marcus Aurelius (121–180), the Roman emperor (161–180), is best known today as a Stoic philosopher and author of inspirational writings published under the title *Meditations*.

6: al-Ma'arri (973–1057), a famous freethinker in Arabic verse, held atheistic views and is controversial even to this day. Almost a thousand years after his death, the al-Nusra Front destroyed a statue of him in his home town of al-Ma'arra in northern Syria during the civil war.

7: St Thomas (first century), one of the twelve apostles of Jesus, was born in Galilee and later travelled to India and possibly China. In Catholicism he is the patron saint of travellers. The Gospel of St Thomas is one of the 'lost' books of the Bible, discovered near Nag Hammadi in Egypt in December 1945. Its place of origin may have been Syria.

8: The Bible (King James Version), Acts 22:6. Acts is the fifth book of the New Testament of the Christian Bible. It tells of Paul (a Jewish man born in Tarsus in present-day Turkey), who is on the way to Damascus from Jerusalem (31–36) under directions to seek out and arrest followers of Jesus. He is hit by a blinding light and spoken to by Jesus, and is unable to see, eat or drink for three days. Once in Damascus he becomes a Christian and an ardent missionary spreading Christianity widely across the first-century world. The phrase 'the road to Damascus' is used in the English language to refer to a sudden turning point or realisation. The King James Bible is an early-modern translation published in 1611 and is one of the most important literary influences on the English-speaking world.

9: Qur'an, Sura 13. The Qur'an is the central religious text of Islam, believed by Muslims to be an oral revelation from God directly to the Prophet Muhammad through the angel Gabriel over a period of twenty-three years beginning in 610. Sura 13 is said to have inspired the mosaics in the Umayyad Mosque (Burns 2009). The Qur'an has had a seismic impact on Arab and Muslim literature, poetry and culture (Mackintosh-Smith 2019).

10: Adonis (b. 1930) is a political writer and highly influential contemporary poet who writes in Arabic. He was born near Latakia, Syria, but has lived in exile since 1956.

11: al-Munsif al-Wahaybi (b. 1949) is a poet, writer and academic. He was born in Tunisia.

12: Labid (c. 560–661), from Hejaz in modern-day Saudi Arabia, is considered the most important pre-Islamic poet; he was a companion to the Prophet Muhammad and converted to Islam. This exert is from one of the seven poems by pre-Islamic poets which were said to have hung on the curtains which covered the Kaaba at Mecca.

13: Gülten Akın (1933–2015) was a highly influential poet from central Anatolia, Turkey. Only some of her work is available in English translation.

14: Kajal Ahmad (b. 1967) is a feminist Kurdish poet from Kirkuk, Iraq.

15: Abu'l Atahiya (748–828) was a pioneering writer of religious poetry during the Abbasid caliphate in what is now Iraq; he was one of the first poets to break away from traditional desert themes which had become outmoded in the urban society of the Abbasid caliphate.

16: Forugh Farrokhzad (1934–67), from Tehran, is the best-known Persian-language woman poet inside or outside of Iran. Controversial, feminist, modernist and iconoclastic, her writings were banned during the revolution of 1979.

17: Azita Ghahreman (b. 1962) was born in Mashhad, Iran. She has lived in exile in Sweden since 2006.

18: Hafez (1320–91) is regarded by many Iranians as one of the greatest writers of Persian literature. His collected works called the Divan are often found in homes in Iran, and Iranians learn his poems by heart and use them as everyday sayings. Hafez (also sometimes transliterated as Hafiz) was born in Shiraz, Iran.

19: Sara Mohammadi-Ardehali (b. 1976) is a poet from Tehran.

Notes on the Chapter Epigraphs and Their Authors

20: Jami (1414–92) is commonly called the last great classical poet of Persia. He was born in Khorasan, Iran and was the leader of the Naqshbandi Sufi order.

21: Granaz Moussavi (b. 1976) is a poet, film director and screenwriter from Tehran.

22: Magtymguly Pyragy (c. 1724–1807), born near Gonbad-e Kavus, is the national poet of the Turkmen people. A poet-philosopher, Sufi and traveller, his poems, which are often sung, contain many images of horse riding, the desert and steppe.

23: Rudaki (c. 858–940) was born in present-day Tajikistan and became a Samanid court poet. In Iran, he is acknowledged as the 'founder of New Persian poetry' and in Tajikistan as the 'father of Tajik literature'.

24: Sanai (c. 1080–1141) was born in Afghanistan. His poetry has had an enormous influence on Persian literature, including on the writings of Rumi.

25: Anna Akhmatova (1889–1966) is one of the most significant Russian-language poets of the twentieth century. She was born in Odessa and lived in Tashkent from 1942–44. There were long periods when she was officially in disfavour.

27: Freya Stark (1893–1993) was an explorer and travel writer of British–Italian heritage. She wrote many books on her travels in the Middle East and Afghanistan. *The Valleys of the Assassins* documents Stark's journey into the mountains on the border between current-day Iraq and Iran.

29: Samuel Taylor Coleridge (1772–1834) was a British poet and founder of the Romantic movement, which drew heavily on Orientalist themes. 'Kubla Khan: or A Vision in a Dream' was composed following an opium-influenced dream he'd had after reading an account by English writer Samuel Purchas (1625) which gave a secondhand description of Shangdu (Xanadu) in China based on Marco Polo's travels (1278).

30: Omar Khayyam (1048–1131) is most famous in Iran, the country of his birth, as a mathematician who developed a general theory of cubic equations. He was also an astronomer, a philosopher and a poet. His poetry became very popular in English thanks to an 1859 translation by Edward Fitzgerald of his *Rubaiyat*, which became a key text of orientalism.

31: Nasir-i Khusraw (1004–88) was an Ismaili poet, philosopher and traveller from Khorasan. As a missionary for the Ismaili Fatimid caliphate, he was a key figure in the spread of Ismailism in Central Asia. He died in exile in Badakhshan.

32: John Wood (1812–71) was a Scottish naval officer, surveyor, cartographer and explorer, principally remembered for his exploration of Central Asia and his journey to the source of the River Oxus (Amu Darya). The passage quoted is about his camp near Lake Zorkul with Kyrgyz herders in February 1838.

33: Mir Dard (1720–85) was a Sufi poet whose ancestors had migrated from Bukhara to India. He was born in Delhi during the time of the Mughal Empire.

34: Aziz Isa Elkun (b. 1970) is a poet from Uyghuristan (East Turkistan/Uyghur Autonomous Region, China). He has lived in exile in the UK since 2001, where he is an academic at SOAS in London.

35: Abu al-Qasim al-Shabbi (1909–34) was born in Tunisia. His poems, including 'The Will to Live', became a source of inspiration for Arab protestors during the revolutions of the Arab Spring.

36: Rawia Morra (b. 1966) was born in Beirut. She spent time as a refugee in Lebanon before going to Sweden. She is a translator, writer and teacher.

Selected Bibliography

The Nation's Favourite Poems, BBC Books, 1996

Adonis, *Selected Poems*, trans. Khaled Mattawa, Yale University Press, 2010

Akhmatova, Anna, *The Complete Poems of Anna Akhmatova*, trans. Judith Hemschemeyer, ed. Roberta Reeder, Canongate, 2021

Azzam, Itab and Mousawi, Dina, *Syria: Recipes From Home*, Trapeze, 2017

Badkhen, Anna, *The World is a Carpet: Four Seasons in an Afghan Village*, Riverhead Books, 2013

Barr, James, *A Line in the Sand: Britain, France and the Struggle that Shaped the Middle East*, Simon & Schuster, 2012

Bell, Gertrude, *The Desert and the Sown: Travels in Palestine and Syria*, Dover, 2008

Bell, Gertrude, *The Letters of Gertrude Bell Volume One*, Ernest Benn Ltd, 1928

Burnes, Alexander, *Travels into Bokhara: A Voyage up the Indus to Lahore and a Journey to Cabool, Tartary and Persia*, ed. Kathleen Hopkirk, Eland, 2012

Burns, Ross, *The Monuments of Syria: A Guide*, I.B. Tauris, 2010

Butcher, Sally, *Persia in Peckham: Recipes from Persepolis*, Prospect Books, 2007

Byron, Robert, *The Road to Oxiana*, Macmillan & Co., 1937

Christie, Ella, *Through Khiva to Golden Samarkand*, John Murray, 2022

Crawford, James, *The Edge of the Plain: How Borders Make and Break Our World*, Canongate, 2022

Davis, Dick (ed.), *The Mirror of My Heart: A Thousand Years of Persian Poetry by Women*, Penguin, 2021

Dean, Aimen, Cruickshank, Paul, Lister, Tim, *Nine Lives: My Time as MI6's Top Spy Inside al-Qaeda*, Oneworld Publications, 2018

Eden, Caroline, *Red Sands: Reportage and Recipes Through Central Asia from Hinterland to Heartland*, Quadrille, 2020

Elkun, Aziz Isa (ed.), *Uyghur Poems*, Everyman's Library, 2023

Elliot, Jason, *Mirrors of the Unseen: Journeys in Iran*, Picador, 2006

Fatah, Rebwar (ed.), *My Poetry Depicts You: An Anthology of Contemporary Kurdish Poetry*, Meriwani Art, 2019

Ferdowsi, Abolqasem, *Shahnameh: The Persian Book of Kings*, trans. Dick Davis, Penguin, 2016

Frankopan, Peter, *The Silk Roads: A New History of the World*, Bloomsbury, 2015

French, Patrick, *Younghusband: The Last Great Imperial Adventurer*, Flamingo, 1995

Gyatso, Palden, *Fire Under the Snow: Testimony of a Tibetan Prisoner*, trans. Tsering Shakya, Harvill Press, 1997

Hafez, *Poems from the Divan of Hafiz*, ed. and trans. Gertrude Bell, Independently published on Amazon, 2021

Hammond, Marlé (ed.), *Arabic Poems*, Everyman's Library, 2014

Handal, Nathalie (ed.), *The Poetry of Arab Women*, Interlink Books, 2015

Ibn Battutah, *The Travels of Ibn Battutah*, ed. Tim Mackintosh-Smith, Picador, 2003

Ibn Fadlan, *Ibn Fadlan and the Land of Darkness: Arab Travellers in the Far North*, trans. Paul Lunde and Caroline Stone, Penguin Classics, 2012

Jami, *The Persian Mystics: Jami*, ed. and trans. Frederick Hadland Davis, J. Murray, 1908

Kociejowski, Marius, *The Street Philosopher and the Holy Fool*, Sutton Publishing, 2006

Lemmon, Gayle Tzemach, *The Daughters of Kobani: The Women Who Took on the Islamic State*, Swift Press, 2021

Lord, Stephen, *Adventure Cycle-Touring Handbook: Worldwide Cycling Route & Planning Guide*, Trailblazer Publications, 2006

Lowe, Rebecca, *The Slow Road to Tehran*, September Publishing, 2022

Maalouf, Amin, *Samarkand*, Abacus, 1994

Mackintosh-Smith, Tim, *Arabs: A 3,000-Year History of Peoples, Tribes and Empires*, Yale University Press, 2019

Maclean, Fitzroy, *Eastern Approaches*, Penguin, 1991

Middleton, Robert, Thomas, Huw, *Tajikistan and the High Pamirs*, Odyssey, 2012

Murphy, Dervla, *Full Tilt: Ireland to India with a Bicycle*, Eland, 2011

Murray, Craig, *Murder in Samarkand: A British Ambassador's Controversial Defiance of Tyranny in the War on Terror*, Mainstream Publishing, 2007

Nasir-i Khusraw, *Divan of Nasir-i-Khusraw*, ed. and trans. Paul Smith, New Humanity Books/Book Haven, 2021

Navoi, Alisher, *Selected Poems*, ed. and trans. Paul Smith, New Humanity Books/Book Heaven, 2018

Newby, Eric, *A Short Walk in the Hindu Kush*, Popular Book Club, 1958

O'Neill, Shaun, *A Church of Islam: The Syrian Calling of Father Paolo Dall'Oglio*, Wipf & Stock Publishers, 2019

Orwell, George, *Down and Out in Paris and London*, Penguin, 2001

Polo, Marco, *The Travels of Marco Polo*, Arcturus Publishing, 2019

Rogerson, Barnaby, *The House Divided: Sunni, Shia and the Making of the Middle East*, Profile Books, 2024

Rudaki, *Selected Poems*, ed. and trans. Paul Smith, New Humanity Books/Book Heaven, 2013

Rumi, *Selected Poems*, trans. Coleman Barks, with John Moyne, A.J. Arberry, Reynold Nicholson, Penguin, 1995

Smith, Paul (ed.), *A Quilt of Women Spiritual Poets of the Middle-East & India*, New Humanity Books/Book Heaven, 2014

Starr, S. Frederick, *Lost Enlightenment: Central Asia's Golden Age from the Arab Conquest to Tamerlane*, Princeton University Press, 2013

Stewart, Rory, *The Places In Between*, Picador, 2005

Stone, Peter F., *Oriental Rugs: An Illustrated Lexicon of Motifs, Materials, and Origins*, Tuttle, 2013

Tabatabai, Sassan, *Father of Persian Verse: Rudaki and his Poetry*, Leiden University Press, 2010

Thesiger, Wilfred, *The Marsh Arabs*, Penguin, 2007

Thubron, Colin, *Shadow of the Silk Road*, Vintage, 2007

Tucker, Jonathan, *The Silk Road: Central Asia, Afghanistan and Iran*, Tauris Parke, 2015

Washington, Peter (ed.), *Persian Poems*, Everyman's Library, 2000

Permissions

Every effort has been made to obtain permission to quote from authors and translators. The author regrets any inadvertent errors or omissions and will be happy to make corrections in future editions.

Chapter 1: Quotation of Mohsin Hamid from *Exit West* by Mohsin Hamid published by Hamish Hamilton. Copyright © Mohsin Hamid, 2017. Reprinted by permission of Penguin Books Limited.

Chapters 2, 6 and 26: Quotations of Rumi from *Selected Poems* by Rumi published by Penguin Classics. Copyright © Coleman Banks, 1995. Reprinted by permission of Penguin Books Limited.

Chapter 3: Quotation of Nizar Qabbani, trans. Nayef al-Kalali used with permission of Taylor & Francis InformaUK Ltd – Books, from *Republic of Love*, Lisa Kavchak (ed), 1st edition, 2016; permission conveyed through Copyright Clearance Center, Inc.

Chapters 4 and 11: Quotation of Fadwa Tuqan, trans Patricia Alanah Byrne, Salma Jayyusi and Naomi Shihab Nye and Quotation al-Munsif al-Wahaybi, trans Salma Khadra Jayyusi and Naomi Shihab Nye used with permission of Columbia University Press, from *Modern Arabic poetry: an anthology*, Jayyusi, Salma Khadra, 1st edition, 1987; permission conveyed through Copyright Clearance Center, Inc.

Chapter 10 and Notes on the Chapter Epigraphs and Their Authors: Quotations of Adonis from *Selected Poems*, reproduced with permission of Yale Representation Limited through PLSclear.

Chapter 13: Quotation of Gülten Akın reproduced with permission of Yapı Kredi Kültür Sanat Yayıncılık Ticaret ve Sanayi AŞ. Copyright © Gülten Akın, Yapı Kredi Kültür Sanat Yayıncılık Ticaret ve Sanayi A.Ş., 2002, 2023.

Chapter 16: Quotation of Forugh Farrokkhzad from *Sin: Selected Poems of Forugh Farrokkhzad*, translated by Sholeh Wolpé. Copyright © 2007 by Sholeh Wolpé. Reprinted with the permission of The Permissions Company, LLC on behalf of the University of Arkansas Press, uapress.com.

Chapter 21: Quotation of Rudaki reproduced with kind permission of the translator Paul Smith.

Chapter 28: Quotation of Rumi, from *Unseen Rain: Quatrains of Rumi*, translated by John Moyne and Coleman Barks. Copyright © 1986 by Coleman Barks. Reprinted by arrangement with The Permissions Company, LLC on behalf of Shambhala Publications Inc, Boulder, Colorado, shambhala.com

Chapter 34: Quotation of Aziz Isa Elkun reproduced with kind permission of the author Aziz Isa Elkun.

Glossary

A large number of languages are spoken across the region covered by this book and its linguistic history is complex. Here words are coded according to the location of usage encountered as opposed to linguistic etymology. Turkmen, Uzbek, Kyrgyz and Uyghur are Turkic languages; Iranian and Tajik are Persian languages. Arabic words are in universal usage given that Arabic is the language of the Qur'an. Russian is commonly used throughout Central Asia. When communicating with people in Central Asia we often relied on trying words of Russian, Turkish, Persian and Arabic origin.

A: Arabic; CA: Central Asia; I: Iran; S: Syria; T: Turkey

abaya (S) – woman's cloak
Abbasids – eighth- to sixteenth-century caliphate originally from Khorasan that governed mainly from Baghdad; successors to the Umayyads
adhan (A) – the first Islamic call to prayer, usually recited by a muezzin at five times of the day in a mosque, traditionally from a minaret
amin (A) – amen, we noticed it in particular usage during mealtime prayer in Central Asia when accompanied by passing cupped hands together in front of the face
andron – classical Greek house for entertaining men
atlas (CA) – Uyghur ikat
ayran (T) – cold, salty yogurt-based beverage
banya (CA) – public bathhouse or steam bath (Russian)
Bedu (S) – Bedouin; pastorally nomadic Arab tribes; derived from the Arabic 'badawi' or 'desert-dweller'
boteh (I/CA) – teardrop-shaped motif with a curved upper end, a Zoroastrian symbol of life and eternity commonly found on Persian rugs and other Central Asian textiles. The motif is referred to as paisley in English after the town in Scotland where the design was first produced in the Western world in imitation of designs found on Kashmir shawls imported by the East India Company
caravanserai – a Persian origin word for a travellers' inn or khan

chador (I) – open-fronted cloak worn by some Iranian women and pulled close to cover the head and body
chaikhana (CA) – teahouse and eatery
dallah (S) – traditional Arabic pot used for brewing and serving coffee
dishdasha (A) – long tunic robe worn by men of the Arabian Peninsula
dizi (I) – traditional Iranian meat broth also referred to as abgoosht
doogh (I) – cold, salty yogurt-based drink commonly flavoured with mint
doppi (CA) – Uzbek or Uyghur round or square skullcap
durtlik / bosma (CA) – a stamp creating lots of tiny holes, sometimes made from reused bicycle spokes to give bread (*non*) a unique design and to allow steam to escape during the baking process
fesenjoon (I) – stew of pomegranate and walnut sauce commonly made with chicken
ful (S) – cooked fava beans served with olive oil and cumin and optionally with chopped parsley, lemon juice and other vegetables; often made in a large copper pot as street food in Syria
Hadith (A) – reports, sayings or traditions of the Prophet Muhammad. Hadith is used to refer both to the collective and individual reports, which are revered by Muslims as a major source of religious law and moral guidance
hafiz/a (A) – an honorific title to a man or woman who has memorised the entire Qur'an
haftseen (I) – an arrangement of seven symbolic items whose names start with the letter 'س' (pronounced as 'seen'), traditionally displayed at Nowruz
hijab (A) – headscarf commonly worn by Muslim women to cover the hair
iwan (A) – in Islamic architecture a rectangular hall or space, walled on three sides, with one end entirely open
khan – see *caravanserai*
khobez (A) – bread
Khorasan – historical area and cradle of ancient civilisations that encompassed, broadly speaking, the east of modern-day Iran and parts of Afghanistan and Central Asia
kora (CA) – both a type of pilgrimage and meditative practice in Tibetan Buddhism
laghman (CA) – thick, pulled wheat noodles; loanword from the Chinese for noodles *lamian*

madrasa (A) – educational institution, often for Islamic instruction
manteau (I) – French-origin word for the long coat worn by Iranian women
manti (CA) – dumplings generally filled with ground lamb
muezzin (A) – the person who calls the faithful to prayer in Islam
nargileh (S) – water pipe for smoking tobacco; *qalyan* in Iran; commonly referred to as hookah or shisha by English speakers (words with Hindu and Arabic etymology)
niqab (A) – a long garment worn by some Muslim women to cover their entire body and face, excluding their eyes
non (CA) – circular flatbread
Nowruz – widely celebrated Zoroastrian-origin festival and New Year celebration of the spring equinox
piala (CA) – tea bowl or cup with no handles
pide (T) – a savoury pizza-like stuffed bread dish of Turkish Black Sea origin, widely eaten across Turkey
pishtaq (I) – the formal gateway to the *iwan*
plov (CA) – rice dish with lamb and carrot; similar to pilaff
qalyan (I) – Persian water pipe (see *nargileh*)
salwar kameez – an outfit of a tunic shirt and trousers worn in many local style variants across Asia and Eastern Europe
samsa (CA) – pastry turnover typically filled with lamb
shahadah (A) – Islamic declaration of faith
shemagh (S) – traditional headdress worn by men of the Arabian Peninsula, also known as keffiyeh or *kufiyyeh*; the black and white keffiyeh is commonly associated with the Palestinian nationalist movement; the most common design in Syria is red and white
shorba (CA) – lamb broth; also a generic name for soup in Turkic languages
suzani (CA) – embroidered fabric
takbir (A) – the name for the Arabic phrase 'Allahu akbar'
tapchan (CA) – tea bed; seating arrangement in a teahouse
turbah (A) – a small disc of soil or clay used during daily prayer, principally by Shia Muslims
Umayyads – caliphate of the seventh and eighth centuries, the first great Muslim dynasty, with an empire that extended from Spain to India

za'atar (S) – spice mixture of dried thyme, toasted sesame seeds, dried sumac, often salt, and more
zawj; *zawja* (A) – husband; wife

Kit List

The *Adventure Cycle-Touring Handbook: Worldwide Cycling Route & Planning Guide* by Stephen Lord is highly recommended for planning a trip of this nature.

Joint
- tent: Hilleberg Nallo 2 GT (chosen for its good porch), stored inside a waterproof roll-top rucksack
- Primus OmniFuel stove with repair kit, fuel adaptors and 2 fuel bottles (1l, 0.75l)
- 1 kettle, 2 pans, 2 bowls, 2 sporks, 2 mugs
- 3 water bottles (0.75l)
- thermos (1l)
- Ortlieb 5l water carriers x2
- Steripen water-purification system (used rarely)
- Ortlieb folding 'kitchen sink' bucket (used as a washing machine, bath and for inner-tube mending)
- elastic washing line
- bike repair kit: spare chain per bike (changed over to keep wear even); 2 spare inners; 2 spare folding tyres; brake and gear cables; brake blocks; Next Best Thing cassette-remover tool
- sewing kit: including heavy-duty needles and thread (used a lot)
- pannier and Therm-a-Rest repair kits
- sterile syringe and dental repair kit
- first-aid kit with selection of antibiotics
- solar charger
- mobile phone
- camera
- binoculars

Individual
- bike: Koga-Miyata WorldTraveller with 26-inch tyres, simple caliper brakes (easy to replace) and gears with granny ratios
- Tubus racks
- Ortlieb front roller panniers x2
- Ortlieb back roller panniers x2
- Ortlieb bar bag with map case
- bike lights
- head torch with spare batteries
- pump
- Topeak ALiEN multitool
- Rab down sleeping bag
- Therm-a-Rest rollmats (3/4 length for Helen)
- down jacket
- waterproof jacket and trousers
- set of thermals (extra set in winter and in the Pamirs)
- zip-off trousers
- Rab Vapour-Rise mid-layer
- gilet

- long-sleeved trekking shirt x2 (or tunic shirts)
- gloves, hat and buff
- sunhat, sunglasses and suncream
- cycling gloves
- helmet and waterproof helmet cover
- change of light clothes for wearing in town (adapted/replaced as appropriate)
- warm socks
- pants
- rubber washing-up gloves for cycling in bad weather
- dayglo vest
- dayglo Velcro bike clips
- walking boots
- sandals

Thanks

The first thanks in this book must go to the many generous people along the way who fed us, gave us beds for the night and provided an endless supply of tea. Sometimes this was done at personal risk and we never encountered any request for reward. Thanks also to fellow travellers who provided encouragement and friendship *en route*. I especially note here also the great work of Citizens UK and the many remarkable people I have met through planning and participating in refugee sponsorship. Events in this book are real, but names have been changed throughout to protect identities.

The writing journey has been long and has unfolded in fits and starts, around life, a career, voluntary work and a pandemic. I am grateful to the following people who have provided feedback, encouragement and writing advice at various stages which have encouraged me to keep going: Elizabeth Findlay, Jim Turner, Jonathan Lorie, Helen Moat, Liz Cleere and members of the Itinerant Writers Club, Adrian Phillips and the competition team at Bradt for giving me some early writing breaks, Raymond Ross of Find Your Voice, Jim Wilson of Poetry in Practice, Andy Dobson, and my fantastic editors, Lucy Ridout and Ross Dickinson. I am very grateful to David Mallon, Helena Crow, Richard Bown, Manouk Wilkinson, Rosie Tudge, Mark Senn, Stephen Senn and Victoria Senn for providing feedback on drafts of the book. Also thanks to the team at Journey Books, including Anna Moores, Claire Strange, Neil Matthews and Ian Spick as well as Louisa Keyworth at Lovell Johns and and illustrator Ollie Davies for helping me see this through to completion.

Thanks to friends Rosie, Bev, Joanna, Ellie, Miles and Jon who have often enquired about progress on 'the book', to Basma for all her kindness, and to Irina and Miroslava for their support and interest in my writing while staying with us. I am grateful to former St Andrews University Mountaineers and the Lost Sheep Mountaineering Club, skipper Andy and his crews and Drumguish TT runners – for company in the hills and at sea, proving that mutual enjoyment of type-two fun is a solid basis for friendship and sanity. And to long-distance cycling friends Kieran Craven and Jarrod Hadfield, who gave us sage advice before we set off.

Of course, this book could not have been written without the help of Ed Watson, who has not only stuck with me on the road to China but also for the journey since, providing love, encouragement and adventure. I drew heavily on Ed's, much more meticulously kept, journals and most of the photographs are his.

Thanks to our family Derek, So Young, Nick, Wendy, Mark, Helena, and all of our lovely nieces and nephews, Rosie, Paul, Joshua, Nathan, Ruth and all the Tudges. I can't finish this book without an acknowledgment to my wonderful late grandparents, Teddy and Elizabeth Senn, who taught me so much about life and literature, and who are ever with me when I am in the mountains. Finally and most of all, thanks to our parents, George and Diane, and Stephen and Victoria, for everything they gave us to make us the people we are, their love and unending support.